Buddhist Feminisms
and Femininities

Buddhist Feminisms and Femininities

Edited by

Karma Lekshe Tsomo

Cover art by Yue Juan.

Published by State University of New York Press, Albany

For information, contact State University of New York Press, Albany, NY
www.sunypress.edu

Library of Congress Cataloging-in-Publication Data

Names: Karma Lekshe Tsomo, 1944– editor.
Title: Buddhist feminisms and femininities / edited by Karma Lekshe Tsomo.
Description: Albany : State University of New York Press, 2019. | Includes
  bibliographical references and index.
Identifiers: LCCN 2018003552 | ISBN 9781438472553 (hardcover : alk. paper)
  | ISBN 9781438472560 (pbk. : alk. paper) | ISBN 9781438472577 (ebook)
Subjects: LCSH: Women in Buddhism. | Women—Religious aspects—
  Buddhism.
Classification: LCC BQ4570.W6 B79 2018 | DDC 294.3082—dc23
LC record available at https://lccn.loc.gov/2018003552

10 9 8 7 6 5 4 3 2 1

Contents

Preface

Language is powerful and words can express more than mere concepts. Since this volume is replete with different cultural heritages that reflect the social evolution of many, widely varied cultures and traditions, the terms used in specific areas of the text remain true to their own traditions. For example, chapters that focus on Theravāda traditions use Pāli terms, while those that focus on Mahāyāna traditions use Sanskrit, Chinese, Japanese, Korean and Tibetan. Terms in Pāli and Sanskrit may be the same or similar. For example, *bhikkhunī* is the Pāli term for a fully ordained nun and *bhikṣuṇī* is the Sanskrit, Dhamma is the Pāli term for the Buddhist teachings and Dharma is the Sanskrit equivalent, and so on.

Two Fulbright Scholar Awards and numerous Faculty Research Grants and International Opportunity Grants from the College of Arts and Sciences of the University of San Diego have given me first-hand experience and knowledge of the lives and perspectives of women in diverse Buddhist communities around the world. I would like to express my sincere appreciation for these opportunities and for the kindness of all those who have warmly opened their hearts to me.

All the contributors to this volume have been wonderful companions on the path to completion. The editors, my close friends Margaret Coberly and Rebecca Paxton, have shared their skills with exceptional kindness, dedication, and generosity. In a stroke of good fortune, the well-known artist Yue Juan offered the cover art, "Lotus Flower from Pond," reproduced from an original brush painting in Gongbi style. The lotus flower symbolizes pure illumined perception arising undamaged from the muck of the world, and is an apt metaphor for women's awakened potential. The smoothly gliding fish, finding their way through constantly shifting circumstances, represent the many fortunate women today who are doing the same. I

am deeply grateful to the women who have contributed to this volume and to all women everywhere, throughout history, who navigate
through the muck and arise victorious by realizing their true nature.

Introduction

Conceptualizing Buddhist Feminisms and Images of the Feminine

Karma Lekshe Tsomo

This volume began with a propitious accident. When the Buddhism section of the American Academy of Religion solicited suggestions for topics, I chimed in with the idea of Buddhist feminisms. The following week, when the ideas went out over the internet, I was surprised to see a call for papers on Buddhist femininities, a topic that made no sense to me at the time, so I quickly changed it to Buddhist feminism(s). To my further surprise, waves of innovative proposals poured in on both topics, enough for two conference panels and more. The present collection grew from this felicitous misunderstanding.

The question of Buddhist feminisms and femininities is not a simple philosophical query, or simply a matter of women's personal and social self-perceptions. The question has profound implications for social justice—in the home, monastery, workplace, social structures, body politic, and environment. Buddhist feminisms emerge within specific cultural contexts, influenced by unique and diverse social and philosophical factors. It would be a travesty to flatten or distort them to match preconceptions about how feminism can or should be done. While the rich models of feminist thinking that have developed in other texts and contexts are clearly relevant in many ways, such as prompting us to consider the links between economic, environmental, political, and gender justice—the models that have emerged in Western societies may or may not be useful for an analysis of Buddhist societies. For example, a Buddhist feminism based on the notion of individual rights may not hold up to scrutiny since, in Buddhist thought, there is no source or bestower and no concrete self on whom to bestow the rights.[1]

The alternative taxonomies of feminism proposed thus far, liberal as well as radical, are largely products of Western women's experiences and may or may not be useful for Buddhist feminist thinking.

The study of women and gender is now a familiar component of liberal arts education in Europe and North American universities, but it is well to remember that higher education is still limited to privileged elites in much of the world, especially for women. Even if university-educated Buddhist women take an interest in gender issues and are curious to understand how feminist thinking emerged and where it is going, it is unrealistic to expect Buddhist feminisms to be like or look like theories developed in the West. Naturally, Buddhist feminisms, emerging from entirely different cultural, social, and historical contexts, will take their own unique forms. Western feminist thinking may seem tiresomely analytical and largely irrelevant to women struggling for survival and, although it would be foolish to ignore decades of extraordinary reflection, the rejection of feminist ideas remains quite strong in Buddhist societies. If people have even heard of it, feminism is often viewed as an unnecessary and undesirable imposition of foreign cultural mores. The task of exploring Buddhist feminisms is therefore fraught from the onset.

A Buddhist deconstruction of feminism is not a dismissal of the extraordinary scholarly work that feminists have done, nor is it a rejection of critical inquiry. It is simply an attempt to develop different, culturally attuned ways of thinking about gender that do not rely on hyper-analysis and "perpetual reflexivity."[2] Taking a cue from black feminist thinking, Buddhist feminists are likely to question the arbitrary dichotomy between theory and experience, as bell hooks enjoins.[3] The point is not how Buddhist women understand the varieties of feminism that have developed in Western philosophies and cultures, but how feminist thinking and sensibilities are emerging unscripted in Buddhist communities, imagining and creating equitable spaces for women within traditionally patriarchal Buddhist philosophies and cultures. To apply alien, standardized feminist frameworks to women's diverse experiences may be as patronizing, misleading, and repressive as imposing patriarchal frameworks has been. Perhaps it would be best to begin afresh and allow the questions and categories to emerge on their own among women in other parts of the world. It has been suggested that a sort of "protofeminism" can be discerned in Asian women's histories and biographies,[4] but the record is mixed, with realized Buddhist women decrying their female rebirth and praying to be reborn in a male body.[5] A range of attitudes toward women can be found in Buddhist literature—valorizing, denigrating, and often profoundly ambivalent—attitudes still evident in Buddhist societies up to today, internalized by women and men alike. The chapters in this volume will engage with these attitudes in representative feminist histories and narratives from Asia. Our hope is that these writings can help us understand Buddhist influences on attitudes toward women and also introduce original expressions of feminist thinking in different parts of the world in ways that may constructively inform contemporary feminist discussions.

Buddhist feminism and notions of femininity are evolving spontaneously and creatively as traditional cultural values are being re-evaluated, rejected, revalued, and re-envisioned. The geographical and ethnic diversity of women in Buddhist societies, from the tropics of Southeast Asia to the steppes of Siberia, argues against a uniform method or process. The enormous variations in Buddhist societies over space and time are daunting, and enliven the conversation. Whatever can be said of one can surely be refuted by evidence from another. The landscape expands as we move through time and the rapid changes that are occurring in Buddhist societies today and in Buddhist communities around the globe. In every corner of the world, preconceptions about what women value and how they would like to live their lives are shaped both by traditional cultural values and by ideas of democracy, human rights, capitalism, scientism, and consumerism. Contemporary culture adds a whole new set of trends being disseminated through social media. The diversity of Buddhist women around the world and across generations is staggering. If Buddhist feminists appear somewhat naïve in avoiding overt intellectualization, the counternarratives they present are original and exciting.

The chapters in this book speak to themes and elements of the feminist conversation, including new orientations to the phenomenology of Buddhist women's communities and new theoretical approaches to understanding Buddhist texts and practices in a new, feminist hermeneutics. From a variety of perspectives and in different cultural contexts, the writers approach the sticky issues implicit in the term "Buddhist feminism." Coming from diverse backgrounds and disciplines, and speaking from different points in their careers, they approach the topic using a broad range of methodologies. The chapters are linked by a common interest in the relationship between texts and communities, culture and context. Each writer contributes unique understandings of Buddhist thought and culture as sources for feminist reflection and social action.

Questioning the Constructs

The English term "feminism" is a construction of Western culture that has many definitions and interpretations. Recitals of the typographies, arguments, and critiques of each iteration have already been published. As myriad scholars have noted, much feminist thinking to date has tended to universalize "women's experience" and has been based largely on the experiences of privileged women facing gender-based inequalities in society. In reality, however, even for Western women, women's experiences differ enormously in relation to class, ethnicity, physical appearance, vocation, ability, and numerous other social markers. The central takeaway of feminist literature to date is that we must be careful to distinguish between collective representations of "women" ("woman," "the female," "the feminine") and the living, breathing variety of human beings who identify as women. Rather than measure Buddhist women's experiences against a standardized alien grid, the aim of this volume is to understand Buddhist perspectives and images of women on their own terms. This is enormously challenging, due to the vast diversity of Buddhist cultures, but in this volume we shall make a start.

As Chandra Talpade Mohanty and other scholars have demonstrated, the representation of feminism as "Western" in its authentic form is deeply problematic, and perpetuates imperialistic agendas in its flattening of non-Western women's agency.[6] Women's movements in Japan, Korea, and China are often associated with the introduction of Western education in these cultures and may ignore indigenous social histories and philosophies, including Buddhism, in the development of local feminist thinking. Historians and sociologists of Asia may also ignore the experiences of ethnic minority women in documenting social and political movements with feminist goals. The writings included here seek to explore new understandings of women and gender in Buddhist communities—their lives, ideas, aspirations, self-perceptions, and relationships to power—contributing to the growing body of literature, critical analysis, and alternative ways of thinking about the world's women.

Buddhist women's experience validates many of the insights that have been elucidated by pioneering Asian and transnational feminists. As Kumari Jayawardena points out, elite feminisms are worlds away from most ordinary women's experiences and may represent only a small fraction of them. Significantly, she also points out that those who wish to keep women subordinate "find it convenient to dismiss feminism as a foreign ideology."[7] She admirably analyzes feminist movements in Asia in relation to nationalist struggles and modernization. While it is true that the evolution of women's feminist awareness cannot be understood apart from the particular cultural, social, and political context of their experience, it is impossible to generalize the experiences of Buddhist women, which vary in different societies and strata of society. While Buddhist feminism may appear to be relatively unsophisticated or even naïve from a highly intellectual Western perspective, it is growing organically from Buddhist women's own authentic perspectives. The literature criticizing elitism is itself elitist and that criticizing colonialism is itself colonialist. The hyper-intellectualism of much feminist literature appears pretentious and weird to many indigenous women. The heart of the Buddha's teachings is to see things "as they are," without mental fabrications; the ultimate experience of awakening is to be free from conceptualization altogether.

If gender were a fixed concept, it would be immutable, but from a Buddhist perspective, no concept is immutable. All compounded phenomena are impermanent, contingent, and interdependent. Changing sex is not taboo in Buddhist texts; in fact, it is mentioned as a fact of life.[8] Sex change was natural—"a rather ordinary thing"[9]—and nonreprehensible. The impermanent, transmutable nature of genitalia seems taken for granted in commentaries on the monastic codes. In the *Kṣudrakavastu*, a Sanskrit *vinaya* commentary, a revered monk named Upali asked the Buddha:

> "Venerable, if a *bhikṣuṇī* changes sex, what should be done with regard to her?" and the Lord replied, "Upali, place that one at the same age among the *bhikṣus*. Moreover, that becomes full ordination and *bhikṣu*-hood."[10]

The representations of sex change in the *vinaya* texts reflect the interdependent nature of things and show that there cannot be something essentially unique to either gender. All that changes are the genitals.[11] When a nun takes the features of a male, he is fully accepted as a member of the order of monks, without having to reordain, and is exempted from rules pertaining to nuns; when a monk takes the features of a female, she is fully accepted as a member of the order of nuns and is exempted from rules pertaining to monks.[12] These references to gender fluidity in the texts call into question definitive notions of masculine and feminine. Still, although passages describing sex change are included in the *vinaya*, admission into the monasteries is restricted to the normative categories of male and female, and biological sex is the chief determinant of gender assignment; people with both female and male sexual characteristics are not admitted. However, as the *vinaya* texts cited above indicate, the male/female dichotomy is not absolute. Genitalia may change, and therefore gender identities are transmutable, not intrinsic. As we conceptualize what form(s) Buddhist feminism may take, the flexible, even ineffable nature of gender distinctions should be kept in mind. On one hand, the generic nature of the monastic robes obviates sex distinctions; on the other hand, gendered monastic restrictions designed to enforce celibacy reinscribe the male/female binary.

In her work on Theravāda Buddhist texts and traditions, Kate Crosby notes several examples of male-female sex distinctions. First, there are whole genres of canonical texts that are gender specific, for example, the codes of monastic discipline for monks and nuns (*Bhikkhu* and *Bhikkhunī Pāṭimokkha* and their corresponding *vibhaṅga*) and the *Therīgāthā and Therīgāthā* (Verses of the Elders, male and female). Second, in postcanonical texts, she notes the use of gendered complementary pairs of beings in *saṃsāra*—male and female *brahmins*, male and female renunciants, male and female beggars, ordinary men and women, and so on. Only the high status positions of minister, general, viceroy, or watchman have no female complement.[13] Crosby surmises that both of these examples could be taken as examples of either gender inclusivity or gender essentializing. A third example, however, veers decidedly toward essentializing gender characteristics. The Dhammasaṅgaṇi, the first text of Abhidhamma, describes "two faculties of sex, the faculty of femininity (*itthindriya*) and the faculty of masculinity (*purisaindriya*). These faculties define physical appearance, marks, traits, and deportment peculiar to the state of femininity (*itthibhāva*) and the state of masculinity (*purisabhāva*), respectively."[14] A fifth-century commentary takes the bifurcation further, stating that the two faculties do not simply define female and male appearance and so forth, but are *causes* of it. To what extent these essentialized notions of gender were known outside a small set of male Buddhist monastic scholars is unknown. The idea that male and female sentient beings are inherently different by virtue of possessing these two distinct faculties that define their appearance and deportment seems very much at odds with Buddhist philosophical rejections of essentializing phenomena. Nevertheless, it is possible that this Abhidhamma bifurcation of masculinity and femininity influenced attitudes toward sex and gender in Buddhist societies.

A key concept of Buddhist philosophy is the acknowledgment that sentient existence entails dissatisfactions, frustrations, and sufferings, caused by ignorance, desire, and assorted mental afflictions. Through awareness and insight into the true nature of things, it is possible to awaken and become liberated from these afflictions and live a contented, happy life. As illustrated in Buddhist legends and histories, awareness and insight are accessible to all, regardless of race, class, gender, or other variables, so it follows that women can achieve the ultimate goal of awakening. Buddhist feminists point out that Buddhist and feminist articulations of liberation are compatible, and may even be mutually entailing. Buddhist feminists confront some major challenges, however. First, they need to reconcile the sufferings of women with the theory of *karma* (cause and effect). This theory of actions and their consequences, extending over lifetimes, has traditionally led to the assumption that women have bad *karma* and to the preconception that a female body is less fortunate than a male body. As a consequence, many Buddhists aspire for a male rebirth and devalue or even despise a female rebirth, leading to gender inequities and amalgamations of male power in Buddhist societies.

Second, Mahāyāna teachings on Buddha nature and emptiness—that all sentient beings have the potential for awakening and that all phenomena, including sex and gender, are empty of intrinsic existence—have been deployed to try to salvage the situation, but these teachings do not adequately explain, justify, or serve to correct the blatant gender inequalities in Buddhist societies that are the source of many miseries. To correct these inequalities, Buddhists must reconcile the long-term goal of spiritual liberation with the immediate need for social solutions to gender violence, exploitation, and inequality, in addition to racism, poverty, and other injustices. One unique contribution of Buddhist feminism is its emphasis on generating impartial loving kindness equally to all sentient beings, rehearsed in meditation and practiced in every aspect of everyday life. Among other practical tools, loving kindness is a useful antidote to rage.

It is commonly said that in Buddhism "there is no male, no female" and that "enlightenment is beyond gender."[15] These statements can be taken at face value or can mean that enlightened beings are beyond attachment to gender concepts, since ultimately, like all existent phenomena, gender distinctions are empty of true existence. Buddhist texts do not deny sex or gender distinctions; in fact, Buddhist texts are full of references to sex and gender. For example, the ideal Buddhist society is comprised of male and female householders and male and female renunciants. Buddhist householders avoid sexual misconduct; Buddhist renunciants avoid sex altogether. These designations and countless other references in the texts, while heteronormative, are gender-specific, so it cannot be said that Buddhism denies sex or gender distinctions. This misconception derives primarily from misinterpretations of the concept of emptiness (śunyatā). The Mahāyāna Buddhist assertion that all phenomena are empty of true, inherent, or independent existence does not mean that all phenomena are nonexistent, which is belied by our own experience. Nor does it mean there are no distinctions among phenomena, a misconception also contradicted by everyday experience. Things exist on the conventional level; most human beings can easily verify distinctions between heat and cold, night and day, far and near, fast and slow, and so on. These distinctions are relative, though, which is why conventional truth is also sometimes called relative truth.

The assertion that perfect awakening is beyond gender is a philosophical claim, not an observation of social realities.[16] Although the claim could be deployed in an apologetics to excuse gender discrimination, and sometimes is, perfect awakening is defined as a state of enlightened awareness utterly free of destructive emotions, misconceptions, and, in fact, all conceptualization whatsoever. All of these ideas have much to contribute to burgeoning Buddhist feminist thinking, but are inadequate to define it. They are important for illuminating the complex influences of politics, economics, bioethics, and colonialism on the lives of women, but are inadequate to address what the powerful ideal of the *bodhisattva* or the concept of spiritual liberation means for women. The religious dimension of women's experience is often overlooked in Western conceptualization of women's concerns.

Buddhism and Gender Identity: Texts, Theory, and Social Realities

From a Buddhist perspective, the ultimate purpose of life is to wake up from the illusions we have about ourselves and the world. Human beings are not created in the image of God; in fact, they are not created at all. Instead, sentient beings evolve due to causes and conditions, taking a variety of forms in successive states of existence. All beings with consciousness have the potential for awakening, regardless of sexual characteristics or gender identity. Sentient beings (beings with consciousness) take rebirth in different states of existence with different identities from one lifetime to the next—visible, invisible, human, nonhuman, female, male, and so on. Rebirth as a human being is regarded as the optimal state of existence for making progress on the spiritual path and achieving liberation from delusions and suffering. The primary delusions, which include attachment, aversion, and ignorance, are problematic because they give rise to unskillful actions that in turn give rise to suffering and dissatisfaction. For example, attachment to a particular gender identity can become a source of suffering if one is unable to satisfactorily embody that identity.

Records tell us that Buddha Śākyamuni affirmed women's capacity to achieve spiritual liberation and, indeed, countless women became *arhatī*s (female liberated beings) at the time of the Buddha. The *Therīgāthā* (Verses of "Elder Nuns) includes seventy-three verses of liberation, recorded in Pāli, that recount the distinctive qualities of pre-eminent nuns by name. These verses, which are the earliest recorded poetic expressions by women, have inspired Buddhist women and men for generations.[17]

For Buddhists, the question of identity begins with a consideration of what constitutes a person, as distinct from other types of phenomena. In other words, we need to get an overview of the general category "human being" before we get down to specifics, such as "male" and "female." From an Indian Buddhist philosophical perspective, the first cut is to distinguish between existent phenomena and nonexistent phenomena. Among existent phenomena, we can distinguish between animate phenomena and inanimate phenomena. Among animate phenomena, we can distinguish between sentient and nonsentient phenomena, those with consciousness and those without. From there, things become a bit more complicated, as there are said to be six states of existence that sentient beings may inhabit in the realm of desire, and many more in the form and formless realms. The Buddha explained personal identity as something imputed by terms and concepts on the basis of the five aggregates (*skandha*s) that comprise a person: form, feelings, perceptions, mental formations, and consciousness. Sexual characteristics pertain to the first aggregate, form, and allude to the body. Gender identities, as social constructs, pertain to the third aggregate: perceptions, recognitions, or discriminations. Like all compounded phenomena, which are dependent on constituent factors and perceptions, constructions of gender lack independent existence or essence.

Many early Buddhist texts reflect remarkably positive images of women as respected members of society at the time of the Buddha. Relative to many other societies, women in Buddhist societies generally enjoyed considerable independence and authority in the family, were free to marry or not, not obligated to produce a dowry, free to divorce and remarry, and assured of their potential to attain the fruits of the spiritual path.[18] Unlike in many societies even today, women in Buddhist societies had options other than marriage and family: they could refuse marriage, engage in business, or live a spiritual life, either at home or in a monastery.

At the time of the Buddha, numerous women achieved prominence in his newly founded religious community. Dhammadinnā and Sukkha were renowned for their teaching skills, Mahāprajāpatī for her leadership skills, Khemā for her exalted wisdom, Patācārā for her impeccable discipline, Nandā for her meditative attainments, Kuṇḍalakesā for her debating skills, Uppalavanā for her supernormal powers, and Somā for her joyful, energetic effort. The Buddha publicly lauded the achievements of these eminent women disciples. To refute the notion that women are incapable of spiritual realization, the Buddha encouraged Mahāprajāpatī to demonstrate her supernormal powers, which she did, dispelling onlookers' doubts about women's capabilities.[19]

The verses of realization preserved in the *Therīgāthā* are said to be the earliest recorded examples of poetry composed by women. The seventy-three verses in this collection are songs of liberation from the bondage of cyclic existence, including mental delusions and social expectations, often related to gender. These nuns challenged the prevailing preconception that women lack intelligence. When she was a laywoman, a *bhikkhunī* named Somā had been castigated by her husband for her "two-finger wisdom," deriding her as unable to judge whether rice was cooked without testing it between two fingers. In response, she declared that for women of knowledge and insight, gender is irrelevant.[20] Contrary to the prevailing perception in India at the time that women were intellectually deficient, Somā retorted that one who is concerned with gender distinctions is deluded and easily distracted from the path. The texts make it clear that, like Somā, many women gained realizations through hearing, contemplating, and practicing the Buddha's teachings, and many became fully liberated *arhatīs*.

The majority of these illustrious women were nuns, but the Buddha also praised outstanding laywomen for their special qualities.[21] Viśākhā, the devout daughter of a wealthy family, was praised for her integrity and generosity to the *saṅgha*. Khujjuttarā was lauded for her knowledge, Sāmāvatī for her kindness, Uttarā for her prowess in meditation, Suppiyā for nursing the ill, Kātiyānī for her loyalty, Kālī for her faith, and so on. In all likelihood, the first person to take refuge in the Buddha's teachings, the signifier of a Buddhist follower, was the laywoman Sujātā, who famously offered the milk rice that ended the Buddha's six years of austerities. Overall, women at the time of the Buddha made a very good showing indeed, with countless women attaining the highest goal of liberation (*nirvāna*) and the other fruits of the path. Inevitably, some women also failed to make the mark. The most notorious of these was Thullanandā, who regularly stirred up mischief and, along with her followers, was castigated for her rather outlandish behavior.[22]

Buddhist Images and Representations of Women

Although we lack historical records to document the lives of the early Buddhists, we are fortunate to have texts that describe their lives. The Indian reciters of oral texts during the early centuries of Buddhist history had prodigious memories, though it must be noted that the reciters were monks and that orally transmitted literature is liable to error. Scholars note that the details, tone, and even the identities of characters in the narratives sometimes vary in different accounts over time.[23] Insofar as Buddhist tradition regards these figures as having been real people, however, their lives are significant. Even if the narratives do not accurately describe the lives of historical figures—and we will never know with certainty whether they lived or not—the extant biographies are significant for what they tell us about Buddhist historical memory regarding nuns and the issues that women, particularly renunciant women, have faced. Although it would be difficult to rely on the Buddhist texts as a source of history, in comparison with contemporaneous literature from other cultures, these texts are rich in detail about the daily life experiences of Indian women during the early years of Buddhist development.[24] Both Collett and Bhikkhu Analayo notice that attitudes toward nuns do change over time, usually to the nuns' detriment, with the canon generally "more favourable towards women than the commentaries."[25]

The portraits or snapshots of Buddhist women that we find in texts and popular media, including village dramas and modern-day films, are not reality. The literary images, of unknown origin, were recounted orally by male redactors for hundreds of years before being committed to writing. Today, visual and digital images are proliferated with good will but with little semblance of historical accuracy. The shape-shifting nature of these literary and visual portraits should not be a source of great surprise or consternation to Buddhists. The unreliable and contested distinction between image and reality, conventional appearance and ultimate truth, is a staple of Buddhist thought, reflected throughout culture in myriad ways. The classic Chan vignette of the finger pointing to the moon alludes to the distinction between the textual teachings and ultimate realization. Literary and cinematic images of a falling cherry blossom wordlessly convey the impermanent nature of life. The tendency of human beings to embroider, misapprehend, and distort perceptions is a staple of Buddhist psychology. If all perceptions are mistaken and fleeting, then it goes without saying that perceptions of gender are subject to misconception.

For many Buddhist scholars and practitioners alike, the topic of gender is a source of confusion. Many writers use terms such as "woman," "femininity," and "feminism" without adequately defining them or exploring their many layers of meaning or their intersectionality. These oversights have led to many facile assumptions, denials, and oversimplifications; the claim, "In Buddhism, men and women are equal," comes to mind. These problems are compounded by ignoring the diverse social and historical contexts in which the terms may be applied. The tools of feminist analysis developed in recent decades can now be used to re-examine feminine imagery in Buddhist texts, gendered representations, and philosophical analysis of gender, but with careful precautions, taking into account the limitations of pre-packaged theoretical paradigms. A thorough investigation of Buddhist femininities comparable to John Powers's groundbreaking work on Buddhist masculinities has yet to appear.[26] This is not that work, but we hope the chapters included here help encourage and anticipate a similarly significant exploration. For starters, we need to investigate how Buddhist concepts of self and no-self intersect with contemporary concepts of identity, especially gender identity and especially for women. Further, we need to examine how the female body, sexuality, and femininity are constructed, construed, and contested in diverse

Buddhist cultures. Placing Buddhist insights and understandings of gender identity alongside insights and understandings from other cultures—on an equal footing—will facilitate informed analysis and help avoid both cultural imperialism and bland, misinformed expediency.

Buddhist Feminism(s): Texts and Communities

This collection explores representations of "the feminine" and the enduring questions of female renunciant identity from multiple Buddhist perspectives. The chapters traverse many disciplines, drawing on philosophy, history, anthropology, sociology, and cultural studies to investigate understandings of femininity and gender construction in a variety of Buddhist contexts. The chapters of the book are organized into two parts. Part I explores the question of whether and how Buddhist feminism(s) can be articulated. Part II examines the question of femininity in diverse Buddhist contexts.

The first chapter, Karen Lang's "Reimagining Buddhist Women in India," sets the stage by surveying the images of women that appear in the Pāli canon, which includes some of the earliest texts ever committed to writing. To do this, Lang takes a textual approach that reorients this ancient archive, discussing ways to re-read classical Buddhist materials—oral, written, official, and unofficial—employing a feminist hermeneutic. Her explicit aim is to locate constructive representations of feminine beauty and the female body in literature and visual culture. Looking beyond images of women as vain and narcissistic snares and seducers, the chapter reassesses a common theme— the rejection of the female form—by analyzing representations of women's bodies in the early Buddhist narratives. In this endeavor, she proposes a fresh epistemological stance, exploring the potential for awakening in a female body.

In chapter 2, "Women Who Did Not Follow the Rules: The Religious Piety of Buddhist Women in Chosŏn Korea," Eun-su Cho documents historical changes that profoundly affected women's religious lives and awareness over many centuries in Korea. During the Three Kingdoms Period (57 BCE–668 CE) and Koryŏ Dynasty (918–1392), Buddhism took root and flourished in Korea, and women were actively engaged in spiritual pursuits. During the Chosŏn Dynasty (1392–1897), however, the government became dominated by Neo-Confucian norms and policies that were oppressive to both Buddhists and women. Cho documents the strategies that Buddhist women devised to subvert the system and protect their religious identity and interests in ways that were "often surprisingly bold and defiant." Working from historical records, she recounts how women defied legal prohibitions and risked public censure to enter Buddhist temples and seek ordination as nuns, providing a valuable account of how women resisted efforts to suppress women and prevent them from exercising their religious choices.

Women's experiences in Buddhist temples and their resistance to societal norms take varied forms in different parts of the world. In chapter 3, "Raichō Hiratsuka and Socially Engaged Buddhism," Christine A. James tells the story of a key figure in the feminist history of modern Japan who led a sexually and spiritually daring life. The Meiji Era was a time of great intellectual ferment accompanied by an awakening of feminist awareness among educated Japanese women. Just at that historical moment, the unconventional Raichō Hiratsuka combined her interests in Western literature and Zen Buddhist practice to produce *Seitō* (Bluestocking), a feminist literary magazine and forum that challenged the gender expectations and limitations of her day. Setting aside the negative views of women inscribed in some traditional Buddhist texts, she embraced the egalitarian rhetoric of Zen nondualism and achieved *kenshō*, a glimpse of enlightenment that may have spurred her feminist insights and activities.

Ching-ning Wang explores the nondualistic rhetoric of Chan/Zen further in "A Great 'Man' is No Longer Gendered: Chan Nuns' Gender Identity and Practice in Contemporary Taiwan," taking up the frequently heard claim that enlightenment is beyond gender. Focusing on a community of Chan Buddhist nuns in contemporary Taiwan, she discusses a radical nondual form of gender identity that is beyond male and female, self and no-self, in a "pedagogy of *prajña*," or wisdom. This rejection of gender essentialism stands against the traditional Chan Buddhist identification of a *da zhangfu* (great person) as male. Unsatisfied by a simple rejection of the term *da zhangfu* as androcentric, patriarchal, or dualistic, this community embraces the concept of nondual gender identity. The nuns' insights contribute to the genealogy of Asian feminist movements through a discussion of their community's experience of how to read Buddhist practice in a feminist way.

In chapter 5, "*Sikkhamat*: The Aesthetics of Asoke Ascetics," Robekkah Ritchie explores the aesthetic dimensions of female renunciant identity, taking as an example the unique redefinition of femininity among nuns in the politically controversial Santi Asoke movement in Thailand. Originating in Thailand in the 1970s, this new order of female renunciants is distinct from the far more numerous white-robed Thai *mae chee* who observe eight precepts, as the Santi Asoke *sikkhamat*s very strictly observe ten precepts. Even though the quota on their numbers is limited to a fraction of the number of monks, these nuns occupy respected positions and wield considerable influence in their communities. After their founder was expelled from the Thai *saṅgha* and the monastics were jailed for contravening institutional norms, the *sikkhamat*s began wearing brown and gray robes. The renunciant identity of the Asoke *sikkhamat*s is thus signaled by the unique style of their robes, which distinguishes them both from mainstream female renunciants and the monks of their own communities. By creating an alternative renunciant identity and a new visual representation of female monasticism, these nuns have redefined the landscape of Buddhist ordination options for women in Thailand and reimagined what a nun can and should wear. Their choices thus raise issues of feminine identity as related to political experience and the challenges that female renunciants pose, both to secular society and to Buddhist institutional stagnation.

In the last chapter in this section, "New Buddhist Women across Borders: Buddhist Influences and Interactions in Alternative Histories of Global Feminisms," Amy Holmes-Tagchungdarpa traces feminist histories from across Asia to identify Buddhist influences in twentieth-century feminist initiatives. Rejecting imperialistic agendas that ignore the influence of indigenous religious and cultural systems such as Buddhism, she explores the genealogies of Asian feminist movements. Further, she proposes tools for thinking about the relationship between feminism and local Buddhist communities, with the aim of developing a critical history of Buddhist feminisms.

Buddhist Femininities:
Demystifying the Essential Feminine

The second part of the book explores concepts of femininity in Buddhist cultures and what these concepts have meant for women at critical junctures in history, up to today. In chapter 7, "Only Skin Deep? Female Embodiment and the Paradox of Beauty in Indian Buddhism," Lisa J. Battaglia proposes a new archive in which Buddhist scriptures be re-examined with reference to living, breathing women in order to answer questions about beauty, ugliness, and plainness in assessing a woman's appearance. Who sets the standards? Battaglia is especially concerned to locate positive images of women and female beauty in Indian Buddhist literature and art, and to question whether and how virtue and beauty may coexist. In numerous Buddhist texts, vanity and attachment to sense pleasures are castigated as hindrances to the cultivation of renunciation and liberation, and female beauty is often portrayed as seductive and dangerous, at least to monks. Although women in Indian society are frequently described as paragons of beauty, they are also seen as potential lures; the female body is cast as the very emblem of sense desires that delude and distract the seeker. To forestall desire and overcome attachment to sense pleasures, the Buddha instructed his followers to meditate on the foulness of rotting corpses at the charnel ground. When speaking to monks, his main audience, he recommended contemplating the rotting corpses of decaying women. If his audience had been nuns rather than monks, he might have recommended the decaying corpses of men, instead. Out of context, however, the listener is left with the impression that female bodies are foul. Over generations, such descriptions have no doubt affected attitudes toward women's bodies negatively, including women's attitudes toward their own bodies. The Buddhist prescription for liberation from desire is the exemplary model of enlightenment, but that model is typically male, which has been interpreted to mean that women must divest themselves not only of their femininity, but also of their female identity.

Chapter 8, Matthew Mitchell's "Conflicts and Compromises: The Relationship between the Nuns of Daihongan and the Monks of Daikanjin within the Zenkoji Temple Complex" looks at an understudied form of Buddhist femininity in early modern and modern Japan through social and legal lenses. From the middle of the seventeenth century until the middle of the twentieth century, the nuns of Daihongan engaged in sporadic lawsuits against the monks of the Daikanjin Monastery over administrative and ritual rights. These disputes between the Daihongan Convent and the Daikanjin Monastery provide nuance to understandings of the relationship between male and female monastic communities in Japan and how those relationships were mediated legally, not just through Buddhist doctrine or practice. Just as important, however, is that these suits provide a window into the ways that the monks and others viewed the nuns and the ways that the nuns deployed precedent and convent legends in an attempt to counter these views and maintain (or regain) their place in the temple complex. In these lawsuits, we can see the nuns enacting a legally savvy Buddhist femininity that expands our understanding of what it meant to be a female monastic.

In chapter 9, "Gendered Hagiography in Tibet: Comparing Clerical Representations of the Female Visionary, Khandro Tāre Lhamo," Holly Gayley recounts the story of nonmonastic Buddhist practitioners living in a vastly different social and cultural sphere. Her study chronicles the religious partnership of a renowned tantric couple who lived and practiced in the remote Golok region of Tibet during the twentieth century. The "shared destiny" of this tantric couple over lifetimes culminates in a relationship to heal both the personal and collective cultural trauma sustained by the people of Tibet. Taking rebirth in the physical body of a woman to benefit sentient beings, Khandro Tāre Lhamo manifests the "*ḍākinī* principle" to activate spiritual evolution in the material world. This form of practice demonstrates the transformative power of tantric practice by linking the erotic and the revelatory, the exotic and the ordinary, throughout many different lifetimes and gender identities.

In chapter 10, "Feminine Identities in Buddhist *Chöd*," Michelle J. Sorensen discusses the sense of identification nuns feel with wisdom *ḍākinīs*, feminine embodiments of enlightenment, in the Tibetan tradition. She explains how, in contrast to nuns in earlier Buddhist cultures, the renunciant identity of nuns in two Himalayan communities (in Pharping, Nepal, and Dharamsala, India) is signaled by their practice of *chöd*. This Tibetan Buddhist recitation and visualization practice derives from Machik Labdrön, a female adept whose life spanned the eleventh and twelfth centuries. Although the practice is accessible to both women and men, it is especially popular among women, many of whom draw inspiration from female enlightened embodiments such as the *ḍākinī* Thröma Nagmo. This chapter raises issues about the social implications of feminine religious imagery and, more broadly, about gendered paradigms of enlightenment. In exploring contemplative practices, it addresses the spiritual dimensions of women's experience.

Chapter 11, Jeff Wilson's "Mindfully Feminine, Mindfully Masculine: Meditation and the Marketing of Gendered Lifestyles," shifts focus from the Himalayas to North America and from the eleventh century to the present day. Wilson considers the gendered ways in which mindful lifestyles are marketed to women in the contemporary West. Three case studies that investigate both text and visual representations illustrate how trendy constructions of feminine identity at different stages of life are used to promote, and in turn are promoted by, appeals to a fulfilling, mindful lifestyle. From "mindful extravagance" to "mindful motherhood," both mindful awareness and quasi-Buddhist femininities have become commodities designed and sold as the answer to a woman's every dilemma. This trend adds another layer of confusion to the demystification of Buddhist femininities.

The Questions Raised and Remaining

The topic of Buddhist femininities raises many important methodological issues, especially questions of epistemology and representation, or what is sometimes called "feminist standpoint theory." Setting diverse approaches to Buddhist feminine identity side by side clearly illustrates the constructed nature of gender and enables a Buddhist critique of fixed notions of self and their gendered manifestations. From monastery to mindfulness-based motherhood, each of the writers presents a fresh approach to a Buddhist analysis of gender, and they all suggest potential directions for the deployment of theoretical engagement with gender identities.

In recent years, especially amidst the debate that besieges full ordination for Buddhist women, non-Asian women stand accused, because of their "feminist agendas," of trying to talk Asian nuns into seeking higher status. This critique seems to assume that feminism is an invention of the West and a contrivance to manipulate hapless Asian women to feminist ways of thinking against their will. While this "critique of the feminist perspective" presumably aims to encourage indigenous voices, it also seems to imply that Asian women have failed to recognize gender inequities or to resist oppression on their own. The cross-cultural feminist conversation is richly complicated by a panoply of perspectives, including those of Western-educated Asian women, Asian-educated Western women, monks, nuns, laywomen, and laymen, feminist and otherwise. A close reading of Buddhist women's history and the burgeoning Buddhist feminist movement exposes many ironies. Building on the work of Kumari Jayawardena, Inderpal Grewal, and others, the papers in this volume examine elements of national and transnational feminist discourse to assess the usefulness of poststructuralist theory for understanding the contemporary Buddhist feminist movement, both in Asia and globally. The aim here is not simply to commemorate exceptional women, but also to investigate the claim that Buddhist feminism is a Western imposition and to examine indigenous Buddhist women's initiatives on their own terms.

Buddhist feminist theories share commonalities with Western feminist theories.[27] For example, passages in both early and late Buddhist texts speak about women as if they had a specific nature identifiable on the basis of their physical and/or psychological characteristics. Followers of Sarvāstivāda, an early school of Buddhism that developed in India, asserted that phenomena exist as they appear to exist. This type of thinking veers toward essentialism in that it is liable to concretize phenomena; in that sense, it is similar to the gender essentialism described by Simone de Beauvoir, bell hooks, and others. Many Buddhist feminists accept the theory that gender characteristics are social constructions. At the same time, it is clear that social constructions affect the ways women perceive themselves and each other, and lead to assumptions about "the way women are" and "what women like."

From a Buddhist perspective, human identity is contingent on the five aggregates mentioned above, and also on the five elements: earth, water, fire, air, and ether. Beyond these constitutive components, human beings have no enduring essence, independently existent self, or soul. Like all compounded phenomena, the identities of sentient beings are impermanent and fluid. The contingent nature of identity, including all our identities and all aspects of our identities, implied by the concept of *anātman*, or absence of inherent or independent existence. As one component of identity, gender identities are also impermanent, changing from lifetime to lifetime, and contingent on physical characteristics, inclinations, and social constructions of gender. Human beings commonly buy into the constructs they have been raised to accept and unthinkingly adopt the gender categories proffered by the communities of their birth, blithely assuming the standard definitions, depictions, and stereotypes they learn in the process of socialization. Assumptions about gender identities have enormous consequences for human beings' psychological and spiritual health and development. Consider how many women have been inducted into the commodification of women, reducing themselves and other women primarily to their physical attributes, thus becoming complicit in their own subjugation by assuming stereotypical attitudes and behaviors. Breast implants and facelifts come to mind.

In an analysis strikingly similar to modern theories of gender fluidity, Buddhist thinkers assert that human beings' identities are constantly in flux. In line with the fundamental assertion that all compounded phenomena change from moment to moment, gender identities are also mutable. Not only are gender categories fluid—as seen in the *vinaya* texts where males become females and vice versa—but sentient beings may also assume different gender identities as their impermanent streams of consciousness continue through successive existences or lifetimes.[28] This is not as farfetched as it may seem. We can confirm the notion of changing identity by considering, for example, that individuals change constantly, both on the molecular level and over time, from conception to birth, childhood, youth, adulthood, and throughout the process of aging, until the end of their lives. Gender categories, like all composite phenomena, also inevitably change in accordance with causes and conditions, as do social and psychological constructions of gender. This is especially evident in the vast array of Buddhist cultures that have developed over the past 2,500 years. Buddhists are as diverse as the Shan and Mon populations of Burma, the Chakma and Marma of Bangladesh, the Buryats and Kalmyks of Russia, the Newars and Sherpas of Nepal, the Chinese, Japanese, Korean, Mongolian, Sinhalese, Thai, Vietnamese, and so on. Perceptions of women and gender overall have also changed over the course of history, during various dynasties and eras of Buddhist history, up to the present. As Buddhism was gradually adopted in new lands, it adapted to the indigenous cultures of the people. This process of Buddhist cultural adaptation continues today in places as diverse as New York, New Zealand, Brazil, and Uganda.

From a Buddhist perspective, the obvious physical differences exhibited by sentient beings are not nearly as important as their similarity in possessing consciousness. When gazing into the eyes of an animal, it becomes difficult to deny the common link of consciousness. In a Buddhist theory of human evolution, consciousness, defined as knowing and awareness, holds primary importance and overshadows the other aspects of personhood, because it is through consciousness that a human being is able to recognize suffering and its causes, and cultivate the wholesome mental factors and actions that lead to liberation from suffering. It is through the refinement of consciousness that a person can achieve mastery over unwholesome mental attitudes and habitual tendencies. This assertion rests on a number of assumptions imbedded in the Buddhist teachings—namely, that actions have consequences in accordance with the law of *karma*, cause and effect, and that through the cultivation of consciousness human beings can achieve a positive evolution, free from harm to oneself and others.

Every woman's experience is unique, yet stereotypes of women abound. We often hear Buddhists, women included, exclaim that Buddhist women are not oppressed, not in need of social liberation, and only need be concerned about liberation from cyclic existence (*samsāra*). Many strongly believe that Buddhists need not speak up about the sexist oppression they experience because, as frequently claimed, "In Buddhism, everyone is equal. Anyone can achieve liberation." In the minds of many Buddhists, women and men stand shoulder to shoulder on the path to enlightenment, and any woman who practices the teachings diligently is capable of achieving enlightenment, the same as any man. Many Buddhist women conveniently attribute any inequalities or sexism in Buddhist texts and societies to the oppressive Brahmanical attitudes enshrined, for example, in *The Laws of Manu*, or to Confucian social dictates. Many strongly believe that discrimination against women is something that happens to non-Buddhists. Analogous to bell hooks's analysis of African American women: when Buddhism is talked about, sexism militates against an acknowledgment of the interests of Buddhist women; when women are talked about, racism militates against an acknowledgment of Asian female interests; in a perverse kind of double jeopardy, Asian Buddhist women are indicted on both counts. Similarly, it may be claimed that, in accepting sexist relationship patterns, they have "had their identity socialized out of existence,"[29] because ". . . sexist-racist socialization had effectively brainwashed us to feel that our interests were not worth fighting for, to believe that the only option available to us was submission to the terms of others."[30] To a very grave extent, such thinking has prevented white feminists from understanding and overcoming their sexist and racist attitudes toward Asian women.

Human beings are not equal in point of fact, for the simple reason that each one is different in both small and large ways. Human beings share many common human characteristics, but each is uniquely constituted. Not only do human beings have distinct genealogies and genetic identities, but also unique karmic genealogies that shape their propensities, capabilities, and temperaments in each lifetime; that is, we are all products of our actions in the past—wholesome, unwholesome, and neutral. Nonetheless, all sentient beings are said to have equal potential to achieve liberation or awakening.

The chapters in this book talk about feminisms and femininities in both theory and practice and include a full round of discussions about how feminism manifests in Buddhist communities. Beginning with a look at archival Buddhist literature and theory, they examine Buddhist thinking about gender norms and how Buddhists interpret and act in relation to these norms in their daily lives. Altogether, the writers seek to engage with both normative interpretations of gender relations and alternate feminist histories garnered from throughout Asia, and to understand the intersectionality between Buddhism and feminism in different parts of the globe. From a variety of non-

Western cultural perspectives, the chapters contribute to a rethinking of the ways in which feminism has been constructed, deconstructed, and reconstructed, usually without the benefit of Buddhist women's voices. A Buddhist rethinking of what feminism connotes will allow for more inclusive representations of women's voices and help to redirect the feminist conversation from abstract theorizing to tangible and socially liberating dimensions of Buddhist women's experience.

Recent highly publicized international incidents of sexual violence, predation, exploitation, and aggression have generated renewed interest in gender issues, both in religion and society, including issues of gender justice and injustice in contemporary Buddhist societies. This collection takes Buddhist texts and narratives as starting points for an exploration of Buddhist approaches and responses to gender studies and feminist studies in religion across a spectrum of issues and traditions. It explores constructions of gender, constructions of motherhood, and images of monastic women through the multifarious lenses of Buddhist textual traditions and continually changing Buddhist societies. By acknowledging this diversity of Buddhist perspectives, sensibilities, and assumptions, we can usefully question what it means to be feminine and cross-culturally re-envision what it means to be a feminist.

Notes

1. Karma Lekshe Tsomo, "Buddhism and Human Rights," *A Companion to Buddhist Philosophy*, ed. Steven Emmanuel (Chichester, West Sussex, U.K.: Wiley-Blackwell, 2013), 651–62.

2. In "Making History: Reflections on Feminism, Narrative, and Desire," Susan Stanford Friedman warns that interminable self-referencing "contains within it the potential of dangerous inaction or, to be more precise, action which in its constant inward turn inhibits an outer-directed energy for social change." *Feminism Beside Itself*, ed. Diane Elam and Robyn Wiegman (New York and London: Routledge, 1995), 25.

3. bell hooks, *Talking Back: Thinking Feminist, Thinking Black* (Cambridge, MA: South End Press: 1999).

4. Janet Gyatso and Hanna Havnevik, *Women in Tibet* (New York: Columbia University Press, 2005), 3.

5. See, for example, Kurtis R. Schaeffer's discussion of this theme in "Autobiography of a Medieval Hermitess: Orgyan Chokyi (1675–1729)," Ibid., 85–109.

6. See, for example, Chandra Talpade Mohanty, *Feminism without Borders: Decolonizing Theory* (Durham, NC: Duke University Press, 2003); Rosalind C. Morris, ed., *Can the Subaltern Speak?: Reflections on the History of an Idea* (New York: Columbia University Press, 2010); and Judy Tzu-Chun Wu, *Radicals on the Road: Internationalism, Orientalism, and Feminism during the Vietnam Era* (Ithaca, NY: Cornell University Press, 2013).

7. Kumari Jayawardena, *Feminism and Nationalism in the Third World* (Brooklyn, NY: Verso, 2016).

8. Carol S. Anderson, "Changing Sex or Changing Gender in Pāli Buddhist Literature," *Queer/Religion* 14:2(2017).

9. Ibid.

10. Damchö Diana Finnegan, " 'For the Sake of Women, Too': Ethics and Gender in the Narratives of the Mūlasarvāstivāda Vinaya," Doctoral dissertation, University of Wisconsin-Madison, 2009, 133–34.

11. Ibid., 133.

12. Vin III.35. For discussions of sex change, gender equality, and sexualities, see Peter Harvey, *Introduction to Buddhist Ethics* (Cambridge: Cambridge University Press, 2000), 353–434; and Serinity Young, *Courtesans and Tantric Consorts: Sexualities in Buddhist Narrative, Iconography, and Ritual* (New York: Routledge, 2004).

13. Kate Crosby, *Theravada Buddhism: Continuity, Diversity, and Identity* (Chichester, UK: Wiley Blackwell, 2o14), 252.

14. Ibid., 252–253.

15. For a discussion of these views, see Rita M. Gross, *Buddhism Beyond Gender: Liberation from Attachment to Identity* (Boulder, CO: Shambhala Publications, 2018).

16. Lucinda J. Peach takes up this question in 'Social Responsibility, Sex Change, and Salvation: Gender Justice in the Lotus Sutra," *Philosophy East and West* 52:1(2002): 50–74.

17. Translations and studies of these verses include Kathryn R. Blackstone, *Women in the Footsteps of the Buddha: Struggle for Liberations in the Therigatha* (Delhi: Motilal Barnassidas, 2007), 127–35; Charles Hallisey, *Therigatha: Poems of the First Buddhist Women* (Cambridge, MA: Harvard University Press, 2015); Ria Kloppenborg, "Female Stereotypes in Early Buddhism: The Women of the Therīgātha," *Female Stereotypes in Religious Traditions*, ed. Ria Kloppenborg and Wouter J. Hanegraaff (Leiden, New York, and Köln: E. J. Brill, 1995), 151–69; and Anagarika Mahendra, *Therigatha: Book of Verses of Elder Bhikkhunis* (Roslindale, MA: Dhamma Publishers, 2017).

18. The four fruits or successive stages of the Buddhist path are *sotāpanna* (stream-winner), *sakadāgāmī* (once-returner), *anāgāmī* (nonreturner), and *arahant* (liberated being).

19. Gisela Krey, "On Women as Teachers in Early Buddhism: Dhammadinnā and Khemā," *Buddhist Studies Review* 27:1(2010): 18.

20. Bhikkhu Bodhi, *Discourses of the Ancient Nuns* (Kandy: Buddhist Publication Society (1997), quoted in Justine McGill, "The Silencing of Women," *Women in Philosophy: What Needs to Change?* ed. Katrina Hutchison and Fiona Jenkins (New York: Oxford University Press, 2013), 198–99.

21. For example, the commentary on the *Etadagga Vagga* in the Anguttara Nikāya describes the special qualities of distinguished laywomen, nuns, laymen, and monks. See Nyanaponika Thera and Hellmuth Hecker, *Great Disciples of the Buddha: Their Lives, Their Works, Their Legacy* (Somerville, MA: Wisdom Publications, 2003), 245–316.

22. Reiko Ohnuma, "Bad Nun: Thullananda in Pali Canonical and Commentarial Sources," *Journal of Buddhist Ethics* 20(2013): 17–66.

23. For further discussion, see Alice Collett, *Lives of Early Buddhist Nuns: Biographies as History* (New Delhi: Oxford University Press, 2016); and Jan Nattier, *Once Upon a Future Time: Studies in a Buddhist Prophecy of Decline* (Nagoya: Nanzen Institute for Religion and Culture, 1991).

24. Collett, *Lives of Early Buddhist Nuns*, 3–17.

25. Collette, *Lives*, xxv.

26. For a thorough study of sexuality and gender in early Buddhist thought, see José Ignacio Cabezón, *Sexuality in Classical South Asian Buddhism* (Somerville, MA: Wisdom Publications, 2017).

27. Here I am drawing on the useful presentation of feminist thinking presented by Jennifer Hockenbery Dragseth, *Thinking Woman: A Philosophical Approach to the Quandary of Gender* (Eugene, OR: Cascade Books, 2015).

28. The question of how sentient beings take rebirth in successive existences if they have no independent self or essence is explained in chapter 4, "Contemplating Self and No Self," in Karma Lekshe Tsomo, *Into the Jaws of Yama, Lord of Death: Buddhism, Bioethics, and Death* (Albany, NY: State University of New York Press, 2006), 43–61; and in Chapter 6, "No Self: Personal Continuity and Dependent Arising," in Rupert Gethin, *The Foundations of Buddhism* (New York: Oxford University Press, 1998), 133–62.

29. bell hooks, *Ain't I a Woman?* (Boston: South End Press, 1981), 7.

30. Ibid., 9.

Part I

Buddhist Feminisms

Texts and Communities

Chapter 1

Reimagining Buddhist Women in India

KAREN LANG

Feminism in its varied forms, methods, and goals is as diverse as Buddhism, which spread widely throughout Asia over two millennia and, more recently, into the West. Nonetheless, there are points of convergence. Many Buddhist scholars and practitioners share feminist commitments to the recovery of women's histories, to understanding the past cultural constraints and textual interpretations that marginalized women, and to call for equal access to educational opportunities and leadership roles within religious institutions. The retrieval of Buddhist women's religious history involves taking a critical look at canonical texts using a hermeneutic of suspicion that acknowledges the dominant role of an elite body of monks in their production and preservation.

Studies on Buddhism and gender have raised questions about the prevalence of negative stereotypes about women. Even when we have reason to think that nuns were the originators of works, such as the *Nuns' Verses* (*Therīgāthā*), monks most likely were responsible for writing down oral texts, contributing commentaries, and redacting the texts over many centuries. Compilations and redactions of works reflect the editing choices of those who collected texts, preserved them, and, in some cases, translated them. These choices were almost certainly influenced by the cultural environment of the time. It is not difficult to find in some Buddhist texts portraits of women

as sexually insatiable, greedy, jealous, and untrustworthy. Although
we should not ignore or downplay negative and restrictive attitudes
that monastics express about women in some of these texts, we see in
other texts positive portraits of women as nurturing mothers, generous donors, intrepid nuns, and inspirational teachers. The Buddhist
canon is vast, and there is not a monolithic picture of the Buddha's
female disciples; we find both negative and positive portrayals of
laywomen and nuns.

The monastic codes of conduct (*vinaya*) and the discourses (Pāli:
sutta, Sanskrit: *sūtra*) are important sources of information on Buddhist women, but equally important are the numerous noncanonical
narratives and commentaries. In none of these sources, however, are
we likely to hear women's voices that haven't been altered in some
way over time. The women depicted in noncanonical narratives and
Mahāyāna discourses are literary characters who reveal more about
their creators' views than historically accurate information about Buddhist women. In reading these works, we may need to read between
the sanctioned lines or "against the grain" when looking for evidence
of women's roles and their concerns.

The First Buddhist Women

When modern translators of Buddhist texts depict the Buddha as
addressing a large audience as "monks" (*bhikkhu*), it seems that
women have been left out. To read women back into the Buddhist
community, which in its broadest sense includes monks, nuns, laymen, and laywomen, it is worth noting, as Bhikkhu Anālayo and Alice
Collett do, that this form of address "can refer to all those gathered
who show reverence, or it can mean one who is a monk, nun, layman
or laywomen, or it can be said, more specifically, to be an address to
the elder monks in the community."[1]

Going Forth from Home to Homelessness

Women faced resistance from their families, who opposed their choice
to live a celibate religious life, and they also faced resistance from the
Buddha. According to traditional accounts of the establishment of the
nun's order, the Buddha was initially reluctant to establish an order
of nuns. When his aunt and foster-mother, Mahāpajāpatī Gotamī,

asked for permission to leave the household life, he declined three times to grant her permission. This resolute woman refused to take no for an answer, even from the Buddha. Saddened but determined, she cut her hair, put on ochre robes, and followed him. Ānanda saw her tired, covered in dust from the journey, and weeping. Moved by her tears and her resolve, he approached the Buddha with her request. He asked the Buddha whether a woman is capable of attaining enlightenment if she leaves home and follows his teachings and monastic discipline. When the Buddha affirmed this, but still declined to grant women permission, Ānanda made the request more personal. He reminded him that Mahāpajāpatī Gotamī raised him and fed him with her own breast milk after his mother died. The Buddha finally gave his consent to her request but with the stipulation that she must accept eight conditions, namely, that monks participate in the ordination of nuns, determine the dates for the twice a month confessional meetings, participate in the interrogation of nuns who transgress disciplinary rules, and help decide the penalty, and further that nuns must live under monks' supervision during the rainy season retreat, nuns must never criticize monks, must never reprimand monks, and even senior nuns must defer to newly ordained monks.[2] Mahāpajāpatī Gotamī agreed and entered the monastic community along with five hundred of her companions.

The canons of different Buddhist schools contain variant versions of this story. Bhikkhu Anālayo draws attention to a Sarvāstivāda school's version that suggests a different reading of the Buddha's refusal to grant ordination to women. The Buddha proposed to Mahāpajāpatī Gotamī that she shave her hair and wear ochre robes but remain at home. This alternative, Anālayo suggests, "changes a flat refusal to grant ordination to women into what appears to express a concern that embarking on the life of a wandering mendicant at a time when the Buddhist monastic order was still in its formative stages may involve hardships and dangers for women."[3] Despite the recognition that women have equal capacity with men to reach enlightenment, the deference to social norms and the imposition of conditions uniquely binding on women who seek to become nuns perpetuated male control over women. Society's expectations that women as children should be subject to their father's control, as wives to their husband's control, and in old age to their son's control were codified in ancient Indian legal texts. But as Stephanie Jamison points out, we find a countervailing attitude expressed in ancient Indian religious texts; the Vedas and the epics abound in stories of resourceful, energetic women capable of independent action in the face of resistance.[4] In Buddhist texts also we find resilient women who overcome their families' resistance to their ordination and intrepid nuns who reject any attempts to deter them from seeking enlightenment.

In Young Chung challenges the accuracy of these traditional accounts of the establishment of the nuns' order on historical grounds based on her detailed comparison of monastic rules for nuns and monks in the *vinayas* of the Dharmaguptaka and Theravāda schools. Most of the eight rules or conditions concern probationary training for nuns, which was a much later development. Moreover, most of the eight rules are nearly identical to minor rules that require only that nuns confess them when they break them. She concludes that these rules are "so different in character and tone" that they are late interpolations "appended by the compilers, and not indicative of either the intentions of Gautama Buddha himself, or of the Buddhist traditions as a whole."[5] Other canonical sources support Chung's argument that these eight rules were later developments. With the words "Come, monk," the Buddha ordained the first monk, Aññāta Kondañña. The Buddha extended the same invitation to Bhaddā:

> After I left my daytime shelter on Vulture Peak,
> I saw the stainless Buddha honored by the Monastic
>   Community.
> I kneeled down, paid homage to him, and facing him, put
>   my raised hands together.
> "Come, Bhaddā," he said to me. That was my ordination.
>   (Thī vv.108–9)[6]

Both passages suggest that ordination in the early formative years of the Buddhist community was much less formal than it would become in later years.

Monks were expected to teach nuns, but not all of them did so willingly. According to the eight rules, nuns were to request teaching from the monks and never to criticize them. But we do find in the *vinaya* indications that not all nuns observed these rules. Several nuns criticized the monk Cūlapanthaka for not giving them a detailed and thorough explanation of each of the eight rules. He was renowned for his skill in meditation and his supernatural power. His response to their criticism was to show off his supernatural power by rising into the sky, where he remained reciting until dark. The nuns had to wait until the nunnery gates opened the next morning. The consequences of his action were mixed: the nuns were suitably impressed with his skill, but townspeople spread rumors that the nuns and the monk had broken their vows of chastity. The rumors reached the Buddha, who made the rule that monks must never teach women after the sun goes down. Nothing in this account indicates that the Buddha reproved the nuns for initially criticizing Cūlapanthaka's teaching skills.[7]

Regardless of whether these eight rules were later interpolations or even strictly observed, women chose to follow Mahāpajāpatī Gotamī. A collection of biographical narratives (*apadāna*) of the Buddha and his disciples were composed circa first and second centuries BCE in the Pāli language and added to the canon of the Theravāda school (the tradition followed in Sri Lanka, Thailand, and Myanmar). The *Narratives about Nuns* (*Therī-apadāna*), which narrates the lives (including many lived under previous *buddha*s) of the Buddha's prominent female disciples, provides, Collett asserts, a "female past" for the Buddhist tradition.[8] One of these narratives, *Gotamī's Story* (*Gotamī-apadāna*), traces Mahāpajāpatī Gotamī's achievement of the enlightened status of an *arhat* to the virtuous actions that she had done in her past lives as a slave girl, a rich man's daughter, and a goddess (nuns were always female in their past births). For the nuns who wrote Gotamī's story in a way that paralleled the lives of Gotama Buddha, she becomes "the Buddha for women." Their enlightenment depended not on Gotama Buddha, but on Gotamī, who opened a path for nuns to reach the goal.[9] But, Jonathan Walters reminds us, her story was not written only to inspire women.

> Finally, it is worth noting that *Gotamī-apadāna* also addresses a male audience, namely, the androcentric ecclesiastical hierarchy of early Buddhism. The vindication of woman's spirituality does not only encourage women; it also serves as a corrective to men who belittle women's spiritual potential. Misogynist attitudes, explicitly and implicitly, are countered by the example of Gotamī.[10]

If the *Narratives about Nuns* were authored by women, as Walters suggests, it provides further evidence for women's active engagement in the Buddhist community: "There is clear epigraphic evidence that Buddhist nuns actually participated in the imperial building projects which they advocated through their performances of the *Apadāna* stories."[11]

Thullanandā and the Formation
of Monastic Rules for Nuns

Monastic codes of conduct prescribe many more rules for nuns than for monks. Chung notes that many of these additional rules for nuns deal specifically with situations that women face, ranging from the serious issue of a possible pregnancy to monks' petty requests for nuns to wash their robes for them. These additional rules for nuns were also generated because the conservative culture of ancient India did not support women's renunciation and not infrequently maligned women who became nuns as harlots or whores.[12]

> These insults—like most insults—probably point to real or perceived social differences or perceptions, and Buddhist sources themselves suggest that it was an ongoing problem to mark and maintain a clear distinction between Buddhist nuns and prostitutes or loose women. In fact the "brahmin" insult could even be read as a perfectly reasonable if not very nicely expressed cultural assumption since the only other group of "single" women who lived together in an Indian city . . . would have been prostitutes, their mothers, and daughters.[13]

Visākhā, an influential laywoman, was concerned that the public might confuse nuns and prostitutes seen bathing naked at the same place and offered to provide bathing clothes for the nuns. The Buddha, who accepted her offer, then made the rule that it was an offense for nuns to bathe naked. The highly disciplined life that these monastic rules depict elevated the low status of women, including ex-prostitutes. Entrance in the nuns' order provided them with the training that enabled them to live purposeful lives. Despite cultural biases against female renunciation, Buddhist monastic institutions enabled single women—those who were never married, those who were widowed, and those who became prostitutes—to leave home, or the streets, for a secure refuge.

"Human nature being what it is," Peter Skilling observes, "we should not expect all learned nuns to be model members of the Sangha." The nun he had in mind was Thullanandā, renowned more for her greed and inappropriate behavior than for her erudition and teaching skills.[14] *Vinaya* texts depict her as a learned nun with many students, an excellent preacher, whose teaching inspired King Pasenadi to reward her with expensive gifts and attracted many other lay supporters. But Thullanandā's notorious behavior was responsible for the promulgation of more disciplinary rules than any other nun. Among the many perceived offenses of this enterprising nun and her gang of six accomplices were operating a tavern, a slaughterhouse, and a brothel near their nunnery. Schopen claims the success of these ventures and the resulting conflict and criticism that came from "other working women and the community at large" were the major motivating factors for rules prohibiting such conduct. Schopen does note, however, that nuns' business ventures were often connected with the difficulty nuns had in supporting themselves and their urban monasteries.[15] Thullanandā also challenged in court a wealthy landowner who had intended to repossess a shed his father had donated to the nuns. She brought a case against him, whereupon he insulted her by calling her a "bald-headed whore." She had him brought up for slander, and the court again ruled in her favor. He then incited others to abuse nuns until finally he was locked up. The bitter dispute generated a public uproar that reached the Buddha's ears and, as a result, monastics were prohibited from bringing lawsuits. Reiko Ohnuma suggests that we could read this story in a way that depicts Thullanandā as a "protofeminist." The story's "gendered framework" that pits the nun Thullanandā, who on behalf of other nuns speaks up to defend their property rights against a wealthy male householder, "implies that her main offense was not in bringing about a lawsuit but in failing to show the proper deference toward men in power."[16]

Thullanandā's conflicts were not confined to the lay community. The rules that nuns should never criticize monks did not restrain her at all. When the elder monk Mahākassapa criticized Ānanda, she responded quickly and in anger. She overheard Mahākassapa rebuke Ānanda for wandering with a group of undisciplined young monks, who return to lay life. Thullanandā rebukes Mahākassapa: "How dare master Mahākassapa, who was once an ascetic of a heterodox sect insult Ānanda, a wise sage, by calling him a fool!"[17] It is never a prudent move to insult a senior and powerful figure. Mahākassapa took offense and launched into a vigorous self-serving defense of his loyalty to the Buddha. The monastic redactors of this scripture conclude at the end of this story that Thullanandā fell away from the religious life. The version of this scripture found in the *Mahāvastu* is a good deal harsher and much more explicit about the location into which she fell: "And as she had hardened her heart against the venerable Mahākāśyapa she was reborn in one of the great hells."[18]

Ohnuma raises a pertinent question: In what specific ways is Thullanandā a "bad nun" (or perhaps, to use the modern idiom, "a badass nun")? The evidence Ohnuma uncovers indicates that Thullanandā's desire for alms, possessions, wealth, fame, and her favoritism for Ānanda and others violates the expectation that all members of the monastic community should be treated equally. She proposes instead that we read Thullanandā's favoritism " 'against the grain,' as it were—a subtle challenge to the kind of renunciatory detachment advocated by the monastic path."[19] When the other nuns wondered whether her sister Sundarīnandā had sex and became pregnant while still a nun, Thullanandā informed them that she did, and they criticized her for concealing her sister's offense. Ohnuma concedes Thullanandā's behavior in this instance is wrong but says:

> I prefer to read it otherwise: as a highly emotional plea in defense of the sisterly bond—monastic regulations be damned. . . . To some extent, of course, whether Thullanandā serves as a marker for a "pro-woman" stance or a "pro-emotion" stance perhaps boils down to much the same thing—for women, in the world of Indic scripture, often stand for the realm of excessive emotions and particularistic attachments, and are opposed to a renunciatory detachment that is implicitly gendered as male.[20]

Thullanandā's passionate defense of other nuns and of Ānanda, while not marking her as an ideal ascetic, makes her seem much more like a genuine human being.

Exemplary Laywomen and Nuns

Buddhist laywomen sustained the monastic community through their gifts of food, clothing, medicine, and other necessities. Because of their important role in providing food and other sustenance for monastic community, laywomen sometimes seem more highly regarded than nuns.[21] In the "Section on the Best" (*Etadagga-vagga*), the Buddha singles out ten female lay disciples for special commendation. First among them is Sujātā, the young woman who fed him when he was starving, thus giving him the strength to proceed to Bodhgayā, the site of his enlightenment. The Buddha tells Princess Suppavāsā, "the best donor of excellent alms food," that donating food gives the recipient life, a healthy appearance, strength, and happiness, and assures the donor of rebirth in heaven. Suppiyā, "the best of those who comfort the sick," cuts a slice off her own thigh to make a broth for an ailing monk when meat was unavailable in the marketplace. When informed of her extraordinary generosity, the Buddha heals her wounds through his supernatural power before making a rule that monastics must never eat human flesh.[22]

Married laywomen could donate their wealth independently of their husbands. Visākhā used money from the sale of one of her golden ornaments to build a monastery near Śrāvastī. She also does not hesitate to criticize monks' behavior. Visākhā had invited the Buddha and his disciples for a meal. The young slave girl she sent to tell the monks that the meal was ready saw a group of naked men in the monastery's courtyard. The confused maidservant returned and told her that there weren't any monks in the monastery—just naked ascetics! After the meal was over, Visākhā told the Buddha what her slave girl had seen, criticized the monks' nakedness, and asked if she could donate clothing for them to wear in the rain and while bathing, to which he readily agreed.[23] Narratives like this one indicate the important role that laywomen played in monastic life not only as generous donors but also as critics of monastic behavior.

These exemplary laywomen exhibit the virtues often attributed to good women: they comfort the sick, provide food for the needy, remain faithful, and treat others with loving kindness. The Buddha praised Kātiyānī and Kālī for their faith. Faith was important also in the lives of Nakula's parents, the ideal married couple, who were praised as "the best of those who are intimate companions." According to the "Compatibility Scripture" (Samajīvi Sutta),[24] the Buddha visited the elderly couple and told them that their mutual devotion and their compatibility in faith, virtue, and generosity ensured they would be together in all their future lives. He praised two laywomen, Uttarā and Queen Sāmāvatī, for their practice of loving kindness. When a jealous prostitute dumped a pot of boiling oil over Uttarā's head, the oil did not burn her because of the power she had acquired through meditating on loving kindness and compassion.[25] Queen Sāmāvatī's story is intertwined with that of her enterprising servant, Khujjuttarā, who habitually spent only half the money the queen gave her to purchase flowers and kept the rest. After hearing the Buddha preach, Khujjuttarā was so transformed by what she had heard that she confessed her previous dishonesty. Queen Sāmāvatī forgave her and asked her to repeat everything the Buddha had said. Khujjuttarā, now freed from servitude, went daily to hear the Buddha teach and returned to teach the queen and her attendants exactly what the Buddha said. For this reason, the Buddha recognized her as the most learned of laywomen. This ex-slave and laywoman was recognized for her important role in transmitting the Buddha's teachings. Peter Skilling states:

> Although early literary and epigraphic evidence thus shows that nuns contributed to the transmission of the texts—as is only to be expected—their role seems to have eventually been forgotten or ignored. Furthermore, no commentaries or independent treatises composed by nuns are known to have survived. It may be that they were never written down, or, if they were, they were not preserved in later ages, when the influence and status of the order of nuns waned. This may have been a decision made by the monks, who controlled the redaction of the scriptures.[26]

The canonical collection of discourses *This was Said* (*Itivuttaka*) contains the 112 discourses she had heard from the Buddha and repeated verbatim to Queen Sāmāvatī.[27]

Wealthy courtesans also supported the Buddhist order, though none is cited in the "Section on the Best." The most generous of these courtesans was Ambapālī. The *vinaya* records that tax revenue from Ambapālī's business was so large that influential merchants persuaded King Bimbisāra to invite a courtesan to set up business in the capital.[28] *Mahāparinibbāna sutta* records that toward the end of the Buddha's life, after Ambapālī heard him teach, she invited him and his disciples for a meal. When later confronted by several young men of the ruling Licchavī family, she refused to be intimidated or bribed into giving up her invitation. Annoyed that a mere woman had bested them, the arrogant aristocrats approached the Buddha with an invitation of their own. But the Buddha refused them, as he had already accepted her offer. That evening, Ambapālī served the Buddha and his disciples food she had prepared, and after the meal she offered him the gift of her mango grove, which he accepted.[29] This episode subverts ancient Indian cultural norms that privilege the power and prestige of high-caste males; the honor of serving the Buddha is granted to a prostitute.

Ambapālī became a nun late in life after her best assets—her beautiful face and figure—had depreciated. In the *Nuns' Verses*, she describes in detail from head to toe how her physical attractiveness had changed over time.

> My hair adorned with flowers was fragrant
> Like a scented box.
> Now because of old age
> It has the stench of dog's fur.
> No teller of truth would say otherwise. (Thī v.253)

> In the past my breasts were beautiful,
> Plump, round, firm, and high.
> Now they hang down like empty water bags.
> No teller of truth would say otherwise. (Thī v.265)

> In the past my feet were lovely
> Soft as if padded with cotton.
> Now because of old age
> They are cracked and wrinkled.
> No teller of truth would say otherwise. (Thī v.269)[30]

As an educated courtesan, Ambapālī would have been familiar with the standard images that secular erotic poetry selects to describe female beauty. She juxtaposes these familiar images with phrases that demonstrate her insight into Buddhist teachings on impermanence. This insight into impermanence marks her attainment of enlightenment.

The Pāli "Section on the Best" identifies thirteen exemplary nuns, beginning with Mahāpajāpati Gotamī, who is praised for the length of time she has been a nun. The fourth century C.E. Chinese translation of the *Numerical Discourses* (*Ekottarika agama*) lists fifty-one praiseworthy nuns. Both sources honor Khemā (Sanskrit: Ksemā) and Uppalavaṇṇā (Sanskrit: Utpālavarṇā) as models for other nuns to emulate. Khemā and several other nuns are honored for their knowledge of the Buddha's teachings. Dhammadinnā is recognized for her knowledge of her knowledge of the Buddha's discourses, and Paṭācārā for her knowledge of the monastic code. The *One Hundred Narratives* (*Avadānaśataka*) relates that, since she is renowned for her great wisdom and teaching skills, King Pasenadi asked Khemā to teach him. When the king later approached the Buddha with the same questions, he found that the Buddha delivered exactly the same teaching as she had. The nun Dharmadinnā's explanations to her ex-husband were said to match exactly how the Buddha said he would have explained the same points.[31] The Indian hierarchical model that places rulers above subjects and men above women is subverted through these stories that empower women to teach men (although not monks). Uppalavaṇṇā is one of several nuns recognized for their skill in meditation and the acquisition of the supernormal powers that result from meditation. These nuns, Anālayo points out, should not be considered exceptional cases. A nun would be recognized as the best or foremost in some respect only if other nuns possessed similar qualities.[32]

The Voices of Enlightened Women

The *Nuns' Verses* (*Therīgāthā*), "the first anthology of women's literature in the world,"[33] contains verses attributed to enlightened nuns (*therī*), including the exemplary women listed above. Because the *Nuns' Verses* was compiled and written down long after its authors' deaths, it is difficult to determine whether the individual nuns actually composed the verses attributed to them. Some of the longest selections appear to have been written about or addressed to, rather than composed by, the nuns associated with them. While there is no reason to think that women would have written about their religious experiences in a way that differed markedly from their male counterparts, differences appear in the experiences they describe and the images they use. Muttā, the daughter of an impoverished brahmin, was given away in marriage to a hunchbacked man who finally agreed to free her from marriage. She says:

> I'm free. I'm free from three
> crooked things: the mortar,
> the pestle, and my hunchbacked husband.
> All that drags me back is cut! (Thī v.11)

Compare this verse with its counterpart in the *Monks' Verses* (*Theragāthā*). Sumaṅgala celebrates his freedom from hard work in the fields and welcomes the opportunity for a life dedicated to meditation.

> I'm free from three crooked things:
> Sickles, ploughs, curved spades.
> Enough of them! Meditate
> Sumangala, meditate Sumangala,
> Remain vigilant, Sumangala. (Tha v.34)

They use gender-related images to describe the life they left behind. Muttā described her liberation from the hard work of cooking with mortar and pestle for an ungrateful husband. Sumaṅgala spoke of the back-breaking labor of working in the fields. These paired verses convey the message that the Buddha's spiritual path is open to women as well as men.

Women's Motivations for Entering the Nuns' Community

The *Nuns' Narratives* and Dhammapāla's "*Commentary on the Nuns' Verses*" (*Therīgāthā-atthakathā*) describe various motivations for these women to adopt the homeless life of a Buddhist nun. The responsibilities of family life made heavier demands on women than on men, but few nuns mention escape from the burdens of marriage and motherhood as their motivation for entering the nuns' community. Dhammapāla relates that a monk's teaching the Dhamma inspired Vaḍḍha's mother to join a nunnery and leave her son in the care of relatives. Years later, after he became a monk, she encouraged him to renounce worldly desires, cultivate self-discipline, and pursue meditative practices that will end all suffering. Vaḍḍha put his mother's advice into practice, and he also became enlightened.[34]

These narratives, as Alice Collett observes, "can be seen as speaking directly to women about female experience and as seeking to show that in any situation in which a woman might find herself, progress can be on the path to awakening."[35] The very painful situation of losing a child or a husband often motivated women to become nuns. Reiko Ohnuma argues that the death of a child has a greater impact on women than on men and leads not only to more profound and prolonged grieving, but also to a greater confrontation with compelling, existential questions, which can result in greater religious involvement. Several nuns described how their anguish over the death of their children drove them insane and how the Buddha healed their suffering and put them on the path to liberation.[36] The commentaries provide the details of Kisāgotamī's painful life and her recovery from madness. Her husband's family scorned her until she finally gave birth to a son. When this beloved child died, she refused to believe that he could not be revived. She carried his small corpse from house to house, unable to find any medicine to heal him, until an old man pointed her in the Buddha's direction. The Buddha promised her medicine if she brought back a mustard seed from a home in which no one had ever died. After a futile search, she understood the universal nature of death and left her son's body on the cremation

ground. She returned to the Buddha, asked to become a nun, and
after deepening her insight into impermanence became enlightened.

> I've cultivated the noble eightfold path that leads to
>   never dying.
> I've realized *nibbāna*. I've seen the teachings as a mirror.
> The dart has been extracted from me and my burden
>   laid down.
> I've done what needed to be done. (Thī vv.222–23)[37]

Patācārā has a similarly harrowing story about the deaths of her husband, her two sons, her parents, and her brother. While pregnant, she
set out for her parents' house, but labor pains and a violent rainstorm
stopped her. While trying to build them a shelter from the rain, her
husband died from a poisonous snake's bite. She gathered up her
newborn son and her older child. She took the youngest child across
the river first. As she returned for the older child, a predatory hawk
seized the newborn baby, and the boy, hearing his mother's screams,
drowned in the river trying to reach her. Alone, she traveled on, only
to find that, in the fury of the previous night's thunderstorm, her parents' house had collapsed on them. Intense grief over these untimely
deaths drove her insane. In village after village, uncaring villagers
chased her away until the Buddha intervened to restore her sanity.
He told her that the tears she had shed over the deaths of her loved
ones in past lives would fill with water four oceans. His advice, "Relatives are no refuge for anyone griefstricken by death," motivated her
to seek refuge in the nuns' community. Soon afterward she had this
liberating insight:

> I washed my feet and watched water trickle down.
> I focused my mind as if I were training a thoroughbred
>   horse.
> I took an oil lamp and entered my cell. I prepared my
>   bed and sat down on it.
> Then I took a needle and pulled out the wick.
> The complete liberation of my mind was like extinguish-
>   ing that flame. (Thī v.114–16)

As Dhammapāla's commentary explains, when she first poured the
water over her feet, streams of water spilled on the ground. As she

watched these streams of water flow across the floor, she realized that, just as some streams travel only a short distance and others much further, some people die young, others die in middle age, and others die in old age, just as had her own children, her brother, and her parents.[38]

Sonā's story also conveys the message that relatives are no secure refuge. She bore ten sons and a daughter. After her husband left her, she divided the family wealth among her children and kept none for herself in the mistaken belief that her sons would take care of her. The neglect and contemptuous treatment she received from her sons and daughters-in-law led her to seek ordination. The nuns initially did not treat this poor old woman much better. When they went out for teachings, Sonā remained behind to perform menial chores. Told to heat water, she put the pot over the fire, sat down, and meditated. When the nuns returned wanting hot water, she heated the water through power she had acquired through meditation and gained their respect. Through meditation, she had attained the liberating insight that all the physical and mental components that make up a human being are impermanent, painful, and empty. She then knew: "Now I will not be reborn."[39]

Some young women recognized early that marriage was more likely to be a source of pain than pleasure. Their stories indicate that not all daughters willingly passed from their father's control into the hands of a controlling husband. Rohiṇī and Sumedhā both chose a nun's celibate life over marriage.

Rohiṇī, born into a wealthy brahmin household, became a Buddhist after hearing the Buddha speak. When she shared the Buddha's teachings with her parents, they too became faithful Buddhists and supported her decision to enter the nun's order. She remembered the initial conversation she had with her father:

"You give a lot of food and drink to ascetics, Rohiṇī.
Now I ask you: Why do you like ascetics so much?
They don't like to work, they're lazy, they live off what
others give, full of expectation, lusting after sweet things—
Why do you like ascetics so much?" (Thī v.272)

She replied:

"You've been asking me about ascetics, for a long time
    father;

I praise them for their wisdom, their ethical behavior,
  and their efforts.
They have gone forth, are from various families
and from various countries,
and yet they are friendly to one another—
that's why I like ascetics so much." (Thī v.274)[40]

In a reversal of societal expectations that a good daughter would never dispute her father's words, Rohinī did not hesitate to correct her father's every mistaken opinion. Her superior powers of persuasion, moreover, not only convinced her father to let her join the nuns' order but also convinced him to become a lay disciple.

Sumedhā's parents and her handsome royal suitor tried to convince her to marry. But she replied that she would rather die than marry and threatened to starve herself if she does not receive their permission to go forth. Why should she value a stinking, disgusting body? Even you, she reminded her parents, will find its stench disgusting after it is discarded on the cremation ground, left to be eaten by maggots and vultures. She dramatically took matters into her own hands: "Sumedhā cut her thick, soft, black hair with a knife, closed the palace door, and entered into her first meditative absorption." When her handsome would-be husband came to change her mind, she warned him that sensual pleasures are the bait that traps human beings in the cycle of death and rebirth. Don't suffer "like the fish that swallowed the hook." In a final defiant gesture, she threw her severed hair down at his feet. Now convinced, he joined her efforts to persuade her parents to become a nun and they gave their consent.[41] Rohinī and Sumedhā are both shown as being capable of independent action, even in the face of opposition from family members.

Escaping Māra and the Snare of Sexuality

The lure of sensual pleasures has no power over these intrepid nuns. Subhā's verses relate how she successfully liberated herself from a would-be rapist who seized her as she made her way through the woods. He first propositioned her:

You're young and beautiful. What's the point of living a
  religious life?

Take off your robes, let's have sex in the woods while the
flowers are in bloom. (Thī v.373)

He also warned her that the forest is a terrifying, lonely place. Kevin
Trainor observes:

A threat of physical coercion seems implicit in the rogue's
action given the seclusion in which the incident takes
place and in light of his audacity in physically obstructing
her. . . . Appealing first to sensual desire, then to fear, he
evokes emotions that renunciation is explicitly intended
to overcome"[42]

Unafraid, Subhā firmly rejected his unwelcome sexual advances. She
informed him that the body he lusts after is just perishable carcass,
like those that fill the cremation grounds, and her eyes, which he
had compared to blue lotuses, are just lumps of flesh. She then took
decisive action, gouged out an eye, and handed it to him. His lust
immediately vanished, and he asked for her forgiveness.[43] This narrative shatters the stereotype of women as being both physically and
morally weaker than men. Subhā does not yield either to sexual temptation or fear of male physical aggression.

Māra, known as the Evil One, tried to lure the Buddha's disciples away from the path to enlightenment back toward the realm
of sensual desire, over which he exercised his control. Māra is also
known as the Lord of Death, a hunter who baited his snare with the
bodies of beautiful women.[44] The ex-prostitute Vimalā explained how
she utilized her body profitably many times to lure men through the
brothel's door:

I adorned this beautifully painted body.
I stood at the brothel door and accosted fools,
Like a hunter, after laying out the snare. (Thī v.73)

Dhammapāla indicates that she was the harlot who had tried
unsuccessfully to entrap Moggallana, one of the Buddha's senior disciples. Instead of attraction, he felt disgust and denounced her as a
flesh-covered bag of excrement. His strong denunciation made her

ashamed of her body and the use to which she put it. Vimalā became a lay supporter of the Buddha and later joined the order.[45]

Despite Māra's association with demons and death, he is also portrayed as a handsome and powerful god, resembling Kāma, the Indian god of love. In the *Connected Scriptures about Nuns* (*Bhikkhunī-Samyutta*) Māra approached ten nuns, each quietly meditating alone in the forest.[46] He came to these nuns not only as the Lord of Death, but also as the Lord of Lust. All ten of these enlightened nuns respond with calm detachment to Māra's sexual aggression, and he went away defeated and disappointed. As Collett explains,

> Māra is representative of male sexuality, which is positioned as a potential danger for the women he approaches. Appealing to (what in the verses is portrayed as) their natural female sexual desire, Māra is attempting to seduce the nuns away from the good path. . . . Instead, in an instance of the sort of similitude that would be expected under a purview of sexual equality, as the female form is seen as a snare of Māra for men, so a sexual male is a snare of Māra for women.[47]

Māra expected Ālavikā, the first nun he encountered, to respond in typical female fashion—with fear and terror—when he told her: "There is no escape in the world. So what's the point of your seclusion? Enjoy sensual passion and don't be regretful later!" But he misjudged his target. Her mind never wavered. She responded that through insight she had found a way to escape the world. Sensual desire, she informed him, is like a cleaver that cuts through a chopping block. She recognized him as the Lord of Death and sensual desire as his weapon of destruction. Defeated, Māra tried again with Vijayā: "You're young and beautiful. And I'm a young man in my prime. Come on, lady, and let's enjoy ourselves while the music plays!" She too recognized him and rejected his unsolicited advances. Māra went on to insult Kisagotamī with his insinuation that she has sought the forest's seclusion only for an assignation with some man. She replied sharply that she had dealt already with her son's death and had no further desire for men (or sex).

When Mara approached Uppalavaṇṇā, he praised her stunning beauty and then asked if she wasn't afraid of rapists. She boldly responded, "Even if a hundred thousand rapists like you were to come here, I wouldn't be afraid, not a single hair would stand on end!" She taunted him with references to her skill in magical powers: "I can make myself disappear or I can penetrate your body. I can stand between your eyebrows and you can't see me!" This seems a stunning reversal of the image of female vulnerability to sexual penetration. She implies that he ought to worry that she can easily slip inside him without being detected!

Even monasteries are not always safe places for women. The *vinaya* identifies Uppalavaṇṇā as a rape victim who was assaulted by a brahmin youth in her meditation hut. When the incident was brought to the Buddha's attention, he ruled that she committed no offense because she did not give her consent.[48] According to the "Hundred Stories on Karma" (*Karmaśataka*), Uppalavaṇṇā used her supernatural powers to rescue an abducted nun from sexual slavery. One of King Ajātaśatru's ministers saw Bhaddā Kāpilānī and snatched her while she was out collecting alms. He had her bathed, perfumed, outfitted with beautiful clothes and ornaments, and then presented her to the king. His lust aroused, the king sexually assaulted her. Uppalavaṇṇā used her powers to enter the palace undetected, where she taught her skills to Bhaddā, who then used them to escape and return to the nuns' community.[49]

There are several versions of Māra's encounter with Somā. He insulted her by saying that as a woman she had just enough intelligence to judge if rice is cooked by testing it between her two fingers. She replied that gender has nothing to do with the practice of meditation and the cessation of suffering. "After clarifying that gender is simply irrelevant, once the mind is concentrated," Anālayo says, "she tells Māra that with such talk he should better go to those who are still caught up in identifications with being a woman or being a man."[50] While Somā is not among the thirteen exemplary nuns mentioned in the Pāli canon, the Sanskrit anthology, the *One Hundred Narratives*, identifies her as the best among nuns who retain what they have heard. Somā memorized the entire collection of monastic rules after hearing it once from the Buddha. When monks asked the Buddha how she was able to remember so much, he told them it was the result of a vow she made in a past life under the Buddha Kāśyapa. In her present life, she studied first under her brahmin father and later, after she became an ordained nun, she studied under Mahāprajāpatī and became an *arhat*.[51]

Gender and the Bodhisattva Path

During the long night the Buddha spent under the fig tree at Bodhgayā, he remembered all his past lives and understood how his actions had an impact on the course of his subsequent rebirths. In all of the stories of his past lives, whether as a human or as an animal, the Buddha was male. Maleness is the thread that strings together all of these diverse "birth stories." "The fact that he was always male," Anālayo says, "would have easily resulted in the notion that the path to Buddhahood, at least in its final stages, requires one to be male."[52] Naomi Appleton points out that the Theravāda tradition that explicitly excludes women from the *bodhisatta* (Sanskrit: *bodhisattva*) path belongs to the later commentarial layer on these past life stories, which presented the stories as part of the *bodhisatta*'s path to Buddhahood. The exclusion of women from the *bodhisatta* path reinforced the idea that changing into a man overcomes both the social and the spiritual limitations of being female.[53]

The few stories of sex changes in the Theravāda tradition do not challenge the position that gender is soteriologically irrelevant. Women can and do become enlightened. But these stories do portray gender as morally relevant. For example, in the *Mahānaradakassapa Birth Story*, a princess tried to convince her father of the importance of moral actions by telling him about her own previous births. As a result of one birth in which she was a man who seduced other men's wives, she suffered in hell. After that, she was reborn as a monkey whose testicles were bitten off by the leader of the herd, then as a castrated ox, and finally as a human who was neither man nor woman. As the result of previous good *karma*, she was eventually reborn as a heavenly nymph, followed by her present birth as a princess. She explained that she can't become a man until all her bad *karma* from seducing other men's wives is exhausted.[54] Men change into women only as a result of immoral conduct, as in the example of the brahmin who had improper thoughts about the *arhat* Mahākaccāna. The change is immediate, involuntary, and unwelcome. When Soreyya saw Mahākaccāna's beautiful, golden-skinned body, he desired that he would become his wife or else that his wife would have the golden complexion. As a result of this impure thought (homoerotic?) about a pure *arhat*, Soreyya was instantly transformed into a woman. He remained unhappily female until he offered a meal to Mahākaccāna, was forgiven, and then transformed back into a man.[55] These rare stories of changing sex support the idea that birth as a woman is the result of immoral actions and that women should aspire to be reborn as men. Wendy Doniger explains that "where men are usually cursed to become women, women often choose to be men—a not surprising asymmetry, since the culture regards male status as higher than female."[56]

In the Theravāda *vinaya*, when the Buddha was asked about a monk whose sexual organs (*liṅga*) changed from male to female and a nun whose organs changed from female to male, his response concerned how these sex changes affected these two monastics' teachers, their seniority, and the relationship to the new order of nuns or monks to which these two transformed monastics should now belong. The *Samantapāsādika* commentary explains that the sudden transformation occurred in the middle of the night; a monk's male sex disappeared due to bad karmic actions, and a nun's female sex disappeared due to good karmic actions. The commentary, as Carol S. Anderson notes, also offers advice on what monastics should do under such circumstances:

> One wakes with female *liṅga* (or genitalia or gender or features), and the initial reaction, the commentary tells us, is not to recoil in horror or surprise but to console his or her friend with the observation that this sort of thing occurs in *saṃsāra*, and not to worry overmuch—nuns and monks can still be enlightened (a noteworthy claim in the commentaries in and of itself). The rest of the passage explains, in rather legalistic terms, just what one is supposed to do for one's monk friend, who now has female *liṅga*—i.e., take her to a nunnery to find her some companions, and so on.[57]

While the *vinaya* and its commentary reflect the cultural assumption that male gender is preferable, the Buddhist message is clear that both nuns and monks can seek and attain enlightenment.

When the Buddha was a Woman

There are several versions of a past life story in which the Buddha was known as Princess Munī. One is a late addition to a Chinese translation of canonical scriptures, the *Numerical Discourses*; the others are noncanonical medieval texts. All versions attempt to reconcile the story of the Buddha's past birth as a woman with the traditional belief that in his past lives the Buddha was always male. In the *Numerical Discourses* story and in the *Scripture of the Wise and the Foolish*, Princess Munī's exceptional beauty was the result of her devotion to previous *buddhas*. She met an old monk begging for oil to light lamps as an offering to the Buddha Ratnaśikhi and provided him with oil. The Buddha Ratnaśikhi predicted that in the future the monk would be reborn as Dīpaṃkara Buddha. When she heard from the monk that he had received a prediction but that she had not, she got in her carriage and went out to confront the Buddha. Princess Munī asked him why she, the donor of the oil, had not received a prediction, as she was the donor of the oil. He replied that she could not become a Buddha because she was a woman. When she asked whether she would attain enlightenment, he told her that she would attain enlightenment in the future; the monk who would become Dīpaṃkara Buddha would give her the prediction.[58] The presumption, though unstated, is that she would be reborn as a man when she receives the prediction to Buddhahood.

In *The Scripture of the Wise and the Foolish (mDo mdzangs blun)*, when Princess Munī inquired why she didn't receive a prediction, the Buddha did predict that she would become Śakyamuni Buddha. Bhikkhunī Dhammadinnā notes a discrepancy between the Tibetan and Chinese translations of this story. The Tibetan translation does not include any transformation of Princess Munī into a man. She concludes that the differing versions of Princess Munī's story suggest that transmitters of these narratives about how a *bodhisattva* who receives a prediction to become a Buddha did not always perceive the change of sex from female to male as a necessity, which "would have proven especially inspirational to a female audience."[59]

Pāli medieval biographies of the Buddha's past lives also include a version of the Princess narrative. Her female birth, which these biographies attribute to the effect of past immoral actions, accounts for the Buddha's refusal to predict the princess's Buddhahood. In the episode "The Princess Who Gave the White Mustard Oil" from the *Sotaṭṭhakī*, the princess wondered why, despite being the original provider of the offering, only the monk receives a prediction. She then took "her own (present and future) life in her hands" and approached the Buddha for an answer. Her female birth prevented him from making such a prediction in the present, but he did predict that in the future she would receive a prediction of becoming a Buddha.[60] Karen Derris points out that this "prediction of a prediction" is a new understanding of the *bodhisattva* path:

> This "predicted prediction" creates a space for a woman to
> be acknowledged as progressing along the bodhisatta path
> while clearly remaining mindful of the canonical and com-
> mentarial conditions obstructing that progress. The narrative
> pushes very hard against the gendered rule of the bodhisatta

path. It does not technically subvert the canonical structure limiting predictions to male bodhisattas, but instead it invents an entirely new category of prediction in order to establish firmly that this woman is indeed a bodhisatta and capable of progress and attainment on that path.[61]

Another version of the story emphasizes the beauty of the princess's face, body, and voice as outward signs of her inner virtues. The description of the beauty of her voice is identical to the description of the Buddha's voice in an earlier commentarial work on the canonical biography of the Buddha, the *Buddhavaṃsa*. "This intertextual reference," Derris claims, "makes a very strong implicit argument: this female Bodhisatta is progressing on the path to Buddhahood to the extent that she is beginning to physically resemble a Buddha in her present lifetime."[62]

The story of a female past life of the Buddha in the *Divine Stories* (*Divyāvadāna*) and in the *Garland of Birth Stories* by Haribhaṭṭa (ca. fifth century CE) also reinforces the idea that only males become *buddhas*. In *Rūpavatī's Narrative* (*Rūpavatī Avadāna*) from the *Divine Stories* collection, a beautiful young woman named Rūpāvatī cut off her breasts to feed a starving woman about to devour her newly born child. After feeding the starving woman flesh and blood from her breasts, she went home to fetch more food. Her astonished husband restored her severed breasts through an act of truth: "If it is true that such an amazing act has never before been seen, let your breasts reappear." Her generous act astonished even the god Indra, who was worried that she might oust him from his divine realm through the extraordinary power generated by her generosity.

> When I attain incomparable perfect enlightenment, may I educate those who are uneducated, liberate those who are unliberated, console those who are inconsolable, and bring to nirvana those who have not reached nirvana. By these true words of truth, may my female body disappear and may I have a male body.[63]

She immediately became a man, Rūpāvata, who was so admired that he was made king. After ruling as a just king for sixty years, he died and was reborn twice as a male *bodhisattva*: first he gave his body to feed ravenous vultures and, reborn again, gave his body to feed a starving tigress about to devour her cubs.[64]

Haribhaṭṭa's *Rūpavatī's Birth Story* (*Rūpyāvatījātaka*) follows the plot of *Rūpavatī's Narrative* but with a much greater emphasis on the *bodhisattva*'s gender. He takes for granted that a woman can be a *bodhisattva* yet prefers that *bodhisattva*s be male. He recognizes the power of her sacrifice but undercuts it with the concession, "even as a woman." In the very first verse he uses the stereotype of female weakness to suggest that a male *bodhisattva* would be even stronger and more skillful in helping people.

> Even as a woman, the bodhisattva cut flesh from her own
> body and gave it away. But how much more [successful
> would a bodhisattva be] as a man, being stronger and more
> skillful in working for the benefit of others. (v.1)

Rūpyāvatī is clearly identified as a *bodhisattva* on the path to enlightenment: "You surely embody for the world's benefit what people seeking enlightenment know as the perfection of wisdom." (v.27) But in the next verse Haribhaṭṭa again returns to the issue of her gender.

> What a contrast between her womanhood and her sharp
>   mind,
> Between her generosity and her delicate nature.
> This virtuous woman's generosity exceeds everyone's
>   donations
> And puts to shame other generous men. (v.28)

Haribhaṭṭa emphasizes the singularity of Rūpyāvatī's action in this verse on her husband's act of truth; yet the phrase "even as a man" again indicates his preoccupation with gender.

> If such an act of generosity has never been heard of
> in another, even a man, then by this truth,
> let my wife's breasts immediately appear! (v.29)

Verses 30 and 31 focus on Rūpyāvatī's breasts. Haribhaṭṭa uses a common Sanskrit poetic image when he describes her breasts as so large that her upper body bends under their weight. In the next verse he employs an elaborate series of metaphors that link the female body with nature: Rūpyāvatī's body is a lotus pond made beautiful by a white lotus (her face) with luminous filaments (her teeth) and a pair of sheldrake ducks (her breasts) that glide over its surface. When Indra appeared before her and asked about her intention, she uttered her own act of truth in which she clearly expressed her wish to become a man. Haribhaṭṭa here explicitly associates maleness with virtuous qualities:

> She then spoke truthfully to the Lord of the gods:
> I seek Buddhahood in order to bring peace to the three
>   worlds.
> If this is true, O brahmin, let me immediately
> become male, the recipient of virtuous qualities in this
>   world. (v. 34)

Her breasts, the signifier of her female identity, act on their own when the sign of masculinity—a black mustache—surfaces on her face; they vanish from shame (or modesty):

> After her two breasts, bulging like the frontal lobes of an
> elephant in rut, saw a mustache, black like a smudge of
> collyrium, appear on the moon of her face, they immediately
> disappeared, as if from shame. (v. 36)

Haribhaṭṭa concludes his story with the observation that if the Buddha could give away his flesh, even when he was reborn as a woman, then anyone reborn as a man should not desire material things. His frequent reminders that if even women can be generous men should be more generous suggest that he wrote primarily with a male audience in mind.

Sex Changes in Early Mahāyāna Scriptures

Although the origins of the Mahāyāna movement remain obscure, most scholars agree that it developed in monastic circles. The anonymous authors of new scriptures believed the Buddha spoke to them in their meditations, visions, and dreams. They remembered his words, wrote them down, taught these new scriptures, and encouraged people to disseminate them. The Buddha was the implied narrator of these scriptures that describe a new path toward becoming a *buddha*. The *bodhisattvas* who pursue Buddhahood are no longer seen as rare, but they are rarely female. Although Mahāyāna Buddhism recognized the spiritual potential of nuns and laywomen, early

Mahāyāna scriptures were written primarily as guides for men training to become *bodhisattva*s. To ensure that these men remained undefiled, they observed strictly all precepts relating to sexual activity and, if married, relinquished all attachment to their wives and children. This reveals the extent to which these scriptures were written from a male point of view, as *bodhisattvas* are never urged to regard their husbands as demons and sources of suffering.[65] Paul Harrison writes:

> Compared with the situation in the Pāli Canon, in which women are at least as capable as men of attaining the highest goal, arhatship, the position of women in the Mahāyāna has hardly changed for the better, since women cannot attain buddhahood, and even the title of bodhisattva is withheld from them. Of course all this reflects the attitudes of the men (probably monks) who produced these texts, but this does not make the conclusion any less inescapable: although both men and women can ride in the Great Vehicle, only men are allowed to drive it.[66]

While men occupy the dominant position in these early Mahāyāna scriptures, some scriptures allow women to travel on the *bodhisattva* path up to a certain point. Unlike arhatship, which both women and men could attain, Buddhahood required that women become men either in a future life or through a sudden transformation of her sex in her present life. In the *Perfection of Wisdom in Eight Thousand Lines* scripture (*Aṣṭasāhasrikā Prajñāpāramitā*), the Buddha predicts that Gangādevī will be reborn eventually as Suvarṇapuṣpa Buddha. First, she must undergo a change of sex. The Buddha told Ānanda that Gangādevī will transform from a woman to a man and afterward will be reborn in the paradise of Akṣobhya Buddha.[67]

Two texts from a collection of Mahāyāna scriptures describe the change from female to male in different ways. In *Viśuddhiśraddhā's Questions* (*Viśuddhiśraddhāpṛcchā*), the princess Viśuddhiśraddhā asks the Buddha what a woman must do to transform her female body. The Buddha replies that a woman must avoid envy, stinginess, flattery, and anger, must be truthful, slander no one, abandon desire and wrong views, revere the Buddha and his teaching, make offerings to monastics, give up attachment to home and family, accept the precepts, have no evil thoughts, be indifferent to her female body, persist in the intention to seek enlightenment and the qualities of a Buddha, and regard worldly life as if it were an illusion or a dream. She agrees to the conditions, and the Buddha then predicts the princess will be reborn in the Tuṣita heaven and after countless eons will become a Buddha.[68] In *Sumatī's Questions* (*Sumatīdārikapṛcchā*), the transformation of Sumatī into a male is instantaneous. When the *bodhisattva* Mañjuśrī asks the eight-year-old why she hasn't changed her female body, she retorts that the femaleness of her body is untenable, for things are neither male nor female. She then performs an act of truth: "If it is true that I will become a Buddha, then may I now change into a man." In confirmation of the truth of her declaration, the requested transformation takes place immediately.[69] The swift sexual transformation underscores her precocious awareness that the terms "male" and "female" attach to bodies that are conventionally considered male or female, but which ultimately have no real transformable nature.

In stories of confrontations between monks and female characters, the *arhat* Śāriputra, known for his wisdom, is the usual interlocutor. Dhammapāla explains in his commentary on the *Nuns' Verses* that Bhaddā Kuṇḍalakesā's skills as a debater developed as she traveled around India as a Jain ascetic challenging others to debate with her. She met her match in the monk Sāriputta (Sanskrit: Śāriputra), recognized by the Buddha as "the best of those with great wisdom." Kuṇḍalakesā lost the debate and became a Buddhist nun.[70] In Mahāyāna narratives, however, Śāriputra emerges as the loser. Even an eight-year-old female—human or nonhuman—is superior in wisdom to the best of the earlier tradition's enlightened *arhats*. In the *Lotus of the True Teaching* (*Saddharmapuṇḍarīka*), Mañjuśrī describes the remarkable wisdom of the eight-year-old daughter of the *nāga* king, Sāgara. Śāriputra refuses to believe that the princess attained so much so quickly because her body is female and the *bodhisattva* path takes immeasurable eons to complete. When he asks her how she could attain Buddhahood so quickly, she quickly hands the Buddha a precious jewel and tells Śāriputra that she could attain Buddhahood even quicker. Immediately the *nāga* princess transforms into a man, and, as a male *bodhisattva*, s/he attains enlightenment.[71]

Śāriputra appears again as the fall guy in a comic episode in the *Teaching of Vimalakīrti* (*Vimalakīrtinirdeśa*). After listening to the lay *bodhisattva* Vimalakīrti teach, a goddess expresses her joy by showering flowers over the audience. Śāriputra is upset when the flowers land on him and stick there (the rules on monastic conduct prohibit monks from wearing flower garlands) and do not stick to the *bodhisattvas*. The goddess informs him that his fear of the world produced his discomfort with all of its sensual pleasures (including lovely fragrant flowers). Evidently unsettled by a female assuming a teacher's role, he challenges her: "If you're so smart, why don't you change your female body?" Through her supernatural powers, she instead changes him into an exact replica of herself and throws the question right back at him: "Why don't you change your female body?" She then educates him about the empty nature of both male and female bodies.

John McRae observes that this episode in which a goddess upstages the stodgy monk Śāriputra interests modern readers because of its statement about gender. For medieval readers, it was primarily a statement about emptiness.[72] Although gender is an important part of a feminist analysis of these scriptures, the statements about emptiness and ultimate truth are also important. Lisa Battaglia Owen sees similarities between these *sūtras'* construction of gender/sex and the work of feminist theorist Judith Butler. The goddess's performance of sexual transformation is one among many examples of female beings who change sex. This change marks the instability and fluidity of sexual differentiation. In an instant, the goddess effects Śāriputra's transformation into a female form, as simultaneously she assumes his male form. Ultimately there is neither sex nor gender. Battaglia Owen states:

> Considering that sex/gender exists only on the level of conditional reality (i.e., illusory and created), it emerges as ultimately, soteriologically irrelevant. Yet, how does one resolve the tension between the irrelevance of sex/gender in ultimate reality (i.e., perceiving through emptiness) and the apparent relevance of sex/gender in conventional reality? The ultimate irrelevance of sex/gender does not alleviate the oppression that women suffer as "women."[73]

These *sūtras* on sex change have shock value because male experience was normative and men and women were often seen in a hierarchical relationship that placed men on top and women on the bottom.

These Mahāyāna scriptures share the view expressed by Somā when responding to Māra: gender is ultimately irrelevant when seen from the perspective of someone who is enlightened. But even monastic institutions are full of unenlightened individuals. Scriptures may reflect the conventional truths of the time, in which women did not exercise authority over men. Such a limited understanding would restrict women to secondary roles, helpers rather than leaders, listeners rather than teachers.

Women as Good Friends and Dharma Teachers

Lay disciples and monastics serve as good friends who offer help and spiritual guidance to people traveling on the Buddhist path. Two influential scriptures, the *Perfection of Wisdom in Eight Thousand Lines* and the *Supreme Array Scripture (Gaṇḍavyūha Sūtra)*[74] tell of the journey of young men seeking enlightenment who are helped along the way by women in the secondary role of good friends. The last chapters of the *Perfection of Wisdom in Eight Thousand Lines* tell the story of Sadāprarudita, a young man whose name translates as "always weeping." In the solitude of the forest he hears a voice telling him to go east if he wants to learn the perfection of wisdom. When he remembers that he hasn't asked the voice how far east he should go, he stops abruptly and bursts into tears. A *buddha* seen in a vision tells him to travel five hundred miles to Gandhavati, where the *bodhisattva* Dharmodgata taught. Since Sadāprarudita has no gift to offer Dharmodgata, he tries to sell himself to raise money. No one will buy him, so he weeps again. Finally, Indra offers to buy his blood for use in a sacrifice. From her upstairs window, a wealthy merchant's daughter witnesses the bloody spectacle of Sadāprarudita cutting his veins. She realizes what needs to be done, comes down, and tells him to stop cutting himself. The merchant's daughter takes charge of the bloody, tear-stained Sadāprarudita, persuades her wealthy family to provide the necessary funds and the chariots for the journey, and travels with him and her five hundred female companions to Gandhavati. Once they arrive, the gift giving begins. Sadāprarudita gifts his own body to Dharmodgata; the merchant's daughter and her companions gift their bodies to him; and he presents them to Dharmodgata, who accepts them, immediately returns them, and enters a meditative state. At the end of seven years, Sadāprarudita hears a voice telling him that in seven days Dharmodgata will emerge from meditation and teach. Together with the merchant's daughter and her five hundred companions, he prepares the ground and arranges a throne for Dharmodgata. At the story's end, Sadāprarudita sees *buddha*s teaching the perfection of wisdom in countless galaxies in all directions; his knowledge has become as vast as the ocean; and in all his births he is reborn only where *buddha*s taught. Unfortunately, the Sanskrit version of the text is silent about what happens to the merchant's helpful daughter and her companions. The Chinese translation's ending differs. Sadāprarudita receives a prediction that he will become a *buddha*. The women will be transformed into men first and then become *buddha*s in the distant future.[75] Counter to stereotypes about male and female behavior, Sadāprarudita emerges as a more passive and emotional character in this narrative. Had the merchant's daughter not coolly assessed the situation, taken control, and marshaled the chariots to move forward, he might well have been left still weeping.

The *Supreme Array Scripture* (*Gaṇḍavyūha Sūtra*) relates Sudhana's quest in search of enlightenment. Along the way, this young man encounters fifty-three good friends who give him the visionary knowledge that will lead to his final encounter with the *bodhisattva* Samantabhadra. Twenty-one of these good friends are beautiful, wealthy, and accomplished women who teach from jeweled thrones in paradisal locations. Half of the text concerns Sudhana's encounters with these women, who include a queen, a princess, a nun, a courtesan, the Buddha's wife, Gopā, and his mother, Māyā. Douglas Osto concedes that this scripture "privileges the male gender as spiritually ideal," but argues that "descriptions of female good friends and their prominent role within the narrative point to a spiritual equality between the genders that is unparalleled in Indian Mahāyāna Buddhist literature."[76] There is a spiritual equality among the good friends that guide Sudhana, but they still play secondary roles in helping Sudhana fulfill his vision quest.

None of the laywomen Sudhana encounters on his journey receives the title of *bodhisattva*, although their accomplishments imply that they are *bodhisattvas* even if they are not explicitly identified as such. Sudhana asks Queen Āśā how long ago she conceived the aspiration for enlightenment, an act that marks the beginning of the *bodhisattva* path. Queen Āśā then relates a series of past lives in which she honored past *buddhas*, before she sent him on his way. Prabhūtā can feed countless beings from a single bowl. The sight of Acalā's extraordinary beauty can free everyone from all afflictions. Princess Maitrāyaṇī enables Sudhana to see *buddhas* reflected in all jewel-encrusted objects in her palace. The nun Siṃhavijṛmbhitā teaches Sudhana the perfection of wisdom and assures him he will not turn back from the path to perfect enlightenment. The courtesan Vasumitrā's spiritual power enables her to transform herself into the female form of any creature in order to teach beings through embraces and kisses. Her beauty and intimate actions never arouse passion, but instead inspire all those who come to her to become dispassionate.[77]

When Sudhana meets Gopā and asks how she achieved liberation, she relates a story about her past life eons ago as Sucalitaratiprabhāsaśrī and her marriage to Prince Tejodhipati. As a devoted wife, she helped the future Śakyamuni Buddha during countless lifetimes until he attained Buddhahood. Gopā directs Sudhana to visit Queen Māyā, who magically appears in the location at Bodhgayā where her son had attained enlightenment. Seated on a jeweled lotus throne, she tells him that she took the vow to become the mother of all *bodhisattva*s and *buddha*s in all worlds and in all eons.[78]

Osto claims the *Supreme Array Scripture* was probably composed in South India during the third-century CE Ikṣvāku Dynasty, when the Buddhist community benefitted from the patronage of wealthy female donors, many of them connected to the royal family. That the text had this female audience in mind, he says, "would explain several distinctive features of the narrative, such as its emphasis on devotion rather than asceticism, its positive portrayal of female beauty, and the prominent role given to its female teachers."[79]

The Lion's Roar of Queen Śrīmālādevī (*Śrīmālādevī Siṃhanāda Sūtra*) may also been composed during Ikṣvāku Dynasty.[80] Like other Mahāyāna scriptures, its author is unknown, though Richard King buries in a footnote the comment that "The 'feminist' aspects of the *Śrīmālā Sūtra* suggest the possibility of a female author."[81] King doesn't elaborate on what these "feminist" elements might be, but this scripture is unique in having a woman, Queen Śrīmālādevī, as its main character. She is praised for her intelligence, not her beauty, although her beauty seems to be taken for granted. When Śrīmālādevī meets the Buddha, he predicts that in the future she will become Samantaprabha Buddha. Śrīmālādevī then conceives the thought of enlightenment and begins to follow the *bodhisattva* path. After she tells the Buddha that all *bodhisattva* vows are contained in one great vow, the acceptance of the true teaching, he praises her profound wisdom and her skillful actions. She taught the doctrine that all beings contain within them the essence of enlightenment, the potential to become a Buddha. Queen Śrīmālā first taught the women of her kingdom, then her husband, and finally the rest of the men.

This text raises questions about the relationship between gender and the spiritual accomplishments of women on the *bodhisattva* path. Male commentators on this text have debated whether Queen Śrīmālā was on the beginning stages of the *bodhisattva* path or at an advanced level or even whether she was a woman at all.[82] For Buddhists who believed this scripture's teaching that women and men equally had the nature of a *buddha* within them, the possibility arose that women could be *buddha*s in their present lives without changing their gender. As Diana Paul explains, "If women were truly capable of having buddha-nature in this lifetime without denying their female gender, this would implicitly indicate that women were not biologically determined as religiously, psychologically, and physically inferior to men."[83]

Conclusion

Laywomen and nuns were active participants in early Buddhist history. The Buddhist canon is vast, and the texts it contains offer contrasting portraits of women. Alongside descriptions of women as weak, passive, and in need of male control, we find evidence that women led active, fulfilling, and independent lives. Married women who chose to marry controlled their own wealth and were generous donors to monastic institutions. Single women, including widows and ex-prostitutes, who were often at the bottom of the social hierarchy, entered the nuns' community, controlled the direction of their lives, and moved forward toward liberation. The religious life also provided them with an opportunity for an education, often denied them in lay life. Because an ancient patriarchal society defined women's roles as procreative, a young woman's choice of a celibate life faced more resistance from family members. Their patience, determination, and persuasive arguments enabled them to overcome their fathers' and husbands' opposition and gain permission to leave home. The *Nuns' Verses* is the earliest anthology we have of these women writing their own stories. Its inclusion in the Buddhist canon, its preservation, and the commentaries written on it attest to its influence in ancient Buddhist communities. It is possible that monks who compiled and redacted canonical texts may have obscured or even failed to preserve other women's achievements. We will never know. Work is underway on translations of the *Narratives about Nuns*, and with more people involved in the translation of numerous untranslated Buddhist texts, we will likely have access to more information about women's lives.

But what about the texts we do have? The multifaceted images of women in these ancient Indian works reflect their unknown creators' differing views on gender and class as well as societal changes that took place over a thousand or more years. As Appleton points out, the Theravāda exclusion of women from the *bodhisattva* path, which belongs to a later commentarial strata, reinforced the idea that changing into a man overcomes both the social and spiritual limitations of being female. Early Mahāyāna scriptures allow women to progress along the *bodhisattva* path only up to a certain point, where they change into men. No commentaries or treatises composed by women that might have presented an alternative view survive. Skilling speculates that women's writings might never have been written down or that they were not preserved by monks who controlled the redaction of scriptures. But Buddhism has never represented itself as resistant to inevitable change. Living in the twenty-first century, we might need to re-evaluate some of these texts. Does the text present a message that transcends particular cultures? Is it tied to a particular stance on gender and class more appropriate to a past time and not to the present? Narrative innovation in medieval Theravāda commentaries inserted female past lives into the Buddha's biography; and in Mahāyāna scriptures women assume the role of spiritual guides on the path to Buddhahood. These narratives can inspire contemporary Buddhists to action. Inspired by Paṭācārā's story, Polly Trout, a layperson with nonsectarian Dharma practice, founded Patacara Community Services, a nonsectarian Buddhist community whose mission is "help people overwhelmed by grief and despair as she has once been."[84]

Innovative commentaries that reinterpret and reimagine the lives of some of these ancient Indian women's stories have already been written. In *The Hidden Lamp: Stories from Twenty-Five Centuries of Awakened Women*, Florence Caplow and Susan Moon have compiled and edited stories of Sujāta, Mahāprajāpatī, Bhaddā Kuṇḍalakesā, Kisagotamī, Uppalavaṇṇā, Somā, Vasumitrā, Śāriputra and the goddess, and many others, and coupled them with commentaries and reflections by contemporary Buddhist women, both lay and monastic. We need to reclaim these long-dead women as part of our own human history, even Thullanandā and her gang of six.

Notes

1. Alice Collett and Bhikkhu Anālayo, "Bhikkhave and Bhikkhu as Gender-inclusive Terminology in Early Buddhist Texts," *Journal of Buddhist Ethics* 22(2014): 774.

2. For different interpretations of Mahāpajāpatī's request and the Buddha's response, see Bhikkhu Anālayo, "Mahāpajāpatī's Going Forth in the Madhyama-āgama," *Journal of Buddhist Ethics* 18(2011): 268–317; Bhikkhu Anālayo, "The Going Forth of Mahāpajāpatī Gotamī in T 60," *Journal of Buddhist Ethics* 23(2016): 1–31; Gisela Krey, "Some Remarks on the Status of Nuns and Laywomen in Early Buddhism," in *Dignity and Discipline: Reviving Full Ordination for Buddhist Nuns*, ed. Thea Mohr and Jampa Tsedron (Boston:

Wisdom Publications, 2010), 49–50; Amy Paris Langenberg, "Mahāsaṅghika-Lokottaravāda Bhiksunī Vinaya: Intersection of Womanly Virtue and Buddhist Asceticism," *Women in Early Indian Buddhism: Comparative Textual Studies*, ed. Alice Collett. (Oxford: Oxford University Press, 2014), 80–96; Reiko Ohumna, *Ties That Bind: Maternal Imagery and Discourse in Indian Buddhism* (Oxford: Oxford University Press, 2012), 86–112; Lisa Battaglia Owen, "On Gendered Discourse and the Maintenance of Boundaries: A Feminist Analysis of the Bhikkhunī Order in Indian Buddhism," *Asian Journal of Women's Studies* 4/3(1998): 8–60, and Liz Williams, "A Whisper in the Silence: Nuns Before Mahāpajāpatī," *Buddhist Studies Review* 17:2(2000): 167–73. On Ānanda's role, see Ellison Banks Findly, "Ānanda's Case for Women," *The International Journal of Indian Studies* 3/2(1993): 1–31.

    3. Analayo, "The Going Forth of Mahāpajāpatī," 19.

    4. Stephanie Jamison, *Sacrificed Wife/Sacrificer's Wife: Women, Ritual and Hospitality in Ancient India* (New York: Oxford University Press, 1996), 15–16.

    5. In Young Chung, "A Buddhist View of Women: A Comparative Study of the Rules for *Bhikṣunīs* and *Bhikṣus* based on the Chinese *Prātimokṣa*," *Journal of Buddhist Ethics* 6(1999): 9–105.

    6. Thī vv, pp. 108–109. The translation of this verse and others from the *Therīgāthā* is mine, cf. Charles Hallisey, *Therīgāthā: Poems of the First Buddhist Women* (Cambridge, MA: Harvard University Press, 2015), 65. For the commentary on Dhammapāla's attempts to show that there was no comparable ordination for women, see William Pruitt, trans., *The Commentary on the Verses of the Therīs* (Oxford: Pali Text Society, 1999), 142n2, 379–81. Krey, "Some Remarks on the Status of Nuns and Laywomen," 45–48; and Williams, "A Whisper in the Silence," 172–73, find his argument unconvincing.

    7. See Ellison Banks Findly, "Women Teachers of Women: Early Nuns: 'Worthy of My Confidence,'" *Women's Buddhism, Buddhism's Women: Tradition, Revision, Renewal.* (Boston: Wisdom Publications, 2000), 136, 152.

    8. Alice Collett, "The Female Past in Early Indian Buddhism: The Shared Narrative of the Seven Sisters in the *Therī-Apadāna*," *Religions of South Asia* 5:1/2(2011): 209–13.

    9. Jonathan Walters, "A Voice from the Silence: The Buddha's Mother's Story," *History of Religions* 33:4(1994): 375–76; and Jonathan Walters, "Gotamī's Story: Introduction and Translation," *Buddhism in Practice*, ed. Donald S. Lopez, Jr. (Princeton, NJ: Princeton University Press, 1995), 113–38. See also Bhikkhunī Dhammadinā, "The Parinirvāṇa of Mahāprajāpatī Gautamī and Her Followers in the Mūlasarvāstivāda Vinaya," *The Indian International Journal of Buddhist Studies* 16(2015): 29–61.

    10. Walters, "A Voice from the Silence," 377.

    11. Ibid., 371.

    12. Chung, "A Buddhist View of Women," 35–36, 49–50.

    13. Gregory Schopen, "Separate but Equal: Property Rights and the Legal Independence of Buddhist Nuns and Monks in Early North India," *Journal of the American Oriental Society* 128:4(2008): 238.

14. Peter Skilling, "*Eṣā agrā*: Images of Nuns in (Mūla-)Sarvāstivādin Literature," *Journal of the International Association of Buddhist Studies* 24:2(2001): 148–49.

15. Gregory Schopen, "The Urban Buddhist Nun and A Protective Rite for Children in Early North India," *Pāsādikadānam: Festschrift für Bhikkhu Pasadika*, ed. Martin Straube et al. (Marburg: Indica et Tibetica Verlag, 2009), 376–77. Midwifery was one of occupations prohibited for nuns by the *vinaya*. Amy Paris Langenberg "Female Monastic Healing and Midwifery: A View from the Vinaya Tradition," *Journal of Buddhist Ethics* 21(2014): 155–90.

16. Reiko Ohnuma, "Bad Nun: Thullanandā in Pāli Canonical and Commentarial Sources," *Journal of Buddhist Ethics* 20(2013): 55.

17. For a translation of this episode, see Bhikkhu Bodhi, *The Connected Discourses of the Buddha: A New Translation of the Saṃyutta Nikāya*, vol. 1 (Boston: Wisdom Publications, 2000), 676–79. My translation of Thullanandā's rebuke differs slightly by taking *kumaraka* ("youngster") as a synonym for *bāla*, which means both child and fool.

18. Ohnuma, "Bad Nun," 48.

19. Ibid., 32.

20. Ibid., 35, 59–60.

21. See Nancy Auer Falk, "The Case of the Vanishing Nuns: The Fruits of Ambivalence in Ancient Indian Buddhism," *Unspoken Worlds: Women's Religious Lives in Non-Western Cultures*, ed. Nancy A. Falk and Rita M. Gross (San Francisco: Harper and Row, 1980), 207–24.

22. G. P. Malalasekera, *Dictionary of Pali Proper Names*. Vol. II. (Oxford: The Pali Text Society, 1997), 1224–25.

23. See I. B. Horner, *The Book of the Discipline (Vinaya-Pitaka)*, vol. 4 (London: Luzac & Company LTD, 1971), 413–419. For more information on Visakhā, see Nyanaponika Thera and Hellmuth Hecker, *Great Disciples of the Buddha* (Boston: Wisdom, 1997), 247–55.

24. See Bhikkhu Bodhi, *The Numerical Discourses of the Buddha, An Anthology of Suttas Anguttara Nikāya* (Boston: Wisdom Publications, 2012), 95–96.

25. Thera and Hecker, *Great Disciples of the Buddha*, 285–93.

26. Peter Skilling, "Nuns, Laywomen, Donors, Goddesses: Female Roles in Early Indian Buddhism," *Journal of the International Association of Buddhist Studies*. 24:2(2001): 253–54.

27. Khujjtuttarā's role in transmitting is also discussed by Maria Heim, "She Who Heard Much: Notes on Receiving, Interpreting, and Transmitting Buddhavacana," *International Journal of Hindu Studies* 19(2015): 144–48.

28. I. B. Horner, *The Book of the Discipline (Vinaya-Piṭaka)*, vol. 4, 379.

29. Ibid., 315–17. On her life story, see also Pruitt, *The Commentary on the Verses of the Therīs*, 260–69; and Thera and Hecker, *Great Disciples of the Buddha*, 300–303.

30. For a complete translation of her twenty verses, see Hallisey, *Therīgāthā*, 129–41.

31. See Anālayo, "Outstanding Bhikkhunīs in the *Ekottarika-āgama,*" *Women in Early Indian Buddhism,* 97–115; Skilling, "Female Roles in Early Buddhism," 247–49; On Khemā's life see Nyanaponika Thera and Hellmuth Hecker, *Great Disciples of the Buddha,* 263–69; Pruitt, *The Commentary on the Verses of the Therīs,* 164–76; and Mabel Bode, "Women Leaders of the Buddhist Reformation," *Journal of the Royal Asiatic Society* 25:3(1893): 529–39. On Dhammadinnā's life, see Pruitt, *The Commentary on the Verses of the Therīs,* 25–31; Bode, "Women Leaders of the Buddhist Reformation," 562–66; and Anālayo, Chos sbyin gyi mdo: Bhiksunī Dharmadinnā Proves Her Wisdom," *Chung-Hwa Buddhist Journal* 24(2011): 3–34. On Uppalavaṇṇā's life, see Pruitt, *The Commentary on the Verses of the Therīs,* 232–51; Bode, "Women Leaders of the Buddhist Reformation," 540–55; and Serinity Young, "Female Mutability and Male Anxiety in an Early Buddhist Legend," *Journal of the History of Sexuality,* 16(2007): 14–39.

32. Anālayo, "Outstanding Bhikkhunīs in the *Ekottarika-āgama,*" 112.

33. Charles Hallisey, *Therīgāthā: Poems of the First Buddhist Women,* vii.

34. See Pascale Engelmajer, *Women in Pāli Buddhism: Walking the Spiritual Paths in Mutual Dependence* (London: Routledge, 2014), 74–76.

35. Collett, "The Female Past," 221–22.

36. Reiko Ohnuma, *Ties That Bind: Maternal Imagery and Discourse in Indian Buddhism* (Oxford: Oxford University Press, 2012), 36–65.

37. On Kisāgotamī's life, see Pruitt, *The Commentary on the Verses of the Therīs,* 222–32; and Mabel Bode, "Women Leaders of the Buddhist Reformation, cont," *Journal of the Royal Asiatic Society* 25:4(1893): 793–96.

38. See Pruitt, *The Commentary on the Verses of the Therīs,* 143–54; Collett, "The Female Past," 222–24; and Bode, "Women Leaders of the Buddhist Reformation," 556–61.

39. Pruitt, *The Commentary on the Verses of the Therīs,* 126–132; and Bode, "Women Leaders of the Buddhist Reformation, cont.," 768–70.

40. For a complete translation of Rohinī's twenty verses, see Charles Hallisey, *Therīgāthā: Poems of the First Buddhist Women,* 141–49; for Dhammapāla's commentary on them, see William Pruitt, *The Commentary on the Verses of the Therīs,* 269–77.

41. For a translation of "The Great Chapter," see Hallisey, *Therīgāthā,* 213–39.

42. Kevin Trainor, "In the Eye of the Beholder: Nonattachment and the Body in Subhā's Verse," *Journal of the American Academy of Religion* 61(1993): 64.

43. For a translation of the verses, see Hallisey, *Therīgāthā,* 183–95. For Dhammapāla's commentary on them, see Pruitt, *The Commentary on the Verses of the Therīs,* 310–28.

44. See Karen Christina Lang, "Lord Death's Snare: Gender-Related Imagery in the *Theragāthā* and the *Therigāthā,*" *Journal of Feminist Studies in Religion,* 11:2(1986): 63–79.

45. Pruitt, *The Commentary on the Verses of the Therīs*, 100–104.

46. See Bhikkhu Bodhi, *The Connected Discourses of the Buddha*, 221–30; and Anālayo, "*Saṃyutta-nikāya/ Saṃyukta-āgama*: Defying Māra: Bhikkhunīs in the *Saṃyukta-āgama*." In *Women in Early Indian Buddhism*, 116–39.

47. Alice Collett, "Historio-Critical Hermeneutics in the Study of Women in Early Indian Buddhism," *Numen* 56(2009): 112.

48. Young, "Female Mutability and Male Anxiety," 21.

49. Skilling, "*Eṣā agrā*," 153. Also see F. Anton von Schiefner, *Tibetan Tales Derived from Indian Sources* (London: Kegan Paul, Trench, Trubner & Co, 1906), 204–205.

50. Bhikkhu Anālayo, "The *Bahudhātuka-sutta* and its Parallels on Women's Inabilities," *Journal of Buddhist Ethics* 16(2009): 137.

51. Skilling, "*Eṣā agrā*," 143–47.

52. Bhikkhu Anālayo, "The Buddha's Past Life as a Princess in the *Ekottarika-āgama*," *Journal of Buddhist Ethics* 22(2015): 103–104.

53. Naomi Appleton, "In the Footsteps of the Buddha? Women and the *Bodhisatta* Path in Theravāda Buddhism," *Journal of Feminist Studies in Religion* 27:1(2011): 41.

54. Ibid., 44.

55. John Powers, *A Bull of a Man: Images of Masculinity, Sex, and the Body in Indian Buddhism)* Boston: Harvard University Press, 2009), 137–38; Appleton, "In the Footsteps of the Buddha?" 46; and Anālayo, "The Buddha's Past Life as a Princess," 111–12.

56. Quoted in Bhikkhu Anālayo, "Karma and Female Birth," *Journal of Buddhist Ethics* 21(2014): 112n.11.

57. Carol S. Anderson, "Changing Sex or Changing Gender in Pāli Buddhist Literature," *The Scholar & Feminist Online* 14.2 (2017): 4. sfonline.barnard.edu/queer-religion (accessed June 12, 2017).

58. Anālayo, "The Buddha's Past Life as a Princess," 95–137.

59. Bhikkhunī Dhammadinnā, "Predictions of Women to Buddhahood in Middle-Period Literature," *Journal of Buddhist Ethics* 22(2015): 489.

60. Karen Derris has translated the story in "My Sister's Future Buddhahood, A *Jātaka* of the Buddha's Lifetime as a Woman," *Eminent Buddhist Women*, ed. Karma Lekshe Tsomo (Albany, NY: State University of New York Press, 2014), 13–24.

61. Karen Derris, "When the Buddha Was a Woman: Reimagining Tradition in the Theravāda," *Journal of Feminist Studies in Religion* 24:2(2008): 36.

62. Ibid., 38.

63. E. B. Cowell and R. Neil, eds., *The Divyāvadāna: A Collection of Early Buddhist Legends* (Amsterdam: Oriental Press, 1970), 473. The text reads *strīndriyam* and *puruṣendriyam*, "female controlling faculty" and "male controlling faculty," but I have translated it more freely. On these controlling faculties, see Powers, *A Bull of a Man*, 132–33.

64. See Reiko Ohnuma, "The Story of Rūpavatī: A Female Past Birth of the Buddha," *Journal of the International Association of Buddhist Studies* 23:1(2000): 103–45. Michael Hahn's edition of the Sanskrit text is found in *Haribhaṭṭa and Gopadatta, Two Authors in the Succession of* Āryaśūra: *On the Rediscovery of Parts of their* Jātakamālās, 2nd ed. (Tokyo: Studia Philologica, 1992), 51–57. Reiko Ohnuma's translation, "Rūpyāvatī Gives Away Her Breasts," appeared in *Buddhist Scriptures*, ed. Donald S. Lopez, Jr. (London: Penguin Press, 2004), 159–71. Michael Hahn has also translated the text and, in his notes, corrects some of his own editing errors and Ohnuma's translations: "In Defence of *Haribhaṭṭa*," *Pramāṇakīrtih: Papers Dedicated to Ernst Steinkellner on the Occasion of His 70th Birthday*, Part 1, ed. B. Kellner, H. Krasser, Horst Lasic, M. T. Much, H. Tauscher (Vienna: Wiener Studien zur Tibetologie und Buddhismuskunde, 2007), 215–29. See also Dragomir Dimitrov, "Two Female Bodhisattvas in Flesh and Blood. Aspects of the Female in Indian Culture," *Proceedings of the Symposium in* Marburg, Germany, July 7–8, 2000, ed. Ulriche Roesler and Jayandra Soni (Marburg: Indica et Tibetica Verlag, 2004), 3–15. Dimitrov was the first to notice Haribhaṭṭa's "gender issue" (p. 8). However, I disagree with his conclusion (p. 11): "If one ventures to speculate about the poet's view on the gender issue, it will have to be admitted that the text clearly reveals the author as being a fairly liberal man and perhaps even a philogynist."

65. Paul Harrison, "Who Gets to Ride in the Great Vehicle? Self-Image and Identity Among the Followers of the Early Mahāyāna," *Journal of the International Association of Buddhist Studies* 10:1(1987): 75.

66. Ibid., 79.

67. P. L. Vaidya, *Aṣṭasāhasrikā Prajñāpāramitā* (Darbhanga: The Mithila Institute, 1960), 181. For a translation of the Chinese text, see Diana Y. Paul, *Women in Buddhism: Images of the Feminine in Mahāyāna Tradition* (Berkeley: University of California Press, 1985), 182–84.

68. For a summary of this text, see Nancy Schuster, "Changing the Female Body: Wise Women and the Bodhisattva Career in Some *Mahāratnakūṭasūtras*," *Journal of the International Association of Buddhist Studies* 4:1(1981): 36–37.

69. Ibid., 29–31; and Paul, *Women in Buddhism*, 201–11.

70. Pruitt, *The Commentary on the Verses of the Therīs*, 132–43. Also see Bode, "Women Leaders of the Buddhist Reformation, cont.," 777–79; and Alberto Todeschini, "The Maiden Who Fell in Love with a Thief: Considerations on the Story of the Nun Bhaddā Kuṇḍalakesā," *Dharma Drum Journal of Buddhist Studies* 13(2013): 153–86.

71. This is a much-discussed episode. For example, see Jan Nattier, "Gender and Hierarchy in the Lotus Sutra," *Readings of the Lotus Sutra*, ed. Stephan F. Teiser and Jacqueline I. Stone, 83–106; Lisa Battaglia Owen, "Toward a Buddhist Feminism: Mahayana Sutras, Feminist Theory, and the Transformation of Sex," *Asian Journal of Women's Studies* 3:4(1997): 5; Paul, *Women in Buddhism*, 185–90; Lucinda Joy Peach, "Sex Change, and Salvation:

Gender Justice in the *Lotus Sutra, Philosophy East and West* 52(2002): 50–74; and Schuster, "Changing the Female Body," 42–45.

72. John R. McRae, *Vimalakīrti Sūtra* (Berkeley, CA: Numata Center for Buddhist Translations and Research, 2004), 62. Also see Battaglia Owen, "Toward a Buddhist Feminism," 5–6; Paul, *Women in Buddhism*, 221–32; and Schuster, "Changing the Female Body," 41–46.

73. Battaglia Owen, "Toward a Buddhist Feminism," 6.

74. Douglas Osto, "The Supreme Array Scripture: A New Interpretation of the Title *Gaṇḍavyūha Sūtra*," *Journal of Indian Philosophy* 37(2009): 273–90.

75. Paul, *Women in Buddhism*, 133–34.

76. Douglas Osto, Power, Wealth and Women in Indian Mahāyāna Buddhism: The *Gaṇḍavyūha-sūtra* (London: Routledge, 2008), 33.

77. Ibid., 89–96. Also see the translations of these women's stories in Paul, *Women in Buddhism*, 98–102, 134–62; and the discussion of Vasumitrā in Douglas Osto, "Proto-Tantric" Elements in the *Gaṇḍavyūha-sūtra*, *Journal of Religious History* 33:2(2009): 165–77.

78. Osto, *Power, Wealth and Women*, 100–104. On Gopā's story, also see Douglas Osto, "Soteriology, Asceticism and the Female Body in Two Indian Buddhist Narratives," *Buddhist Studies Review* 23:2(2006): 205–8.

79. Osto, *Power, Wealth and Women*, 105–16.

80. Alex Wayman and Hideko Wayman, *The Lion's Roar of Queen Śrīmālā* (New York: Columbia University Press, 1974), 2.

81. Richard King, "Is 'Buddha-Nature' Buddhist?: Doctrinal Tensions in the Śrimālā Sūtra: An Early Tathāgatagarbha Text," *Numen* (1995): 19n.45.

82. Paul, *Women in Buddhism*, 286–87.

83. Diana Paul, *The Sūtra of Queen Śrīmālā of the Lion's Roar* (Berkeley, CA: Numata Center for Buddhist Translations and Research, 2004), 6.

84. patacara.org (accessed June 12, 2017).

Chapter 2

The Religious Life of Buddhist Women in Chosŏn Korea

Eun-su Cho

Buddhism came to Korea around the fourth century, introducing the Three Kingdoms Period (57 BCE–668 CE) to a systematic spiritual worldview that challenged and virtually displaced the existing shamanistic understandings of the world.[1] The Kingdom of Silla, in particular, actively promulgated Buddhism to the masses not only to cultivate an ethic based on the ideas of *karma* and rebirth but to develop the social consciousness that drove its unification of the Korean peninsula. Buddhism was revered as a national religion through Unified Silla (668–935 CE) and the Koryŏ Dynasty (918–1392 CE), where the spiritual pursuits of women were encouraged and praised under this aegis of prestige. However, the succeeding Chosŏn Dynasty (1392–1897 CE) was established through a coup by Confucian politicians, whose patriarchal and anti-Buddhist policies challenged the Buddhist order and faith from various directions. Buddhist temples within cities were demolished; temples were forced to eke out their existence in the remote mountains, creating the moniker "Mountain Buddhism." Monks and nuns were ostracized as the lowest untouchables, lower than the peasant; they were denied entry into cities and subject to being pressed into forced labor.

Yet through these challenges Buddhist practice managed to survive, even thrive. In the face of economic and social hardship and the endless attacks from Confucian ideologues, the Buddhist temples and monasteries continued to operate. Though banned in the public sphere, Buddhist faith never lost its foothold in private; for women in particular, Buddhism remained a part of everyday emotional and spiritual life.[2]

The Women Who Did Not Follow the Rules

Whereas men were at home in the Confucian social order, women were marginalized, such that religious faith played a more important part in the lives of many women. Not only were women persecuted for being Buddhists, they were marginalized by the patriarchal views of Confucianism. Thus, women often turned to Buddhism in private for spiritual refuge, but they frequently had to suffer for their faith. The *Annals of the Chosŏn Dynasty* (*Chosŏn wangjo sillok*), the official historical record of the court, includes innumerable records about Buddhist women. There were women investigated for defying the national edict that prohibited women from entering temples; fully ordained nuns (*bhikṣuṇīs*) who attracted public censure for abandoning their families of nobility to live a monastic life or were arrested under suspicion of having committed sexual misdeeds; petitions criticizing Buddhist functions being held at shrines within the palace walls; and endless recommendations by officials throughout the six-hundred-year history of the dynasty to order the destruction of all Buddhist temples because of these issues.

Yet these negative records about Buddhist women serve to reveal the times during which Confucian control of women and policies of Buddhist persecution surged and anti-Buddhist rhetoric gained the upper hand in political discourse, as well as how Confucian fundamentalists of the time viewed women. The biased nature of these records makes it difficult to say that they accurately depict how Buddhism functioned in society or what Buddhist practice looked like for women. Indeed, the very fact that these events kept coming up in the records provides powerful evidence that the tradition of women's Buddhist practice persisted and thrived against odds. By the Confucians' own admission, these women "did not fear any prohibitions, acting freely and without reluctance";[3] the light of their faith could not be extinguished.

Buddhist Women: The Hated and Reviled

Almost no records survive of what Buddhist faith looked like for the common people during the Chosŏn Dynasty. Nameless commoners were not included in records; in fact, names were recorded in the *Annals* only if someone had committed a crime or aroused social censure. Thus, to deduce what religious life was like for the everyday person is nearly impossible. Nevertheless, paradoxically, the barrage of petitions prohibiting displays of Buddhist faith and the records of women persecuted for going to temple provide proof that Buddhism never lost its relevance among the common people.

Expressions of Buddhist faith were controlled and prohibited through various social and legal restraints. For instance, Chosŏn society had an almost neurotic obsession with the chastity of women, and numerous public monuments were made in honor of women who kept their chastity after being widowed or faithfully serving their late husbands' family. Behavior that deviated from this norm was immediately condemned, to the point where even women who had been taken captive during war were shunned for not remaining faithful to their husbands. This ideology of sexual virtue could be used to pressure and condemn women, and Confucian politicians formed anti-Buddhist laws on this pretext. In the foundational legal text of the Chosŏn Dynasty, *Kyŏngje yukchŏn* (The Six Law Codes for Governance), an explicit prohibition states that if a woman and a monk go to the same temple, they will be found guilty of 'losing their virtue' [*silchŏl*]." Social custom at the time prohibited men and women from sharing the same space. By the same token, a woman spending the night at a temple where monks lived was itself considered a grave violation of their chastity. Although it may seem excessive by today's standards that women's "sexual purity" could be lost merely by sharing the same space as a man, this obsession over sexual purity was used effectively to suppress Buddhist women.

In 1704, during the mid–Chosŏn period, the petitions of ministers in the *Annals of King Sukchong* (r. 1674–1720) provide examples of the degree of vitriol levied against these women:

> The long-standing ban on monks and nuns entering the cities that has been effect since the founding of the Kingdom was to rectify the public by taking action against the crafty and lustful. But now [the temple] is a place where hordes of women who betrayed their fathers and their masters [their husbands], and widows who lost their way after becoming widowed early, fight amongst each other to attend. There they fornicate and commit obscene acts; in more than one place they seduce and disturb the public morals.[4]

In spite of such vitriol and prohibitions, women never ceased to visit temples and offer their prayers. Earlier, in 1494, when the sister-in-law of King Sŏngjong (r. 1469–1495) founded a temple called Hŭngboksa and held a service, women from the nobility and gentry flocked to enter its doors. However, the fact that they stayed at the temple together with monks and nuns became a national issue, resulting in petitions from the Sahŏnbu (Ministry of Prosecution) and Saganwŏn (Ministry of Internal Audit) demanding that the monk who led the service be interrogated and the women who attended the temple be punished. King Sŏngjong quashed their demands, stating, "These women uphold and believe in Buddhism for the sake of their husbands and parents. How could we raze all the temples, or indeed ban the faith entirely?"[5]

It is interesting to observe that, in the *Annals*, it is always the king or queen who acts as the protector and speaks out against these petitions to close temples, reform Buddhism, or force the nuns in the court nunneries to renounce their vows so that they could be controlled in a central location in Seoul. In April 1434, during the sixteenth year of King Sejong (r. 1418–1450), a king who was initially pro-Confucian but became pro-Buddhist in his later years, a service was held to commemorate the renovation of Hoeamsa, a temple intimately related to the early kings of the Chosŏn Dynasty.[6] According to *The Annals of King Sejong*,

> Monks, using the excuse that the Buddha Hall [of Hoeamsa] was in disrepair, traveled Seoul and the countryside with flyers [*kwŏnsŏnmun*; lit., statement of encouraging goodness] urging the people to donate. The ignorant women and the rich merchants flocked to them and they raised a fortune. Even the king bestowed rice and linen to help.[7]

When the renovations were finished, a ceremony was held to celebrate the temple's completion. Many noblewomen and *bhikṣuṇī*s attended. The abbot gave a Dharma talk, and women listened to his talk in the same hall. Even some officials were in attendance. Then the monks performed a Buddhist drama called the "Non-obstruction Play," to which the women donated their expensive clothing on the spot, the king's mother-in-law among them. This incident prompted fierce petitions from the Confucian scholars for two months. The gathering, the sleepover, sitting with men in the same space—all were protested in vehement petitions. In July, after two months' investigation, the prosecutors' office sentenced the accused: flogging for the twenty or so wives and nuns who had stayed over at the temple, as well as punishment for the scholar-monks involved. The wives, daughters, and the daughters-in-law of vassals of merit were released after fines were collected.[8]

However, throughout this long process, King Sejong himself forbade regional officials from raiding temples and tried to smooth over the petitions to prosecute and hand down sentences. In the *Annals of King Sejong*, there are ten entries about Hoeamsa that pertain to this incident alone, and forty-eight entries altogether in that one year, most of which are long, boring, and vehement petitions and appeals from Confucian scholars and the ministries of Internal Audit. The following year, in 1435, the king donated salt to the temple; he ignored a petition from the Ministry of Prosecution stipulating that donations to the temple and the renovations requested by his older brother Prince Hyoryŏng (who was a pious Buddhist and lived almost like a monk) be rejected. Even afterward, he argued that donations to the temple should not be stopped.[9]

Thus, the problem of Buddhism in the Chosŏn Dynasty must be understood not only in terms of Confucian-Buddhist conflict, but also in terms of power struggles and the system of checks and balances between the king and his ministers, which were located within Neo-Confucian concepts of governance. An examination of conflicts within these circles of power surrounding perceptions of Buddhist women and their responses may lead to new understandings about the inner workings of the Chosŏn Dynasty. At any rate, although appeals to prevent women from meeting with monks and nuns at temples were continuous during the history of the dynasty, women's attendance at Buddhist temples could not be stopped by strictures.

The *Bhikṣuṇī*: Straddling the Boundaries of a Woman of Virtue

Bhikṣuṇī is a Sanskrit term referring to a female monastic or nun, parallel to the *bhikṣu* or male monastic. Due to the request of a woman, the Buddha approved the creation of an order of female monastics. Buddhism is rather unique in having had male and female monastic orders since the inception of the religion. In Korea, the first recorded nun is Sa, the sister of Morye, who played an instrumental role in the adoption of Buddhism in Silla, as recorded in *Memorabilia of the Three Kingdoms* (*Samguk yusa*). The *Chronicles of Japan* also contain a record that *bhikṣuṇī*s from the Korean kingdom of Paekche (18 BCE–

660 CE) spread Buddhism in Japan, and that three Japanese women visited Paekche thereafter to receive their *bhikṣuṇī* vows.[10] During the Unified Silla period, the *bhikṣuṇī*s were so notable that records indicate a *bhikṣuṇī* minister of government. Although women could not take the official entrance exams to become a monk during the Koryǒ Dynasty, many *bhikṣuṇī*s nevertheless devoted themselves to Buddhist practice. The tombstone of Hyesim, the pupil of Pojo Chinul—one of the most famous monks in Korean history—lists several *bhikṣuṇī*s among his pupils. These nuns came from various backgrounds; most of them joined the order after their husband's death, while some joined because they could not afford marriage due to poverty. *Bhikṣuṇī*s of noble birth sometimes built and lived in temples next to their families.[11]

In the Chosǒn Dynasty, many women joined the monastic order after being widowed, stating as their rationale their desire to pray for the repose of their husbands and to maintain their faithfulness. Lady Yun entered the order after her husband's death; the *Annals of King Sejo* (r. 1455–1468) record the matter thus:

> Lady Yu, the wife of Yu Chahwan, was the daughter of Prime Minister Yun Hyǒng. She was extremely jealous, wild and loose in character; she consorted in secret with nuns even before Yu Chahwan's passing. After her husband's passing she did not show the slightest hint of grief, and when his family prepared to take his coffin from Seoul to his hometown, she behaved as if she would follow the procession. However, the day the coffin was to be borne out she snuck away at night, going off to join the monastic order [lit., leave home] that very day instead of going to the funeral. She shaved her head and became a nun, going around various mountains to meet with monks to receive the Buddhist teachings, while staying many nights at temples; although she claimed it was to pray for the fortune of her dead husband, she was in fact going wherever she wanted and doing as she pleased.[12]

This passage is clearly a condemnation of Lady Yu's behavior. However, when read another way, the record describes the decision of a religiously inclined housewife of the gentry who awaited the opportunity to join the order; in order to avoid opposition by the family who surrounded her, she had little choice but to run away from home on the day of the funeral procession. The records later show that Lady Yu became the abbess of the temple Chŏngŏpwŏn, demonstrating the depth of her practice and the respect she garnered from other *bhikṣuṇīs* as well as her lay devotees. Rather than choosing the restricted life of a widowed "woman of virtue," she made the choice to leave home to pursue the path of a practitioner.

Not only widows, but unmarried women also became *bhikṣuṇīs*. These women eagerly frequented temples to offer prayers and listen to sermons delivered by monks. The *Annals of King Sŏngjong* (r. 1469–1495) contain a vitriolic condemnation of these religious activities as unforgivable, obscene, and abominable:

> The flow of unmarried women and widows shaving their heads does not cease; they crowd together, make friends, and intermingle with monks, using the excuse that [Buddhism] recommends virtue, or that they were only having a picnic in the mountains with their friends. Their obscene and abominable acts send the order of their families into disarray.[13]

Although a widow might become a nun with the express intention of keeping her virtue, she was constantly subjected to criticism for "intermingling with monks and committing obscene and abominable acts." By rejecting the social demand that a widow become a confined "woman of virtue" and instead become a nun, such a woman rebelled head-on against the Confucian family order of the time.

Under the Confucian view of the family, the status of unmarried women was fundamentally unstable; the fact that such women left home to follow the Buddha's teachings inevitably made them a target of criticism:

> The nuns today are not only the daughters of commoners but also the gentry; they shave their heads and become nuns though their husbands have passed away only recently. Inappropriately, even young, unmarried women clamor to shave their own hair. It is only human nature that a man takes a wife and a woman has a husband. If a young woman becomes a nun and does not take a husband, this will bring about disaster by breaking the harmonious order [of the family]. I beseech you to call them back to secular life and have them return to their homes.[14]

Although women of the gentry were not normally allowed to join the order, in many cases unmarried women became nuns when enforcement became lax. Yet an unmarried woman living alone was an act against the harmony of nature. *Bhikṣuṇīs*, who gathered together in communities to practice, aroused more discomfort than any other group. They were considered renegades who followed Buddhism, a religion forbidden by the state, and by accepting Buddhist teachings as truth, they were perceived as stubbornly refusing to bend their opinions. The way of life of these women was not only a deviation from the Confucian order and its customs, but also a deviation against the order of the universe itself.

Throughout the Chosŏn Dynasty, pleas attempted to force young nuns to return to the secular world, grow their hair, and get married. The only possible exceptions were those who became nuns to preserve their virtue after becoming widowed.

> The [Confucian] canon states that "in the home, let there be no resentful woman; outside, let there be no lamenting husband." This shows the importance of the harmony between yin and yang in the married couple. Now, young nuns accumulate sexual desire within while outwardly they feign fidelity to their principles. Although in their minds they would like to get married right now, they end their lives sighing every day because they cannot dare express this; how could anyone say that they have no hidden resentment? How about ordering the central and regional authorities to have nuns under the age of 30 grow out their hair and marry?[15]

Despite strictures, suppression, and criticism, the existence of *bhikṣuṇīs* is repeatedly confirmed by these measures throughout the existence of the Chosŏn Dynasty. Nevertheless, aside from some cases of religious friendships with upper-class women, material support from the court, and patronage by wealthy sponsors, many *bhikṣuṇī* temples remained exceedingly poor. Overall, in addition to enduring the hatred and loathing of normative Confucian patriarchal society, nuns had to overcome the obstacles of social ostracism and economic hardship in their struggle to survive throughout the dynasty's six-hundred-year history.

"How Could I Stop Her?"

The Chosŏn Dynasty's policy on Buddhism took different forms depending on the attitude of the ruling monarch. After the invention of Hangul (the native Korean script) by King Sejong, several successive reigns saw the translation of many Buddhist texts into Hangul by the order of the king or queen mother. The intended audiences for these texts were women and commoners and the texts selected for translation focused mainly on prayers for good fortune or rebirth in the Pure Land in the next life rather than doctrinal education. Even after the national office for the publication of Buddhist texts ceased to exist, the publication of Buddhist texts continued unabated until the mid–Chosŏn Dynasty.

As an example, let us focus here on the Buddhist faith of members of the Chosŏn royal family, who served as pillars of support for Buddhism. This faith, which was most prominent among women of the royal family, such as King Sŏngjong's mother Queen Mother Insu (1437–1504) and the mother of King Myŏngjong (r. 1545–1567), Queen Mother Munjŏng (1501–1565), has drawn widespread attention and even been the subject of historical dramas on TV. The *Annals of King Sŏngjong* include a vivid case of the king coming under pressure from his ministers due to the Buddhist activities of Queen Mother Insu:

QUEEN MOTHER INSU: I heard that there was a violent debate in the court about the fact that I copied Buddhist scriptures [as a form of practice] at Pongsŏnsa Temple, is that true?

KING SŎNGJONG: Yes.

INSU: Why did you not tell me this?

SŎNGJONG: How could I bother Mother's ears with nonsense?

INSU: It seems I have brought harm to His Majesty by copying the scriptures. For generations, our previous kings did not get rid of Buddhism despite saying that they are false teachings. I came to the palace when I was young and parted from the late king forever, not having served him properly for even a day [due to his early death at age twenty]. How can I properly express this sorrow now?

Praying for the departed is a traditional thing to do; I have never once stopped caring for the late king above and attending to the current king [Sŏngjong] with all my heart. Sejo, our previous king [Sŏngjong's grandfather], took into consideration my sorrow and allowed me to pay respects at my husband's grave every spring and fall. But now, as mother of the people, I have to fear the arguments of the court and nothing I do is of my own volition. Is it not true that Confucians have rejected the Buddha since long ago only because of the fear that if the king was too deeply devoted to Buddhism he would make the people suffer by squandering the nation's wealth building temples and entertaining monks? Yet the court becomes embroiled in this much controversy when I spend only my own personal wealth to publish Buddhist scriptures without any harm to the nation. What am I to do? If the Buddha's teachings are empty, then why have we continued to hold ceremonial services on behalf of the deceased king and his consort, or hold rites for the guardian spirits of the major mountains and rivers on behalf of the nation? But if the Saganwŏn (Ministry of Internal Audit) forces this issue, I will stop the copying of scriptures.

After this, Sŏngjong called forth his ministers from the Saganwŏn and demanded an answer. "For what reason do you dare speak about this when you are aware that it is the Queen Mother's prerogative? Do you think your actions are right or wrong?"

After the minister of audit said, "It is our wrongdoing," the king replied, "I am glad that you freely admit it is your own offense."

Hardliners among the court angrily protested, saying, "How could an old fogey like you who accepts the stipend of the king and bears the title of Minister of Speech [the ministry also having functioned as the press] only respond in such a feeble way?" and tried to launch an appeal with the help of others. More moderates argued that "people commonly hold ceremonial rites at temples on behalf of their fathers and give offerings to monks; why should it be harmful to the country that the queen mother copies Buddhist scriptures on behalf of the late king?" The hardliners lamented, "The king says he can't stop it because his mother does it on behalf of the late king. You ministers say you should leave it alone because it is only the Queen Mother's doing and not the King's, and that it won't harm the rule of this country. When then can we stop the worship of the Buddha in the palace?"[16]

Although this is a small cross-section of an event within the palace during the reign of King Sŏngjong, arguments along these lines took place throughout the dynasty. When the queen mother, the queen, or the royal concubines of the late king kindled their Buddhist faith and carried out services to comfort themselves or asserted that their practice was conducted on behalf of deceased monarchs, it was difficult to stop them, especially a king who felt affection and respect toward those who had raised him.

Royal Temples:
Prayers for the Prosperity of the Chosŏn Royal Family

It is important to examine the position of Buddhism in Chosŏn from multiple angles in a nuanced manner. Until very recently, books on Korean history generally painted a black-and-white picture, claiming that Buddhism flourished as the national religion during the Koryŏ Dynasty and died out during the Chosŏn Dynasty due to policies ostracizing and suppressing Buddhism. This binary characterization reached Korean Studies scholars outside of Korea without any critical filtering, causing some Western scholars to label Buddhist suppression during the Chosŏn "persecution," portraying images of heretics being burned alive and executed much like medieval times in Europe. Although Chosŏn had consistently upheld Confucianism and excluded Buddhism as a matter of national policy, Buddhist ritual practices for the prosperity of the royal family persisted throughout its history. When Buddhism was disseminated among ordinary people, it was regarded as a threat to society; when Buddhist practices were not aimed at the public, as in the palace, they were regarded as a private matter.

The Royal Temples (lit., Prayer Temples) of the Chosŏn Dynasty serve to illustrate how Buddhist faith manifested within the royal family. Royal Temples were supported by the royal family to pray for the souls of departed kings and to effect the continued prosperity of the family. Such temples included Pongsŏnsa in Namyangju, and Pongguksa in Seoul. From the standpoint of the public, Confucianism provided values and norms necessary for people to function in society, but it was unable to provide satisfactory answers to key questions about the uncertainties of life, such as human suffering and what lies beyond death. Buddhism, on the other hand, provided a spiritual view of the world and a moral compass for both the present life and what lies beyond, based on the theory of rebirth. For this reason, Buddhism retained relevance in the spiritual hearts of the people.

Chŏngŏpwŏn: The Existence of Royal Nunneries

Buddhism remained popular during the Chosŏn Dynasty, espe-cially among the women of the court. Royal nunneries such as the Chŏngŏpwŏn, Chasuwŏn, and Insuwŏn, located immediately outside the palace walls, were sites for Buddhist functions such as prayer, ceremonial rites, and the Lantern Festival, in addition to housing the ancestral tablets of the royal family.[17] Royal concubines and women of the court joined the order, received land and slaves from the king, and enjoyed state-sponsored financial support on par with other gov-ernment offices. Among these nunneries, Chŏngŏpwŏn existed before the dynasty's founding. Chasuwŏn and Insuwŏn lasted until late in the dynasty, mainly housing the royal concubines of the late kings who had taken monastic vows. What began as a place for the women of the court and royal concubines to live near the palace after the king's demise naturally evolved into quasi-temples, populated as they were by women who became nuns to spend the rest of their days in Buddhist devotion. By holding prayers and rites, these nunneries functioned very much like full-fledged temples.

The abbess of the nunnery was usually a member of the royal household and appointed by the queen mother. The *Annals of King Sejong* record that "Ŭibin [a title] Lady Kwŏn and Sinnyŏnggungju [a title] Lady Shin shaved their heads and became nuns without even consulting the king. The royal concubines competed to shave their heads and prepared chanting instruments, practicing Buddhism day and night; even the King could not stop them despite his pro-hibition."[18] The tone of this pronouncement demonstrates how the women's devotions were perceived as an eyesore by officials at the court, and students of the Confucian academy persistently demanded the abolition of the nunneries to keep Buddhism in check. However, because these nuns were generally members of the royal family or in some way related to the court, the kings of the Chosŏn Dynasty had no choice but to take special care of them and treat them with respect.

The pro-Buddhist King Sejong endured criticism and resistance from his ministers throughout his reign, due to issues such as the creation of new nunneries, the relocation of Royal Temples, and the printing of the Buddhist canon, ultimately resulting in the temporary closure of the Chŏngŏpwŏn nunnery. King Sejo (r. 1455–1468) shifted to pro-Buddhist policies, reopened Chŏngŏpwŏn, and actively supported it with land and slaves, a pattern that continued through the reign of King Sŏngjong (r. 1469–1494). During the latter's reign, Chŏngŏpwŏn flourished greatly after a renovation funded by Queen consorts Chŏnghŭi and Sohye. Sŏngjong's successor Yŏnsangun (r. 1494–1506), furious at King Sŏngjong's former concubines over the deposal of his mother as queen, evicted the nuns of Chŏngŏpwŏn and forced nuns outside the palace walls into slavery. This effectively marked the end of the nunnery.

The *Annals of King Myŏngjong* (r. 1545–1567) record a threatening petition issued in 1553:

Now, [the kingdom] has spent the labors of the people to build Insugung [i.e., Insuwŏn], where widows who shaved their hair can live. These hordes follow teachings that respect neither the father nor the king, nor do they grow silkworms or weave cloth. They ring their bells and shout out their chants next to the palace; if passersby are surprised by the sight and sounds, how would the heavens themselves react upon seeing and hearing this? Lately the weather has been strange, and it would not even be surprising if we should now see floods and droughts.[19]

Alongside these dire predictions were rumors that hot-blooded Confucians were planning to set fire to the newly built Insugung. Ultimately in 1661, Insuwŏn and Chasuwŏn, the remaining nunneries, were completely abolished. Nuns who were forty years of age or below were forced to return to secular life, whereas old nuns who had nowhere to go were sent to nunneries outside the city walls. The wood from the demolish temple was used to repair the Sŏnggyungwan, the highest Confucian academy.

Buddhist Faith Framed as Filial Piety

Despite the official national policy that supported Confucianism, Buddhism received steady support from within the private sphere of the palace. The patronage of Buddhist artwork by women of the royal family and nobility is one example. These women also supported the transcription, printing, and distribution of Buddhist scriptures, and commissioned statues and paintings of the Buddha and various *bodhisattvas*.[20] Of these figures, the scriptures and artwork portraying the *bodhisattva* Ksitigarbha was the most popular. Judging from the donation records for these works of art and printing, the benefactors were mostly queen mothers, court women, or women of the gentry.[21] Ksitigarbha's status as the *bodhisattva* who provides salvation to all beings, who suffer not only on this earth but particularly in the hells, explains his popularity among those who commissioned these works, which represented a prayer for the souls of their departed parents. This patronage was thus a fusion of Confucian filial piety and the Buddhist resolve to alleviate suffering. Perhaps these wives were looking for a way to express their faith by funding the renovation of temples and the printing of scriptures, and by commissioning various works of art. Yet, these large donations could not have been made without the notice and approval of their husbands, demonstrating that the Confucian gentry were inclined to accept Buddhist faith within the framework of filial piety.

After the sixteenth century, royal support for Buddhism gradually began to decline. Following the large-scale suppression of Buddhism during the reign of Yŏnsangun, royal patronage for Buddhist art and culture began to dissipate. Although there were several pro-Buddhist rulers in the late eighteenth century, such as King Chŏngjo (r. 1776–1800), they lacked the influence to bring about a new revival of Buddhist culture, calling on Buddhism primarily to protect the royal family and its succession. The major patrons of Buddhist art during the eighteenth and nineteenth centuries were women at court. High-ranking women at court were particularly prominent in commissioning many projects that influenced the development of Ksitigarbha paintings; some made offerings together with the queen and royal concubines. During the nineteenth-century reign of Kojong (r. 1863–1907), a record exists of high-ranking women at court offering a sizable donation to sponsor the reprinting of the Tripitaka Koreana.

After the mid–Chosŏn Dynasty, Buddhism quickly weakened, and its ideological traditions began to fade away, diluted by its syncretism with folk beliefs. Doctrinal study withered, and Buddhism persisted mostly in the form of Sŏn (Japanese: Zen; Chinese: Chan) meditation and prayers to be reborn in the Pure Land by chanting the name of Amita Buddha. Buddhist ideals also persisted in the folk-lore of ordinary people. The *Togang Koga Pusa* (Story of a Woman Who Married a Blind Man from Togang), an epic poem said to have been written by Tasan Chŏng Yagyong (1762–1836) based on a story he heard while in exile, tells the following tale: A girl who lived in Kangjin Province was pressured by her father and deceived by her matchmaker into marrying a violent old man. Unable to stand her husband's beatings and the abuse of her in-laws, she ran away to a temple, shaved her head, and became a nun. Her husband reported this to the officials, who dragged her away to court. This story shows that even in the eighteenth century, the temple served as a kind of emotional and physical hideout for women. Within a society con-trolled by the patriarchal Confucian social order, women attempted to kindle inner strength through their Buddhist faith in order to over-come the endless challenges they faced in life. For women, Buddhism is both infused in daily religious life and a place to find personal peace.

Conclusion

The historical record reveals a multilayered site of contention involv-ing gender roles and social norms imposed on women by the Chosŏn Dynasty. During this time, Buddhist women devised strategies to counter the long-held public disdain toward Buddhism fomented by the anti-Buddhist policies of the Chosŏn government, and the legal and cultural oppression of women authorized by Neo-Confucian ide-ology. Though every attempt was made to marginalize and stigma-tize Buddhist women, they found ways to navigate the complex and oppressive political and social structures of the Chosŏn Dynasty and remain relevant in Korea up until today. In the process, female Bud-dhist followers showed how even within the narrow confines of the monastery, they could not only provide a spiritual refuge for women, but also create a positive self-image and constructive Buddhist prac-tice overall. Thus, they show that religious ideals and achievements are not only for men, but for women as well.

   Although Buddhist women may seem unlikely protagonists, they have been heroes in helping break down the gender stereo-

types and constraints of traditional society. Their efforts throughout
the years shine through in the contemporary Korean Buddhist landscape, where nuns have become equal and indispensable partners
with monks, regardless of whether this fact is acknowledged. Time
and time again, Korean Buddhist women have proven their selfless
dedication, resourcefulness, and compassion. By taking their education and training into their own hands, they have created a strong
sense of personal, social, and religious identity that empowers them
to confidently excel in studies, meditation, caregiving, and activism—
taking to the streets to voice the concerns of human society, the natural world, and all that is wholesome. Even in the face of political
and economic uncertainties, women continue to demonstrate that they
may be Buddhism's most valuable asset.

Notes

1. This work was supported by an Academy of Korean Studies (KSPS)
Grant funded by the Korean Government (MOE) (AKS-2012-AAZ-104).

2. For more information on Korean Buddhist nuns and laywomen, see
Eun-su Cho, ed., *Korean Buddhist Nuns and Laywomen: Hidden Histories, Enduring Vitality* (Albany: State University of New York Press, 2011).

3. [King] *Sejong sillok*, 19th year (April 27, 1437).

4. *Sukjong sillok*, 30th year (October 28, 1704).

5. *Sŏngjong sillok*, 25th year (April 17, 1494).

6. King T'aejo, the founder of the dynasty, used to come to Hoeamsa
to visit his mentor, the monk Muhak, during his last years, after yielding his
throne to his ambitious son King T'aejong. King T'aejong eventually had to
visit to plead with the abdicated king to return to the palace.

7. *Sejong sillok*, 16th year (April 10, 1434).

8. *Sejong sillok*, 16th year (July 7, 1434).

9. *Sejong sillok*, 17th year (March 9, 1435).

10. There is a record that three Japanese nuns, whose names are
recorded as Zenshin-ni, Zenzo-ni, and Kenzen-ni, came to Paekche in 584
and received novice precepts as well as full ordination in 588, an event that
marks the beginning of Japanese Buddhist nuns. See Akira Hirakawa (trans.
Karma Lekshe Tsomo), "The History of Buddhist Nuns in Japan," *Buddhist-
Christian Studies* 12(1992): 143–58.

11. For a history of Korean Buddhist women in antiquity, see Eun-
su Cho, "Reinventing Female Identity: A Brief History of Korean Buddhist
Nuns," *Seoul Journal of Korean Studies* 23:1(2009): 31–35.

12. *Sejo sillok*, 13th year (February 25, 1467).

13. *Sŏngjong sillok*, 9th year (November 30, 1478).

14. *Sŏngjong sillok*, 22nd year (May 22, 1491).
15. *Sejong sillok*, 25th year (May 16, 1443).
16. *Sŏngjong*, 8th year (March 7, 1477).
17. Kiun Lee, "Chosŏn sidae Chŏngŏpwŏn ŭi sŏlch'iwa Pulgyo sinha-eng (The Installation of Chŏngŏpwŏn and Buddhist Faith in the Chosŏn Era)," *Chonggyo yŏn'gu* (Study of Religion) 25(2001); and Kiun Lee, "Chosŏn sidae wangsilŭi piguniwŏn sŏlch'iwa sinhaeng (The Installation of Royal Nunner-ies and Faith in the Chosŏn Era), *Yŏksa hakbo* (Journal of History) 178(2003).
18. *Sejong sillok*, 4th year (May 20, 1422).
19. *Myŏngjong sillok*, 8th year (June 26, 1553).
20. Hŭijŏng Kang, *Chosŏn hugi pulhwawa hwasa yŏn'gu* (Buddhist Paint-ings and Painters of the Late Chosŏn Dynasty) (Seoul: Iljisa, 2003).
21. Chŏnghŭi Kim, *Chosŏn sidae chijangsiwangdo yŏn'gu* (Study on the Chosŏn Era Paintings of Ksitigarbha) (Seoul: Iljisa, 1996).

Chapter 3

Raichō Hiratsuka and Socially Engaged Buddhism

CHRISTINE A. JAMES

Hiratsuka Raichō (1886–1971) was a major feminist in Japan during the Meiji era. Her education incorporated both Western literature and Zen Buddhist practice, which combined to shape her perspective and inspired her to produce a new literary magazine, *Seitō*. She is regarded today as a leading figure who argued for women's rights, including suffrage and the right to divorce. The publication of her autobiography in Japanese[1] and its translation into English[2] provide a unique opportunity to understand the role of religious practice in Raichō's life.

Raised in a traditional, wealthy family in Tokyo, during her college years at the Japan Women's University, Raichō began Zen practice, crediting it with helping her through physical and social difficulties throughout her life. She achieved *kenshō* (the first stage of Zen enlightenment) at an unusually early age. Michel Mohr utilizes Raichō's testimony as a way to understand the religious practices and the primarily male religious leaders of her time. In contrast to Zen, depictions of women in traditional Japanese Buddhism (via the Buddhist teachings from India and China) were traditionally negative or limited to specific physical roles and sexually coded duties. But in Zen Buddhism, Raichō claimed to find the way to focus her thinking and empowered herself to become a self-aware and active feminist. Raichō's Zen Buddhist practice gave her a way to transcend the physical roles and expectations of women in her time. By understanding the historical Buddhist texts that described women, the Rinzai masters she studied with during her lifetime, and her current status as a figure who inspired socially engaged, activist Buddhism, we can better understand how her Buddhist practice defined her experience as a woman and feminist.

Haru Hiratsuka, whose pen name was Hiratsuka Raichō, was a co-founder and the first editor of a Japanese women's literary journal called *Seitō*. Born to a wealthy family in 1886, she was raised to value education and intellectual pursuits. She graduated from Japan Women's College in 1906, specializing in domestic science, which she ultimately found unfulfilling. She then began to privately study both Western philosophy and Zen Buddhism to expand her knowledge and to better understand her inner world.[3] Her approach to life's challenges, which combined Zen Buddhism and individualism, gave her the strength to stand publicly for women's freedoms. In 1911, Raichō became the editor of *Seitō* (Bluestocking). The metaphor that she used to describe women's lost spiritual independence and self-determination—"In the beginning, woman was the sun"—was featured in the first edition of *Seitō*.[4]

That Raichō was able to take high-profile stands in support of Japanese women's freedoms is a direct result of her study of Buddhism—not only the practice of Buddhism, but her awareness of Buddhism's historical views of women. Hiratsuka immersed herself in Western thought and Zen Buddhism, and witnessed firsthand both the positive insights into coping that result from Buddhist practice, and a variety of problematic assumptions about sexuality among the competing Rinzai masters she encountered in Japan during her early adulthood. She decided to follow an independent path. In the process, she caused a scandal with her love life, but found lasting happiness in an unconventional marriage. Raichō's advice that women should pursue self-awareness and cultivate their "hidden genius"[5] still resonates today as an influence in socially engaged Buddhism.[6]

One way to explore the influence of Raichō in socially engaged Buddhism is to look at her Buddhist practice as well as her literary efforts within the feminist journal *Seitō*. In the French journal *Ebisu*, Christine Lévy discusses *Seitō* as a literary and feminist project:

> The magazine undoubtedly brought together women who have played a vital role in the feminist movement in the social, political and literary sphere in Japan. It opened a

door to the symbolic emancipation of women, assigning a liberating role to the literary domain. From the first issue, the tone is feminist. As for Raichō, it is a cry of revolt and hope that she signs with (the famous phrase) originally, woman was the sun [*Genshi, josei wa taiyō de atta*].[7]

The representation of the female and the female body as a reproductive and biological entity was also a clear focus from the first issue of *Seitō*, which included a story by Tamura Toshiko (1884–1945) titled "Ikichi" (Living Blood) about a man and woman spending a night in an inn. The issue was banned because the story was considered threatening to traditional family structure, but it signaled at the outset that the journal was willing to discuss female sexuality, virginity, and chastity. The way in which the journal addressed these important issues owed a great deal to the life and Buddhist knowledge of Hiratsuka Raichō.[8]

Buddhist Historical Texts and Views of Women

To fully understand how Raichō's background in Zen Buddhism influenced her views on women's lives, we must understand the context of Buddhism in Japan before her lifetime, as well as the Buddhist texts she would have studied describing women. Many of the Buddhist texts that were influential in the social context of Raichō's practice list a number of problematic aspects of womanhood, often focused on menstruation. These include the Seven Grave Vices of Women, the Five Obstacles (or Obstructions or Hinderances), and the Three Subjugations. Both lists are related to the Blood Bowl mentioned in the *Blood Pool Sūtra*. The *Blood Pool Sūtra* is described vividly by Momoko Takemi in the article " 'Menstruation Sutra' Belief in Japan."[9] As Takemi notes, various works were referred to as *Ketsubon kyō* (literally, *Blood Bowl Sūtra*), including some associated with Daoist and Shinto shrines. In each case, certain common features can be found. Most of the texts include women suffering in a Blood Pool after having contaminated the deity of the earth with blood in some way, such as shedding blood in childbirth, cleaning blood-stained clothing and allowing the water to contaminate the earth, or using contaminated waters to make tea for a leader or deity. The venerable monk Mokuren sees the women suffering and asks the Buddha how they might be saved. Takemi argues carefully for a likely set of textual "families" and lines of influence, as the *sūtra* was taught and used as a means to save women from an eternal suffering in the "hell" of the Blood Pool. Interestingly, the source of women's contamination appears to have shifted over time: earlier, the emphasis was on the impurity of blood shed at childbirth; later, menstrual blood was included as well:

> The earliest texts explained this damnation in terms of blood shed at childbirth, but that from the beginning of the Edo period the idea of menstrual pollution seems to have been added to the explanations.[10]

The *sūtra* was used in various ways: as a liturgy to save souls of the dead from the Blood Pool, as a way to obtain rebirth in the Pure Land, and as a kind of amulet protecting women who were pregnant and in the process of childbirth when held near them. Practicing a *Blood Pool Sūtra* dedication service for women who died in child-birth was thought to effect a rebirth on lotus petals.[11] There were a variety of such services, but during the Edo period most were trans-formed into services specifically for women, traditions that remained for generations.[12] One such custom involving pregnant women wear-ing a *Ketsubon kyō* charm with the letters of the *sūtra* in Sanskrit in her waistband during pregnancy remained popular until about 1937 in the area around the temple Shōsenji; the custom did not die out entirely until the 1970s.[13]

The history of such practices and the widespread influence of the *Ketsubon kyō* was significant even in Raichō's time. Vivid descriptions of the impurity and putrefaction that result from menstrual blood were present in Japan in multiple forms since the medieval period. In 1300, Muju Ichien, a monk of the same Rinzai Zen school in which Raichō practiced, wrote a popular religious tract that discussed the afflictions of women. He declared, "Many serious instances of the sins of women, among the unregenerate who are all deluded, are cited in the sacred scriptures and commentaries." As evidence, Ichien cited a list of the Seven Grave Vices of Women attributed to the seventh-century Chinese monk Dōsen: "(1) they arouse desire in men; (2) they are jealous; (3) they lack empathy; (4) they are only concerned with their appearance; (5) they are deceitful; and (6) they are without shame. . . . Seventhly, their bodies are forever unclean, with frequent menstrual discharges. Seeing that both pregnancy and childbirth are both foul and the afterbirth unclean, the evil demons vie for posses-sion while the good deities depart."[14]

Dōsen's outline of the vices of women connects directly with two other texts Takemi cites to explain why women are damned. According to the *Kaie rakusōtan: Ketsubon kyō ūshitsu enyu no suishu* (Random Stories about Buddhist Ceremonies: The Origin and Transmission of the *Ketsubon kyō*):

> Because they were born as women, their aspirations to Buddhahood are weak, and their jealousy and evil character are strong. These sins compounded become menstrual blood, which flows in two streams each month, polluting not only the earth god but all the other deities as well. Thus after death they will certainly fall into this Hell (the blood pool), where they will undergo unlimited suffering.[15]

In addition, Takemi cites Yūkokuyain, published in 1821, which includes a section called "The Origin of the *Ketsubon kyō*":

> All women, even those who are the children of high families, have no faith and conduct no practices, but rather have strong feelings of avarice and jealousy. These sins are thus compounded and become menstrual blood, and every month this flows out, polluting the god of the earth in addition to the spirits of the mountains and rivers. In retribution for this, women are condemned to the Blood Pool Hell.[16]

Taken together, the *Ketsubon kyō* and these texts describing the Seven Grave Vices, the Five Obstacles, and the Three Subjugations became an integral part of the understanding of gender in the history of Japanese Buddhism—what Faure calls the "politics of menstruation."[17] The Seven Grave Vices of Women are also described by Muju Ichien, whose views are in line with, and representative of, the sacred scriptures and commentaries that Buddhists had read for generations. The seventh "sin" of women is the one most directly related to women's reproductive bodily processes. Because pregnancy, childbirth, and afterbirth are viewed as foul and unclean, they attract negative forces ("evil demons") and drive away positive forces ("good deities").[18]

In describing the seven grave vices, Dharmacari Jnaanavira notes that this seventh grave vice was interpreted as a punishment for a past action. "While the first six sins of women are character traits that some women might be expected to embody more than others, just as some men might, the last sin is a physiological condition which affects all women equally. It is only the seventh sin that can be characterized as specifically female. A defiled body was the result of some negative past-life action."[19] The dominant Buddhist view in Japan at the time was that women were constantly accruing negative *karma*. It was believed that women lack spiritual aspiration, are jealous, and have an evil nature; these negative tendencies or characteristic actions result in negative karmic propensities, or *samskāras*. Women's menstrual blood is a physical manifestation of these negative characteristics, just as obesity might be a manifestation of greed. It is important to note that many Buddhists would not have held this view or come to this conclusion because of the Buddhist emphasis on the role of intention in action. According to this view, women cannot be blamed for the defiling nature of menstrual blood, as it is not the result of their own intentional actions. "Despite the fact that this position can be undermined using basic Mahāyāna principles, it does not seem to have been criticized by Buddhist teachers in any systematic way. Indeed, the 'defilement' of women became the paradigmatic Japanese Buddhist view."[20]

Another example of negative views of women in Japanese Buddhism are the Five Obstacles (or Obstructions or Hindrances) said to afflict women. In an article titled "Dragon-Girl, Maidenflower, Buddha," Edward Kamens describes the Five Obstructions of Women.[21] According to this widespread belief, women are said to be excluded from five forms of existence, namely, rebirth as a Brahma god, the god Sakra, the tempter Māra, a Wheel-turning Monarch, and a Buddha. In each case, women are limited by their state of defilement related to female bodily functions. The idea behind this doctrine is that women have brought something upon themselves through previous negative actions, something inherent in the state of "woman" that means she cannot, while in female form, attain the very highest or most powerful forms of existence as symbolized by the list of the five great beings.

During their female lifetime, women are also afflicted by the Three Subjugations; that is, they must obey their fathers in childhood, their husbands in marriage, and their sons in widowhood. "Because they are terribly sinful, they are abandoned by the Buddhas of the ten directions and fall into the hells with no hope of salvation."[22] Faure sees the origin of this list as a "technical or juridical restriction" arising from the rules subordinating women to men within the monastic order (*saṅgha*), but points out that within Japanese Buddhism the three subjugations came to be interpreted as a "moral and ontological inferiority" that derive from women's impurity. Rebirth as a woman was not a morally neutral state but resulted from bad *karma*.[23]

Considering these lists of women's negative afflictions in historical Buddhist texts, and given the apparently limited opportunities for her success, one might struggle to understand how and why a woman like Hiratsuka would seek out Buddhist spiritual practice. One way to understand this comes from Faure's work. In his book *The Power of Denial*, Faure makes the point that, paradoxically, Buddhism is neither as sexist nor as egalitarian as is commonly thought.[24] He gives several reasons to support this view.

First, Buddhism in Japan must be understood in a broader social and political context. Buddhism spread from India to many countries in Asia, including Japan. As Buddhism spread, it often adopted and incorporated local gender prejudices, while trying to plant roots in patriarchal societies. Although the patriarchal nature of the Buddhist community (*saṅgha*) can be traced to India, it was influential in Japanese Buddhist practice. Buddhist institutions became decidedly patriarchal, with an element of suspicion of women in general. This suspicion is both a cause and a result of specific practices, such as the gender bias inherent in the eight rules (*gurudharma*) that render nuns subordinate to monks irrespective of seniority. These rules can thus be seen as setting up the *saṅgha* as "a bastion of male privilege."[25] Other scholars of Japanese history note that civil war in later medieval Japan also lowered women's status, perhaps more than particular Buddhist teachings.[26] Women in Japanese Buddhism were defined by their bodies in ways that had no parallels in representations of men. Indeed, women as a class became identified with the flesh and with carnality in a manner strikingly similar to certain streams of Christianity. This suggests that the tendency toward corporeal representations of women are not necessarily Buddhist but more characteristically patriarchal. Faure points out how the male Buddhist establishment was "unable or unwilling to distinguish between biological constraints and the arbitrary constraints imposed by society."[27]

Second, Buddhism certainly places an emphasis on equality, which Faure refers to as a "rhetoric of equality." Rhetorically, the concepts of nonduality, nondifferentiation between men and women from the standpoint of the ultimate truth, and such other postulates provide a counternarrative that appears welcoming to women, even if they were not successful in undermining endemic structures of inequality between the genders. For example, because Japanese Buddhist scholars believed that women had to be reborn as men to have any possibility of salvation, women were excluded from sacred places in Japan until 1873, during the Meiji Restoration. But Faure notes that this prohibition was not accepted meekly by women.[28] The counter-narrative of equality was definitely present, and evidence exists of women mocking some of the lists of vices, obstacles, and subjugations attributed to and imposed on them. Jnaanavira cites *The Tale of Genji*, the classic eleventh-century work by Murasaki Shikibu, as an example.[29] In this novel, the five hindrances are not referred to in usual terms, *itsutsu no sawari*, but by an amusing nickname or circumlocution, *itsutsu no nanigashi*, which can be understood as "the five something-or-others" or "the five what's-its." He explains:

> Murasaki's audience would have had no trouble identifying the "five something-or-others" as the "five obstructions" and would certainly have been able to list them, so it seems that Murasaki had a specific reason to use that different terminology. Perhaps she was indicating a certain disdain for this particular "teaching," or expressing an ironic attitude towards the idea that women are "hindered" by what she lightly refers to as "the five whatsits."[30]

At least some women were apparently well aware of the problematic dissonance between the welcoming narrative of Buddhist equality and the more dominant narrative of women's negative state, and were openly willing to respond to it with ironic wit. This was certainly true in Raichō's time, as women participating in the writing of Seitō addressed issues of women's embodiment directly. But it was also true of certain earlier Japanese Buddhist scholars, whose teachings Raichō would have been introduced to during her own Zen Buddhist training.

One such example is Dōgen, a Japanese Buddhist monk who lived from 1200 to 1253. Dōgen encouraged women to participate in Buddhist practice, and publicly argued against what he called the "evil custom" of keeping lay women and nuns out of training halls and denying them participation in Buddhist rituals.[31] Even more radically, Dōgen called for reform and a return to "something original, that is to the core orthopraxis of Buddhism." This core is specifically *zazen*, seated meditation.[32] This practice is something that Dōgen encouraged both men and women to do, not merely as a "means" to enlightenment, but as an actual practice of enlightenment, an expression of enlightenment already achieved.[33] This practice of enlightenment required mindful engagement in many aspects of everyday life. For Dōgen, this form of mindful engagement could spiritually transform the ordinary day-to-day activities of the average person, including women. Kasulis regards Dōgen's insistence on disciplined practice to be his most valuable contribution to Buddhist practice, and his clearly articulated position encouraging women's practice to be a precursor to Raichō's activism.

One form of rigorous disciplined practice advocated by Dōgen is the use of a *koan*, a traditional story, a painting, or a famous Buddhist metaphor or phrase used in concert with *zazen* meditation.[34] In "Meaning and Context," Dōgen states: "To practice—authenticate yourself by letting the totality of phenomena advance—that's realization . . . authentic buddhas go on authenticating."[35] This emphasis on the process of realization rather than the goal is a hallmark of Zen practice. Raichō's training in Zen practice included careful attention to this process of developing insights, and realization over time became central to her personal development and her work on behalf of women in the context of *Seitō*.

Raichō's Buddhist Affiliations

In later centuries, and in Hiratsuka's beginning Zen practice, further evidence of women's awareness of the issue of equality in Buddhism can be found. For example, Karen Kuo describes and interprets Etsu I. Sugimoto's *A Daughter of a Samurai* through this lens. In this work, Sugimoto identifies Buddhism as the reason for her heart's "morbid tendency," and its strain of hopeless sadness, specifically regarding her status as a female Buddhist.[36]

The perception that Japanese Buddhist women felt sadness, or, on the other hand, felt a need to mock some of the Buddhist assumptions about their womanhood, raises an important question about how Raichō Hiratsuka understood her own study of Buddhism. Did Raichō begin her Buddhist practice with a feminist mindset and an awareness of inequality? The answer is a qualified yes, if we consider the growing trend toward individualism in Japan during the Meiji Era. Note that the growing interaction between Japan and "the West" became highly influential during the Meiji Era:

> It is said that Japanese society is inhospitable to individualism (*kojinshugi*), with the most vocal anti-individualists being conservative educators and politicians; though some of them might defend individualism if it means "economic

self-reliance." Things were different a century ago. Then individualism was a byword for Japan's reforming intelligentsia. . . .[37]

In other words, the reforming intelligentsia of Japan were embracing individual self-determination and economic self-interest. This individualism was a central motivation for Hiratsuka's intellectual pursuits and Buddhist practice, at least as much as her early feminism.

The Rinzai Buddhist masters that Raichō knew and studied with have been written about in detail in the scholarly literature. For instance, Richard Jaffe and Michel Mohr provide thorough studies of the renowned Rinzai master Nakahara Nantenbō and mention Raichō as one of his leading lay disciples. There were many contentious issues between Nantenbō and other Rinzai masters during the time of Raichō's practice. Nantenbō disagreed with other masters who became famous for "rationalized Zen" and for their vivacious scholarly salons, rather than for their rigorous training in *zazen, koan*, and the precepts.[38] Nantenbō appears to have been worried about a popularized and less serious approach to Zen Buddhism and publicly criticized Rinzai masters who led *sesshins* that involved no *zazen* at all, with participants distracted and diverted into gaming rather than careful reverence.[39] As Nantenbō described the issue, the gaming usually involved board games such as Go, a traditional encircling or capturing game played on a board with stones.[40] For example, Zen practice involving *koans* could often be mistaken for a literary game of improvised poetry and wordplay, in which ironic ambiguity and reversal were used not for enlightenment, but for amusement. Arguably, this has to do with the political context in Japan at the time.[41]

Raichō Hiratsuka in Buddhist Practice and Reactions to Her Sexuality

The context of Japanese Zen Buddhist practice that Raichō encountered was imbued with assumptions regarding sexual behavior. As a young woman, Raichō experienced strained relationships with men and was judged by her Zen masters because of her sexuality and physical relationships with men. These experiences prepared and strengthened her for what she would experience later, as a "New Woman," in publishing the journal *Seitō*.

In the summer of 1905, Raichō began Zen practice under the leadership of Rinzai masters in the Engaku-ji line. She was a dedicated student and received the *koan*, "[Show me] your original face before your parents were born." The next year, during a *sesshin*, she began to weep while reciting Hakuin's *Zazenwasan* (Hymn to Aazen). She described it not as an emotional state of sadness or gratitude, but "probably an explosion of the life that was in me." Her first *kenshō* was acknowledged by Sōkatsu in the summer of 1906, and he gave her the Buddhist name Ekun.[42]

Soon after this mark of progress in her Zen training, Raichō was involved in affairs with two men. In March 1908, she ran away with one of her university teachers, Morita Sōhei (1881–1949), who was a disciple of Natsume Sōseki (1867–1916). This event received a great deal of attention in the press and gave Raichō a sexualized reputation. The event was referred to as the Shiobara Incident (*Shiobara jiken*) after the hot spring in Ibaraki Prefecture where they were apprehended. Sōhei wrote a novel after the event titled *Baien* (*Soot and Smoke*).

In addition to the affair with Sōhei, Raichō was involved in a difficult interaction with a young Zen Buddhist abbot while she was engaged in Zen study.[43] In her memoirs she describes the event as her "first kiss." In the spring of 1907, Hiratsuka was sitting *zazen* alone at Kaizen-ji for a couple of hours and suddenly realized that it had become dark and she was late. As she left the temple, she passed in front of the office, and the young abbot, Shūgaku, exclaimed "Oh, you were still there?" As he took a candle and helped her open the heavy door, she unexpectedly kissed him. Raichō explains that she was in a state of complete stillness and that her behavior was utterly innocent, but the monk mistook it as an invitation for a sexual relationship. He asked his teacher Sōen for permission to marry Raichō. The next time she came to Kaizen-ji, she was shocked to have a marriage proposal from Shūgaku.[44] Her reaction to his proposal was to try to disarm him and explain that she simply had other priorities. Her refusal had implications for both Raichō and Shūgaku. This incident ended Shūgaku's monastic career; he had hoped to become an official Dharma successor of Sōen, but his expressed desire to marry left him in the bottom tier of a two-tiered clerical ranking system among Rinzai priests.[45]

Raichō then moved to Kamakura and later to Nagano Prefecture, keeping up her intensive Zen practice and moving to avoid journalists who wanted to write about her story. During her stay in Kamakura she lived in a small hermitage within the precincts of Engaku-ji. In her memoirs she describes the chief abbot as "absolutely unattractive," and she found doing *sanzen* under his direction was unproductive.

When she returned to Tokyo in the winter of 1908, Raichō discovered that Nantenbō was coming every month to the Nihon Zengakudo in Kanda to conduct a *sesshin*, and she started practicing *sanzen*—one-on-one instruction—with him. In the Rinzai school, *sanzen* is also known as *dokusan*, meaning a private interview between student and master. Their first meeting was charged with tension, either because of Nantenbō's criticism of other Rinzai masters (specifically the Engaku-ji group with which she had first begun her study of Zen) or because of her reputation and affairs with men.

During their first meeting in the *sanzen* room, Nantenbō abruptly asked Raichō, "What did you understand by practicing Kamakura Zen? You probably didn't understand anything at all. If your master was indulgent with you and if you therefore believe that you have really got *kenshō*, it is a big mistake."[46] Raichō notes in her memoirs that she could not understand why Nantenbō was so aggressive toward her former Engaku-ji teachers. She conjectured that Nantenbō might have meant to encourage her to return to her beginner's mind and to devote herself to practice with renewed energy. But perhaps Nantenbō made these comments to Raichō because he had heard of her reputation and sexual history with men. Shūgaku was an adopted son of Nantenbō, and he would have known about the kiss and proposal. He also likely learned of the Morita Sōhei affair through the press.[47] His comments to Raichō and his past public criticisms of other Zen masters indicate that Nantenbō was very open and direct in his assessments of others, and his interactions with Raichō may reveal that he distrusted her as a woman.

Eventually, however, Nantenbō accepted and acknowledged Raichō. During December 1909, Raichō went to Kaisei-ji, Nantenbō's temple in Nishinomiya to participate in the *rōhatsu*, the last day of an intensive week-long *sesshin*, which in Japan commemorates the Buddha's enlightenment. During this intense week of training, she passed through the *mu koan* and received the new name Zenmyō from Nantenbō, indicating his full recognition of her accomplishments.[48] Raichō also kept a friendly but platonic relationship with Shūgaku even after rejecting his proposal. In the summer of 1910, he became, just once, her first "love instructor."

Taken together, the stories of Raichō's involvement with Sōhei and Shūgaku give evidence that the environment in which she was studying Zen was highly sexualized and that her identity as a woman could not be ignored. As noted previously, although the Zen Buddhist narrative emphasizes equality, in Japanese Zen Buddhist practice, women were perceived as lacking in specific sexualized ways. Raichō's Zen training still entailed an understanding of her female gender as an obstacle—as something one should strive to transcend.[49] Her experiences appear to have been an important influence on her later work in support of women and their literary talents. Her early Buddhist training not only presupposed that her gender had to be transcended and overcome, it had also attracted very unwelcome media attention focusing on her sexual behavior, formative love relationships, and womanhood. Simultaneously, it appears that Raichō's history with Zen Buddhist contexts and with unwelcome publicity also prepared her for her work with *Seitō*, which changed her mind about gender as a condition to be overcome. Instead, she came to emphasize the positive "possibilities of womanhood."[50]

Seitō Years

Raichō's Western educational background and Zen Buddhist practice came into full force when she established the literary magazine *Seitō* in 1911. The name, which translates as "bluestocking," is a reference to learned women in Western culture, especially British culture. The name alludes to Meiji society's intriguing embrace of Western conceptions of individualism, in combination with a critique of the often stifling "proper" roles for women in traditional Japanese culture. In this context, *Seitō* and the group of women who wrote, edited, and produced the magazine emerged. Known as the Seitōsha, this handful of upper-middle-class, college-educated women founded *Seitō* with the express purpose of providing a place for women to develop their literary talents. Within a year, *Seitō* also became a place to discuss and debate women's issues.

Literary and artistic expression provided a space that was both public and private, a space where women and men could negotiate and experiment with their relationship to modernity, each other, and society.[51] Literary and intellectual pursuits were acceptable in the wealthy, privileged social class in which Raichō had been raised. Most of the women had an interest in reading and writing for themselves, and were fortunate enough to have the educational background, free time, and financial means to undertake this literary initiate. Although their aim was to promote self-awareness and a variety of options for women, the Seitōsha women had to confront a hostile media that usually dismissed them as dangerous, frivolous New Women out to destroy the family and the nation.[52] The dominant narrative for women at this time in Japan was to be a "good wife and wise mother" (*ryōsai kenbo*). Raichō was opposed to the inequality inherent in the "good wife, wise mother" role, but was all for advancing the rights of women by focusing on their special qualities.[53] In order to help inspire women to acknowledge their own special qualities, Raichō included the well-known "starting word of *Seitō*" in the first issue of 1911:

> In the beginning, woman was the sun. An authentic person. Today, woman is the moon. Living through others. Reflecting the brilliance of others, such as the pale moon. We have to regain the sun in ourselves [that has] disappeared. "Demonstrate your sun disappeared and your potential ability."[54]

The reference to the sun connects with Raichō's training in Zen Buddhism. The sun symbolized a source of life in Zen, or *daienkoutai*. "Demonstrate your sun disappeared and your potential ability" was a call for all women to recover their lost life force and rekindle their creative power by rediscovering their individual selfhood. As Junko Kiguchi describes it, Raichō aspired to recover the potential of the female by raising each woman's consciousness.[55]

Along with her own opening words in the first issue of *Seitō*, Raichō also requested a special poem from Yosano Akiko:

The Day the Mountains Move

> The day the mountains move has come.
> I speak, but no one believes me.
> For a time the mountains have been asleep,
> But long ago, they danced with fire.
> It doesn't matter if you believe this,
> My friends, as long as you believe:
> All the sleeping women
> Are now awake and moving.[56]

This description of mountains waking from sleep and moving is a metaphorical description of women as volcanoes, like mountains that move when their consciousness is raised. The use of "sun" and "volcano" as metaphors for women can be taken as a call for women to regain their inner heat, light, and brightness:

> "*Genshi, josei wa taiyō de atta*" ("In the Beginning, Woman Was the Sun") reverses the gendered metaphors of man as the sun and woman as the moon, merely reflective of the sun's heat and brightness, with no identity or power of her own: "In the beginning, Woman was truly the Sun. An authentic person. Now, Woman is the Moon. Living off another, reflecting another's brilliance, she is the moon whose face is sickly and wan." Penning a call to all women, Raichō encourages and compels women to ignite and reclaim their inner sun . . .[57]

In Raichō's view, as women regain their inner sun, their tasks involve a combination of Zen Buddhist enlightenment and self-awareness, including Western individualism and personal responsibility. These influences can be seen in the 1912 issue supplement of *Seito*, in which Raichō comments on a performance of Henrik Ibsen's play "A Doll's House: A Play in Three Acts" staged in Japan in September and November of 1911. The heroine of the play, Nora, was a controversial figure for Japan's educated elites. At first, she seems rather dim; it emerges she has gotten herself and her husband in debt and is working odd jobs and committing fraud to pay off the debt. In the end, she realizes her husband never really loved her, but saw her merely as a doll, a plaything, so she leaves him and strikes out on her own. To Japanese audiences, Nora represented a "New Woman," a woman antithetical to the good wife and wise mother that was the traditional model of what a woman should be. This New Woman, it was argued, might have a negative impact on Japanese society and the family. Male critics in particular felt that Nora set a bad example by "selfishly" walking out on her husband and children. The Seitōsha women discussed the play in *Seitō*, broadening the discussion to question the very nature of intimate relationships and an individual woman's need for self-awareness. Raichō was most concerned with this theme of self-awareness and independent rational thought. She was critical of Nora's naiveté and faulted her for acting prematurely, before she had attained a true sense of herself. For Raichō it was imperative that Japan's New Women enhance society, not destroy it.[58]

The 1912 issue of *Seitō* included a supplement on "A Doll's House" that contributed to public discussions about Nora as the liberated "New Woman" and brought out conflicting understandings of individualism. In the Japanese government's interpretation of gender roles at this time, women who rejected prescribed roles for women were acting from an individualism that threatened morals, family life, and society.[59] Raichō herself might have argued that women who are not self-aware do pose a threat to morals, family life, and society, not because they do not accept their prescribed roles, but because they are unable to participate fully in an equal marriage. If the promise of Zen Buddhism's narrative of equality were to be fulfilled, it would have to be because individuals engage in careful reflection. The institution of marriage would be one possible location for that kind of equality, but Nora's naiveté and lack of self-awareness precluded any such equality.

For Raichō, any marriage based on inequality would be "unreasonable and irrational." Her marriage to the artist Okumura Hiroshi was based on equality and did involve careful reflection. Raichō cohabitated with Okumura for twenty-seven years before agreeing to a formal marriage to prevent discrimination against their children. Although they were deeply in love, Raichō presented her own version of a prenuptial agreement, requiring that he answer eight questions, including, "How would you respond if I said I would not marry you but am willing to live with you?" and "Have you given any thought to our financial prospects?" Her memoirs do not reveal what his answers were, but presumably they were satisfactory. They remained together until he died in 1964.[60]

In a 2012 issue of *Ebisu*, Tomomi Ōta discusses Raichō's ideas on romantic love, which emphasize the work of Swedish feminist Ellen Key.[61] Raichō concludes that love, spiritual and sexual, is intrinsic to women's personal development:

> According to Key, in love, "the two souls share the sensual pleasure and the sensuality gives them the pleasure that makes the soul grow" and "so that the virtue of perfect love may be Preserved, the union of the two must be accomplished by the will of bodies and souls. Love has become a great spiritual force whose genius is comparable to any other creative force for the formation of character. Love must give life, (and) new values. Love must enrich humanity through those who love each other."

Raichō's translations of Key's writings, published in *Seitō* between January 1913 and December 1914, appear to have influenced discussions about love, both among *Seitō* members and male intellectuals of the day. This new concept of romantic love is especially relevant for socially engaged Buddhism because, as Raichō argues, it not only transforms individual romantic relationships, but also the state of humanity at large.[62] Studying Key's work appears to have helped Raichō clarify her own perspective. In line with the Buddhist distinction between romance and love, the type of love she describes indicates a new kind of relationship between men and women in the intellectual and religious communities of her time.

Raichō's Continuing Influence and Socially Engaged Buddhism

Raichō's influence as a pioneer feminist in Japan and in Buddhism continues today. She famously articulated the view that women must attain inner awareness, strength, and knowledge before confronting society at large. She enjoined women to question existing customs and morals, and to search for new avenues to achieve freedom, security, and opportunities. During her lifetime she exposed and spoke out against the legal inequities of Japan's marriage system.[63] As shown in her essay "To the Women of the World," she exhorted women to become economically independent and self-sufficient.[64]

Raichō's influence can also be seen in literature, such as in Etsu Inagaki Sugimoto's novel, *A Daughter of a Samurai* (1925). In her analysis of Sugimoto's work, Karen Kuo highlights the explicit references to Raichō and the Seitōsha. In her writings, Sugimoto explores the possibility of combining the concept of the New Woman (*atarashii onna*) with the roles of a good wife and wise mother (*ryōsai kenbo*). Kuo credits *Seitō* for its literary exploration of the concerns of modern Japanese women, which helped define the roles of women in Japanese society.

Raichō's influence in Buddhist circles, especially including socially engaged Buddhist concerns, continues to be a topic of interest at international conferences. At the 13th Sakyadhita International Conference on Buddhist Women, which addressed the theme of socially engaged Buddhism in many sessions, Akemi Iwamoto explicitly addressed Raicho's work. In her research on Raichō and D. T. Suzuki, Iwamoto shows how the Japanese women's liberation movement was significantly inspired by Zen Buddhism.[65]

The history of Raichō's own work as a feminist and as a Buddhist are discussed in *Ebisu*. For example, in "The Debate in Seitō on the New Woman, Atarashii Onna," Marion Saucier discusses the biological facts of female bodies: "Un autre argument souvent évoqué est celui de la physiologie et des menstruations, ainsi que les grossesses des femmes, qui sont censées les affaiblir et les render moins productives." ("Another frequently cited argument is that of physiology and menstruation, as well as women's pregnancies, which are supposed to weaken them and make them less productive.")[66] Raichō, and *Seitō*, were able to turn these perceived weaknesses of women into strengths by working through the traditional Buddhist teachings such as those referring to the *Blood Sūtra*, and readdressing them as a new life force and creative potential of women. Her Buddhist practice opened the door for Raichō to rediscover the female as her own practice raised her own consciousness.

Hiratsuka Raichō combined influences from Western scholarship and Buddhist practice, sharing lessons she learned in ways that were pivotal in the development of the women's movement in Japan and influential for generations of Japanese women. She used her literary talents to raise women's consciousness and inspired others to do so as well. Her concept of consciousness-raising combined Buddhist interpretations of self-awareness and Western individualist notions of empowerment and personal responsibility—a laudable accomplishment given the social and political context of Japan in her day. Raichō and the women of the Seitōsha provided an important space for women to express themselves freely and explore new definitions of self-awareness that drew from both traditional and modern streams.

Notes

1. Raichō Hiratsuka, *Genshi, josei wa taiyō de atta* (*In the Past, Women Were the Sun*), 4 vols. (Tokyo: Koku-min bunko, 1992). The first edition of this work was published by Ōtsuki Shoten in Tokyo in 1971–73, with different pagination.

2. Raicho Hiratsuka (trans. Teruko Craig), *In the Beginning, Woman Was the Sun: The Autobiography of a Japanese Feminist* (New York: Columbia University Press, 2006).

3. Dina Lowy, "Love and Marriage: Ellen Key and Hiratsuka Raichō Explore Alternatives," *Women's Studies* 33:4(2004): 361–80.

4. Shaun O'Dwyer, "Echoes of an Old Debate on Feminism and Individualism," *Japan Times*, November 14, 2013. www.japantimes.co.jp/opinion/2013/11/14/commentary/japan-commentary/echoes-of-an-old-debate-on-feminism-and-individualism/#.WCmx_i0rLIU (accessed November 14, 2016).

5. Ibid.

6. Anna Halafoff and Praveena Rajkobal, "Sakyadhita International: Gender Equity in Ultramodern Buddhism," *Feminist Theology: The Journal of the Britain & Ireland School of Feminist Theology* 23:2(2015): 122.

7. *Ebisu: Etudes Japonaises* 48(2012).

8. Christine Lévy, "Introduction: Feminism and Gender in Japan," *Ebisu* [online] 48(2012). ebisu.revues.org/568 (accessed May 25, 2017).

9. Momoko Takemi, "'Menstruation Sutra' Belief in Japan," *Japanese Journal of Religious Studies* 10:2–3(1983): 229–46. The *Bussetsu diazō shōkyō ketsubon kyō* (The Buddha's Correct Sutra on the Bowl of Blood) is found in the *Dai nihon zoku zōkyō* (Great Storehouse of Japanese Sutras, con't.), sec. 87, vol. 4, 2999.

10. Ibid., 235.

11. Ibid., 240–41.

12. Ibid., 242.

13. Ibid., 243.

14. Cited in Dharmacari Jnaanavira, "A Mirror for Women? Reflections of the Feminine in Japanese Buddhism," *Western Buddhist Review: Journal of the Western Buddhist Order* 4 (2003): 2. Jnaanavira's article is a response to Robert E. Morrell, "Mirror for Women: Muju Ichien's *Tsuma Kagami*," *Monumenta Nipponica* 35:1(1980): 45–50.

15. *Kaie rakusōtan: Ketsubon kyō ūshitsu enyu no suishu* (*Random Stories about Buddhist Ceremonies: The Origin and Transmission of the* Ketsubon kyō) was published sometime between 1801 and 1803. It is mentioned as an example of an Edo-period text in which stories about the origins of the *Ketsubon Kyō*, various Buddhist prayers, and *dhāraṇī* ("spells"), are found together with explanations as to why women take rebirth in this hell and ways to liberate them. Cited by Momoko Takemi in "'Menstruation Sutra' Belief in Japan," *Japanese Journal of Religious Studies* 10:2/3(1983): 235. This article includes a translated excerpt of such a text (230–32). Curiously, even barren women were in danger of landing in the Blood Bowl (236). However, Lori Meeks contends that male priests during the medieval period in Japan did not necessarily associate women's inferiority or sinfulness with bodily impurity. She further contends that the conflation of the *Blood Bowl Sūtra* with the Mulian narrative, in which the monk Mulian rescues his mother from the hungry ghost realm, is a later development. See Lori R. Meeks, *Hokkeji and the Reemergence of Female Monastic Orders in Premodern Japan* (Honolulu: University of Hawai'i Press, 2010), 272–73. These and numerous other examples make it clear that notions of women's impurity existed in tension with filial concepts of indebtedness to one's mother.

16. Ibid.

17. Bernard Faure, *The Power of Denial: Buddhism, Purity, and Gender* (Princeton, NJ: Princeton University Press, 2003), 333–34.

18. Robert Morrell, "Mirror for Women: Muju Ichien's Tsuma Kagami," *Monumenta Nipponica* 35:1(1980): 68.

19. Jnaanavira, "A Mirror for Women?" 2.

20. Ibid.

21. Edward Kamens, "Dragon-Girl, Maidenflower, Buddha: The Trans-formation of a Waka Topos, 'The Five Obstructions,'" *Harvard Journal of Asiatic Studies* 53(1993).

22. Junko Minamoto, "Buddhism and the Historical Construction of Sexuality in Japan," *U.S.-Japan Women's Journal English Supplement* 5(1993): 92; and Jnaanavira, "A Mirror for Women?"

23. Faure, *The Power of Denial*, 63.

24. Ibid.

25. Ibid., 333–34.

26. D. R. Chaudhry, "The Power of Denial: Buddhism, Purity and Gender," *Tibet Journal* 30/31:4/1(2005): 188.

27. Faure, *The Power of Denial*, 105.

28. Ibid., 235.

29. Murasaki Shikibu (trans. Royall Tyler), *The Tale of Genji* (New York: Penguin Classics, 2002).

30. Jnaanavira, "A Mirror for Women?" 5.

31. Dōgen, "Treasury of the Eye of the True Dharma," cited by Kitagawa Sakiko in James W. Heisig, Thomas P. Kasulis, and John C. Maraldo, *Japanese Philosophy: A Sourcebook* (Honolulu: University of Hawai'i Press, 2011), 1119.

32. Dōgen, "Treasury of the Eye of the True Dharma." Cited by Thomas P. Kasulis in James W. Heisig, Thomas P. Kasulis, and John C. Maraldo, eds., *Japanese Philosophy: A Sourcebook* (Honolulu: University of Hawai'i Press, 2011), 136.

33. Ibid., 137.

34. Ibid., 142.

35. Ibid., 145.

36. Karen Kuo, "Japanese Women Are Like Volcanoes," *Frontiers: A Journal of Women Studies* 36:1(2015): 77.

37. O'Dwyer, "Echoes of an Old Debate."

38. Richard M. Jaffe and Michel Mohr, "Editor's Introduction: Meiji Zen," *Japanese Journal of Religious Studies* 25:1/2(1998): 8.

39 Michel Mohr, "Japanese Zen Schools and the Transition to Meiji: A Plurality of Responses in the Nineteenth Century," *Japanese Journal of Religious Studies* 25:1/2(1998): 189.

40. Ibid.

41. For example, in May 1893, Nantenbō proposed that all recognized Zen masters undertake an examination ascertaining their level of realization. Nantenbō's attempt to curtail the authority of specific Zen masters may have been seen as a problematic return to an earlier time when the imperialist government sought to end the freedoms of the Zen leadership. Faure also makes the case that the shift from the Tokugawa to the Meiji Era was characterized by increasing influence from Christian missionaries in Japan, and that these missionaries' attitudes toward sex contributed to further tensions between

the government and the Zen masters. For further discussion of the political context, see Jaffe and Mohr, "Editor's Introduction," 8; Mohr, "Japanese Zen Schools," 186; Martin Collcutt, "Buddhism: The Threat of Eradication," *Japan in Transition: From Tokugawa to Meiji*, ed. Marius B. Jansen and Gilbert Rozman (Princeton, NJ: Princeton University Press, 1986), 167; Bernard Faure, *The Red Thread: Buddhist Approaches to Sexuality* (Princeton, NJ: Princeton University Press, 1998); William R. LaFleur, Monumenta Nipponica 54:4(1999): 556–58; José Ignacio Cabezón's review of The Red Thread: Buddhist Approaches to Sexuality, *Journal of the American Academy of Religion* 67:4(1999): 880–82; Liz Wilson's review in *The Journal of Religion* 81:1(2001): 179–80; and Christian K. Wedemeyer's review in *International Journal of Hindu Studies* 3:2(1999): 201–202.

42. Mohr, "Japanese Zen Schools," 189.

43. Hiratsuka, *In the Beginning*, 102.

44. Hiratsuka, *Genshi*, 230–31.

45. Toward the end of the Meiji Era, a Rinzai monk who chose to marry would be allowed to do so, but would have to give up all hope of becoming a high-ranking teacher.

46. Mohr, "Japanese Zen Schools," 190.

47. Ibid., 193–94.

48. Ibid., 190.

49. Lowy, "Love and Marriage," 370–71.

50. Ibid.

51. Ibid., 368.

52. Ibid.

53. Ibid., 374.

54. Junko Kiguchi, "Japanese Women's Rights in the Meiji Era." Paper presented at the 37th World Congress of the International Institute of Sociology, Stockholm, 2005, 141. daigakuin.soka.ac.jp/assets/files/pdf/major/kiyou/17_syakai2.pdf (accessed October 14, 2016).

55. Ibid., 141–42.

56. Akiko Yosano, "The Day the Mountains Move," first published in *Seitō* in 1911 and republished in Carole R. McCann and Seung-kyung Kim, eds., *Feminist Theory Reader: Local and Global Perspectives*, 2nd ed. (New York: Routledge 2010).

57. Kuo, "Japanese Women Are Like Volcanoes," 75.

58. Lowy, "Love and Marriage," 369, 377.

59. O'Dwyer, "Echoes of an Old Debate."

60. Ian Neary, "In the Beginning, Woman was the Sun: The Autobiography of a Japanese Feminist," *English Historical Review* 123:500(2008): 247–48.

61. Tomomi Ōta, "When Women Talk about Love . . . : Discourses on Love in *Seitō*," *Ebisu* 48(2012). ebisu.revues.org/619 (accessed May 24, 2017).

62. Ibid. Raichō Hiratsuka published four translations of Ellen Key's writings and speeches in *Seito*: "Ren ai to kekkon Eren Kei cho (*Love and*

Marriage: The Work of Ellen Key)," *Seitō* (January, 1913): 1–19; "Seiteki dōtoku hatten no katei Eren Kei *(Evolution of Sexual Morality: Ellen Key),"* *Seitō* (August, 1913): 72–86; "Ren ai no shinka Eren Kei *(Evolution of Love: Ellen Key)* *Seitō* (October, 1913): 126–33; "Ren ai no jiyu Eren Kei *(Freedom of Love: Ellen Key),* *Seitō* (July, 1914): 80–91.

63. Lowy, "Love and Marriage," 372.

64. Kuo, "Japanese Women Are Like Volcanoes," 67.

65. Akemi Iwamoto, "'New Women' and Zen in Early 20th-Century Japan: Raichō Hiratsuka and D. T. Suzuki," *Buddhism at the Grassroots*, ed. Karma Lekshe Tsomo (Delhi: Sakyadhita, 2012), 67–74. This presentation is cited in Halafoff and Rajkobal, "Sakyadhita International," 122.

66. Marion Saucier, "The Debate in Seitō on the New Woman, Atarashii Onna," *Ebisu* 48(2012). ebisu.revues.org/605 (accessed May 16, 2017).

Chapter 4

A "Great Man" Is No Longer Gendered

The Gender Identity and Practice of
Chan Nuns in Contemporary Taiwan

CHING-NING WANG (CHANG-SHEN SHIH)

In the Chinese Buddhist scriptures and Chan literature, *zhangfu* (man), *da zhangfu* (a great or virtuous man), and *zhangfu xiang* (the form of a great or virtuous man) are concepts that refer to spiritually advanced practitioners. There has been ongoing discussion about the issue of gender and Buddhism both in premodern Chan Buddhism and among Buddhist nuns in contemporary Taiwan. Scholars question the rhetoric surrounding these concepts and see them as androcentric and patriarchal; that is, they use *man* as the standard of sacred or advanced practice. The use of man as the spiritual standard not only ignores women's spiritual achievement in history, but also denies woman the possibility of accomplishing Buddhahood. Moreover, scholars offer a critical account of how gender essentialism, which identifies the biological male body as masculine and determines his gender identity as a man, and which identifies the female body as feminine and determines her gender identity as a woman, is embedded in the institutional patriarchal Buddhist community.

This gender essentialism results in Buddhist women being seen as spiritually inferior to men in Buddhist communities. It is only by denying their femininity in practice that women may become a *da*

107

zhangfu, that is, a "great man" or a "heroic man," a masculine term used in Chinese Buddhist scriptures to refer to spiritually advanced practitioners. Regarding the rhetoric of *da zhangfu* in the literature of Chan Buddhism in relationship to Mahāyāna egalitarianism and gender, scholars point out that, although Chan emphasizes the Mahāyāna doctrine of egalitarianism and sudden enlightenment within which all distinguishing marks—especially binary codes such as male versus female, rich versus poor, old versus young—are dissolved and regarded as nonexistent, the use of *da zhangfu* in the Chan literature is never gender-neutral but is always androcentric and patriarchal.[1]

Indian and Chinese societies have been patriarchal for a long time. However, economic growth in the postwar period, coupled with the government policy in Taiwan that since 1968 has required nine years of compulsory education, has dramatically increased women's access to education. Political, economic, and social changes in contemporary society in Taiwan permit a new understanding of *da zhangfu* and allow for new interpretations of Buddhist scriptures. This chapter will use fieldwork interviews of Taiwanese Buddhist nuns at Dharma Drum Mountain as a case study to explore reinterpretations of scripture and practice among Buddhist nuns in contemporary Taiwan and to reassess scholarship on gender essentialism in Chan Buddhism.

As a first intervention, I will use feminist scholarship on the philosophy of language to re-examine rhetoric about the concept of *da zhangfu* in Chinese Buddhist scriptures. I argue that a *da zhangfu* is not necessarily a man, which contests scholarly conclusions advanced in studies of gender and Chan Buddhism. I argue that *da zhangfu* is a generic term that includes both men and women. It is not that *da zhangfu* is equated with men, but that there is a subconscious androcentric preference in Buddhism toward using the masculine generic term *zhangfu* instead of a feminine or gender-neutral term to refer to spiritually advanced practitioners. This biased use of the term therefore tightens and restricts rather than loosening the hold of the preexisting cultural imagination in patriarchal Buddhist society.

The relationship between Buddhist canonical texts and real practice is not simply a matter of the former influencing the latter, but of ongoing changes related to physical and temporal location and of new interpretations and practices of Buddhist practitioners in the modern age. Therefore, my second intervention is to use fieldwork findings among Buddhist nuns at Dharma Drum Mountain to demonstrate that Chan women in contemporary Taiwan have a more radical interpretation and practice of gender identity. They do not interpret the negative female characteristics described in Buddhist scriptures as a denial of women or as obstacles hindering their attainment of enlightenment; instead, they use the pedagogy of sudden enlightenment and the egalitarianism of Chan and Mahāyāna to empower women in practice. To Chan Buddhist nuns in contemporary Taiwan, the term *da zhangfu* refers neither to man nor woman but to a state beyond dualistic form—that is, to the pedagogy of *prajña* (wisdom) in Chan, to the absence of a doer, and to the mind freed from particularization: the foundations of Mahāyāna egalitarianism in the practice of Chan Buddhism.

Gender and Chan Buddhism

Research on women in Chan Buddhism, though not totally neglected in the past two decades, is still scarce. Among the few critical studies that have appeared since the 1980s, Ding-Hua Hsieh and Miriam Levering focus on female masters in Chan literature during the Song Dynasty (960–1279) in mainland China.[2] Beata Grant studies the sayings of seven women Chan masters recorded in the Jiaxing Tripitaka from the late Ming Dynasty to the early Qing Dynasty (seventeenth and eighteenth centuries).[3] Jingjia Huang focuses on eminent Chan laywomen, analyzing their dialogues (*jifeng duihua*) with male Chan masters in the collections.[4] These studies provide the biographies of Chan women, including their training process under or in interaction with male masters, their efforts to propagate the Dharma, and their social outreach, but are limited to premodern literary and historical analysis and lack empirical findings. An understanding of the real practice of Chan women, their subjective perceptions of Chan, and their substantive pedagogy requires further inquiry.

On the issue of gender equality in Chan Buddhism, Heng-ching Shih studies women in Chinese Buddhist literature and concludes that, among the eight major schools of Chinese Buddhism, Chan has always been the most affirmative toward female practitioners.[5] Many male Chan masters not only directly challenged patriarchy in Chinese culture and the Eight Gurudharmas (Eight Weighty Rules for *bhikshunis*, fully ordained nuns) from the early Buddhist tradition, they also acknowledged the equality of females in terms of their human nature, spiritual potential, and religious accomplishments. In addition, the recorded sayings (*yulu*) and "records of the lamp transmission" (*chuandeng lu*), which are biographies of the Chan patriarchs, include a number of biographies and Dharma talks by female Chan masters, testifying to their indisputable status as Dharma disseminators in the Chan tradition. Most remarkable are the records that illustrate how nuns and female lay practitioners debated with male Chan masters, indicating that the status of their realizations matched or even surpassed those of male Chan masters. Chinese Buddhist literature includes examples of monks who achieve insights and attain awakening through the teachings of female Chan masters—a very rare instance of gender reversal in world literature, be it religious or secular.[6]

Miriam Levering and Bernard Faure disagree with assertions of gender equality in Chan. They argue that Chan women live in patriarchal and androcentric Chan communities whose institutional bias against women ironically contradicts the rhetoric of equality that is based on the philosophy of nonduality in Chan doctrine.[7]

Beata Grant approaches the question from a different perspective. Investigating the writings of seventeenth-century Buddhist monks and laymen who refer to Chan women, she states that these writings reflect an ongoing ambivalence toward religious women, ranging from undisguised disapproval or skepticism to wholehearted support for women's Chan spiritual training on the Buddhist path. These ambivalent and changing attitudes of male writers may stem from the Mahāyāna notion of an absent doer, which made a fluid, performative understanding of gender possible among Chinese Buddhists at the time.[8] Another view is that of Chün-fang Yü who, through her detailed examination of Chinese nuns' and monks' hagiographies, disagrees with the critique that spiritually advanced nuns were unequal in Chinese Buddhism. She concludes that it is hard to detect gender differences amidst the qualities that earned them fame and success, as the nuns described are in no way inferior to monks. Drawing on historical texts, Yü notes that the chief qualities exalted in Buddhist practice, such as "asceticism, ability to work miracles, willingness to sacrifice their lives for the Dharma, expertise in *sutra* expositions, and ability to achieve great feats of chanting scripture," are ungendered.[9]

In sum, scholars hold diverse views on the issue of gender equality in Chan Buddhism, ranging from Mahāyāna egalitarianism with gender equality to critiques of patriarchal and androcentric discrimination that contrast with the pedagogy of Chan teachings on "the mind free from particularization" (*wu fenbie xin*). Some scholars focus their critique on the rhetoric of *da zhangfu* in Chan literature. These scholars contend that, although Chan emphasizes sudden enlightenment and the Mahāyāna doctrine of egalitarianism that dissolves all distinctions—especially binaries such as male versus female, rich versus poor, old versus young—the term *da zhangfu* in Chan literature is never gender-neutral but is instead androcentric and patriarchal.[10]

In Chinese Buddhism, *da zhangfu* is used to refer to the qualities of a spiritually advanced person who is decisive, calm, independent, compassionate, fearless, and so on. Focusing on the question of the demeanor of *da zhangfu xiang*, Meiwen Su contends that the word *zhangfu* does not carry male connotations. She cites the *Treatise on Da Zhangfu* (*Da zhangfu lun*), the Chinese translation of Aryadeva's *Mahāpuruṣa śāstra*:[11]

> One who can only cultivate merit and has no wisdom and compassion is named *zhangfu*. One with merit and wisdom is named a good *zhangfu*. And only one who cultivates merit, wisdom, and compassion is named a great *da zhangfu*.[12]

In this text, *da zhangfu* refers to one who not only cultivates merit, but also wisdom and compassion, and is spiritually superior to those who cannot cultivate all three qualities at the same time. Meiwen Su points out that a bold person means someone who can cultivate merit but has no wisdom or compassion. As such, only one who can cultivate merit, wisdom, and compassion can be called a great bold person. However, Su states that, in a patrilineal and patriarchal society characterized by gender bias, this word refers to men and the ultimate goal of practice is portrayed in the male image.[13]

Yu-chen Li rejects Su's notion that *da zhangfu* was originally gender-neutral. Through an analysis of gender differences and sensual beauty in early Buddhist texts and the disciplinary codes for the monastic community (*saṅgha*), she argues that *da zhangfu* is used only to refer to an accomplished being in the body of a man, not the body of a women. Therefore, the term is not gender-neutral.[14] In line with Li's argument, Bernard Faure criticizes those Chan patriarchs who use the term *da zhangfu* to praise spiritually advanced women. He contends that the term carries implications that deny a woman's sex, valorize maleness, and assign women second-class status in Chan Buddhist communities. In Faure's view, the images of women in Chan stories "imply male dominance and do not let us hear the female voice."[15]

Interestingly, scholars who worked in the field of Buddhist literature in premodern times tended to interpret *da zhangfu* as a gendered term and strongly linked it not only with the male body in a biological sense, but also with maleness as gender identity in a cultural sense. In translating *da zhangfu* as "heroic man," "great male," or "virtuous man" instead of "great person," "bold person," "virtuous person," the translation process acts as a gendering process. Based on this strong tendency to associate *da zhangfu* with the biological and cultural male, the Chan school may legitimately be criticized as being patriarchal and androcentric.

In contrast to English, Chinese pronouns are not gendered; therefore, the Chinese language offers the space for us to imagine gender fluidity. For example, the third-person singular pronoun in Chinese is "*ta*," with the same pronunciation and written form for all genders. The word *ta* did not become gendered, with distinct characters indicating male and female gender, until the early twentieth century. This was a time when China became a modern nation-state that opposed Western imperialism. Through reflection on the gender distinctions between "he" and "she" in English, another Chinese word with a different character but with the same pronunciation was invented to refer to the female third-person singular ("she"), while the original word was used to designate the male third-person singular ("he"). When we check the etymology of the female character, we find that this word did not exist in premodern Chinese. The first appearance of the term was in 1912, when it was expressly devised for the purpose of translating into Chinese the name of Zhongta International, an international organization of women executives in business and the professions that came to be known as Chongtashe.[16]

Similar to the production of the gendered third-person singular pronoun (*ta*), other gendered Chinese words have been created in the context of translation in the past century; people may use either traditional or gendered words according to their preference. The term *da zhangfu*, for example, refers to a great, bold, heroic, virtuous "man" or "person," and may include both men and women. In traditional Chinese society, such a person was usually male but sometimes female. Ever since the word *zhangfu* came into use in premodern Chinese, beginning in the Han Dynasty (206 BCE–220 CE), the term has been used to refer not only to a heroic man but also to a heroic woman, as in *nü zhangfu* or *zhangfu nü*.[17] The terms *zhangfu* and *da zhangfu* sometimes carry gender signification and sometimes do not, depending on the context. Although in Chinese culture and society *da zhangfu* usually refers to a man, it is a generic term that refers to a heroic person, male or female.

As Tze-lan D. Sang explains, a translation is never "just" a translation, but embodies its own historicity. The question of translation is not just a matter of translation from English to Chinese, for example, but is always already a manifestation of embodied experience. The "never fully translatable," articulated in a negative register, does not imply that there is an original text that lacks or loses its true meaning in the process of translation. Sang contends that translation is not about realism, which assumes a universal reality existing independently of observers; translation is a process within which an essential meaning of origin is transmitted. Sang suggests that the process of translation should be understood as creative, that is, a process of producing meaning in relation to society and history.[18] To contextualize the term *da zhangfu*, translated into English as "heroic man," is to elucidate what is embedded in the translation process—namely, different perceptions and concepts of oneself, the relational subjective environment, and the actual bodily experience of these terms. The term *da zhangfu* also raises questions about translation across time and language. The term circulates among languages, yet languages can never fully translate the term.

The critical framework of dichotomies—man versus woman, male versus female, first citizen versus second citizen, masculine versus feminine, maleness versus femaleness, and so on—can become reductive and static. With an awareness of the power relationships implicit or explicit in gender and in Chan Buddhism, it is easy to see how this can also lead to a reductive analysis of the world as divided into only two paradigms, with one being stronger and the other being weaker. The criticism of *da zhangfu* as representing gender bias in the Chan community in premodern Chinese history is not unwarranted. However, this analysis of women and gender issues in Chan Buddhism is typically binary. Such a critique not only risks slipping into a hierarchical gender binary, but also ignores Chan pedagogy and the teaching and practice of nonduality. It is precisely this teaching that underscores the Chan approach of mind free from particularization that makes alternative forms of gender identity and practice possible.

While useful, this binary critical perspective that preconceives the problem of women in Chan Buddhism in binary terms may have its own limitations. Specific patterns in discussing women in Chan Buddhism fall into what Eve Kosofsky Sedgwick calls the "methodological centrality of suspicion," or the "concept of paranoia."[19] As Sedgwick wisely and creatively points out, paranoia is "anticipatory," "reflexive and mimetic," a "negative affect"; it is like setting up a thief in order to catch a thief. When we set a person up to be responsible for a missing wallet in our house, everything that person does becomes suspicious. Every gesture becomes loaded with meaning and is interpreted to support our preconceived assumptions. Even a small gift is assumed to be a tactic the person uses to disclaim guilt. Although a binary critical reading of the term *da zhangfu* effectively calls out the patriarchy in Chan Buddhism, it does not serve to empower women. Instead it risks neglecting both the agency and subjectivity of Chan women in interpreting Chan pedagogy and connecting to real practice. Static and binary gender criticism results in women being seen only as losers or victims in patriarchal Chan structures and not as agents with the potential to change androcentric institutions and cultures.

Is a *Da Zhangfu* a Man? A Feminist Critique

In Chinese Buddhist scriptures, binary and hierarchical rhetoric terms such as superior (*shusheng*) versus inferior (*xialie*), unbounded mind (*lifuxin*) versus bounded mind (*jiefuxin*), or mind (*xinxing*) versus bodily form (*shenxiang*) are used as analogies for the process of liberation process, moving from the latter to the former. In the context of traditional, patriarchal Chinese and Indian Buddhist cultures, this binary and hierarchical rhetoric produces concepts such as "denying the female body form" (*foding nüshen*), "transform the female body into a male one" (*zhuanü chengnan*), and "no women in the Pure Land" (*jingtu wu nüren*), in addition to other descriptions of women's biological and moral faults of women in the Buddhist scriptures.[20] In these scriptures, the male body (*nanshen*), male form (*nanxiang*), and man (*nanzi*) are the analogical superior, likened to unbounded mind, purity, and perfection in the next world (*chu shijian*). By contrast, the female body (*nüshen*), girly demeanor (*nütai*), woman (*nüren*), and woman's mind (*nüren xin*) are the analogical inferior, likened to bounded mind, impurity, vexation, and imperfection in the mundane world. This patriarchal and androcentric binary is analogous to the liberation process, in which the latter (inferior) transforms to the former (superior). In Buddhist scriptural rhetoric, *da zhangfu* equates to man, to realizing Buddha nature, and to accomplishing Buddhahood, whereas woman equates to the opposite. Two paragraphs from the scriptures serve as examples. The first comes from the *Mahaparinirvana Sutra*:

Good men and women! Please listen to the *Mahāyāna Mahaparinirvana Sutra* attentively. We should often scold the female form and strive for male form. Why? In the *Mahaparinirvana Sutra*, it says *zhangfu* form is Buddha nature. What does that mean? It means that if we have not seen our Buddha nature, it means that we do not have male form. What does that mean? It means that if people have not realized their Buddha nature, we call those people women. If people have realized their Buddha nature, we call those people having *zhangfu* form. If women realize their Buddha nature, we should know those women are men, good men.[21]

The second comes from *The Sutra of the Buddha's Preaching on Transforming the Female Body*:

One time, the Lady of Undefiled Light asked the Buddha: "World Honored One I would like to invite all bhikshus, bhikshunis, upasakas, and upasikas present to listen attentively. How do we cultivate good deeds in order to abandon female bodies and become men, that is, to have the determination to attain supreme perfect enlightenment? I wish the World Honored One would explain this for us." In order to benefit and accomplish the four divisions of disciples, Buddha told the Lady of Undefiled Light: "If women can accomplish one thing, they can leave their female bodies and become men. What is this thing? That is, to have strong determination to attain perfect enlightenment. Why? If women have the determination to attain perfect enlightenment, we call this determination the mind of the great person, the *da zhangfu* mind, the mind of the great sage, the non-inferior mind. . . . If women can have this determination, they will not have those women's bounded mind and moral infection. Therefore, they can abandon female bodies and become men."[22]

Heng-ching Shih contends that in Buddhist scriptures influenced by strong negative attitudes toward women and the feminine in traditional Indian society, a concrete example of corporal gender transformation is used as a metaphor for mental transformation.[23] She is explicit that that Buddhist practice is a process of mental transformation, not physical transformation, but she does not offer any further analysis as to how mental cultivation was constructed as gender transformation in the social and cultural traditions of that time. Why should mental transformation entail gender transformation? Why is mental transformation constructed hierarchically in terms of gender? Conceiving the rhetoric of gender transformation in Buddhist scriptures simply as a metaphor for mental transformation, without deeper reflection, risks turning a blind eye to the gender controversy implicit in the pursuit of Buddhahood.

In feminist critiques of the philosophy of language, the false gender-neutral use of terms and the androcentric assumptions that derive from and perpetuate gender bias have been criticized since the 1970s. Tzyh-lai Huang contends that language is one of the important social and cultural tools or mechanisms that shapes us. Androcentric language produces an ideology of gender difference and bias, which manifests in the use of the masculine pronoun as a generic term for both women and men, as well as gender-distinct ways of speaking and behaving, traditional gender-biased divisions of labor, and a dismissing of the roles and contributions of women in history.[24] Generic terms in English linguistic prescriptivism in scriptures, literature, and history are not gender-neutral but laden with embedded gender-specific meaning. Dale Spender points out that generic masculine pronouns and terms such as "he" and "man" treat men as "prototypical of the human species," which directly influences gender cognition and practice in social reality.[25] The word "man" as a generic term presumably refers to all human beings yet, when tested, the theory quickly breaks down; for example, "Man has two sexes; some men are female" and "Man breastfeeds his young."[26]

This false gender-neutrality in generic terms, which takes maleness to be the norm, in fact implies male superiority and renders women invisible in history. As feminist critics in the philosophy of language have clarified, the ambiguous but not accidental use of gender-neutral generic pronouns treats man as normative in society and culture. In this language system, women become invisible and disappear in historical scriptures. Since language is the tool that expresses and regularizes social mechanisms, the use of masculine pronouns as generic terms for human beings not only reflects a biased, unequal state of society but also, at the same time, reproduces it. Marxist feminist Michele Barrett argues that the use of such generic terms is the production process of social ideology because, through it, "meaning is produced, challenged, reproduced, and transformed."[27] Following

Barrett's argument, the use of the masculine pronoun as the generic term for humanity is a cultural practice that produces and reproduces gender ideology. Through language formation, dissemination, and transmission, this cultural practice becomes possible and dominant.

When we track the practice in India and examine the original Sanskrit term for *da zhangfu*, we find that the Buddha is depicted as having "the thirty-two marks of a Great Person," or *mahāpuruṣa* (Pāli: *mahāpurisa*).[28] The term *puruṣa* in Sanskrit has numerous meanings. In the Rigveda, *Puruṣasūkta* is "Hymn to the Cosmic Man." In the Indian Samkhya philosophical system, *puruṣa* means "soul" or "consciousness." However, Sanskrit nouns may be masculine, feminine, or neutral. *Puruṣa* is a masculine noun and often refers to "man," used as a male pronoun. It also refers to "cosmic Man," a divine being that has existed before time, and also to *atman*, or Self, which may be either transcendental and universal or worldly, such as individual selves that are distinct from one another.[29]

From a gender perspective, *puruṣa* can refer to a man, a gender-unspecified "person," or a genderless divine entity.[30] Therefore, translating the Sanskrit *puruṣa* into Chinese as *zhangfu* means that *zhangfu* can also refer to a gender-unspecified "person" or a spiritually advanced practitioner, and could be either man or woman. The Chinese language does not distinguish nouns as masculine, feminine, or neutral. Although *zhangfu* is generally a masculine pronoun, it also can refer to a man, a woman, or a gender-unspecified person. Therefore, although *da zhangfu* is generally a masculine term in the Buddhist scriptures, it can refer to either a man, a gender-unspecified person, or a genderless divine creature. As mentioned above, *zhangfu* sometimes carries gender signification and sometimes does not.

Thus, the androcentrism of Buddhism does not manifest as an absolute equivalency of *da zhangfu* and man. Instead, the androcentrism in Buddhism lies in the use of the masculine term *puruṣa* and *zhangfu* as a generic term for a spiritually advanced practitioner, instead of a feminine or neutral term. I argue that androcentrism in Buddhism manifests not in the use of *da zhangfu* as a gender-specific term equivalent to man, as many scholars contend, but in using the masculine term *da zhangfu* as the generic term for a spiritually advanced practitioner, instead of a feminine or neutral term. A *da zhangfu* embodies attributes such as wisdom, compassion, peacefulness, and gentleness—attributes achievable by any human being. Yet the use of the term *da zhangfu* for *mahāpuruṣa*, a spiritually advanced practitioner that was taken to be male in androcentric Indian society, consequently "genders" and stratifies the path of Buddhahood and makes becoming a *da zhangfu* easier for men than women.

To clarify this argument, I borrow the model of linguist Ferdinand de Saussure (1857–1913). In this model, a sign combines two elements: signifier and signified. The signifier refers to the form that the sign takes, such as a word or image. The signified refers to the concept the signifier represents. The bar referring to the relationship between the signifier and signified is arbitrary.[31] Therefore, using De Saussure's model, especially the arbitrariness of the relationship between signifier and signified, we see that interpreting *da zhangfu* both as a gendered term and also as a generic term not only challenges the androcentrism in Buddhism, but also opens up more space for different interpretations and agency. The diagram below describes the above points as follows:

Signifier : *da zhangfu* (gendered term)	: *da zhangfu* (gender-unspecific generic term)
Signified : man	: spiritual ideal (both men and woman)

People may argue that *mahāpuruṣa* cannot be a non-gender-specific term, because in the Indian tradition one of the thirty-two characteristics of a *mahāpuruṣa*, a Great Man, is a sheathed penis. Therefore, a *mahāpuruṣa*, or Great Man, has a male body and cannot be non-gender-specific. My response to this is that language and reality are separate things. No matter whether the noun *mahāpuruṣa* matches its associated bodily description or not, androcentrism in India manifests in the use of the masculine pronoun and male body in the language that "represents" a spiritually advanced person.

Similarly, we see the use of masculine pronouns such as male body and male form, and masculine nouns such as man used as generic terms to refer to the superior, unbounded mind and to purity and perfection in the transcendent state in the process of translating Indian Buddhist texts into Chinese. According to the *Mahaparinirvaṇa Sutra* and the *Sutra of the Buddha's Preaching on Transforming the Female Body* cited above as examples, "if we have not seen our Buddha nature, it means that we do not have male form," and, "if women realize their Buddha nature, we should know those women are men." These are typical examples of masculine pronouns used to refer to a superior state. In other sections of the same *sutra*s, the use of feminine descriptors such as female body, female form, woman's mind, and women become generic terms that refer to something inferior, likened to bounded mind, impurity, vexation, and imperfection in the mundane world—for example, "scold the female form and strive for male form," "if people have not realized their Buddha nature, we call those people women," and "[i]f women can have this determination, they will not have the bounded mind of women and moral infection. Therefore, they can abandon their female bodies and become men."

We can conclude that the text and translation are not neutral, but are reflections of the biased and ordered gender hierarchy of Indian and Chinese Buddhist societies at that time. Premodern Indian and Chinese Buddhist societies not only produced patriarchal and androcentric language usages, but also, at the same time, participated in disseminating, transmitting, producing, and reproducing them, such that Buddhist patriarchy and the androcentric mechanism became possible. As a result of this gendered cultural and social imagination, not only did gender become ordered, but the practice of Buddhism became a matter of uplifting oneself from the lower, feminine lever of impurity to the upper, masculine level of purity, culminating even in a need for the female body to be transformed into a male one. The fact that women "can abandon female bodies and become men" shows that when women generate a strong determination to attain perfect enlightenment, they can become men.

As another example, Pure Land *sūtra*s such as the *Sūtra of Immeasurable Life* and the *Merit of the Former Vows of the Medicine Tathāgata Sūtra* depict a Pure Land completely absent of women.[32] According to these scriptures, it is not possible to have women in the Pure Land because they represent impurity. Therefore, we find depictions of gender transformation, such as "transform the female body into a male one" and "no women in the Pure Land." Not accidentally, we also find descriptions of the characteristic biological and habitual moral faults of women appearing in Buddhist scriptures.

As mentioned earlier, research on women in Chan Buddhism has not been totally neglected in the past two decades, but most of these studies focus on the biographies of female Chan practitioners, their training under or in interaction with male masters, their efforts to propagate the Dharma, and their social outreach, and have been limited to premodern literary and historical analysis. A lack of empirical data leaves the practice of real Chan women, their subjective perception of Chan, and their substantive pedagogy undocumented and deserving of further inquiry. In the following section, I will use fieldwork findings of Chan women in contemporary Taiwan to explore the interrelationships among gender, Chan Buddhism, and modernity. My findings show that Chan nuns in contemporary Taiwan do not interpret *da zhangfu* as equivalent to man, but regard it as a generic term for a spiritually advanced practitioner, who may be female or male. According to Faure:

> Buddhism . . . was not as passive as we have been led to believe. We need to take into account real practices and subjective perceptions before passing judgment. We also need to get a better understanding of the actual dialectics at play in the exercise of power, and how boundaries between genders were constantly renegotiated.[33]

For Faure, Chan women are not just passive receivers of canonical texts; their subjective interpretations and practice are important fields of inquiry. Gregory Schopen also points out that it questionable for researchers to consider only scriptural texts as representing the reality of Buddhism. Scriptural Buddhism represents an ideal paradigm that cannot represent what really happens. Not only was the production of Buddhist canonical texts controlled by social elites, it was also embedded in the social values and traditions of the time. The study of Buddhism cannot be limited to a consideration of canonical texts, but must also include other resources, such as archaeological and epigraphical materials and, I would contend, fieldwork as well.[34]

The Nondualistic Gender Identity of Chan Nuns in Taiwan

Alan Sponberg suggests four distinct attitudes toward women and the feminine in reading the inconsistencies and multiplicity of voices in early Buddhist texts: soteriological inclusiveness, institutional androcentrism, ascetic misogyny, and soteriological genderlessness in Perfection of Wisdom (*Prajñāpāramitā*) thought and parts of Vajrayāna Buddhism. According to Sponberg, these four attitudes are not totally separate but interrelated in the process of doctrinal and institutional development and change in Buddhist history.[35] Sponberg's analysis of these four attitudes toward women and the feminine in Buddhist texts is also applicable to contemporary practice in Taiwanese Buddhist communities. In Taiwan, because Buddhist and governmental authority is decentralized, gender perceptions are not universal; significant differences in attitude exist among nuns in different *bhikshuni* monasteries. In contrast to Buddhism in China, which depends on the political hierarchy of the Communist party and state, who control the Chinese Buddhist Association, the democratic environment of Buddhism in Taiwan gives different monasteries independence and space to develop. The monasteries are financially and institutionally independent and do their own fundraising according to their abilities, which gives each monastery a unique character.

Li contends that, comparable to the decentralized functioning of Taiwanese Buddhist institutions, the women's rights movement and women's self-awakening in Taiwanese society in past decades has developed variously, sometimes parallel to and sometimes in contrast with, attitudes toward gender identity in other religions in Taiwan.[36] In terms of gender identity, Li contends that Buddhist nuns follow religious doctrine more than feminist thought or the women's rights movement.[37] However, Buddhist scriptures and pedagogy are inconsistent about women's potential to become liberated or enlightened. The emphasis on not being attached to forms (including gendered forms) and the complexity of attitudes toward gender in Buddhist texts—from derogatory ones, such as the eighty-four disagreeable aspects of women, up to more positive ones, such as the Dragon Girl becoming enlightened in one instant in the *Lotus Sūtra*—complicate the concept of gender in *bhikṣuṇī* communities.[38]

Elise DeVido illustrates that some Taiwanese nuns distinguish themselves in their "self-awareness" and "fighting" for gender equality in the women's rights movement in Taiwan. The self-reliant, self-administered, highly talented, and hard-working nuns of Taiwan work for the good of society at large and do not consider themselves feminists, with notable exceptions, such as Bhiksuni Zhao Hui (1957–) and Bhiksuni Xing Guang (1962–), who explicitly identify as Buddhist feminists. Nevertheless, the younger generation of Buddhist nuns in Taiwan who are in their forties or younger may well align themselves with feminist ideas. Some of them even have Women's Studies backgrounds or took Women's Studies courses at university.[39]

In contrast to the women's rights movement in Taiwan, which encourages women's self-awareness, the negative portrayals of women in Buddhist scriptures have continued to influence Buddhist circles. The negative physical and mental traits of women, who are described as *wuhui* (disgusting), *guohuan* (faulty), and *nüguo* (impure, f.), for instance, are highlighted for the purpose of facilitating monks' celibate practice by accentuating aversion to the female form. Moreover, Buddhists often describe the negative nature of femininity as *nütai* (girly), suggesting that women have more obstacles and less potential than men to achieve spiritual goals in their practice. This negative representation of female traits and potential in the Buddhist scriptures easily leads to the construction of a hierarchical, gendered juxtaposition of the spiritually advanced cultivator (*da zhangfu*) in contrast to the disgusting, flawed, impure, and "girly" woman.

Hillary Crane, in interviews conducted at Zhi Guang Chan Monastery (a pseudonym) in Taiwan, concludes that Taiwanese Buddhist nuns strategically create a complex gender cosmology. That is, they identify both as male and female in gender in order to accommodate textual contradictions without denying their spiritual abilities. When they identify themselves with the male gender, the nuns assert that their spiritual abilities are no different from those of men, without seeing this as contradictory to textual assertions about women and men. On the other hand, nuns identify themselves as women biologically in order to follow the *vinaya*, the monastic discipline of the *saṅgha*, and live separately from monks.[40] In Crane's findings, Buddhist nuns in Taiwan are influenced by the texts and teachings of their tradition and interpret *da zhangfu*, *nanshen* (male body), and *nanxiang* (male form) literally as pertaining to men, and specifically associate spiritually advanced practitioners with men. On the negative pole, they interpret *nütai* (girly), *nüshen* (female body), and *nüxiang* (female form) as pertaining to women.

DeVido concurs that nuns are influenced by negative portrayals of women in Buddhist scriptures and argues that this has created a kind of gender essentialism in Taiwanese Buddhist communities. The presupposition of gender essentialism emphasizes purported natural differences between men and women. As a result of this presumption, *da zhangfu* is characterized as having a male quality. In order to become *da zhangfu*, women need to shed the negative aspects of their female nature, such as envy and judgmentalism.[41] Although a number of male masters in Taiwan, such as Bhiksu Xingyun and Bhiksu Sheng Yen, support education for Buddhist nuns and have helped re-establish *bhikshuni* ordination in other Buddhist traditions, DeVido contends that they hold to the idea of gender essentialism, emphasizing motherhood and being a wife as part of a woman's nature, leading women to be more willing than men to sacrifice themselves for their family. Because women spend much of their time and energy supporting their husbands' careers and taking care of children, they do not have as much time to engage in Dharma practice as men. These masters contend that the "natural instincts of a woman" constrain her potential for spiritual cultivation.[42]

Instead of denying the femininity of biological women, another aspect of gender essentialism in Taiwanese Buddhism is to positively emphasize the so-called feminine aspects of women's nature, such as gentleness and loving kindness. These "female qualities" make it easier for women to resonate with compassion and other positive qualities emphasized in Buddhism and to conclude that women are more suitable for Buddhist practice than men. Hwei-syin Lu points out that the female master Bhiksuni Cheng Yen (1937–) of Tzu Chi Foundation (Buddhist Compassionate Relief) considers love, empathy, and compassion to be feminine characteristics inborn in the nature of women. She encourages women to develop these feminine attributes, not only in caring for their families but in caring for all sentient beings, so that their feminine energy can be used in charity in the public sphere.[43] The operations of Tzu Chi therefore make use of women's traditional tendencies toward caring and generosity, transforming them into Buddhist compassion through caring for and benefitting others, thus transcending and expanding care for the secular family to a much larger religious family. Lu illustrates that in this transformation women play an essential role in the "influence of family on religion" (*zongjiao jiating hua*) and the "influence of religion on family" (*jiating zongjiao hua*). As a result, the endeavors of women, including organizational interactions, operations, and communications, have become paramount to Tzu Chi 's success.[44]

My fieldwork has shown that Chan nuns in contemporary Taiwan interpret the term *da zhangfu* as a generic pronoun that refers to spiritually advanced practitioners, including both women and men, who embody attributes such as wisdom, compassion, peacefulness, and gentleness. The term is not understood to be gender-specific or equated with males, as interpreted by many scholars. For Chan Buddhist nuns in contemporary Taiwan, to become a *da zhangfu* is to go beyond identifying as either a man or a woman and to thereby avoid dualistic forms altogether. Use of the term *da zhangfu* thus signals a more radical gender identity and reinscribes Chan as an egalitarian practice of the mind free from particularization. In contrast to the gender identities that scholars have found to be characteristic of other monastic communities of nuns in Taiwan, the nuns of Dharma Drum Mountain do not identify themselves as men and also do not believe that women represent all things negative. Although *bhikṣuṇī*s and *bhikṣuṇī*s live in the same monasteries, *bhikṣuṇī*s see no difference between men and women in practice.[45] FG[46] said:

In terms of Buddhist practice, men and women are spiritually equal and have equal potential to reach enlightenment. Yet, in the application of practice methods, some methods may not be suitable for women, such as practicing reflections on repulsiveness (*baigu guan*) in cemeteries, a traditional meditation method of contemplating thirty-one parts of the body, because it usually requires one to do a solitary retreat in the mountain.[47]

According to YE:

I do not think that there are specific differences between men and women in practice. Basically, I see no differences among them. If there really are any differences, and women are considered inferior to men, I would like to know what they are and how to overcome such obstacles.[48]

Compared to other places where *bhikṣuṇīs* and *bhikṣus* live in the same monastery, Dharma Drum Mountain educates monastics to practice the Chan doctrine of "no marks"' and "no thought," in which the mind free from particularization breaks through imagined characteristics (*fenbie xiang*). YH said:

If biological women have female characteristics that are obstacles to their practice, so do men have male ones. To practice is to cast off all such characteristics, such as being bashful or rough, all of which are undesirable.[49]

HI said:

Personally, I do not consider that women or men are born with specific characteristics. Women may have male qualities and vice versa. With regards to practice or Chan cultivation, I would not intentionally consider the difference between men and women.[50]

CG voiced a somewhat different view:

If a woman behaves in a way that is too feminine or too masculine, it makes people feel weird. And the same is true for men. If a man is too feminine or behaves like a muscleman, it also looks weird.[51]

For the nuns at Dharma Drum Mountain, gender identity comes close to an example of the "nondualistic" experience cultivated in Chan. When I asked them whether gender affects their practice and the dissemination of Buddhadharma, most nuns said there is no difference between men and women in terms of practice and leadership. They often answered, "I do not particularly think about the gender issue." Among the nuns I interviewed, GG's response made a special impression on me. We had just sat down, and before the interview started, she asked me straightforwardly with great curiosity, "Is there any difference between males and females?"[52]

On the other hand, though most Dharma Drum Mountain nuns have a nondualistic view of gender identity, a few nuns do feel there are inherent gender differences in terms of practice. They noted the physical differences between men and women; women experience inconveniences such as menstruation and lack the physical strength of men. However, to most nuns at Dharma Drum Mountain, *da zhangfu* refers to the purity of Buddha nature and the reality of Dharma; that is, it signifies ultimate truths such as impermanence rather than phenomenal truths or dualities such as male and female bodies or masculinity and femininity. The Chan school, based on wisdom imbued with insight into emptiness, *prajña*, and inherent Buddha nature, denies the essential nature of imagined characteristics and educates sentient beings to transcend all worldly discriminations to achieve Buddhahood. Many practitioners of this school disagree with the view that women face more physical obstacles. According to CI:

> Well, regarding the assertion that women cannot practice as well as men due to menstruation, let's stop debating that. The physical makeup of men and women was never the same in the first place, and the obstacles that they come across during practice are also different. It is not possible to make comparisons, and there is no need to underestimate oneself. If there are people who would like to impose restrictions on themselves, then just don't fuss over it with them. What is important is not to make comparisons between men and women, but to look at the degree of freedom in the mind. In the course of our practice, if we are bound by conditioned concepts, then we are not liberated, no matter whether we are a man or a woman.[53] Most nuns think that the gender hierarchy in the Buddhist community in Taiwan today is caused by patriarchal Chinese culture and the androcentric monastic ethics in traditional Buddhism.

Without the Buddhist "right view," one could easily become influenced and attached to the phenomenal male or female form, generating arrogance due to having a male body or feelings of inferiority due to having a female body, which diverts the focus of one's practice from the mind.[54]

HO expressed a similar view:

> *Da zhangfu* does not refer to men. It means purity of one's body, speech, and mind, and has nothing to do with one's sex. As long as one is cultivating purity of one's body, speech, and mind like the Buddha, one could be considered a *da zhangfu*. One can actually feel the compassion, wisdom, and peacefulness of some senior monks or nuns, or those who have devoted themselves to society or even the whole world, for a long time. They don't make people frightened, but magnetize others with their very steady, very pure, and peaceful energy. Shifu once mentioned in class that at some dwelling places of some senior monastics, one could actually smell a light fragrance that comes from their practice.[55] If one treats others with an unbiased, non-discriminating mind, one is a *da zhangfu*. In order to become a *da zhangfu*, what one really needs to learn are not masculine or feminine characteristics, but the mind and behavior of the Buddha. A man will not necessarily be considered a *da zhangfu*. Some men are so rough and attached that they ask others to obey them, but the Buddha is not rough at all. Those who think that *da zhangfu* refers to a man lack correct faith and correct view. They learn the Chan pedagogy very superficially, getting attached to appearances instead of cultivating the mind, which is really pathetic.[56]

In the interviews I conducted with the Dharma Drum Mountain nuns, I found that most do not think the idea of *da zhangfu* refers to a man, in contrast to the conclusions reached in previous studies. Moreover, the nuns at Dharma Drum Mountain maintain a nondualistic gender identity. To them, *da* (great) signifies not being attached to and being liberated from dualistic differences between male and female bodies or forms. To become a Buddha or a *bodhisattva* is not to become a man or a woman and to be reborn in the Pure Land is to be neither a man nor a woman. A somewhat radical view of gender identity of Chan nuns in contemporary Taiwan emerged in my interviews with the Dharma Drum Mountain nuns. To their minds, *da zhangfu* refers neither to man (an androcentric term), nor to man and woman (a generic term), but to a spiritually advanced state that transcends the dualism of male and female gender categories and therefore deconstructs the hierarchical gender order in the practice of Chan. According to YG:

> To be a *da zhangfu* does not require one to be very masculine. It does not refer to one's external appearance, but to the disposition of some internal characteristics. Some celebrities may look quite masculine, but would definitely not be considered *da zhangfu*.[57]

YI explained:

> I think that the idea of *da zhangfu* is without gender significance. Women can be *da zhangfu*. The idea of *da zhangfu* is to remind us to be open-minded and to return to the original teachings of the Buddha, the ultimate reality. This reality or truth was not invented, but was discovered by the Buddha. The Buddha shared his findings to help us free ourselves from our own deluded thoughts. The form of a *da zhangfu* is neither gendered nor androcentric. If you take a good look at Buddha statues, most of them are gender-neutral, without much sexual significance. Rather than having the dualistic forms of men and women, Buddhas and *bodhisattvas* embody and manifest different pure forms in order to liberate sentient beings. A few days ago, I read *sūtras* that mentioned the so-called eighty-four disagreeable aspects of women. Honestly, I don't think those negative qualities that the Buddha described were aimed at nuns specifically, but rather were a reminder to both monks and nuns. Men or women may fall prey to that kind of mindset. Or, it might be that the Buddha was teaching some nuns, but his intention was just to warn the practitioners in general, instead of attributing these qualities to women only.[58]

L2 concurred, saying:

> The ideal of becoming a Buddha or a *da zhangfu* has to be realized through cultivating the mind. It has absolutely

nothing at all to do with one's being a man or woman. In my mind, there is hardly any connection between gender and practice. Being feminine is great, and I kind of like it personally, but I don't find it an obstacle or a help in any particular way. I think the Buddha teaches us to meditate on the impermanence of all things. Whatever phenomenon or characteristic manifests itself, just try to contemplate its dependent origination. There's no inherent self-nature within.

In contrast to gender essentialism, nuns in Dharma Drum Mountain view the manifestation of *da zhangfu* as resulting from the culmination of Buddhist practice. For them, *da zhangfu* is not restricted to men, but is the fulfillment of certain qualities, which are neither masculine nor feminine and do not naturally belong to men or women, a perspective that deconstructs gender essentialism. Regarding debates on the relationship among gender, biological differences, and cultivation, YN believes that the essence of Chan is to "develop one's potential":

Shifu said that meditation helps cultivate one's potential. We should not restrict the limitless potential of women in any respect. For example, is it true that women are inferior physically? I know of one monastic who is small and short yet can easily lift and move heavy things that usually require the strength of two people. Perhaps because we are a Chan monastery, we tend to be gender-neutral. We don't generally give the impression that men are superior to women, but instead emphasize relationships of mutual respect. Monastic practice entails cultivating the marks of a *da zhangfu*, which is a spirit of independence and non-reliance, rather than a physical characteristic. Being a *da zhangfu* does not mean that one should be masculine, but rather use the spirit of Chan to reflect inwardly on one's body, speech, and mind and develop one's potential. Actually, Shifu does not teach his disciples with any gender presumptions. Once as I listened to Shifu's morning talks in the early years, Shifu asked a monastic who was present: "Venerable X, do you have self-confidence? Ven. YY, how about you?" Those monastics were nuns. Shifu knew that, due to the socialization process of patriarchal-patrilineal Chinese society, women easily lack self-confidence. This is why Shifu told those nuns that they should have confidence in themselves. Practice requires self-confidence and it is true that Chan practice can help develop one's potential.[59]

Dharma Drum Mountain nuns are taught and practice the Chan pedagogy that one must first have great faith; second, great vows; third, great determination; and fourth, great doubt.[60] Faith comes first, and it means to have faith in wisdom (*prajñā*), egalitarianism, and nonduality in Mahāyāna and Chan doctrine, and to practice accordingly. Chan practice, therefore, is to overcome all dualistic thinking, deconstructing dualistic forms, including the concept and practice of gender essentialism.

Conclusion: Some Methodological Reflections

Drawing from feminist critiques of the philosophy of language and critical readings of Buddhist scriptures, I argue that *da zhangfu* as a generic term is a critique of both the androcentric use of masculine pronouns in Chinese Buddhist scriptures and of scholarly uses of textual scripture that overlook real practices in society. Moreover, *da zhangfu* as a generic term deconstructs the hierarchical dualism of man as advanced and woman as primitive that is embedded in gender essentialism. Therefore, there is no necessity for a woman to become a man first in order to reach Buddhahood, which is a common interpretation of Buddhist scriptures.

Whereas first-wave feminists in the nineteenth century focused on equal rights, criticized mandated inequalities in property rights, and advocated for the right to vote, second-wave feminists in the twentieth century addressed gender differences along with a range of social practices that emphasize women's ability to exercise agency and achieve self-fulfillment. Within second-wave feminism, one view in discussing the production of gender difference is social constructionism. In social constructionist thinking, the tendency is antiessentialist: biological determinism is rejected, and the body is defined as nothing more than a social construction. Drawing on criticisms leveled by postcolonial theories, women of color, and queer theories, Liz Wilson contends that debates in feminist theory since the 1980s have questioned the homogeneity of the category "women" and have offered examples of exclusion to show that women's experiences are multiple and cannot be adequately categorized by monolithic models.

Moreover, deconstructionist and poststructuralist theories question the universality of the category of "female" or "women," which as unified objects of inquiry or identity cannot offer analytical precision.[61]

From these paradigm shifts in feminist methodology and epistemology, we can see that research on women in Buddhism is mostly still trapped in binary modes of man versus woman, first versus second, and criticism following this line of thought. Although pioneering feminist critics in Buddhist studies have offered powerful analytic structures and criticism, they have neglected certain productive insights that can further empower women. The question now is how to borrow feminist theories to deepen our analysis and encourage women's active agency rather than seeing women as passive victims of patriarchy or androcentrism in Buddhist communities. Although Indian and Chinese societies remain patriarchal, economic growth and compulsory education have dramatically increased women's access to education. With the lifting of martial law, since 1987 Taiwan has become a democracy with flourishing social movements. The women's rights movement in Taiwan has flourished since then, arguably making Taiwan the most gender-open society in Asia. Following the implementation of the Gender Equity Education Act in 2004, universities and schools have been required to promote gender equity and gender studies.

These political, economic, and social changes in contemporary Taiwan permit new understandings of *da zhangfu* and new interpretations of Buddhist scriptures. This exploration of the gender identity as understood by Chan nuns in contemporary Taiwan has shown how the concept *da zhangfu* goes beyond binary modes of thinking about gender in Buddhism and avoids the consequences of this dualistic thinking. Influenced by Chan doctrine, the nuns engage in productive ways of thinking to reconsider gender and Chan Buddhism that also empower women in practice. By contrast, I have argued that the analytical frameworks of many scholars are trapped in biological and cultural gender dualities: male versus female, man versus women, masculine versus feminine, and so on. Reflections on gender identity voiced by Chan nuns in contemporary Taiwan render these frameworks problematic, replacing them with a view of Chan women surpassing gender difference and exalting them as *da zhangfu*—a male-oriented term used in patriarchal Chan community. Previous critics understood *da zhangfu* as a denial of female characteristics and a suspicious Chan rhetoric of equality. However, previous criticism of Chan Buddhism's treatment of Chan women as culturally and institutionally inferior is itself a consequence of gender essentialism. By foregoing timeless definitions of feminine identity, Chan nuns' in contemporary Taiwan are exploring sexual difference in ways that go beyond the usual binary and hierarchical tropes. This turn frees Chan women from the fixed and dualistic frameworks that have not only essentialized "man" and "woman," but also ordered them hierarchically in constructs that invariably relegate women to a secondary, "other" category.

This research demonstrates that Chan nuns in contemporary Taiwan neither interpret the negative aspects of females described in Buddhist scriptures as a denigration of women nor as an obstacle for their attainment of enlightenment. Most see the negative attitudes toward women in the scriptures as part of the cultural imagination constructed in ancient patriarchal Indian and Chinese societies and contrast it with the essence of Chan Buddhism, which is the pedagogy of *prajña*. In the absence of a doer, *da zhangfu* is neither androcentric nor a generic dualistic gender form, but a nondualistic term for one whose mind is free from particularization, who embodies *prajña*, wisdom beyond dualistic forms and concepts. This nondualistic approach to gender identity among Chan women in contemporary Taiwan provokes new thinking, stimulating further research in the study of gender and religion.

Notes

1. Miriam Levering, "Lin-chi (Rinzai) Ch'an and Gender: The Rhetoric of Equality and the Rhetoric of Heroism," *Buddhism, Sexuality, and Gender*, ed. José Ignacio Cabezón (Albany: State University of New York Press, 1992), 137–56; and Bernard Faure, *The Power of Denial: Buddhism, Purity, and Gender* (Oxford & Princeton, NJ: Princeton University Press, 2003), 119–42.

2. Miriam Levering, "Miao-tao and Her Teacher Ta-hui" and Ding-hua E. Hsieh, "Images of Women in Ch'an Buddhist Literature of the Sung Period," *Buddhism in the Sung*, ed. Peter N. Gregory and Daniel A. Getz, Jr. (Honolulu: University of Hawaii Press, 2002), 188–219; and Miriam Levering, "The Dragon Girl and the Abbess of Mo-Shan: Gender and Status in the Ch'an Buddhist Tradition," *Journal of the International Association of Buddhist Studies*, 5:l(1982): 19–35.

3. Beata Grant, *Eminent Nuns: Women Chan Masters of Seventeenth-Century China* (Honolulu: University of Hawaii Press, Honolulu, 2009).

4. Jingjia Huang, "Zhihui de nüxing xingxian—chanmen denglü zhong chanpo yu chanshi de duihua" (Profiles of Sagacious Women: The Dialogues

of Old Women and Masters in the Collections of Biographies of the Zen Masters) *Journal of the Center of Buddhist Studies* 7(2004): 127–54.

5. Heng-ching Shih, "Chinese Bhiksunis in the Ch'an Tradition," *National Taiwan University Philosophical Review* 15(1992): 181–207.

6. Yeshe Tsogyal and Machik Labdron in the Tibetan Vajrayāna tradition were female masters who enabled the enlightenment of male practitioners.

7. Levering, "Lin-chi (Rinzai) Ch'an and Gender," 137–56; Faure, *The Power of Denial*, 119–35.

8. Beata Grant, "Da Zhangfu: The Rhetoric of Female Heroism in Seventeenth-Century Buddhist Writings," *Nan Nü: Men, Women and Gender in China* 10:2(2008): 177, 211.

9. Chün-Fang Yü, *Passing of the Light: The Incense Light Community and Buddhist Nuns in Contemporary Taiwan* (Honolulu: University of Hawaii Press, 2013), 13.

10. Levering, "Lin-chi (Rinzai) Ch'an and Gender," 145; Faure, *The Power of Denial*, 130–31.

11. Aryadeva (third century CE), a disciple of Nagarjuna, was one of the important founders of the Indian Madhyamika school.

12. CBETA, T30, no. 1577, p. 265, b26–28; CBETA, T12, no. 374, p. 422, a28–b6.

13. Meiwen Su, "Nüxing chanshi de daoying: cong 'xiezhen yu min-gyan' tanxi qiyuan chanshi zhi xingxiang." *Journal of the Center for Buddhist Studies* 10(2005): 259.

14. Yuchen Li, "Fojiao piyu wenxue zhong de nannü meice yu qingyu: zhuiqiu meili de zongjiao yihan" (Religious Desire and Religious Beauty: Gender Difference and Sensual Beauty as Represented in the Avadaana Literature), *Xinshixue* 10:4(1999): 56–59.

15. Faure, *The Power of Denial*, 131.

16. Ministry of Education, R.O.C. *Jiaoyu bu chongbian guoyu cidian xiuding ben* (*Revised Chinese Dictionary*), 2015. http://dict.revised.moe.edu.tw/cgi-bin/cbdic/gsweb.cgi (accessed October 13, 2016).

17. Ibid. In this use of the terms *nü zhangfu* and *zhangfu nü*, *zhangfu* is a generic term. For clarification, the word "female" (*nü*) is placed before or after as an adjective to indicate that the heroic subject is a woman.

18. Tze-lan D. Sang, *The Emerging Lesbian: Female Same-Sex Desire in Modern China* (Chicago: The University of Chicago Press, 2003), 30.

19. Eve Kosofsky Sedgwick. *Touching Feeling: Affect, Pedagogy, Performativity* (London & Durham, NC: Duke University Press, 2003), 38, 123–51.

20. Binary gender rhetoric and analogy are often seen in Buddhist scriptures, such as the Agamas in early Buddhism and in Mahāyāna texts such as the *Lotus Sūtra*, the *Merit of the Former Vows of the Medicine Tathagata Sūtra*, the *Mahāratnakūta Sūtra*, and many other scriptures throughout Buddhist history.

21. *Mahāparinirvāna Sūtra* (*da bo niepan jing*), vol. 9, Tathagatha-nature, ch. 4. CBETA, T12, no. 374, p. 422, a28–b6.

22. *The Sutra of the Buddha's Preaching on Transforming the Female Body (fo shuo zhuan nüshen jing)*, vol. 1. CBETA, T14, no. 564, p. 918, c2–14.

23. Heng-ching Shih, "*Putidao shang de shan nüren*" (Sakyadhita on the Bodhi Path) (Taipei: Dongda, 1995), 89.

24. Tzyh-lai Huang, "Yingyu yuyan xingbie chayi yu yingyu jiaoxue—cong nüxing zhuyi pipanyingyu tanqi" (Sex Variation in English and English Language Teaching). *Bulletin of National Taiwan Normal University* 41 (1996): 245–46.

25. Dale Spender, *Man Made Language* (London: Pandora, 1980), 18.

26. Jennifer Saul, "Feminist Philosophy of Language," *Stanford Encyclopedia of Philosophy*, 2010 (accessed online on October 14, 2016).

27. Michele Barrett, *Women's Oppression Today: The Marxist/Feminist Encounter* (London: Verso, 1980), 97.

28. Robert E. Buswell, Jr., ed., *Encyclopedia of Buddhism* (New York: Macmillan Reference, 2004), 179.

29. Lindsay Jones ed., *Encyclopedia of Religion*, 2nd ed., vol. 1 (Detroit: Thomson Gale, 2005), 338; and Constance A. Jones and James D. Ryan, eds., *Encyclopedia of Hinduism* (New York: Facts on File, 2007), 338.

30. Concerning the meaning of the word "*puruṣa*," I am indebted to Catherine Wessinger and Wei-jen Teng for their erudition in Sanskrit.

31. Ferdinand de Saussure (trans. Roy Harris), *Course in General Linguistics* (London: Duckworth, 1983), 67.

32. In the first volume of the *Merit of the Former Vows of the Medicine Tathagata Sūtra*: "The Medicine Buddha's land is permanently pure, without women or other evil destinies or the sounds of suffering." CBETA, T14, no. 450, p. 405, c2–3. In the *Sutra of Immeasurable Life*, vol. 1: "There are women in the immeasurable and inconceivable Buddha lands of the ten directions who have heard my name, rejoice in faith, awaken the aspiration for enlightenment, and wish to renounce womanhood. If, when I attain Buddhahood, these women after death are reborn again as women, may I not attain perfect enlightenment." CBETA, T12, no. 360, p. 268, c21–24.

33. Faure, *The Power of Denial*, 7.

34. Gregory Schopen, *Bones, Stones, and Buddhist Monks: Collected Papers on the Archaeology, Epigraphy, and Texts of Monastic Buddhism in India* (University of Hawaii Press, 1997), 1–14.

35. Alan Sponberg, "Attitudes toward Women and the Feminine in Early Buddhism," ed. Jose Ignacio Cabezon, *Buddhism, Sexuality, and Gender* (Albany: State University of New York Press, 1992), 7–27.

36. Yuchen Li, "*Fojiao de nüxing, nüxing de fojiao: jin ershi nianlai zhong yingwen de fojiao funü yanjiu*" (Buddhist Women, Women in Buddhism: Studies of Women and Buddhism in the Past Twenty Years), *Taiwan bentu zongjiao yanjiu de xin shiye he xin siwei* (Searching for a Paradigm: New Perspectives on the Taiwanese Religious Studies), ed. Canteng Jiang and Shun Chang (Taipei: Nantian, 2003), 507.

37. Yuchen Li, "Siyuan chufang li de jiemei qing: zhan hou taiwan fojiao funü di xingbie yishi yu xiuxing" (The Jiemeiqing in the Monastic Kitchen in Post-War Taiwan: The Gender Identity and Community Solidarity of Buddhist Women), *Funü yu zongjiao: kua lingyu de shiye* (Women and Religions: Interdisciplinary Scopes, Methods, and Approaches) (Taipei: Liren, 2003), 316.

38. The "eighty-four disagreeable aspects of women" are referenced in the *Mahāprajāpatī Bhikṣuṇī Sūtra*. For example, the second volume states that: "women have eighty-four disagreeable aspects which bewitch and delude people and make them unable to attain enlightenment." CBETA, T24, no. 1478, p. 954, a6–7. In the *Lotus Sūtra* (vol. 4), the Daughter of the Dragon King appears to become a Buddha: "At that time Śāriputra spoke to the Dragon King's Daughter and said: "You say that you will attain the highest path soon. What you say is difficult to believe. Why? The female body is impure and polluted so is not a vessel for the Dharma. How can you use the female body to attain highest enlightenment? . . . Later the assembly there all saw the Dragon King's Daughter instantly transform into a man and perfect the *bodhisattva* practices. He then went to the World of No Impurity in the south, sat on a jeweled lotus flower, and attained highest and complete enlightenment." CBETA, T09, no. 262, p. 35, c6–17. The *Lotus Sūtra* is one of the "sex change" *sūtra*s in which a female must transform into a male in order to become a Buddha.

39. Elise DeVido, "Buddhism, Women, and Civil Society in Taiwan," *Renjian fojiao xinhuo xiangchuan: di si jie yinshun daoshi sixiang zhi lilun yu xueshu lunwen ji* (Transmission of Humanistic Buddhism: The Proceedings of the Fourth Conference on Studies of Master Yin Shun's Theory and Practice), Taoyuan: Hongshi Foundation, 2003. http://www.hongshi.org.tw/dissertation.aspx?code=212AAFBD714B393A2B713C93B53A3427 (accessed October 14, 2016).

40. Hillary Crane, "Becoming a Nun, Becoming a Man: Taiwanese Buddhist Nuns' Gender Transformation." *Religion* 37(2007): 117–121.

41. Elise DeVido, "*Taiwan de xingbie benzhi zhuyi yu dangdi fojiao de fazhan*" (Taiwan's Gender Essentialism and the Development of Taiwanese Buddhism), *Zongjiao wenhua yu xingbie lilun* (Religious Culture and Gender Ethics) (Taipei: Fajie, 2008), 332–34.

42. Ibid., 339.

43. Hwei-syin Lu, 1999a, "Xiandai fojiao nüxing de shenti yuyan yu xingbie chongjian: yi ciji gongdehui weilie" (Body Language and Gender Reconstruction of Contemporary Buddhist Women: A Case Study of the Tzu Chi Merit Association), *Bulletin of the Institute of Ethnology*, Academic Sinica 88(1999): 284, 296.

44. Hwei-syin Lu, " 'Jiating zongjiao hua' yu' zongjiao jiating hua': fojiao nüxing de xinyang shijian" ('Religion in the Family and the Family in Reli-

gion': The Religious Practice of Buddhist Women), Proceedings of the Chinese Family and Ethics Conference (Taipei: Chinese Studies Center, 1999b), 297.

45. Since 2012, I have conducted an ethnographic survey and interviewed forty nuns in Dharma Drum Mountain about their Chan practice, learning, and gender perspectives. There are approximately 250 nuns in Dharma Drum Mountain. The interviews I quote are part of the research I have done over the past few years.

46. I have identified nuns by the first and last letters of their names.

47. Interview with FG, Dharma Drum World Center for Buddhist Education, New Taipei City, January 24, 2012.

48. Interview with YE, Dharma Drum World Center for Buddhist Education, New Taipei City, January 24, 2012.

49. Interview with YH, Dharma Drum World Center for Buddhist Education, New Taipei City, February 12, 2013.

50. Interview with HI, Dharma Drum Yun Lai Temple, Taipei, January 27, 2012.

51. Interview with CG, Dharma Drum World Center for Buddhist Education, New Taipei City, February 5, 2012.

52. Interview with GG, Dharma Drum Yun Lai Temple, Taipei, January 28, 2012.

53. Interview with CI, Dharma Drum Mountain World Center for Buddhist Education, New Taipei City, March 5, 2013.

54. Right view is one of the factors in the Noble Eightfold Path, one of the principal teachings of Buddhism. Right view refers to having the right perspective and understanding of reality and how it works, that is, the Four Noble Truths: knowledge of suffering, knowledge of the origination of suffering, knowledge of the cessation of suffering, knowledge of the way of practice leading to the cessation of suffering. Right view gives direction to the seven other factors of the path and leads toward self-awakening and liberation.

55. Shifu is a title used for Buddhist teachers or masters by their disciples. In DDM, monastics refer to their teacher and the founder of Dharma Drum Mountain, Master Sheng Yen, as Shifu.

56. Interview with HO in Dharma Drum Mountain World Center for Buddhist Education, New Taipei City, February 8, 2013.

57. Interview with YG in Dharma Drum Mountain World Center for Buddhist Education, New Taipei City, February 9, 2013.

58. Interview with YI in Dharma Drum Mountain World Center for Buddhist Education, New Taipei City, February 8, 2013.

59. Interview with YN in Dharma Drum Mountain World Center for Buddhist Education, New Taipei City, March 1, 2012.

60. Sheng-Yen. Xinxing ming jianglu (Commentary on Faith in Mind) (Taipei: Fagu, 1999), 32. "To practice Chan, one must first have great faith; second, great vows; third, great determination; and fourth, great doubt. Therefore, it

is correct to first have faith. Believing that we are originally unified, believing in 'oneness,' then practicing according to the method. . . . An equal and nondualistic mind is what *Faith in Mind* teaches us, and it is also the starting point for practice." (My translation.)

61. Liz Wilson, "Buddhism and Gender," *Buddhism in the Modern World*, ed. David L. McMahan (New York: Routledge, 2012), 258–63.

Chapter 5

Sikkhamats

The Aesthetics of Asoke Ascetics

ROBEKKAH L. RITCHIE

At 3:30 in the morning, while many may consider resting the body and mind, the *sikkhamats* rise for their morning chanting, chores, or meditations. They comprise a small but dedicated group of women throughout Thailand who have chosen an alternative path of renunciation under the leadership of the Thai monk, Phra Bodhirak. Over the past forty years, the *sikkhamats* have become well known throughout Thailand as their new communities, known as Asoke or Santi Asoke, have emerged across the country.[1]

This chapter examines how the Asoke system of Thai Buddhist renunciation has developed a distinctive aesthetic to reflect and signal the unique identity of their female monastics, the *sikkhamats*. This aesthetic is not only embodied in their spiritual practice, indicating how they engage and behave in their communities, but also signals that they are serious Buddhist renunciants and teachers, eco-friendly, highly ethical, and educated. Further, as dedicated social activists, they have made a unique contribution to the development of new systems that allow women to take up active and respected roles in monastic communities.[2]

The chapter begins with a brief introduction to various forms of ordination available for women in Theravāda countries, particularly those who undertake eight to ten precepts, in comparison to fully ordained *bhikkhunī*s who follow the 311 rules prescribed by the *vinaya*, the monastic code of conduct. In Thailand, although *bhikkhunī*s are not presently recognized by the Thai Ecclesiastical Council, some nuns have begun receiving full ordination according to the *vinaya* in Sri Lanka and elsewhere. Both these *bhikkhunī*s and the Asoke monastics wear colored robes rather than white, which denotes lay status. I will explore themes of embodied morality and the importance of the many identification choices, such as the colors of the robes, as markers of renunciation, and their nuances in the context of Thailand. The focus will be on the aesthetic aspects of Asoke, investigating their integration of ethics and embodiment in Asoke's aesthetic ideals, and how these values are expressed visually, embodied in daily life by the monastics and lay members. Last, the threads exploring morality, color, and aesthetics will be brought together in a discussion of the lives and ordination progression of the *sikkhamat*s. Aesthetic expression is a multifaceted system of communications touching and informing individuals as well as groups, personal beliefs, and societal structures. Through these interactions and manifestations, a dialogue surrounding expressions of femininity, feminism, and renunciation in Thailand emerges.

Mae Chees, Sikkihamats, and Bhikkhunīs

Becoming a *mae chee* is the most socially accepted and viable option for women who wish to become renunciants in Thailand. Women who become *mae chee*s wear white, shave their heads, and follow the eight precepts. In the past few decades, the status of *mae chee*s has begun to improve and they have gained access to more resources. Still, many live in poverty, and are expected to dedicate their time and energy to washing, cooking, and cleaning for monks.[3]

In the 1970s, a new group called Asoke was founded, further shaping the landscape of Thai Buddhism. After breaking away from mainstream norms and being expelled from the official Thai *saṅgha* in the 1990s, Asoke was considered an unusual and controversial expression of Buddhism in Thailand. Currently, nine main centers exist across Thailand, consisting of both monastic and lay communities that house schools, health centers, vegetarian restaurants, stores, recycling centers, organic agricultural production, and other community resources. Numerous other smaller Asoke projects are also found throughout the country, such as rice fields, gardens, and educational farms.[4]

Marja-Leena Heikkilä-Horn observes that: "the Asoke group consists predominantly of a network of four major wings engaged in spiritual, agricultural, social, and political activities. What unites the wings is their self-identification as disciples of Bodhirak."[5] Approximately one hundred *samana*s and twenty-five *sikkhamat*s live in Asoke communities throughout Thailand, numbers that have fluctuated little in the past decades. Along with the ordained members of Asoke, lay-persons and students at the Asoke schools live in the communities. Lay members range from being highly involved, living or working in an Asoke center, to supporters who only participate in special events throughout the year. Others involved with Asoke include farmers interested in the Asoke style of organic agriculture or vegetarianism, former students of the Asoke schools, and those with similar political beliefs, such as supporters of Major-General Chamlong.

Today in most Theravāda countries there are few opportunities for women to receive *bhikkhunī* ordination, which is equivalent to the ordination of a fully ordained monk or *bhikkhu*. In some cases, as in Thailand, *bhikkhunī* ordination is prohibited by law. Evidence suggests that *bhikkhunī*s existed in India and Sri Lanka until the end of the first millennium, but it is unclear whether fully ordained nuns lived in Southeast Asia.[6] A slow revival has begun in recent decades, based on unbroken *bhikkhunī* lineages from East Asian traditions. In Sri Lanka, *bhikkhunī*s are now socially accepted, and a few small international *bhikkhunī* communities have developed in Western countries, such as the United States and Australia. The struggle for acceptance for fully ordained nuns in Thailand continues to face a variety of legal, cultural, and political hurdles, including some vocal opponents and efforts to deter monks from ordaining or supporting the ordination of women.[7] The internationally known scholar Bhikkhuni Dhammananda estimates that approximately one hundred fully ordained *bhikkhunī*s currently reside in Thailand, in comparison to an estimated 300,000 monks, but they still face challenges and possible arrest for wrongfully impersonating monks.[8]

The topic of ordination has come to the forefront of discussions in the academic study of women and Buddhism in a wide array of Buddhist contexts in recent years. Theravāda nuns around the world, including *mae chee*s in Thailand, *dasa sil mata*s in Sri Lanka, *thilashin* in Burma, and fully ordained *bhikkhunī*s the world over, are gaining greater exposure with an increase of literature and dialogue. Many authors have explored the various expressions of ordination in countries where *bhikkhunī* ordination is not available and have offered insights from renunciant women regarding their own beliefs and experiences. For several decades now, the topic of higher ordination for women and the technicalities involved in the ordination process, such as the eight *garudhammas,* dual ordination, and lineage legitimacy have been of scholarly interest throughout the world.[9]

Introduction to Asoke

The Asoke group was founded in 1975 by the Thai monk, Bodhiraksa. Born in 1934 as Mongkol Rakpong, he became known as Rak Rakpong before ordaining, and later became known by his current title of Bodhiraksa.[10] He studied at Poh Chang Art College in Bangkok, and went on to work at the Thai Television Company, where he gained popularity as a TV entertainer, singer, and songwriter. Rak Rakpong became a household name among TV viewers. In his personal life, he became more interested in Buddhist teachings and began to simplify his lifestyle, which included shaving his head, walking barefoot, and eating a vegetarian diet. He ordained in 1970 at Wat Asokaram, a Thammayut monastery, and was given the Pāli name Bodhiraksa, often shortened to Bodhirak.[11] Three years after his ordination, he resigned from that Thammayut monastery and was re-ordained in 1973 at a Mahanikai monastery.[12] As Bodhirak explained in an interview, he continued to be dissatisfied with the way Dhamma was being practiced and chose to leave and create his own monastic center in 1975.[13] Although Bodhirak returned his monk's certificate when he left Wat Asokaram, he did not formally disrobe from the Mahanikai order at the time he formed his own center, which caused confusion as to his status as a monk within the mainstream *saṅgha.*[14]

Asoke community membership continued to grow. The first community, located near Nakhon Pathom, was called Daen Asoke, referring to Wat Asokaram and the fact that Bodhirak had given Dhamma talks under Ashoka trees. The group began publishing small booklets under the name "Asoke," and the residents became known as "Chao Asoke" or "People of Asoke." This new community emphasized the *vinaya* and a simple way of life that encouraged the monastics to practice diligently.[15] The female and male monastics both wore dark brown robes and did not shave their eyebrows as is required practice in the Thai *saṅgha.* For these reasons, along with Bodhirak's strong political beliefs and their strictly vegetarian one meal per day, the Asoke movement began to be seen as controversial by various monastic authorities in the Mahatherasamakom (Council of Elders, or Ecclesiastical Council).[16] The abbot of a nearby temple began to receive pressure from the provincial *saṅgha* governor and the Council of Elders to force change within the Asoke community regarding their brown robes.[17] Since Bodhirak and the monastics refused to change their attire, the abbot was admonished and Asoke was ordered to dismantle all living accommodations at Daen Asoke.[18] Daen Asoke moved to a nearby location and was renamed Pathom Asoke, where it has become one of the larger communities. In 1976, Santi Asoke on the outskirts of Bangkok, Sri Saket in northeastern Thailand, and Sali Asoke in Phai Sali in central Thailand were established.

In August 1975, Asoke was formally created as an independent group. The monastics were re-ordained and Bodhirak announced that the Asoke community would not conform to or be regulated by the authority of the Thai Ecclesiastical Council.[19] Jackson argues that as a consequence of Bodhirak's break from the mainstream, the Asoke movement "effectively represents the formation of a third, although as yet unofficial, *nikaya*[20] or order within the Thai *Sangha*."[21] Bodhirak is quoted as saying, "I do not wish to be either Mahanikay or Thammayutnikay because in the time of the Buddha there was no *nikaya*."[22] In an early article by Sanitsuda Ekachai, Bodhirak states that his intention of creating a new place of monastic practice was not to create a division between the mainstream sects but to bring together the best of both by "going back to the fundamental teachings and practices of ancient times," and that his "mission is to revive Buddhism in Thailand."[23]

Physiomorality, Identity, and the Buddhist Women's Robes

In the mid-1970s, before much discussion about the status of women monastics had taken place, Bodhirak began creating a new category of female clergy by ordaining *sikkhamat*s, brown-robed nuns, who live by ten precepts. This has significance for various reasons: not only were these women visually represented as monastics by wearing brown instead of white, they were also integral community members, leaders, and teachers. White symbolizes a lay renunciant, and is worn by *mae chee*s and novices, whereas brown and saffron are reserved for fully ordained monastics, thereby providing visual cues as to how they should be treated inside and outside of their communities. As we explore the implications of these cues, we will find that in Bodhirak's commitment to creating a visually identifiable presence for Asoke in Thai culture, even subtleties in color variation and monastic appearance are important markers, ripe with meaning. The choice of brown as the robe color for women denoted that this new and valuable system of Thai Buddhist monasticism was serious and to be respected.

Thailand has a long tradition of color association for the days of the week, for the representation of royal figures, and for determining the status of religious persons. In Theravāda Buddhism, saffron, ochre, and brown tones are typically associated with monastic attire. The dying of the robes was intended to distinguish the followers of the Buddha from the followers of other renunciant groups and to diminish the value of the cloth.[24] The *vinaya* provides detailed guidelines for dying, drying, and creating appropriate colors for the cloth used to make robes.[25] Although a range of saffron, ochre, and brown tones may be worn, in Thailand monastic attire is most often a bright orange or saffron color.[26] Some monks, such as those associated with the Thai Forest Tradition, typically wear darker hues, including ochre and brown tones, which has become associated with more austere monastic practice. After the founding of Asoke, all monastics wore brown robes—the *sikkhamat*'s long sleeves and a slightly lighter colored outer robe was the only visual means of differentiating between the nuns and their male counterparts.

An account from a monk who has lived in Asoke since 1981 illustrates the important associations between monastic practice and the color of the robes in Thailand. Before he knew about the existence of the Asoke group, Samana Tissa had ordained in the mainstream *saṅgha*. He did not consider the typical bright orange color appropriate for a serious monastic practice, however, and on his own chose to dye his robes a darker hue. Because of his appearance, in darker robes, he was approached by laypeople who asked whether he was a member of Asoke. These encounters eventually led to his coming into contact with Bodhirak and joining the group.[27] This brief account demonstrates the significant nuances of colors as a form of communication and representation of beliefs in Thai monastic practice. Bodhirak used darker colored robes to symbolize a more austere and dedicated practice, conveying a sense of authenticity and visually emphasizing the seriousness of the newly formed group. The darker color further distinguished Asoke as a separate entity and reinforced an aspect of material culture that is equally distinct to female and male Asoke renunciants.

The intentional use of a distinctively darker color for the robes of both male and female Asoke renunciants took on greater significance with the emergence of a small group of women wearing robes that signified something other than lay status. Not only did gender differences become somewhat muted by the color of the robes, but female renunciants in Asoke also assumed active roles within their communities and lived a lifestyle that varied little from their male counterparts. Exploring the significance and nuances of color in this context is an important aspect of understanding the implications of female renunciant attire in Asoke and other Theravāda countries.

Although *sikkhamat*s, *thilashin*, and *dasa sil mata*s differ in many ways, they are all examples of precept nuns whose robes visually set them apart from the white attire of laypeople. The precept nuns of Burma known as *thilashin* wear pink robes, with an orange underrobe and an orange or brown shawl. *Thilashin* receive scriptural and meditation training similar to monks, are able to take the same examinations, and have considerably larger communities than Thai *mae chee*s. For these reasons among others, *thilashin* appear to have a higher social status than *mae chee*s. Ingrid Jordt mentions that "controversy raged" in the early nineteenth century over renunciant women wearing a color other than white. According to Jordt, *thilashin* are currently seen wearing only colored robes, "never the white, which is the mark of the lay practitioner," and this "has further served to blur the role of *thilashin* in the religious structure by symbolically juxtaposing them with the monk's order."[28] According to Jordt, *thilashin* are currently seen wearing only colored robes, "and never the white, which is the mark of the lay practitioner." She concludes that this "has further served to blur the role of *thilashin* in the religious structure by symbolically juxtaposing them with the monk's order."

In Sri Lanka, nearly all *dasa sil mata*s wear yellow or orange robes, though Nirmala Salgado reflects that "heated debates" occurred regarding the right of *dasa sil mata*s to wear colored robes.[29] Harris mentions that "all *dasa sil mata*s risk being accused of wearing the orange robe falsely," and cites an example of a prominent monk who condemned nuns for wearing anything other than white, since he believed "they are no more than lay-people."[30] Again, the differentiation in visual cues between lay and ordained practitioners is reflected in Salgado's observation that in Sri Lanka, "a renunciant in white is usually thought of differently from one wearing attire that is yellow, orange, or brown—colors that are used by *dasa sil mata*s, and by *bhik-khu*s and *bhikkhunī*s, who are generally considered to practice a stricter form of renunciation."[31]

The examples of these various groups of women wearing colored robes—*thilashin*, *dasa sil mata*s, *sikkhamat*s, and *bhikkuni*s in Thailand—involve reoccurring themes of tension and animosity in relation to their attire, specifically regarding its color. The intertwining of morality and color becomes relevant both to assumptions about gender and about a practitioner's seriousness and dedication to renunciant practice, linked in a hierarchical relationship. This connection between morality and bodily expression (or in Mrozik's terms, "physiomorality") is signaled through "various forms of bodily inscription such as dress, posture, and movement," which for Buddhist monastics are "most obviously constituted as such by shaven head, monastic robes, and the absence of conventional forms of adornment such as jewelry."[32] In considering the colors of the robes of female renunciants, even subtle shifts in robe color can influence the expression and reception of morality. Although the color white signifies purity in Buddhist cultures, it is also associated with the religious practice of householders and the temporary or periodic observance of precepts on *uposatha* days, in contradistinction to the colored robes of dedicated monastics observing the precepts continuously. Considerations of physiomorality are pivotal to a deeper exploration of Asoke aesthetics and lifestyle.

Asoke Aesthetics and Politics

From the beginning, political participation has been a prominent feature of Asoke. Members of the group have participated in rallies and political events and have played a role in shaping the Thai political arena in the past decades. These political interactions have also informed the aesthetics of Asoke, particularly those of monastics. One prominent example of this can be seen in the Asoke court cases of 1989, which received both media and scholarly attention.[33] Due to the long-term implications of these formative years within Asoke, a brief account of the early political involvement and the legal action against Bodhirak and Asoke monastics is necessary.

Asoke also gained publicity through its collaboration with Major-General Chamlong, a devout Buddhist who served for six years as Governor of Bangkok, among other politically influential positions.[34] Due to Asoke's political involvement in the 1988 elections, the group again came under scrutiny, despite the disappointing election results.

The group received a list of demands from the Department of Religious Affairs and the Council of Elders requiring Asoke to conform to their regulations. The rejection of these mandates by Asoke led to a gathering of 150 senior monks who came to a consensus to formally defrock Bodhirak.[35] In June 1989, the *Bangkok Post* reported that Bodhirak would comply with the disrobing and had agreed to change his attire to a "new long-sleeved uniform similar to the robes worn by Mahanayan or Annam sects in China, Tibet and Mongolia."[36] Bodhirak stated: "We [Asoke] have no attachment toward uniform or name," and the council had no objection to the new uniform because, according to their description, the Asoke monastics would no longer be Buddhist monks.[37] Regardless of the uniform change, Bodhirak was arrested soon thereafter on charges of failing to comply within seven days of receiving the order to disrobe, a criminal charge carrying up to six months in prison, and he was forced to change into white clothes.

On August 8, 1989, all 106 monks and *sikkhamats* were arrested. A day later, twenty-six of them were released after findings concluded that they were "properly ordained as monks."[38] The remaining seventy-nine monastics, including all of the *sikkhamats*, were regarded as illegally donning Buddhist robes, because they were ordained solely by Bodhirak.[39] White robes were issued to all the monastics while in custody to represent the invalidity of their ordinations. This is another example of how colors play a prominent role in Thai society, particularly as they differentiate monastics and householders, where saffron represents monkhood and white represents a nonordained, lay status. The discharge of the Asoke monastics from police custody was only temporary. They were asked to return to the public prosecutor's office the following October "for a decision on whether investigators had gathered sufficient evidence to support prosecution."[40]

The change of Bodhirak's robes from brown to white while he was in custody was meant to remove his status as a monk. Because of the privileged status of monks, this was seen as a way to demote Bodhirak to lay status. After the court cases, which were postponed until 1995, all Asoke monks and *sikkhamats* wore white during a two-year probation period, and then reverted to wearing brown again. As straightforward as this may seem, with white signifying lay status and brown symbolizing ordained status, the change was significant in allowing a group of brown-robed female renunciants to maintain their distinctive renunciant identity. I would argue that this simple change of color altered the *sikkhamats'* status, both inside and outside the Asoke communities.

After the court cases and probation period ended, the monks (now referred to as *samanas*) and the *sikkhamats* changed the color and style of their robes to distinguish themselves from mainstream monastics in terms of dress. It was important for the *sikkhamat*s to wear colored robes, both so that they would be recognized as monastics and differentiated from *mae chee*s. Despite the risk of again being charged with impersonating monks, which potentially entailed imprisonment, the *sikkhamat*s chose brown and gray robes, which they continue to wear today. Regardless of the ordeals they experienced, Bodhirak and Asoke members continue to be politically involved up to the present.

Art, Morality, and Embodiment in Asoke

When discussing the aesthetics of the Asoke *sikkhamat*s, various intersecting factors must be taken into account—not just their dress, but how they live and engage with their community. Bodhirak has a particular interest in the embodiment of aesthetics and art, and describes the necessity of both action and appearance to encompass the Asoke interpretation of the Dhamma wholeheartedly. Michael Carrithers comments on this approach: "The aesthetic standard so understood is different from a morality or rules in that it is partly embodied, that is, it exists partly as a quality of bodily movement, or as a physical posture or as a propensity in speech and action."[41] One focus throughout daily life for Asoke monastics and members is to express Bodhirak's teachings and their understanding of the Dhamma in action rather than still, closed-eye meditation. Carrithers finds this focus on movement important because "the aesthetic standard is essentially fuzzy and indeterminate . . . it does not fully prescribe actions, but only a quality of actions."[42] This "quality of actions" further connects with explorations of physiomorality—expressing how movement and posture can be indicators of moral practice and a practice of embodied Dhamma. For Bodhirak, the central point is for Asoke community members to be committed to a quality of action that contains the spirit of Dhamma, which in Asoke is predominantly based on *sīla*, or moral practice.

Bodhirak's interest in aesthetics can be seen throughout the Asoke communities, with an abundance of murals, statues, paintings, carvings, reliefs, and other forms of art. He describes himself as an artist, instead of a painter or sculptor, stating that his "element, or medium is the happenings of life, catching every detail and composing them into a living art."[43] Bodhirak's interweaving of aesthetics and morality can be understood in the connections between art and life, expressing the Dhamma and Asoke beliefs. His outline of five levels or kinds of art provide insight into Asoke aesthetics and ideals for its monastics, lay members, and centers.[44]

The first level of art, described as the lowest, is lustful art that contains or insinuates conceptions of erotica or depicts violence, including through color, in ways that arouse passions in the viewer. This kind of art is described as very raw and superficial.

The second level of art, Bodhirak explains, is less raw than the first stage, but more persuasive. Using the metaphor of bitter medicine coated in sweetness, this kind of art uses color or other appealing aesthetics to cover the bitter intention of the art. This art is seen as persuading the viewer toward luxury, sensuality, anger, and other defilements. This stage is less graphic, but viewing it will eventually lead to indulgence. Realizing that human beings are vulnerable to the defilements (*kilesas*), artists selectively, seductively mix them into their art.[45] Bodhirak explains the need for literature or painting to add color and sweetness to what might otherwise be bitter or unpleasant. Without this kind of beautification, the content would be purely academic, like a documentary.

The third level of art still attempts to coat its messages, because the artist understands that, without using the persuasion of the (*kilesas*), viewers will find the essential meaning of the art too academic. Artists of this kind seem to believe that the pure look of the art will not be of interest to people, so they turn to more technical methods of composition, harmony, focus, and so on.

The fourth kind of art incorporates Dhamma, the teachings of the Buddha, through various representations, including the ideals and teachings of Bodhirak. The stage is set when the artist adds the "aroma, glance, or glare" of Dhamma to the work. Because it contains the essence of Dhamma, Bodhirak believes that this type of art benefits those who come in contact with it. The goodness of this art is not merely representational, but inherently meritorious on various levels.

The fifth and final level of art is transcendent, supramundane (*lokuttara*) art. Bodhirak reveals that he has not yet seen any art of this kind,[46] but that it is his mission to achieve it. "Every day, I am living and working on art," he says. "Few people understand that I am an artist, painting the world and painting life."[47] Integrating the spirit, or spiritual values and mindful qualities, into his life art is the essential key. Thus, for Bodhirak and Asoke, these stages are not only descriptors of art, but reflections of the foundation of aesthetics and moral intent, intertwined to create a living expression of Asoke Dhamma. These concepts are integrated into Asoke in a variety of ways, represented and communicated through the aesthetics of the members and in their communities. These teachings are reinforced in the daily lives of monastics, lay members, and students through Bodhirak's daily Dhamma talks, Asoke literature, and the media, including Asoke's television channel (FMTV), Dhamma study, practice, and discussion. Members often emphasize the importance of action—working and embodying Asoke beliefs—reflected in their daily activities and schedules. Samana Kayakayan emphasizes this:

> [Asoke monastics and lay members] practice seriously—we are serious practitioners. When you believe things, you are just believing. . . . The purpose of Asoke is to really behave it—you have to behave it, and live it.[48]

One physical manifestation of the Asoke aesthetics, particularly moral conduct, is the attention Asoke monastics and lay members give to their posture and physical movements. The body both expresses and provides access to Buddhist teachings. As Steven Collins explains, "The composed, pure, and autonomous body of the monk or nun presented in social life instantiates for lay supporters the immediate existence of that sacred, immaterial, and underlying Truth which their own bodily concerns make impossibly distant from them, and with which they can thus be connected by their material support of its human embodiments."[49] In Asoke, lay supporters are also encouraged to strive to embody these qualities, and those living in and around the communities often act with composure similar to that of the monastics. Many monastics and lay members explain they were first attracted to Asoke way of life through observing these physical qualities.[50] For some, seeing the physical embodiment of a hardworking, ascetic, and modest life was a catalyst spurring them to ordain in Asoke or become committed to the group.

The potency of the monastic image is particularly significant in Buddhist countries. For Asoke, the portrayal of the renunciant ideal is interwoven in their validation of the group as a more moral, austere, and "true" version of Buddhism. Asoke monastics and lay members alike are taught to be highly self-controlled and respectful while walking, sitting, standing, or lying. When meeting a monk in an informal situation, such as in passing on a road, members kneel on the ground and *wai*, pressing their palms together while bowing, until the interaction is complete. Gestures of respect such as this, performed with eyes downcast, are active expressions of the Dhamma in daily live at Asoke. Walking, talking, and interacting with these embodied Dhamma qualities express the pure intentions and aspirations of monastics, lay members, and students who are taught in the Asoke schools. The practice of striving to embody the Dhamma is not unique to Asoke; many passages in the *vinaya* prescribe the physical movements appropriate for monastics. By placing an emphasis on moral development, Asoke has created a distinct interpretation of *vinaya* practice for both lay and ordained members, expressed and embodied by individuals in the physical spaces where they live and work. These values are exemplified in every aspect of the Asoke communities, including the austere practice of precepts, modesty, attire, architecture, and physical layout of living spaces.

Bodhirak's articulation of five levels of art, correlating morality and an aesthetic sensibility, can be used as a basis for transformation, with tangible expression in the bodies and spaces of Asoke. It is within this complex tapestry, woven with aesthetics and embodiment, visual cues expressing Dhamma and morality, that the Asoke *sikkhamat*s emerge.

Lives and Aesthetics of *Sikkhamats*

*Sikkhamat*s are highly respected members of the Asoke community, with a wide range of duties, depending on their interests, skills, and capabilities. They take on leadership roles and are responsible for female aspirants, residents, and guests. The *sikkhamat*s' responsibilities are distributed throughout the Asoke communities. Many teach in the schools and perform other educational functions for Asoke members and unaffiliated visiting groups. Others counsel laypeople and female aspirants, give Dhamma talks, and appear on Asoke's television network. According to their individual skills, the *sikkhamat*s contribute as respected and highly visible members of the community. They are also engaged in political activity. For example, during 2013 and 2014, the majority of members of the Asoke communities, including *sikkhamat*s and *samana*s, relocated for months to downtown Bangkok to participate in anti-Taksin, anti-Yinluck rallies. Living under tarps and sleeping on cement, they endured tear gas and bomb threats to publicly express their views.

A considerable number of the *sikkhamat*s are well educated, some speaking many languages. Consequently, the multilingual *sikkhamat*s spend time with all varieties of visitors and, in many ways, become

Asoke's connection to other parts of the world. Through their frequent engagements with visitors, both from Thailand and abroad, the *sik-khamats* have gained much public exposure. Yet, although they have respected roles and are fully engaged in their communities, discrepancies remain between the *samanas* and *sikkhamats*. One of these is the fixed ratio regarding the number of *sikkhamats* at Asoke at any given time. According to this policy, *sikkhamats* may comprise between a quarter and a third of the monastic community. Generally, the ratio is four to one: four *samanas* to one *sikkhamat*. When the number of *samanas* increases to over one hundred, the ratio becomes three to one. If the quota is already filled, which has typically been the case because there is little fluctuation in the number of Asoke monastics, the *krak* (female aspirants) must either wait for more *samanas* to ordain or wait until there are fewer *sikkhamats*, either due to passing away or disrobing. Heikkilä-Horn speculates that this ratio exists so that the *sikkhamats* do not outnumber the *samanas*; as she puts it, "If all the Asoke laywomen were ordained, this would most certainly be the case."[51] During an interview, Bodhirak stated that he felt the ratio was simply an appropriate balance for their community.[52]

When one ordains in the Asoke community, the decision is assumed to be a lifetime commitment, and typically it is. Only approximately ten *sikkhamats* have disrobed in the history of Asoke.[53] *Sikkhamats* who disrobe do so often for personal reasons and remain active contributors to the Asoke communities. A requirement states that applicants be under fifty years old when ordaining as a *sikkhamat*; however, considering the relatively long waiting period and the slowly aging Asoke population, this rule may become obsolete.

The physical appearance of Asoke monastics and laypeople is considered a mirror of Asoke beliefs, not just in the quality of actions but in the visual social cues transmitted by the robes. The monastics' dark brown robes signal not only their renunciation, but an austere version of it. Within Asoke, the *sikkhamats* visually complete a vision of the four-fold *saṅgha* (monks, nuns, laywomen, and laymen) that constitutes a stable, ideal Buddhist society.

Cloth as visual symbol reveals and communicates a great deal, especially if it is flexible and can be shaped to transmit a variety of messages. As Jane Schneider and Annette Weiner express it, cloth has an "intimate association with the body . . . putting it in a metonymic relationship to the self. Signifying rank, status, sexuality, power, ideals, it individuates the person. But it can also dissolve a person's social identity as in uniforms and sackcloth."[54] Cloth shaped and identifiable as monastic robes has a particularly salient potency as a representation of piousness, morality, and the sacred. Robes are perhaps the most visually defining characteristic of the monastic community, marking a sense of identity for those who wear or are surrounded by them. One could argue that monastics' appearance is as significant to their identity as their beliefs, in that the robes reflect their beliefs. The importance of the monastics' visual appearance can be gauged from the various *vinaya* rules that specify the acquisition, use, and appropriate mode of wearing the robes.

Sikkhamats are not the only women in Asoke to whom visual markers of renunciation apply; changes in dress mark a series of progressive transformations that signal increased renunciation for aspirants and lay members.[55] Both women and men interested in ordaining must undergo an extensive process, and distinctive markers such as clothing style, color, and a shaven head visually represent these various stages toward monastic life. These changes in appearance further reinforce the power of visual cues to identify how certain members and their roles are recognized within the community. A shift in outward appearance, especially a drastic change such as shaving one's head or wearing monastic attire, also alters the religious and social experience of the aspirant.

The process of becoming a *sikkhamat* can be lengthy, with guidelines prescribing the length of each step. Aspirants may advance in the standard amount of time or more slowly, as the community of *sikkhamat*s assesses their readiness.[56] One of the first aesthetic alterations a person undertakes when entering Asoke, either as a temporary or permanent guest, is to forgo beautification by any means, including makeup, jewelry, and adornments such as amulets and fashionable clothes.[57] Many choose to wear blue "peasant" attire consisting of a long-sleeved, high-collared shirt and a sarong (or pants for men), which has become a kind of Asoke "uniform." If a permanent resident has lived at Asoke for at least a year and a half, and wishes to ordain, she may undergo the necessary interviews and begin living as a *pa*.[58] A *pa* changes from the typical blue uniform to a brown sarong and lighter colored blouse. Brown is important because it signals the color of a renunciant, but at this stage the style of clothing remains similar to the lay clothes of an aspirant. Use of the color brown serves a dual purpose: it represents piousness and is also a practical color to wear for those engaged in physical labor and agricultural work. A *pa* is not required to shave her head, but her hair must be worn shorter than ten centimeters.

After at least six months of living as a *pa*, the aspirant may progress to become a *krak*. To indicate this further stage of renunciation, her hair must be shaved regularly and she may wear a brown shawl for meals, ceremonies, and other important events. These changes—the shaved head and the use of a brown shawl resembling the outer robe of a monastic—more closely mirror the appearance of a renunciant and thereby signal a progression toward a more monastic lifestyle. The aspirant begins to visually occupy a space between the lay and monastic communities. After living as a *krak* for a year and a half, if all requirements are met, an ordination ceremony may be held at which the *krak* undertakes the discipline of observing the ten precepts and is given the robes and a bowl of a *sikkhamat*. The robes she receives are brown in color, with a gray outer robe. This final shift in the color and style of the robes is accompanied by instruction in how to appropriately fold, wrap, and wear the robes. Learning how to wear the robes further influences the aesthetics of the *sikkhamat*'s physicality, namely, her posture and movement. *Sikkhamat*s are often seen quietly folding, rearranging, and adjusting their outer robes so as to wear them as neatly as possible.

Through these visual transitions, members of the community and visitors from outside begin to interact with the aspirant differently than before, which reinforces the new role that the practitioner has assumed. These changes represent increased renunciation with each step, expressing a moral progression and dedication on the spiritual path and in the Asoke community. In this way, visual cues communicate the virtue and discipline of the monastics, which in turn conveys a certain authority, respect, and status in the community.

Buddhist monastics typically have three robes that they arrange or wear in different styles, depending on the appropriate context.[59] The *antaravāsaka*, or inner robe, covers the lower half of the body from above the navel to below the knees and is secured by folding and cinching around the waist with a cord or belt. The *uttarāsanga*, or upper robe, wraps around the body, either leaving the left shoulder bare or covering both shoulders, as is common when monastics leave the grounds of the monastery. Last, the *sanghāti* is an extra outer robe that can be worn either folded across the right shoulder, wrapped around the body, or used for warmth. For monks, it has become the custom in Thailand to wear an *angsa*, a one-shouldered vest or undergarment worn under the *uttarāsanga*, typically fastened at the waist. Instead of wearing an *uttarāsanga*, or *angsa*, the *sikkhamat*s wear a long-sleeved, knee-length tunic sewn at the sides and with slits outside the thighs to allow mobility. Because Asoke places such emphasis on work, including physical labor, many *sikkhamats* and *samanas* wear informal attire while engaged in these activities, and may leave behind their outer robes or add sweaters, hats, or socks in cold weather. Considerable flexibility can be seen regarding dress within the confines of the monastery; monastics may often be seen wearing just an *antaravāsaka* and *angsa*, especially while working. The *sanghāti* is worn during alms rounds, sermons, meals, and more formal community interactions—brown for the *samanas*, gray for the *sikkhamats*. The style and color of the robes to be worn by the *sikkhamats* was a communal decision adopted after the court cases and after a probationary period of wearing white. The *sikkhamats* explain that their gray and brown tunics were designed to be an amalgamation of the long-sleeved robes worn in China, Tibet, and Mongolia, along with traditional Indian elements.[60] The result is a modest, functional, and monastic-looking set of robes.

Unlike Thai monks, Asoke monastics do not shave their eyebrows. As insignificant as eyebrows may seem, in the Thai monastic context, this is a relevant and meaningful detail. Sikkhamat Rinpah explains why Thai monks began shaving their eyebrows:

> Lord Buddha said you have to shave your hair, beard and moustache . . . because, if not, your hair will get longer and longer . . . but, your eyebrows will never grow longer than this. That is reasonable—the Lord Buddha never does anything unreasonable. But then why do Thai monks shave their eyebrows? Because in ancient times, Ayutthaya was the capital of Thailand—the Burmese, enemies of Thailand, came to Thailand to fight in Ayutthaya. They sent people who snuck into Thailand wearing robes like Thai monks. So, we know this, and the Thai monks said, "If you are a Thai monk, shave your eyebrows so we can catch the Burmese monks." . . . So after that the Thai monks have no eyebrows . . . now only monks in Thailand have shaved eyebrows.[61]

The simple gesture of keeping their eyebrows is another aspect of the Asoke aesthetic, one that further separates Asoke monastics from the mainstream. This has not gone unnoticed, and the point has been used to criticize Asoke. In 1988, Sangwian Poorahong, the president of the Parian Dhamma Association, criticized Asoke monks because they "did not shave their eyebrows and had renounced the Ecclesi-astical Council." He feared that "other monks worldwide would also renounce the Ecclesiastical Council and stop shaving their eyebrows." If Asoke were not stopped, "trouble will reign in Sangha society."[62] Sangwian's comment is telling, and underscores the importance of visual conformity. Citing unshaven eyebrows and the rejection of the Council of Elders as the main points of dissonance and rebellion highlights the gravity of both acts, even though the shaving of eye-brows could have been viewed as a much less subversive act than crossing the council of *sangha* elders. Chamlong came to the defense of the Asoke monastics, saying, "the centre follows the teachings of the Buddha and is in no way out of line," and further, "people who wonder why the monks at the centre did not shave their eyebrows, wear robes of a different color, and eat no meat should go there and make up their own mind."[63]

A complaint was made to the police in 2006 from a group called the Buddhist Network, stating that Bodhirak was imitating a Bud-dhist monk and Asoke is "in total contradiction to Buddhist precepts by . . . expressing political opinions."[64] Bodhirak replied: "I have changed the color of my robe and stopped shaving my eyebrows. So, I don't have anything more to say and it's up to them if they still view me as a monk impersonator."[65] This comment implies that Bodhirak stopped shaving his eyebrows to further distinguish Asoke from the mainstream, rather than adherence to scriptural traditions. Under the circumstances, unshaven eyebrows fulfill a dual purpose: to express Asoke's "authenticity" and devotion to scriptural accounts about how monks lived during the time of the Buddha, and also to visually dis-tance themselves from mainstream Thai monastics. Although the shift may seem inconsequential, this example underscores the importance of a monastic appearance, even in regard to details such as shaving one's eyebrows.

Being barefoot is nearly a necessity for the Asoke monastics and lay followers. It is unusual to see anyone wearing footwear, either inside or outside of their communities. This is partially due to the emphasis on an ascetic lifestyle and also to the believed health benefits of walking barefoot, which are likened to receiving natural reflexol-ogy, or foot massage, throughout the day.

Unordained members of the community can also manifest their beliefs through their appearance by adopting the lay "uniform," a dark blue peasant suit, and short cropped hair, in addition to going barefoot. All the school children wear similar blue uniforms with *bodhi* leaf patches on the breast pocket to identify them. During larger festivals and at yearly gatherings of Asoke schools from multiple communities, different-colored scarves are added to the students' uniforms to designate the center at which they study. Themes of embodied morality, simplicity, hard work, and spiritual striving are expressions of "authentic" Buddhism that run throughout many aspects of Asoke aesthetics. This is not confined only to the visual culture of Asoke, but also influences members' daily practices, community projects, manufacturing of goods, and provision of services, in addition to physical spaces.

Members of Asoke not only strive to maintain a clean, orderly appearance externally, but also stress the importance of internally cleansing. Cleanses of the liver, intestines, and bowels are done by many monastic and lay residents on a regular basis, with designated detox centers run by nurses, herbalists, and health practitioners located in the communities. Vegetarianism and organic farming play integral parts in the concept of inner purification. This is not the sole reason why the Asoke communities are strictly organic and vegetarian. They believe that eating meat is a violation of the first precept: to refrain from taking life. Asoke community members extend the interpretation of this precept to mean striving to protect and nurture life. Since pesticides and chemical fertilizers harm the earth and the body, Asoke has developed its own organic fertilizers and agricultural systems to revegetate barren land.

Temple dwellings reflect Asoke's aesthetic beliefs and lifestyle, too, with small clusters of *kutī*s (huts) with thatched roofs. The *sikkhamat*s, female residents, and female guests are always grouped together, while the monks, male residents, and male guests stay nearby. Each *sikkhamat* has her own hut, consisting of a mosquito net on a raised platform with a thatched roof. Many permanent residents also live in these small *kutī*s. The Asoke temple aesthetic integrates many organic elements, such as natural building materials, and often features water in the form of ponds, streams, and waterfalls. The centers include common halls, communal kitchens, meditation *sālā*s, libraries, schools, vegetable gardens, health centers, media rooms, and factories for producing tofu, soy sauce, soaps, herbal remedies, and other natural products. In many monastic dwellings at Asoke centers corpses are preserved and graphic images of disease and death displayed to inspire reflection on the impermanence of the somatic form.

Although Asoke communities typically strive for an aesthetic of simplicity, they also embrace media and technology to spread their message. The programs of FMTV, the Asoke-run television station, are produced at Santi Asoke in Bangkok. The channel airs daily talks by Bodhirak, as well as interviews and discussions with other *samanas* and *sikkhamats,* and political reports. The presence of active *sikkhamats* on FMTV contributes a feminine cast to Asoke's public presentations that is often lacking in Thai Buddhist circles.

Conclusion

Asoke's creation of a unique visual appearance for a small group of renunciant women in Thailand reflects an alternative status and lifestyle for female monastics, with active and respected roles for women. Asoke's values, embodied by monastics and lay members alike, shape how the *sikkhamats* engage with each other and with lay community members. These values, which include dedicated political activism, in turn, influence their unique aesthetic. Quietly and consciously rejecting the white robes of a *mae chee* that signify lay status in Thailand, the *sikkhamats* have helped redefine renunciation through their visual representation, wearing brown robes to present themselves as ordained members of the community. Their integrated visual presentation as renunciants, holding involved and revered roles within their communities, demonstrates the importance of actively engaged women in the monastic context.

In exploring Asoke's monastic aesthetic, patterns integrating morality, embodiment, and feminism begin to emerge. The aesthetic is not exclusively feminine, as it encompasses lay and monastic members, female and male, in an intricate system of symbolism. At the same time, it is significant that the *sikkhamats* have pioneered new approaches to monastic practice in tandem with new roles for women that integrate ethics, renunciation, art, and aesthetics. It can hardly go unnoticed that they were able to bring these unique expressions into being in an unorthodox, politically proactive movement outside mainstream Thai monastic forms.

Discussing feminisms in the context of Asoke raises questions about the roles of women in orthodox Thai Buddhism, Thai feminism, renunciation, and cultural norms in a devout Buddhist country facing many social, economic, and political challenges. Ordination requires the subtracting of many "feminine" visual markers, such as hair, cosmetics, jewelry, and fashion. The process of removing these substantial, socially mandated aspects of a woman's appearance can lead to a perceived gender neutrality. For many Thai women, a certain standard of "hyper-femininity" can be observed in a variety of ways and is socially encouraged and rewarded. Few women reject this standard in favor of Buddhist renunciation; in fact, the few women who wear colored robes to signify their monastic status are often mistaken for men. This speaks to the blurring of gendered markers and representations, suggesting that ordination can be perceived as a form of "un-gendering," moving toward a kind of visual neutrality. The aesthetic of the *sikkhamat*s communicates a variety of messages related to assumptions about practice, morality, political involvement, and community roles. They visually embody an "un-gendered" status and an aesthetic equality with their male counterparts, while not denying their feminine form. For that, they are neither dismissed as being other nor depreciated for practicing a less serious form of renunciation.

Bodhirak has been the creative guiding force for Asoke from the beginning, and together with the *sikkhamat*s, has developed a system that allows women to be represented and live as monastics. This format relies on the strength of women who are willing to challenge social norms that commonly deprecate women, discourage them from ordaining, and exclude them from the ranks of religious participation, leadership, and power. Many *sikkhamat*s describe the hardships of going against the wishes and expectations of their families and social structures to pursue a monastic life. Not only have the *sikkhamat*s chosen to demonstrate their determination and agency in becoming renunciants, they also have successfully managed to do so in a controversial setting.

Notes

1. Research for this paper was undertaken in various Asoke centers: Santi Asoke (Bangkok), Pathom Asoke (Nakhon Pathom), Sali Asoke (Phai Sali), Ratchathani Asoke (Ubon Ratchathani), and smaller garden projects throughout Thailand. This field research, conducted from February 2013 to February 2014 and overlapping the 2013–2014 political crisis, is the foundation of my PhD research at the Freie Universitat, Berlin.

2. Aesthetic in this context refers to an encompassing sensory experience, not confined to concepts of beauty, however with emphasis on visuality.

3. For further studies on *mae chees* see, Monica Falk, *Making Fields of Merit: Buddhist Female Ascetics and Gendered Orders in Thailand* (Copenhagen: Nias Press, 2007); Chatsumarn Kabilsingh, *Thai Women in Buddhism* (Berkeley:

Parallax Press, 1991); Joanna Cook, *Meditation in Modern Buddhism: Renunciation and Change in Thai Monastic Life* (New York: Cambridge University Press, 2010); and Steven Collins and Justin McDaniel, "Buddhist 'Nuns' (mae chi) and the Teaching of Pali in Contemporary Thailand," *Modern Asian Studies* 44(2010): 1373–1408.

4. These smaller centers may or may not have Asoke monastics, members, or students living on the property. Because Asoke owns numerous pieces of land, often used for agriculture, it is difficult to accurately estimate how many exist and which are actively operating as centers. Heikkilä-Horn reports the existence of twenty-seven Asoke centers in 2007. Marja-Leena Heikkilä-Horn, "Santi Asoke Buddhism and the Occupation of Bangkok International Airport," *Austrian Journal of South-East Asian Studies* (2009): 32.

5. Ibid., 34.

6. Collins and McDaniel, "Buddhist 'nuns' (mae chi) and the Teaching of Pali," 1383.

7. For further discussions on *bhikkhunī* ordination in Thailand, see Ayako Itoh, "The Emergence of the Bhikkhunī-Sangha in Thailand: Contexts, Strategies and Challenges" (PhD dissertation, École Pratique des Hautes Études, 2013); Tomomi Ito, "Questions of Ordination Legitimacy for Newly Ordained Theravāda Bhikkhunī in Thailand," *Journal of Southeast Asian Studies* 43(2012): 55–76; Martin Seeger, "The Bhikkhuni-Ordination Controversy in Thailand," *Journal of the International Association of Buddhist Studies* 29(2006 [2008]): 155–83; Varaporn Chamsanit, "Reconnecting the Lost Lineage: Challenges to Institutional Denial of Buddhist Women's Monasticism in Thailand" (PhD dissertation, Australia National University, 2006); Emma Tomalin, "The Thai Bhikkhuni Movement and Women's Empowerment," *Gender and Development* 14:3(2006): 385–97; Tomomi Ito, "Ordained Women in Yellow Robes: An Unfamiliar 'Tradition' in Contemporary Thailand," *Out of the Shadows: Socially Engaged Buddhist Women*, ed. Karma Lekshe Tsomo (Delhi: Sri Satguru, 2006), 168–71.

8. Voramai Kabilsingh (mother of Bhikkhuni Dhammananda) received *bhikkhunī* ordination in Taiwan in 1972 and wore light yellow robes. See Bhikkhuni Dhammananda, "Bhiksuni Ta Tao: Paving the Way for Future Generations," *Eminent Buddhist Women*, ed. Karma Lekshe Tsomo (Albany: State University of New York Press, 2014), 61–70. Although her ordination was not accepted or validated within Thailand, she was able to avoid charges or forceful disrobing. The first attempt to ordain *bhikkhunīs* in Thailand was in 1928 by two sisters who were then jailed and disrobed. See Kabilsingh, *Thai Women in Buddhism*, 45–48. *Bhikkhunīs* in Thailand still face challenges and discrimination as they are not recognized as members of the *saṅgha* and could be charged with impersonating monks. In 2016, a meditation center run by *bhikkhunīs* in Rayong was badly damaged "by arsonists disgruntled with the role of women in the clergy." Nanchanok Wongsamuth, "Female Monks Blame Sexism for Burning Down of Temple Dormitory in Rayong," *Bangkok Post*,

April 17, 2016, www.bangkokpost.com/archive/female-monks-blame-sexism-for-burning-down-of-temple-dormitory-in-rayong/935737. After a group of over seventy *bhikkhunīs*, *mae chees*, and novices were not permitted entrance to pay their respects to the late king's funeral urn through the gate for monastics in January 2017, Dhammananda was quoted as saying, "This current situation just creates a space for discrimination . . . still, it's up to each one's preference whether to exploit it or not." Melalin Mahavongtrakul, "Monks of a Different Gender: Why Are the Bhikkhuni Experiencing So Much Discrimination in Thailand?" *Bangkok Post*, January 18, 2017, www.bangkokpost.com/lifestyle/social-and-lifestyle/1182233/monks-of-a-different-gender.

9. The *garudhammas*, eight "heavy rules" for fully ordained *bhikkhunīs*, are controversial conditions placed on female monastics that cause them to be subordinate and dependent on the community of male monastics. The historical validity of these rules has been questioned. Disputes about dual ordination and lineage legitimacy make it difficult to reinstate *bhikkhunī* ordination in various countries where the order of nuns has died out, because fully ordained nuns are required to ordain new *bhikkhunīs*.

10. In Thai, Bodhirak, Pothirak, or Phothirak are the most common spellings. Jackson states that Bodhirak was given the Pāli clerical name Phothirakkhito or Bodhirakkhito at his ordination. See Peter Jackson, *Buddhism, Legitimation, and Conflict: The Political Functions of Urban Thai Buddhism* (Singapore: Institute of Southeast Asian Studies, 1989), 160.

11. Wat Asokaram was founded in 1955 by Ajahn Lee Dhammadharo (1906–61), a disciple of the famous ascetic Ajahn Mun (Ajahn Mun Bhuridatta Thera, 1870–1949). Ajahn Mun created the Thai Forest tradition with his mentor Ajahn Sao Kantasīlo. The Thai Forest Tradition has spread internationally and is known as a particularly ascetic branch of Theravāda Buddhism, which is one of the main reasons Bodhirak chose to ordain at Wat Asokaram. Pictures of Ajahn Mun hang in many of the Asoke centers.

12. In Thailand, there are two recognized lineages, the larger and older Maha Nikāya (Mahanikai) and the more recent Dhammayuttika Nikāya (Thammayutnikai) created in 1833 by King Mongkut, Rama IV.

13. Interview with Bodhirak at Santi Asoke, Bangkok, January 30, 2014. Accounts conflict among scholars as to why Bodhirak chose to leave the previous monasteries, particularly Wat Asokaram. Heikkilä-Horn writes that Bodhirak resigned from Asokaram because he was not allowed to organize joint meetings of monks from both the Thammayutnikai and Mahanikai. See Marja-Leena Heikkilä-Horn, *Buddhism with Open Eyes: Belief and Practice of Santi Asoke* (Bangkok: Fah Apai, Ltd., 1997), 44. Jackson asserts that Bodhirak created schisms in the monastery by criticizing other monks for eating meat, smoking, chewing betel nut, being lazy, and in some cases practicing supernatural rituals and magic. See Jackson, *Buddhism, Legitimation, and Conflict*, 159. Swearer also writes that Bodhirak was "forced to disrobe as a *Thammayut* monk because of his unorthodox activities." See Donald Swearer, *The*

Buddhist World of Southeast Asia (Albany: State University of New York Press, 2010), 173. In interviews I conducted with Asoke monastics and members, all these accounts were said to be false. They said that Bodhirak did not try to organize meetings, did not criticize other monastics, and left of his own accord because he wanted a more ascetic practice.

14. Disrobing entails a range of formalities, depending on the tradition and the reason for disrobing. Within the mainstream lineages in Thailand, temporary ordination is quite common, particularly as a rite of passage for boys and young men, and entering and leaving monasteries is quite simple. When returning to lay life, a ceremony generally takes place in which the 227 rules followed by monks are replaced with the five basic Buddhist precepts. If a monk commits certain offenses, he is also automatically disrobed. Monks may ordain several times throughout their lives; however, in the canonical scriptures, ordination is seen as something that should be taken as a lifetime commitment. In the Asoke communities, ordination is assumed to be a life-long undertaking, and since the process or ordination within Asoke is lengthy and strenuous, few Asoke monks and nuns disrobe.

15. *Vinaya* refers to the rules of conduct for monastics. Other aspects of this lifestyle include walking barefoot, going for alms in the early morning, eating one meal a day, and sleeping on simple wooden platforms.

16. The Mahatherasamakom is a collective of prominent senior monks, presided over by the Supreme Patriarch, who is appointed by the king. The Council of Elders is also closely managed and supervised by the government through the Secretary General of the Mahatherasamakom who is also the Director-General of the Department of Religious Affairs. Somboon Suksam-ran, *Buddhism and Politics in Thailand: A Study of Socio-political Change and Political Activism of the Thai Sangha* (Singapore: Institute of Southeast Asian Studies, 1982), 48.

17. According to Jackson, the same provincial *sangha* governor also threatened to notify the police that Bodhirak had violated the 1962 Sangha Act requiring all religious centers to be registered with the Department of Religious Affairs. See Jackson, *Buddhism, Legitimation, and Conflict*, 161. Also see Swearer, *The Buddhist World of Southeast Asia*, 173.

18. Bodhirak responded by requesting to be in direct contact with the Mahatherasamakom rather than having the Nong Kratum temple abbot voice the opinion of the Mahatherasamakom to Bodhirak and the Asoke community. See Apinya Fuengfusakul, "Buddhist Reform Movements in Contemporary Thai Urban Context: Thammakai and Santi Asoke," Doctoral thesis, University of Bielefeld, Germany, 1993, 91.

19. Re-ordination required the Asoke monastics to receive new identity cards and an ordination ceremony presided over by Bodhirak. At the time, Bodhirak did not have the required ten years of seniority as a monk, as is normally required in order to conduct ordinations, which was another factor in seeing the Asoke monastics as subversive and unsanctioned.

20. In Sanskrit and Pāli, *nikāya* means "group," "class," or "assemblage," most commonly referring to various monastic lineages or fraternities.

21. Jackson, *Buddhism, Legitimation, and Conflict*, 159.

22. Ibid., 161. This quote is sourced from Anan Senakhan's book, *Bodhiraksa: The Highly Dangerous Prophet* (Photirak, Saatsadaa Mayaaphay). Although this source is potentially biased, Bodhirak's intention of marrying aspects of various lineages is well known.

23. Sanitsuda Ekachai, "The Man behind Santi Asoke," *Bangkok Post*, July 22, 1989.

24. Vin 1.94. The sewing together of smaller panels of cloth is also meant to reduce the value of monastic robes. For further discussion on washing and dying robes, see Ann Heirman, "Washing and Dyeing Buddhist Monastic Robes," *Acta Orientalia Academiae Scientiarum Hungaricae* 67:4(2014): 467–88; Thanissaro Bhikkhu [Geoffrey DeGraff], *The Buddhist Monastic Code II*, 3rd ed. (Valley Center, CA: Metta Forest Monastery, 2013), 25–36; and Mohan Wijayaratna, *Buddhist Monastic Life: According to the Texts of the Theravada Tradition*, trans. Claude Grangier and Steven Collins (Cambridge: Cambridge University Press, 1990), 32–39.

25. Colors not permitted for robes include black, blue, and crimson, and any fabrics that are multicolored or patterned. Mv. VIII.29. Thanissaro Bhikkhu elaborates, specifying that other forbidden colors include "blue (or green . . .), entirely yellow, entirely blood-red . . . entirely orange, or entirely beige. . . . Pale versions of these colors—gray under 'black,' and purple, pink, or magenta under 'crimson'—would also be forbidden. As white is a standard color for lay people's garments, and as a bhikkhu is forbidden from dressing like a lay person, white robes are forbidden as well." Thanissaro Bhikkhu [Geoffrey DeGraff]. *The Buddhist Monastic Code II*, 3rd ed. (Valley Center, CA: Metta Forest Monastery, 2013), 25.

26. Roots, bark, leaves, flowers, and stalks are permitted for dying. The inner wood of the jackfruit tree is often used to obtain the bright oranges found in Thailand. However, with widespread deforestation, chemical dyes are used more frequently. The materials permitted for making dye are described in Vin I.281.

27. Interview with Samana Tissa in Santi Asoke, June 12, 2014.

28. The controversy was resolved when the official head of the *saṅgha* at the time, following the request of the king, ruled that white and red robes are equally appropriate. Ingrid Jordt, "Bhikkhuni, Thilashin, Mae-chii: Women Who Renounce the World in Burma, Thailand, and the Classical Pali Buddhist Texts," *Crossroads* 4(1988): 37.

29. Nirmala Salgado, *Buddhist Nuns and Gendered Practice: In Search of the Female Renunciant* (New York: Oxford University Press, 2013), 113.

30. Elizabeth Harris, "Reclaiming the Sacred: Buddhist Women in Sri Lanka," *Nivedini: A Sri Lankan Feminist Journal* 8:1(2000): 15.

31. Salgado, *Buddhist Nuns and Gendered Practice*, 114.

32. Suzanne Mrozik, *Virtuous Bodies: The Physical Dimensions of Morality in Buddhist Ethics* (Oxford: Oxford University Press, 2007), 69.

33. Various publications on Asoke feature the detention of Asoke monastics and the court cases. See Jackson, *Buddhism, Legitimation, and Conflict*, 159–198; Heikkilä-Horn, *Buddhism with Open Eyes: Belief and Practice of Santi Asoke* (Bangkok: Fah Apai Co. Ltd., 1997); and Rory Mackenzie, *New Buddhist Movements in Thailand: Towards an Understanding of Wat Phra Dhammakaya and Santi Asoke* (New York: Routledge, 2007). Asoke also published a small book dealing extensively with the court cases. See A. Poompanna, *Insight into Santi Asoke, Part II* (Bangkok: Kittiya Veerapan, 1991).

34. Chamlong has been a central figure in Asoke since the late 1980s and continues to be active in Asoke communities and their political campaigns. For further reading on Chamlong, see Duncan McCargo, *Chamlong Srimuang and the New Thai Politics* (New York: St. Martin's Press, 1997).

35. After discussions between the Council of Elders, the Department of Religious Affairs, the Ministry of Education, and the National Security Council, Bodhirak was approached in September 1988 with various demands put forward by the authorities in order to drop the charges against Asoke. These requirements stipulated that Asoke return under the control of the Council of Elders, that the group be legally registered with the Department of Religious Affairs, that Bodhirak stop criticizing the Council of Elders, and that Asoke discontinue its unorthodox activities. Fuengfusakul, "Buddhist Reform Movements in Contemporary Thai Urban Context," 183.

36. *Bangkok Post*, June 10, 1989.

37. Ibid.

38. *Bangkok Post*, August 10, 1989.

39. In Thailand, it is illegal for a person to dress or use symbols (such as an alms bowl) to wrongfully suggest that one is a monk, priest, or novice of any religion and is punishable by imprisonment or a fine. This prohibition includes dressing as or imitating Buddhist monks without an ordination recognized by the ecclesiastic council.

40. *Bangkok Post*, September 9, 1989.

41. Michael Carrithers, "Jainism and Buddhism as Enduring Historical Streams," *Journal of the Anthropological Society of Oxford* 21:2(1990): 158.

42. Ibid.

43. Interview with Bodhirak at Santi Asoke, Bangkok, January 30, 2014.

44. The following section is based on an interview with Bodhirak at Santi Asoke, Bangkok, January 30, 2014.

45. The *kilesas* are defilements or negative emotions, such as passion (*lobha*), aversion (*dosa*), and delusion (*moha*).

46. Bodhirak stated further that he doubts it is possible to reach this fifth level in the West because of different perceptions of art, but the fourth stage is still possible.

47. Interview with Bodhirak at Santi Asoke, Bangkok, January 30, 2014.

48. Interview with Samana Kayakayan at Santi Asoke, Bangkok, March 9, 2013.

49. Steven Collins, "The Body in Theravāda Buddhist Monasticism," *Religion and the Body*, ed. S. Coakley (Cambridge: Cambridge University Press, 1997), 203.

50. These reoccurring themes were found in my fieldwork, as well as by Juliana Essen in *Right Development: The Santi Asoke Buddhist Reform Movement of Thailand* (Oxford: Lexington Books, 2005); and by Heikkilä-Horn, *Buddhism with Open Eyes*.

51. Heikkilä-Horn, *Buddhism with Open Eyes*, 46.

52. Interview with Bodhirak at Santi Asoke, Bangkok, January 30, 2014.

53. This estimation is based on my own fieldwork and comments by Heikkilä-Horn, *Buddhism with Open Eyes*, 46.

54. Jane Schneider and Annette Weiner, "Cloth and the Organization of Human Experience," *Current Anthropology* 27:2(1986): 178.

55. Some laywomen in Thailand choose to live as an *upāsikā*. The term is derived from "to sit close" or "to attend to" and, although it technically refers to any laywoman, the meaning has shifted to represent one who is particularly devout. A variety of platforms for living and practicing as an *upāsikā* are available; some wear all white and may shave their head. A few women in Asoke choose to live as *upāsikā*s, signified by shaving their head and wearing a black sarong with a white blouse.

56. A similar progression takes place for male aspirants. A *pa* wears brown pants and tunic. A *nak* (male version of *krak*) shaves his head, and his uniform stays the same, with a slight variation of the tunic. Men alter their attire when they progress to living as a *samanutthet*, which is the last stage before full ordination. The *samanutthet* wears a long brown tunic and a brown sarong similar to the *samana* (a stripe on the collar further distinguishes them from the *samana*) and a white outer robe for more formal occasions. This change of clothing style signals a movement towards monkhood; a *samanutthet* without the white outer robe is nearly indistinguishable from the fully ordained *samana*. When all requirements are complete, an ordination ceremony takes place at which the *samana* receives his three robes and bowl.

57. Forgoing these aspects of adornment is taken seriously within Asoke. During an interview, a long-term resident compared attachment to cosmetics and fashion to consuming alcohol, which is prohibited in the five precepts strictly followed in Asoke communities, expressing the seriousness of attachment to cosmetic beautification thus: "Cosmetic is the cause of ruin and decoration is the cause of ruin. . . . Maybe it is worse than drinking alcohol, like, cosmetic for the woman and cosmetic dressing is worse than the man who drinks alcohol . . . addicted to cosmetic, especially Thai ladies. They spend a lot of money. . . . The wife spends much more money than the husband who drinks alcohol and gets drunk. She is drunk also, though, lost and blind, attached." Interview in Pathom Asoke, February 2, 2013.

58. It also takes approximately two years to become a permanent resident.

59. Nuns have two additional robes: the *samakaccikā* is worn under the *uttarāsanga* as a bodice, and the *udakasātikā* is used as a bathing cloth. Vin 2.272.

60. Interview with Sikkhamat Rinpha at Sali Asoke, Phai Sali, February 25, 2013.

61. Interview with Sikkhamat Rinpha at Sali Asoke, Phai Sali, March 1, 2013.

62. *Bangkok Post*, July 18, 1988.

63. *Bangkok Post*, August 19, 1988.

64. Ampa Santimatanedol, "Thailand: Santi Asoke Leader Faces Complaint," *Bangkok Post*, March 9, 2006.

65. Ibid.

Chapter 6

New Buddhist Women Across Borders

Buddhist Influences and Interactions in Alternative Histories of Global Feminisms

AMY HOLMES-TAGCHUNGDARPA

In 1925, the campaign for full women's suffrage in Great Britain, which would extend voting rights to all women over the age of twenty-one, was in full swing. The periodical *The Vote*, published by the Women's Freedom League, published articles on women's politics and their continued struggle for full franchise. They also published on international women's issues, making note of other countries where suffragettes had been successful. One of the more unusual of these globally focused articles appeared in 1925 in an interview titled "Where Women are Really Equal." The subject of the interview was Mrs. Rinchen Lhamo (1901–1929), a recent arrival in the United Kingdom from the distant, mysterious lands of Tibet. Rinchen had moved to London with her husband, a British Frontier Officer, where she was enthusiastically welcomed by a fascinated press as a "Princess" who represented a faraway culture where, unusually, women enjoyed the same privileges as men.[1] The editors of *The Vote* emphasized the fair treatment of women through their access to economic and political influence in eastern Tibet in a move of early twentieth-century solidarity, to make a statement intended to cast the British Empire as comparatively backward.

However, after reading the article and other popular works on Tibet, Rinchen was perturbed by what she found. In her 1926 memoirs, *We Tibetans*, Rinchen Lhamo sought to respond to inaccuracies in Euro-American writing on Tibet, and especially addressed the question of gender equality:

> With us [Tibetans], neither the one sex nor the other is considered the inferior or the superior. Men and women treat each other as equals. The women are not kept in seclusion, but take full part in social life and in business affairs. Husband and wife are companions and partners, but the husband is the head of the household, and not the wife, as some of your writers have it. The status of women in our country is much the same as yours.[2]

Rinchen's statement was a challenge to the claim made by *The Vote* and other British news organizations, for while she did claim men and women were equal in Tibetan society, she tempered this by stating that men still acted as the head of the household and that women in Tibet were still in the same position as women in Britain.

As with other elements of *We Tibetans*, Rinchen's representation of Tibetan women was a complex one. On the one hand, her argument may have been part of a self-conscious attempt to underplay Tibetan exceptionalism and claim equality by emphasizing similarity over difference, which is also seen in her only brief discussion of polyandry, an exotic and foreign family structure to British readers at the time. Alternatively, her move to respond was a sign of Tibetan agency at a time when the popular press was inundated by Orientalist fascination with Tibet.[3]

The emphasis on the exotic nature of Tibetan gender and familial relations was by no means unique. It was a demonstration of the Orientalist trope of feminizing the Other found throughout literature on Asia during this period.[4] What is noteworthy here is the intentional connection between suffragettes and feminists of the colonial metropole and their distant enlightened Asian sisters. The invocation of Rinchen Lhamo as an independent, equal woman in the eyes of editors of *The Vote* was part of broader moves in the early twentieth century to make connections with alternative histories of matriarchal cultures. Chie Ikeya has noted how in colonial Burma, the "traditional" role of women was often emphasized as a stereotype by different colonial and nationalist writers to make power claims.[5] However, an additional complex element in the case of Rinchen Lhamo was her glamorous Buddhist identity, which was also strongly emphasized in public discourse about her and in her book. The connections between indigenous forms of gender equality and Buddhist ideology positioned her within broader global currents of discussions over the gendered nature of Buddhist modernities. In this chapter, I will outline some of the connections that undergird these currents, which have often historically neglected the role of women in global Buddhist movements. Through stories of other key women in these movements, I will explore how, even though women and gender were not at the center of discourses of Buddhist modernism, Buddhist ideas and practice remained a rich resource for concepts of gender equality. To this day the underground connections between Buddhism and feminism continue to see individuals and communities borrow from each other to make claims toward a different and more just world.

The Question of a Gendered Buddhist Modernism

The turn of the twentieth century was a time of global encounter and exploration. Fueled by the technologies of the industrial revolution and exploitation of colonial resources and labor, the networks of travel and commerce that spread globally transmitted ideas and philosophies as much as commodities of empire. In addition to ideologies of exploitation, this period also brought about critical discussions of liberation and freedom in political, racial, and economic terms in the formation of trans-imperial intellectual communities.[6] Two of the key discussions that circulated within these communities were the roles of women and religion in society. Enlightenment ideals espoused that women should be equal to men, and allowed access to independence in the forms of education, livelihood, wealth, and political suffrage. Similarly, religious freedom was seen as a key idea, and the self-critique of colonial ideologies and acceptance of the Orientalist-constructed "mystic East" facilitated the broad acceptance of a number of non-Judeo-Christian religious traditions. While the nontheism of Buddhism bewildered some intellectuals, other of its elements were seen as particularly conducive to global projects and definitions of modernity.[7] As David McMahan has written, much of what is popular about Buddhism today in the public sphere is its popular representation as:

> . . . a religion whose most important elements are medita-
> tion, rigorous philosophical analysis, and an ethic of com-
> passion combined with a highly empirical psychoanalytical
> science that encourages reliance on individual experience.
> It discourages blindly following authority and dogma, has
> little place for superstition, magic, image worship, and gods,
> and is largely compatible with the findings of modern sci-
> ence and liberal democratic values.[8]

This form of "Buddhist modernism," as he has termed it, is by no means new. Multiple projects by multiple intellectual and cultural communities have in turn colluded and competed to construct Buddhist modernisms over the past two hundred years. A number of these parties have used discourses about equality as their central focus. Despite these constructions, however, the treatment of gender as a category of Buddhist modernism has remained underdeveloped. The early links between the intellectual communities mentioned above, who were interested in religious freedom and women's rights, respectively, have often been concealed within other projects. In the case of Buddhism, in the past two decades a number of scholars have discussed connections between Buddhist and feminist ideologies,[9] but as Jean Byrne has recently argued, there still remains much to be debated and explored to demonstrate the viability of Buddhism as a system compatible with feminism, particularly due to the realities of its institutions on the ground in patriarchal societies.[10] Concerns over cultural appropriation and structural inequalities within feminism have arisen that need to be addressed to create fully a representative and inclusive feminism, as well as to consider whether feminism is the most appropriate discourse for discussing issues of gender equality in different Buddhist communities.[11]

The study of Buddhist modernism has often ignored these questions, which is surprising as Buddhist modernists were concerned with social justice issues, including education, class equality, and democracy. However, studies of Buddhist modernists around the world continue to focus on elite, English language–educated, urban men, normally monastics, and leave the involvement of women out of Buddhist modernist histories entirely.[12] Liz Wilson has recently begun the process of rectifying this through examining the importance of first-wave feminist ideals for the early study of Buddhist women in European and American scholarship, using examples such as Caroline Rhys Davids (1857–1942) and I. B. Horner (1896–1981).[13] However, there is still little about the networks of Western and Asian, and inter-Asian networks in the acknowledgment of links between Buddhist and feminist projects in the Age of Empire.[14] The Dhammaloka Project undertaken by Bocking, Cox, and Turner has demonstrated the richness of materials available for understanding more diverse Buddhist communities during this period, with respect to class, through their investigations related to the working-class Irish mystery monk Dhammaloka (c. 1856–1914).[15] This chapter will suggest some similar trajectories for including the category of gender and indigenous collaboration in the examination of Buddhist modernist projects through thinking about alternative resources and archives for examining the women involved in these global networks. They included translators, scholars, and explorers, as well as the patrons that made such projects possible, and inspired active feminist groups and New Women in the pursuit of their goals. Exploring these links can provide us with alternative genealogies of both Buddhist and feminist movements, and allow us to better understand Buddhism as it is currently deployed in discussions about women's rights and ordination, and how this Buddhism developed.

The Absence of Women in Global Buddhist Modernist Networks

The links between Buddhist modernism and feminism are not new, dating back to the nineteenth and early twentieth centuries, a period of global colonial modernity and interaction that fostered the formation of both discourses. As Buddhism was constructed within a tradition of ideas that mirrored Enlightenment thought, the suffragette movement and women's rights also became a concern for Buddhist modernists, along with democratic and scientific ideals. However, these were not of significant concern for many of the male, elite, educated leaders of these movements. Recent scholarship has demonstrated the breadth and diversity of Buddhist responses to colonial modernity. Figures such as Dharmapala (1864–1933), Henry Steel Olcott (1832–1907), Taixu (1890–1947), Shaku Kozen (1849–1924), and D. T. Suzuki (1870–1966) were instrumental in creating new institutions and texts for the global dissemination of Buddhism. They traveled widely, participating in a number of initiatives including global meetings (such as the World Parliament of Religions and lecture tours), creating print organs (such as periodicals, newspapers, and translated texts as well as new scholarly and popular works) and other moments of intercultural contact. While they were proponents of diverse interpretations of Buddhist modernism, women's rights were not taken up as a major theme by any of them, and women's agency remained limited within their movements and aspirations.

For example, Dharmapala was seen as a key figure as an indigenous agent who was committed to the recreation of India as a worldwide Buddhist center while also taking part in many other initiatives through his links to the international Theosophy movement. The lack of discourse related to women, let alone women's involvement in his initiatives, may be demonstrated through looking at the journal he edited, *The Journal of the Mahabodhi Society*, and its various incarnations, printed from 1894. During the first ten years of the journal, only three female writers were featured: the prominent Theosophists Madame Helena Blavatsky (1831–1891) and Annie Besant (1847–1933), and later the mysterious Countess Miranda de Souza Canavarro (1849–1933), a Texan who married a Portuguese Count and after his death moved to Ceylon to establish a girl's school there. This school represents one of the few female-focused Buddhist modernist institutions to emerge at this time, and its focus on education for young women in Buddhist societies is an exemplar of one of the only themes related to women found in the *Journal of the Mahabodhi Society*. Dharmapala sympathized with women's education and saw it as a necessity; he published a few new snippets related to the beginnings of discussions about women's ordination in Burma in 1895, and praised education in the Japanese Empire and the United States, but his view of idealized modern Buddhism was thoroughly masculine. In his own creation of the specialists in his new Buddhist order, which he dubbed *"anagarika,"* or "homeless protector of the Dhamma," and in the schools he created to train such figures, he did not discuss women or their role.[16]

Taixu, another great Buddhist figure of the period based in China, similarly was not focused on women or their participation in the creation of new Buddhist society. While there were institutions founded for nuns, and a short-lived, single-issued newspaper published out of Wuhan,[17] the lack of discussion of women or women's issues in more extensive ways remained absent.

Global Buddhisms, Local Collaborators: Scholars, Translators, Explorers, and Students

This did not mean that women were absent from these movements, however. In actuality, women facilitated the development of these movements in many new spaces through local networks and collaboration, and their concern for including women's issues in their work was an important alternative to male scholarship produced during the same period. While scholars such as Caroline Rhys Davids and I. B. Horner were known for their philological and textual work, they also spent long periods in Buddhist societies, particularly Ceylon. Women inspired by their example followed their lead, including Anna Ballard (dates unknown), a journalist and Theosophist who ended up in Burma in the 1890s, where she apparently spent time with nuns and wrote on discussions about reintroducing full ordination for women there. While she did not name any of her collaborators, she undoubtedly did interact with local women who made her studies possible. The Belgian-French explorer and bestselling author Alexandra David-Néel (1868–1969) was an example of a figure who was hugely influential in the construction of Western knowledge about Buddhism, but also relied heavily on local knowledge. In her many travels throughout Tibet and Asia, she was often accompanied by assistants and interacted extensively with local people, including women.[18] As Erik Mueggler's work has argued, the lack of exact identities and names of local collaborators in colonial scholarship should not be seen as a lack of local cooperation. Instead, power hierarchies and cultural conditions led to the obscuration of certain genealogies of knowledge, which can only later be ascertained through detective work and reading between the lines to create a more nuanced and representative picture.[19]

Buddhist modernist projects also often make the mistake of focusing only on European language discussions. Research into Buddhist texts and the public sphere of local languages reveals more complex gendered authorial histories. For example, recent research by Martin Seeger has discovered that the popular Thai text *Thammanuthamma-patipatti* from the nineteenth century was written by Khunying Yai Damrongthammasan (1886–1944), a wealthy laywoman who spent many years studying Buddhism in southern Thailand.[20] This research demonstrates the importance of reading multiple sources and archives for exploring the global networks at work in the nineteenth and twentieth centuries, as well as being cautious of projecting Victorian-period gender norms onto different cultures in multiple areas.

The Women Behind the Movements: Gender, Associations, and Patronage

Women played important roles as patrons in many modern Buddhist activities and projects. Mary E. Foster (1844–1930) facilitated much of Dharmapala's work, contributing generously to his charity and school projects in India and Ceylon. The Countess Canavarro was also a generous, hands-on patron. In the 1890s, she moved to Ceylon where she headed the Sanghamitta Convent, which was also a school and orphanage. However, it was not only American and European women who played important roles in Buddhist philanthropy; Dharmapala's mother and relatives were frequent contributors to his activities.[21] Burmese noblewoman Daw Kin Kin E (or Mrs. Hla Oung as she was often referred to, 1904–1991) was instrumental to many philanthropic projects, and particularly dedicated to the creation of schools and educational institutions for girls as well as boys.[22] These institutions acted as important exemplars, though they are often obscured in institutional histories in favor of prominent organizations such as the Young Men's Buddhist Association. Women had their own equivalents of these Associations; in post-independence Sri Lanka, for example, the All Ceylon Women's Buddhist Congress was established in 1949 with a broader focus than its male equivalent that included diverse welfare projects.[23] These Buddhist women, using Buddhist modernist discourses of equality to explain their programs, were dedicated to providing girls with educational opportunities that would facilitate economic independence.

Obscured Genealogies:
Buddhism as an Inspiration to Feminist Groups

Despite these goals of female empowerment, however, these Buddhist women and their associations did not call themselves feminists. Feminists did call themselves Buddhists, though, which demonstrates a circulation of ideas between these separate intellectual currents. While many histories of Asian feminist movements discuss the influence of Christianity on the development of local educational institutions for women, the influence of Buddhism has been little discussed. Japan and Korea were both states with active feminist and New Woman movements that aspired for gender equality, women's rights to education and work, and free love. Japanese feminist thought developed in salon-type environments and publications such as *Seito* (*Bluestocking*). While New Women were often derided and ridiculed in the Press for their glamorous, scandalous lifestyles, which saw them engage in torrid love affairs with men and women, married and unmarried, their intellectual contributions to the development of local feminism were key.[24] A number of early intellectuals argue that

Buddhism was a major inspiration to them, particularly the influential writer and labor activist Raicho Hiratsuka (1886–1971), who began practicing Zen Buddhism at university. In her autobiography, Raicho wrote of its importance to her intellectual development and activism on behalf of Japanese women.

> . . . Trampled and despised for generations in a male-dominated world, Japanese women were ready to explore, and I happened to be the escape valve. I was no doubt the right person, for I had practiced Zen for several years and freed myself of the preconceptions and reached that realm where there is no Self. . . .[25]

For Raicho, Buddhist ideology became a resource for her cause, and for her ability to embark on what she saw as an "adventure"[26] for the liberation of Japanese women from patriarchy, allowing her to move beyond social condemnation and judgment through her lack of concern for her ego.

Feminism arrived in Korea through Japanese publications, but inadvertently led to the development of new anticolonial discourses underpinned by goals for women's liberation from Korean Confucian and Japanese colonial patriarchies.[27] While the New Women of Korea were similarly critiqued in the tabloids for their colorful personal lives, a number were also inspired by Buddhism. The most famous was Kim Iryop (1896–1971), a renowned writer in the modern Korean canon who was apparently married no fewer than five times, depending on the biography, who founded the influential journal *Sinyŏja* (*A New Woman*) in 1920. In the Introduction to the first journal, she wrote of the need to radically reform women's roles in Korea:

> What should we rebuild? We should rebuild the whole society. If we want to rebuild society we need to restructure the family which is the basic unit of society. If we want to reorganize the family, we need to liberate women. If we [Koreans] want to live like other people in the world, if we don't want to be defeated by other powerful people, we need to rebuild all aspects of society. In order to do this, we must liberate women.[28]

This call for a complete reconstruction of Korean society demonstrates how Western feminist genealogies (first wave, second wave, third wave) are inadequate for capturing the complexities of what was happening in different societies. Kim's rallying cry was far more radical than many of the suffragettes and bluestockings of Britain and Europe during the same period. Her contributions to Korean feminism were considerable before 1935, when she disappeared into monastic life. Her decision to become a nun came from her own personal experience of loss and tragedy, as she lost her immediate family at a young age, and her torrid love affairs fueled the gossip columns. Monasticism gave her peace, and she continued to write important and influential works on Buddhist thought and practice while mentoring female monastics.[29] For Kim and Raicho, and others like them, Buddhism provided new opportunities through their intellectual affinity with the ideas of no-self and impermanence. Even if official Buddhist modernists were not committed to women's issues, feminists were at the same time reconstructing the boundaries of Buddhist modernism, suggesting the use of Buddhism as a resource for projects of liberation beyond concerns related to politics, patronage, or proselytization. The influence of such ideas remains obscured, but when put together, these networks of education, anti-colonial activisms, and movements for gender equality point to an underground genealogy of links between Buddhist modernists and feminists.

Complicating Feminist Utopias

Complicating this genealogy is the fact that feminist interpretations of already constructed representations of Buddhist cultures were often based on idealized notions. Rinchen Lhamo's discussion at the start of this chapter is an example of her response to one such moment. Another example comes from the Himalayan Vajrayāna Buddhist state of Sikkim, which in 1912 passed legislation that was to be, on the surface, beneficial for women. The centerpoint of this law was a resolution to abolish polyandry among the Bhutia and Lepcha ethnic populations passed by the modernist Crown Prince Sidkeong Tulku. However, the deeper reasoning behind the law actually related to maintaining, rather than subverting, a form of constructed tradition. Here, anxieties about cultural authenticity and civilization were masked as a concern about maintaining cultural purity through maintaining population rates. The resolution stated:

> Though we [i.e., Bhutias and Lepchas] ought to be ruling over a prolific race and populous country without diminishing in number as we are the inhabitants of the sacred hidden land of Guru Padmasambhava yet our Bhutia and Lepcha race is dying out owing to the evils of the marriage customs prevailing amongst us, which allows polyandry the custom of several brothers marrying one wife, besides the Lepcha custom of extravagant expense and price of the girl demanded by a young man to marry at all.[30]

The resolution was also concerned with Lepcha practices of only allowing marriage between members of certain families and marriage of men and women of widely disparate ages. It stated that in the future, "with a view to increase the birth-rate and number of the race the Lepchas and Bhutias must marry each brother one wife to himself . . . ," unless the first wife was barren in which case a second wife could be taken, but only with permission of the first wife, that people of the same age should marry, and that Bhutias and Lepchas should not intermarry with the "Paharias or Madhyasias" (Nepalese or Plainsmen). The resolution also moved to prohibit unreasonably high marriage ritual expenses and dowries, unless families had enough means to present them.[31] The complex reasons for passing this legislation were not necessarily related to gender equality or women's rights. Instead, these laws can be interpreted as a sign of anxiety about the changing demographics within Sikkim due to the arrival of laborers from Nepal and the plains. There also a concern to maintain authority within the Bhutia and Lepcha communities after the British imperial takeover of the Sikkimese administration after the 1880s.

Legislation was also connected to broader moves within Asian societies to assert indigenous forms of "civilization" that contrasted with Euro-American imperialistic claims. Part of this civilizing discourse was tied to the dissemination of Victorian concepts of gender and sexuality that resulted in oppressive rather than liberating changes for women. For example, in Siam (Thailand), the government passed legislation that restricted marriage to monogamous heterosexual couples. This was part of a broader response to a series of unequal treaties with Western powers. This legislation, as well as other forms of cultural reform, resulted from the belief among the elite that a "society that did not at least formally abide by this standard of a civilized marriage was not considered fully modern by other powerful countries, most of which were Western, Christian, and imperialist."[32] Family law thus became connected to anxieties about appearing "civilized," and the abilities for states to retain sovereignty in a competitive environment of imperial predatory threats. It was not always inherently connected to practices of matriarchy or gender equality.

Conclusion

Feminist historians have not engaged in detail with Buddhist modernist movements. Due to the focus in women's history on Western-led movements for gender equality in Asia, Buddhist women's agency has remained obscured. This is particularly the case in relation to the movement for the full ordination of nuns in Vajrayāna and Theravāda communities, where some critics argue that full ordination is an issue more relevant to Western nuns than women of Asian cultural origin. These moments of misrepresentation and the critique of the relevance of Western feminist discourse in different cultural contexts continue to have legacies today in critical discussions of gender equality in Buddhist societies.[33]

These complicated discussions have been enriched by new technologies and an expansion of the public sphere to include multiple new voices from within Buddhist societies. A noteworthy example is the Tibetan Feminist Collective, a blog maintained by Tibetan women from around the world. It is an indigenous movement to discuss gender equality in Buddhist practice and associated issues such as women's rights, ordination, and domestic abuse within the Tibetan community.[34] These women are creating new archives and retracing missing genealogies.

These genealogies, not found in official archives, are of the women who participated in networks to disseminate Buddhist modernist thought throughout the world. The most obvious of these women are the students of the figures we have discussed, as well as readers of their printed materials. Less obvious are women who used new global technologies of communication and transportation, such as female pilgrims who moved throughout Asia traveling by train and automobile to reach the new pilgrimage sites of the modern Buddhist; the urban women in factories and schools who took part in new Buddhist groups and brought new literature; and older women who continued their traditional practices but used new offering materials and read from newly printed texts. These were not only monastic women, who are often the locus of contemporary discussions related to Buddhism and feminism, especially in regards to ordination, but also laywomen and those who identify neither as lay nor ordained. Looking out for such women in their indigenous context may seem obvious—after all, in many Buddhist states it was taken for granted that women were crucial patrons of Buddhist temples and active pilgrims. What is often not noticed, however, are the patterns of continuity between the premodern and modern forms of Buddhism that Anne Blackburn has argued are so often concealed in Buddhist modernist histories. These forms of continuity in regards to concepts of local identity, lineage, and patronage networks were not based on a "developmentalist discourse that approached social problems and their solution through a self-conscious reflection on [their] own era as one that required a compensatory imitation of new forms of political order, ritual and devotion, or education explicitly presented . . . as suitable or new or 'modern' times."[35] Something that was new, however, was the globalized nature of the networks that spread these ideas. These networks were gendered in important ways, and the involvement of women in them in myriad roles points to the need to recognize women's participation in the multidirectional construction of diverse Buddhist modernisms and in mutual imaginings of Buddhism and feminism.

Notes

1. Author unknown. "Where Women are Really Equal," in *The Vote: The Organ of the Women's Freedom League* (1925): 1–2.

2. Rinchen Lhamo, *We Tibetans* (New York: Potala Publications, 1985 [1926]), 125.

3. For more on Orientalism related to Tibet, see Donald S. Lopez, Jr. *Prisoners of Shangri-La: Tibetan Buddhism and the West* (Chicago: Chicago University Press, 1998); and Clare Harris, *The Museum on the Roof of the World* (Chicago: Chicago University Press, 2012).

4. These tropes are discussed in Edward Said, *Orientalism* (New York: Pantheon, 1978); and Anne McClintock, *Imperial Leather* (New York: Routledge, 1995).

5. Chie Ikeya, "The 'Traditional' High Status of Women in Burma: A Historical Reconsideration," *Journal of Burma Studies* 10(2005–2006): 51–81.

6. Leela Gandhi, *Affective Communities* (Durham, NC: Duke University Press, 2006), 2.

7. Some of the definitions are outlined in Jeffrey Franklin, *The Lotus and the Lion* (Ithaca, NY: Cornell University Press, 2008).

8. David McMahan, *Buddhist Modernism* (Oxford University Press, 2008), 5.

9. See, for example, Anne C. Klein, *Meeting the Great Bliss Queen: Buddhists, Feminists, and the Art of the Self* (Boston: Beacon Press, 1996); and Sandy Boucher, *Turning the Wheel: American Women Creating the New Buddhism* (Boston: Beacon Press, 1993).

10. Jean Byrne, "Why I am Not a Buddhist Feminist: A Critical Examination of 'Buddhist Feminism,'" *Feminist Theology* 21:2(2013): 180–94.

11. Chandra Talpade Mohanty, "Under Western Eyes: Feminist Scholarship and Colonial Discourses," *Boundary 2* 12:3–13:1(1984):333–58; and Michelle Hannah, "Transmigratory Buddhists and Traveling Feminism: Globalization and Cross-Cultural Differences," *The Australian Journal of Anthropology* 21:3(2010): 332–49.

12. For example, Anne Blackburn, *Locations of Buddhism* (Chicago: Chicago University Press, 2010); Anne Hansen, *How to Behave* (Honolulu: University of Hawaii, 2007); and Richard Jaffe, "Seeking Shakyamuni: Travel and the Reconstruction of Japanese Buddhism," *Journal of Japanese Studies*, 30:1(2004): 65–96.

13. Liz Wilson, "Buddhism and Gender," *Buddhism in the Modern World*, ed. David McMahan (New York: Routledge, 2012), 257–72.

14. Jaffe, "Seeking Shakyamuni," 65–96.

15. Alicia Turner, Laurence Cox, and Brian Bocking, "Beachcombing, Going Native and Freethinking: Rewriting the History of Early Western Buddhist Monastics," *Contemporary Buddhism* 11:2(2010): 125–47.

16. This is based on a survey of copies of *The Journal of Mahabodhi Society*, 1894–1904.

17. Yuan Yuan, "Chinese Buddhist Nuns in the Twentieth Century: A Case Study of Wuhan," *Journal of Global Buddhism* 10(2009): 375–412.

18. Her travels are outlined in Barbara Foster and Michael Foster, *The Secret Lives of Alexandra David-Neel* (New York: Overlook Press, 2002).

19. Local collaborations are a central theme throughout Erik Mueggler, *The Paper Road* (Berkeley: University of California Press, 2011).

20. Martin Seeger, "Reversal of Female Power, Transcendentality, and Gender in Thai Buddhism: The Thai Buddhist Female Saint Khun Mao Bunruean Tongbuntoem (1895–1964)," *Modern Asian Studies* 47:5(2013): 1488–1519.

21. This philanthropy is mentioned throughout *The Journal of the Mahabodhi Society*.

22. Kim Thida Oung, *A Twentieth Century Burmese Matriarch* (Yangon: Author, 2009).

23. All Ceylon Women's Buddhist Congress, http://www.acwbc.slt.lk/projects.html

24. These movements are outlined in Jan Bardsley, *The Bluestocking of Japan: New Women Fiction and Essays from Seito, 1911–1916* (Ann Arbor, MI: Center for Japanese Studies, 2007).

25. Hiratsuka Raichō (trans. Teruko Craig), *In the Beginning, Woman Was the Sun* (New York: Columbia University Press, 2010), 315–16.

26. Ibid., 320n.5. Hiratsuka Raichō's engagement with Buddhism is discussed in more detail in Christine A. James's chapter in this volume, "Raichō Hiratsuka and Socially Engaged Buddhism."

27. Insook Kwon, "The New Women's Movement in 1920s Korea: Rethinking the Relationship between Imperialism and Women," *Gender and History* 10:3(1998): 381–405.

28. Translated in Bonnie B. C. Oh, "Kim Iryop: Pioneer Writer/Reformer in Colonial Korea," *Transactions of the Royal Asiatic Society, Korea Branch* 71(1996): 18.

29. For more on Kim, see Kim Iryop (trans. Jin Park), *Reflections of a Zen Buddhist Nun* (Honolulu: University of Hawaii Press, 2014).

30. "The Abolition of Polyandry," Sikkim State Archives, Gangtok, Sikkim, 1912.

31. Ibid.

32. Tamara Loos, *Subject Siam* (Ithaca, NY: Cornell University Press, 2006), 7.

33. For more on the ordination debate, see Michelle Hannah, "Transmigratory Buddhists and Traveling Feminism: Globalization and Cross-Cultural Differences," *The Australian Journal of Anthropology* 21.3(2010): 332–49.

34. The Tibetan Feminist Collective can be found at http://www.tibetanfeministcollective.org (accessed August 1, 2016).

35. Blackburn, *Locations of Buddhism*, 212.

Part II

Buddhist Femininities

Demystifying the Essential Feminine

Chapter 7

Only Skin Deep?

Female Embodiment and the Paradox of Beauty in Indian Buddhism

LISA J. BATTAGLIA

"**B**eauty is only skin deep," or so the saying goes.[1] Beauty is superficial, artificial, lacking in integrity, profundity, or so the maxim intimates. External attractiveness has no relation to goodness or essential quality.[2] Physical beauty is shallow, trivial, paling in comparison to a person's intellectual, emotional, and spiritual qualities.[3] The proverb "beauty is only skin deep" is so pervasive and taken for granted that it is virtually unconscionable to suggest otherwise.

In *Merriam-Webster* beauty is defined as (1) the quality or aggregate of qualities in a person or thing that gives pleasure to the senses or pleasurably exalts the mind or spirit; and (2) a beautiful person or thing, *especially* a beautiful woman.[4] In both theory and practice, beauty has particular implications for women. As many feminists have suggested, beauty—that is, the pursuit of beauty and the concomitant unattainable beauty standards expected of women—keep women in bondage. In her bestseller, *The Beauty Myth: How Images of Beauty are Used Against Women*, Naomi Wolf boldly asserts that societal forces compel women to be obsessed with beauty at the expense of claiming political and economic power.[5] Wolf calls into question the ideal of beauty in contemporary America, observing that beauty standards—

dictated by market forces and a multibillion-dollar advertising industry—drain women psychologically and financially.[6] Not only is beauty
a psychological and economic drain, it is also evaluative: "beauty"
becomes the standard by which women are judged and limited due
to their physical appearance. Women are taught that their worth is
proportional to their attractiveness. Physical appearance, one's body
shape, face, hair, clothes—these seemingly trivial concerns *matter*,
particularly to women. Indeed, as Wolf cites, "thirty-three thousand
American women told researchers that they would rather lose ten to
fifteen pounds than achieve any other goal."[7] She continues, "We are
in the midst of a violent backlash against feminism that uses images
of female beauty as a political weapon against women's advance-
ment: the beauty myth."[8] This "beauty myth" (as Wolf coins it) is a
powerful force that keeps women focused on the pursuit of beauty,
at the expense of allegedly worthier pursuits. Wolf's book ultimately
calls for a "new wave of feminism to free women from enslavement
to beauty's dictates."[9]

The tenuous relationship between female liberation and beauty
is hardly new or particular to contemporary American society. While
Wolf and other feminists regard beauty as an institutional and economic trap for women, textual evidence suggests that early Indian
Buddhists considered beauty a psychological and soteriological obstacle for renunciant women (and, circuitously, for men as well). Indeed,
if we switch gears, we can travel back in time and across continents
to ancient India where another "beauty myth" surfaces.

Suffering for Beauty

Buddhist literature abounds with vivid epithets of the human body:
"city of bones," "parade of decay," "elevated mass of wounds," and
"ornamented pot of filth," to name just a few. In order to realize the
true nature of the body—that is, as impermanent and impure—the
Buddha of the Pāli canon advocates meditation on the transience and
foulness of the body.[10] Body-focused meditations include contemplating the thirty-one loathsome parts of the body, observing the nine
stages of the gradual decomposition of a corpse, and meditating on
the ten varieties of a dead body.[11]

Buddhist sources emphasize the deceptive nature of our perceptions: that which we deem pleasurable is, in reality, unsatisfactory.
This is particularly true of bodies: we blindly seek pleasure in our

own or another's body. In the *Visuddhimagga* ("Path of Purification"), Buddhaghosa, the fifth-century Indian Buddhist commentator and scholar, warns that contemplating the body of someone of the opposite sex could inadvertently heighten passion and be a hindrance to chastity. He advises monks to avoid using female bodies as objects of meditation, just as nuns should avoid using male bodies.[12] Nonetheless, Indian Buddhist literature suggests that many monks did not heed this advice: Monks are frequently depicted contemplating the repulsiveness of the specifically *female* body.[13] Buddhist literature underscores the duplicitous nature of the female body: it is a razor blade dripping with honey, its exterior is attractive, its interior repulsive. Women's beauty holds men in thrall and leads wayward monks down the path to temptation. The Buddha of the Aṅguttara Nikāya explains, "Womankind is entirely the snare of Māra."[14] Only the foolish and deceived mistake "walking corpses" and "abject bags of filth" for paragons of beauty.[15] Contemplating a beautiful female body turned rotting bag of bones serves to illustrate two fatal follies on the Buddhist path: mistaking pleasure for pain and purity for impurity.[16]

In Indian Buddhist literature, female bodies are systematically analyzed and dismembered to reveal the pollution and filth that remains obscured by a beautiful, yet artificial and deceptive, veneer. Conjured bodies of women are aged rapidly before enraptured onlookers; monks frequent the charnel fields to meditate on the decaying forms of women. The *bodhisattva* himself departs on his spiritual quest immediately after viewing the grotesque and disheveled forms of sleeping women in his palace. Biographies of the Buddha contain rich descriptions of the attractive women in Siddhāttha's harem: they are "beautiful, faultless, loving women, with bright eyes like jewels, with large breasts, resplendent white limbs, sparkling gems, firm and fine waists, soft, lovely, and black-colored hair, wearing bright red mantles and cloaks, bracelets of gems and necklaces of pearls, ornaments and rings on their toes, and anklets."[17] The erotic is subverted, however, by suggestions of disgust, devastation, and death. Aśvaghoṣa's *Buddhacarita* (*Deeds of the Buddha*) vividly chronicles the notorious harem scene in which Gotama, on his road to spiritual awakening, realizes the deceptive and superficial nature of the women's beauty:

> So one, as she lay there, supported her cheek on an unsteady hand, and as if angry, abandoned the flute in her lap, dear though it was to her, with its decoration of gold leaf.

Another, lying with her bamboo pipe in her hands and her white robe slipping off her breasts, resembled a river with lotuses being enjoyed by a straight row of bees and with banks laughing with the foam of the water.

Similarly a third was sleeping, clasping her drum, as if it were her lover, with arms tender as the hearts of young blue lotuses, so that the bright golden armlets had met together.

So others, decked with ornaments of fresh gold, and wearing peerless yellow garments, fell down helpless with deep sleep, like *karṇikāra* boughs broken by an elephant.

Another lay, leaning against the side of a window with her beautiful necklaces dangling, and seemed with her slender body bent like a bow as if turned into the statue of a *śāla*-plucker on a gateway.

Another again had her lotus-face bowed down, thereby causing the jeweled earrings to eat into the lines of paint, so that it took the likeness of a lotus with its stalk half-curved, as it is shaken by a *kāraṇḍava* bird standing on it.

Others lay in the position in which they had sat down, and, embracing each other with intertwined arms decorated with golden bracelets, appeared to have their bodies bent down under the load of their breasts.

Yet another clasped her mighty *parivādinī*, as if it were her friend, and rolled about in her sleep, so that her golden threads shook and her face had the pendent strings on her ears all disordered.

Another young woman lay, bringing her *paṇava* whose beautiful netting had slipped from her arm pit, between her thighs, like a lover exhausted at the end of his sport.

Others, though really large-eyed and fair-browed, showed no beauty with their eyes shut, like lotus-beds with their flowerbuds closed at the setting of the sun.

Another too had her hair loose and disheveled and with the ornaments and clothes fallen from her hips and her necklaces scattered she lay like an image of a woman broken by an elephant.

But others, helplessly lost to shame despite their natural decorum and endowment of excellent beauty, lay in immodest attitudes, snoring, and stretched their limbs, all distorted and tossing their arms about.

Others looked ugly, lying unconscious like corpses, with their ornaments and garlands cast aside, the fastening knots of their dresses undone, and eyes moveless with their whites showing.

Another lay as if sprawling in intoxication, with her mouth gaping wide, so that the saliva oozed forth, and with her limbs spread out so as to show what should have been hid. Her beauty was gone, her form distorted.[18]

After viewing this grotesque spectacle, the *bodhisattva* concludes: "Such is the real nature of woman in the world of the living, impure and loathsome; yet man, deceived by dress and ornaments, succumbs to passion for women."[19] Upon viewing the women's ugly and corpse-like bodies, Gotama escapes from the palace and immediately embarks on the Great Renunciation.[20]

Elsewhere in the Indian Buddhist narrative repertoire, women are horrifically transformed in order to edify wayward monks. For example, the monk Cittahattha repeatedly leaves the *saṅgha* (monastic community of ordained monks and nuns) to return to his wife and the householder life.[21] On his seventh transgression, Cittahattha returns home to find his wife visibly pregnant and sleeping:

Now his wife had lain down for a nap and was asleep at that moment. Her outer garment had fallen off, saliva was flowing from her mouth, snores resonated in her nasal passages, and her mouth was wide open. She looked like a bloated corpse.[22]

Upon viewing his wife's hideous body, Cittahattha's desire dissipates, and he runs back to the monastery. A few days later, Cittahattha becomes an *arhat*.[23] Contemplating the corpse-like forms of women has a salutary effect on the male onlooker. In another tale from the *Dhammapadā hakathā*, a lovelorn monk is infatuated with the reported beauty of a young woman named Sirimā; although he has never seen her, he becomes engrossed with his imaginings of her. The lovesick monk sets off to see Sirimā, only to find her gravely ill. His passion for her does not abate. That evening Sirimā dies. The Buddha offers the following instructions:

There's to be no cremation for Sirimā. Have her body laid in the charnel field and post a guard, so that crows

> and dogs will not devour it. . . . Three days passed, one
> after another. On the fourth day the body began to bloat,
> and from the nine openings of her body, the nine gaping
> wounds, maggots poured out. Her whole body had burst
> open like a cracked vessel of rice.[24]

The forlorn monk is summoned to come view Sirimā's putrid rotting
body. The Buddha admonishes:

> Monks, look at this available woman adored by so many
> people. In this very city men used to pay a thousand
> *kahāpana*s for the sake of spending one night with this
> woman. Now there is no one who will take her even for
> free. Her beauty has perished and decayed. . . . Monks, look
> at this diseased body. . . . Look at this decorated image,
> an elevated mass of wounds. This diseased thing is highly
> fancied, [although] it's neither permanent nor stable.[25]

While the monk had hoped to set eyes on a vibrant, beautiful Sirimā,
he is instead instructed in the discipline of cremation-ground meditation. In each of these tales, the destruction of a woman's beauty
suffices to destroy a man's desire.[26] As a beautiful female gives way
to disfiguration and decay, women move from the role of temptress
to redemptress. The female body is at once an entrapping and libera-
tive spectacle.

When women spiritual seekers are depicted contemplating the
transience and foulness of the body, they use their *own* bodies as
objects of contemplation. Verse by verse, female aspirants de-beautify themselves on the path to liberation. Consider the story of Rūpa
Nandā, the quintessential "vain nun." Rūpa Nandā is intoxicated with
her physical form and consumed with a "fierce affection for her body."
In order to cure her of her paralyzing vanity, the Buddha conjures up a
phantasm of a beautiful woman—a woman more beautiful than Rūpa
Nandā—for the wayward nun to contemplate. This female phantasm
is described alluringly: "She was the very definition of sweet sixteen,
standing there in his presence dressed in red, wearing all her ornaments, holding a fan, and fanning herself."[27] Rūpa Nandā becomes
enthralled with this attractive female form. However, that which is
lovely quickly turns ugly as the Buddha wields his psychic powers
and causes the spectral woman to age before Rūpa Nandā's eyes.
Rūpa Nandā becomes increasingly displeased as the once-beautiful

woman deteriorates into a toothless, hunchbacked, old woman leaning heavily on a walking stick. The object lesson is not over; as the
grisly spectacle reaches its final, cataclysmic end:

> The Teacher mastered her with disease. Screaming loudly,
> she threw down her stick and fan, fell to the ground, and
> rolled back and forth, wallowing in her own urine and
> feces. Seeing her, Rūpa Nandā was extremely disgusted.
> The Teacher then caused her to see the death of this
> woman. Her body immediately assumed a bloated condi-
> tion; putrid lumps and maggots oozed out through her nine
> orifices. Crows and the like fell on her and tore into her
> flesh.[28]

Upon witnessing the horrific disfiguration of the once-beautiful
woman, Rūpa Nandā realizes the truths of impurity and impermanence and, ultimately, becomes an *arhat*.[29]

The *Therīgāthā* (the enlightenment poetry of early Buddhist
nuns) is ripe with stories of women who attain awakening by contemplating the deceptive and foul nature of their bodies. Vimalā, a
courtesan-turned-nun, contrasts her former physique and occupation
as seductress of men with that of her present condition as a renunciant
who is deliberately unalluring:

> Intoxicated with my glowing skin, my beauty, my luck,
>   and my fame;
> Utterly confident of my youthful charms, I scorned other
>   women;
> Having decorated myself, that attractive body called out
>   to fools.
> Like a hunter putting out his snare,
> I stood at the gate where prostitutes stand in hopes of
>   wealth;
> Showing myself to be well put together,
> I revealed a great deal of what should be hidden;
> I managed all kinds of deception, and made fun of many
>   people.
>
> Today I wander for alms—bald and wearing a robe;
> Seated at the foot of a tree, I've achieved a state of
>   thoughtless trance;

I've cut off all the bonds to which deities and humans
    are subject;
Having destroyed all the afflictions [*āsave*], I'm cool and
    tranquil.[30]

The women of the *Therīgāthā* are wont to contrast point by point their once beautiful and youthful body with their unornamented and aged body. Consider the musings of the nun Ambapālī:

Flashing and brilliant as jewels, my dark eyes were large;
Overcome with age, they are no longer beautiful—
In youth my nose was long, beautiful, and delicate;
with age it has become pendulous—
Adorned with gold and delicate rings my hands were
    once beautiful;
with age they look just like twisted roots—
My body was once beautiful as a well-polished tablet of
    gold;
now it is covered all over with very fine wrinkles—
not other than this are the Truth-speaker's words.[31]

By contemplating her own beautiful-turned-ugly flesh, Ambapālī achieves enlightenment. Limb by limb, body part by body part, she chronicles the deterioration, de-feminization, and de-beautification of her body.

Like Ambapālī, the nun Nanduttarā reflects on the frivolous nature of beautification and the superficial lifestyle of her past:

I used to worship fire,
the moon, the sun,
and the gods.
I bathed at fords,
took many vows,
I shaved half my head,
slept on the ground,
and did not eat after dark.

Other times
I loved makeup and jewelry,
baths and perfumes,
just serving my body
obsessed with sensuality.

Then faith came.
I took up the homeless life.
Seeing the body as it really is,
desires have been rooted out.

Coming to birth is ended
and my cravings as well.
Untied from all that binds
My heart is at peace.

While Nanduttarā's poem insinuates that body modification and attention to the body are superficial and fruitless, anti-body sentiments are perhaps most sharply expressed by the nun Khemā:

I'm disgusted by this body.
It's foul and diseased.
It torments me.[32]

Perhaps the story of Rūpyāvatī, found in a fifth-century Sanskrit collection of *jātakas*—stories of the Buddha's previous lives—bespeaks the de-feminization of the body most explicitly.[33] The story of Rūpyāvatī is exceptional in its status as a rare account of the Buddha assuming a female form in a previous life. Rūpyāvatī, a beautiful young woman who lives in a town plagued by famine, encounters a starving woman who is about to eat her newborn son. In a supremely self-sacrificing religious act, Rūpyāvatī cuts off her own breasts and gives them to the woman, providing her food and sparing her child:

Then Rūpyāvatī said to her, "Wait a moment. First, bring
    me a knife, if you have one here." And the woman
    brought Rūpyāvatī a knife.
Then Rūpyāvatī cut off her breasts with the sharp knife,
Like two golden water-pots gushing with blood.
She gave them to the starving young woman,
Unconcerned with the suffering of her own body. . . .
Then, having given both breasts to the woman,
    Rūpyāvatī went back into her own house.
The charming belt and garment on her beautiful body
Were stained with blood that had gushed forth from her
    severed breasts.
She looked like a golden image
That has been worshipped with saffron powder.[34]

Rūpyāvatī's husband is confused when he sees his mutilated wife and questions what kind of horrible person has cut her breasts from her beautiful body. When he learns of her immensely compassionate act, he performs an act of truth:

> "As no one else—not even a man—
> Has given such a gift before,
> By means of this truth,
> Let my wife's breasts immediately be restored!"
> As soon as the householder had performed his act of truth,
> Her chest was restored, heavy with the weight of her
>   bosoms.
> And then Rūpyāvatī once again adorned the city,
> Like a lotus pond that relieves the thirst of the world
> Through the water of generosity.
> Her heavy breasts were like two Cakravākā birds,
> Her beautiful face was like a lotus,
> And her teeth were like lotus filaments.[35]

What is particularly remarkable about Rūpyāvatī's story is that her femininity and beauty—though initially defiled—are restored and lauded. However, the tale takes a drastic turn as Rūpyāvatī declares:

> As I wish only for the state of a victor [a buddha]
> In order to bring peace to the three worlds,
> O brahmin, by means of this truth of mine,
> Let my sex become male immediately,
> For manhood is an abode of virtue in this world.[36]

As soon as Rūpyāvatī speaks these words, she miraculously becomes a man and incurs the following body transformation:

> And when her two breasts—
> Swollen like the frontal lobes of an elephant in a rut—
> Saw just a few beard hairs as dark as collyrium powder
> Appearing on that moon-like face,
> They immediately disappeared into a broad chest,
> As if out of shame.[37]

By rescinding their beauty and the very "femaleness" of their forms, Rūpa Nandā, Vimalā, Ambapālī, Nanduttarā, Khemā, and Rūpyāvatī become Buddhist exemplars. Yet, as one of the students in my Women and Buddhism course commented, they "are encouraged to ruin themselves for the sake of spiritual awakening." As they change from beautiful women to sexless renunciants (or to men, as in the case of Rūpyāvatī), what was once explicitly female becomes discursively and visually stripped of female gender.[38] If, as the Buddhist record indicates, physical features are indicative of moral status, then to what moral attainments, if any, do female physical features attest?[39] Can the female body, which is repeatedly associated with impurity and deception, ever reflect true beauty and virtuousness? Can moral status ever be inscribed on an explicitly *beautiful* female body?

As the stories of Rūpa Nandā, Vimalā, Ambapālī, Nanduttarā, Khemā, and Rūpyāvatī reveal, the very markers and signifiers of a *female* body—that is, ornaments and adornments, hair and cosmetics, hips and breasts, lips and eyes, skin and flesh—are stripped away as the onlooker or inhabitant (the woman who witnesses her own physical demise) moves from a state of bondage and suffering to a state of liberation and release. What one is left with is an androgynous, asexual form at best, and a sack of bones at worst—*not* a female body, and surely not a beauty. The grotesquely represented "woman," or the transcendent androgyne (who sheds her beauty, femininity, and sexuality on the path to enlightenment), becomes an exemplary model of enlightened "female" embodiment.[40] Yet, can we even consider the resulting embodiment to be "female"? Is "she" still a "woman" at all? Can the beautiful female body ever tell a story of awakening? Let us now turn from the Indian Buddhist narrative record to the artistic landscape.

The Idealized Female Form

In her book, *The Body Adorned: Dissolving Boundaries Between Sacred and Profane in India's Art*, Vidya Dehejia observes that "the sensuous bodily form, female and male, human and divine, has been a dominant feature in the vast and varied canvas of the Indian artistic tradition."[41] A central image in Indian art is the well-formed human body—that is, the beautiful human body. Within the realm of ancient Indian art and aesthetics, the Sanskrit word *"rupa,"* which simply means "form," implies a handsome form, beauty, elegance, or grace.[42] Decorated with fine fabrics, jewels, and flowers, the perfectly formed body of the Indian tradition is always deliberately ornamented. Indeed "ornament" (*alankara*) has a symbolic connotation of auspiciousness, protection, beautification, and completion.[43] Women swathed in jewels, voluptuous, seductively posed, populate the world of Indian imagery, adorning the walls of Hindu, Buddhist, and Jain temples. Indeed, these voluptuous beauties find prominent place on the brackets of *toranas* (gateways) and rail posts of Buddhist *stūpa*s, symbols of worship and veneration.[44] For example, the entryways at the *stūpa* at Bharhut are flanked with sensuous images of semi-divine beings known as *yakshis* and *devatas*—the epitome of female beauty and Indian aesthetics.[45] The female figures at Bharhut, the beautifully carved women who flank the gateways of the *stūpa* at Sāñchī, and the sensuous women on the railing pillars at the Mathura *stūpa* challenge the notion that Buddhists have no concern for, or have transcended, aesthetic beauty.[46] Sensuous, richly adorned, beautiful women populate Indian Buddhist sacred sites, suggesting that Buddhism and beauty may not be antithetical after all.

Surrounding the Buddhist *stūpa* at Bharhut is a tall railing composed of ornately carved pillars, nearly seven feet tall, which enclose a path for ritual circumambulation.[47] Among the various male and female semi-divine beings, human devotees, and warriors carved on these pillars are female *yakshis*, such as the Chandra *yakshi*. She is "a sensuous female with her left leg wrapped around the trunk of a tree, her right hip thrust outward, and her right arm drawing one of its leafy branches down toward her."[48] She is adorned with various jewelry and accoutrements (earrings, headdress, necklace, bangles, anklets, hip-belt) that further accentuate her swelling breasts, slender waist, and curvaceous hips. An inscription names her Chanda (meaning "moon") and describes her as a *yakshi*, a "semidivine, nymph-like being associated with forests, foliage, and fertility."[49] She is joined by other beautiful female figures that contribute to the grandeur and sacredness of the Bharhut site.

Like Bharhut, the Buddhist *stūpa* at Sāñchī features sensuous images of women, most notably carved on the gateways. As Dehejia notes, "Viewers enter the sacred enclosure and passing through each of the four gateways, as they sought to view its sacred narratives, would have passed beneath these sensuous female figures, twenty-four in all."[50] Likewise, numerous *yakshis* were carved into the railing pillars surrounding the *stūpa* at Mathura.[51] It is evident from the iconography that ideal beauty and female fertility are at play in these sacred sites. With large breasts and wide hips, these *yakshis* represent classical India's conception of ideal feminine beauty and fecundity.

The blackening of the breasts and pubis of the Mathura *yakshis* testifies to the ritual practice of pilgrims circumambulating Buddhist shrines and touching the breasts and pubis of *yakshis* to accrue merit and procure blessings. As reliquary mounds, the main purpose of *stūpa*s is to glorify the Buddha and, for devotees, to experience the living presence of the Buddha (believed to be enshrined in the relics). What are we to make, then, of these sensuous female images amidst these sacred sites? Dehejia offers some profound insights:

> We should ponder the significance of such frank and lus-
> cious representation of physical beauty in a space associated
> with the Buddha's relics, a space open to public viewing,
> while keeping in mind that the sensuous figures were often
> gifts from the monastics themselves. While the prime aim
> of the site was to allow visitors to experience the presence
> of the Buddha, it was considered important to surround the
> stūpa with carved representations of semidivine beings of
> more-than-Buddhist significance, several of whom . . . were
> portrayed as offering their homage to the greatness and
> glory of the Buddha.[52]

Rejecting the notion that these images objectify women and are intended for the edification of men, Dehejia offers the following critique: "One has to discard the use of phrases like 'the male gaze' with its inference that the sensuous female figures were created solely for the viewing pleasure of men, for women were responsible for some of these commissions."[53] Moreover, monastics—both Buddhist monks and nuns—commissioned such images, further displacing a strict gender divide or lay/monastic divide. At Sāñchī alone, of the 527 identifiable inscriptions, eighty-four are gifts from nuns (*bhikkhunī*) and sixty-nine are gifts from monks (*bhikkhu*). Indeed, "the monastics community was substantially involved in the construction and decoration of the stūpa."[54] Clearly, one cannot say that these sensuous female images are the creations of men for men, nor that they represent the inclinations and preferences of the laity alone. Further, it is certain that pilgrims to Bharhut consisted of Buddhist men and women, laity and monastics alike, all of whom would have set their eyes on these sensuous beauties. The suspicious, even disdainful attitudes toward women, female embodiment, and beauty so prevalent in Buddhist texts are not reflected in the visual material culture.[55] Within these sacred spaces is an apparently comfortable coexistence of seemingly divergent concepts—the sensuous and the sacred. As Dehejia observes, "That such juxtaposition was totally acceptable in Buddhist . . . sacred precincts indicates a worldview at variance with the one to which we are today accustomed, especially in the West."[56]

With breasts bared, hips full, and expressions of serene pleasure, these quasi-divine female figures evoke the very opposite of the repulsion, impurity, and degradation of the female body evidenced in much Indian Buddhist literature. Of course, as Dehejia discerns, the gendered body of artistic expression (whether literary, sculptural, or pictorial) "is a social construct that rarely reflects life as it is lived."[57] Yet, how do these sensuous and beautiful figures pertain to the Indian Buddhist renunciant who is exempt from such adornments and refinements, save the requisite robe? One might be tempted to say that beauty is beyond the scope of Buddhist monastics, both male and female: in other words, Buddhist monks and nuns have transcended any apparent attachment to beauty, and the seemingly superficial concerns of beauty have no place on the path to enlightenment. However, the Indian Buddhist textual record provides a much more varied and complex relationship between beauty and Buddhist spiritual adepts.

Buddhaful: The Beautiful Buddha

In his groundbreaking work, *A Bull of a Man: Images of Masculinity, Sex, and the Body in Indian Buddhism*, John Powers reveals that the Buddha of Indian Buddhist literature is upheld as the paragon of masculinity, repeatedly and fervently extolled for his extraordinarily beautiful body.[58] Contrary to being portrayed as androgynous, asexual, and ascetic, the Buddha is described in Indian Buddhist texts as "handsome, good looking, graceful, possessing supreme beauty of complexion, with sublime beauty and sublime presence, remarkable to behold."[59] The Buddha's remarkable physical beauty elicits admiration from women and men, and becomes a public signifier of his attainment of spiritual perfection. Indeed, the Buddha's physical appearance alone captures the attention of numerous wandering ascetics and motivates them to listen to his teachings.[60] The Buddha's beauty prompts spontaneous conversion experiences and establishes followers on the Buddhist path. Powers emphasizes the centrality of the Buddha's beauty in the propagating of the Dharma: "the Buddha's physical endowments are not merely peripheral or unimportant: they are essential components of his persona and play a crucial role in his conversion activities."[61] His beauty even sways skeptics: after attaining buddhahood, the Buddha seeks out his five former ascetic companions who had abandoned him earlier with charges of his lax-ity and gluttony; as the Buddha approaches, the former skeptics are mesmerized by his splendor and beauty. They declare, "Venerable Gotama, your features are perfectly clear. Your complexion is per-fectly pure."[62] Securing their confidence through the radiance of his physical presence, the Buddha delivers his first sermon and gains his first disciples.

The Buddha's beauty is neither ambiguous nor androgynous in nature, but resolutely masculine and virile. It is not coincidental that Gotama resolves to impregnate Yaśodharā prior to leaving the householder life to pursue the religious path.[63] He fulfills his sexuality and masculinity, and ultimately produces a male heir.[64] In colloquial terms, the Buddha is studly. He is a "manly man."[65] Even in ascetic robes, the bodhisattva has a profound effect on women: "women looked up at him with restless eyes . . . [The bodhisattva], bright as a golden mountain, captured the hearts of the best women and capti-vated their ears, limbs, eyes and beings with his voice, touch, beauty, and qualities."[66] His magnificent body and sexual virility reflect his accumulated merit and advanced spiritual state.

The Buddha's exceptional beauty is a manifestation of his spiri-tual attainments over many lifetimes. To further contextualize, there is no notion of a mind–body division in Indian Buddhist discourses. Indian Buddhist texts posit an inherent connection between a per-son's body and physical endowments and his (or her?) morality. As Powers observes, "In Indian Buddhism, virtue is beautiful, and the most morally advanced beings are also those with the most attrac-tive physiques."[67] In accordance with the Buddhist doctrine of karma, "Those who are well favored, wealthy, good-looking and long-lived are experiencing the ripening of their past karma, while those who are ugly, misshapen, poor, and sickly similarly are reaping what they have sown."[68] Beauty is the reward of virtue. Yet, the correlation between physical appearance and moral status is highly gendered. It appears that only men are allowed to be male, beautiful, and liberated, all at the same time, whereas women must be stripped of their gender, as well as becoming ugly in the process, in the pursuit of libera-tion (recall Rūpa Nandā, Vimalā, Ambapālī, Nanduttarā, Khemā, and Rūpyāvatī).

The Buddhist linkage between bodily beauty, on the one hand, and moral perfection, on the other, is perhaps most clearly expounded

in the *Lakkhaṇa Sutta,* or *Text on Perfections.*[69] *Lakkhaṇa* (Pāli) or *lakṣaṇa*
(Sanskrit) means "an auspicious mark" and the text that bears the
name describes the thirty-two marks that distinguish a great being
or *mahāpuruṣa.* (Of course, the fully enlightened Buddha is considered
a *mahāpuruṣa.*) Among the thirty-two marks are (4) long fingers and
toes; (5) soft and tender hands and feet; (8) legs like an antelope's;
(10) male organs enclosed in a sheath; (11) a bright complexion, the
color of gold; (12) delicate and smooth skin; (17) a chest like a lion's;
(19) a proportioned body; (24) even teeth; (29) deep blue eyes; and
(30) eyelashes like a cow's.[70]

The *lakṣaṇa*s are at once signs of beauty and signs of worth.[71]
The body of a *mahāpuruṣa* (in this case, the Buddha) is variously
described thusly: "fair to see, and shapely limbed"; "well-formed
above, and beautiful"; "graceful"; and with a body "like fine-wrought
gold . . . more fair than all the gods."[72] The text makes clear that each
of the bodily marks or perfections are the outcome of moral actions:
indeed, "there are karmic reasons for the gaining of them."[73] While
some figures in the Pāli canon exhibit a range of these physical marks,
only *buddhas* possess all of them, and to the greatest degree of clar-
ity and perfection.[74] The thirty-two *lakṣaṇa*s also suggests that only
a man can be considered a *mahāpuruṣa,* given that one of the marks
can appear only on a man (namely number 10, a penis enclosed in
a sheath). As Powers comments, the sheathed penis "is associated
with the retracted members of stallions, bulls, and elephants, all symbolic of masculinity in Indic literature.[75] The tenth mark affirms the
male body as the vehicle for Buddhahood.[76] Or does it? While the
traditional, age-old interpretation of the tenth mark hinges on the
necessity of a penis, and hence manhood, in order to be a Buddha,
several scholars offer subversive readings of the tenth mark. Nancy
Barnes contends that the sheathed penis "symbolizes that his genital
virility is controlled and contained and is replaced by his oral 'virility.' "[77] Sociologists Dean and Juliet MacCannell assert, "Without actually viewing another's genitals, we have no real *proof* of the other's
sex."[78] Thus, we are left to question, *if the "male organ" is covered by a
sheath, how do we know it is really there at all?* Finally, reflecting on the
nature of female anatomy, Rita Gross proposes, "the usual bearers of
a *sheathed* 'penis' are not men at all, but women." This muddling of
seemingly disparate and clear categories resonates with the rhetorical
claim of Dr. Anne Fausto-Sterling: "How small does a penis have to
be before we can call it a clitoris?"[79]

Transposing the trope of the thirty-two *lakṣaṇa*s of ancient India
into contemporary American discourse demonstrates how beauty

standards, as well as standards of masculinity and femininity, shift over time and in different cultural contexts.[80] In Indian Buddhist art and literature, the Buddha's body is upheld as the paragon of the male physique. Yet, even a brief survey of the thirty-two marks reveals how notions of body image and normative masculinity are particular to certain historical and geographic locales. While the Buddha's physique is depicted as the supreme male form, this body image differs significantly from, and even contradicts, contemporary Western standards.[81] Powers explains:

> [I]n the West, attractive male bodies are commonly presented as having a distinctive V-shape, with strongly delineated muscles, while Buddha images made in India generally have no muscle tone and appear effeminate to Western eyes. Buddha is often depicted with flaring hips, with no discernable muscles, and with a slight midriff bulge. He is said to be powerful and athletic in Buddhist texts, but these qualities are not displayed in images and are not associated with muscularity. Rather, male beauty requires smoothness of features, lack of protuberances and bulges, proportion between limbs, and dignified comportment.[82]

While the Buddha's physique may appear "odd" to Westerners, classical Indian artists were selective about how many and which marks to fashion; indeed, to create a figure with all of the thirty-two marks of a *mahāpuruṣa* would run the risk of imaging a "freak" rather than a specimen of human perfection.[83]

Beauty and morality are intricately and cohesively interwoven, at least for male renunciants, the Buddha included. Consider the description of the Buddha's virtue and beauty in the Sanskrit text, the *Lalitavistara*:

> Next to the radiance of the [Buddha]
> . . .
> gold cannot shine; it becomes like ink.
> So it is with the jewels
> adorning the one who is unblemished,
> the one filled with a hundred virtues;
> placed on him the jewels cannot shine.
> [. . .]
> Bearing the signs which are the fruits of former virtue,
> what need does he have of common ornaments,

the work of others?
Let the ornaments be removed!
. . .
Give away these jewels!
Seek the radiance which is truly pure and spotless.[84]

As the *sūtra* conveys, the Buddha's body is so luminous from his meritorious actions and spiritual attainments that no superficial ornaments or adornments are necessary. While the text maintains the linkage between beauty and morality, it discursively strips the spiritual adept of external ornamentation. Likewise, Aśvaghoṣa's *Buddhacarita* reports on the Buddha's golden splendor and its effect on onlookers: "His beautiful body is transformed by the shaving of his head and wearing cast-off garments, but he is still covered in the color of gold [radiating] from his body."[85] Far from being merely skin deep, true beauty is manifest internally and radiates outward.

Yet, where do women fit in this? Are there instances in which female piety and female beauty are validated and deemed worthy simultaneously? I offer up at this point three possibilities from the Indian Buddhist narrative and artistic repertoire: Queen Māyā, the laywoman Visākhā, and the lesser known Kumaradevī.

Queen Māyā

Queen Māyā, mother of Siddhāttha, who later became the Buddha, is represented, both in literature and art, in idealized female form. In various Pāli canonical sources and in Buddha biographies, Māyā possesses qualities of physical and moral perfection that render her fit and worthy to be the bodhisattva's mother, including being "supremely beautiful" and "abundant in merit."[86] She is depicted as possessing thirty-two good qualities (possibly echoing the thirty-two physical marks of a Buddha):

Friends, the woman in whose womb a bodhisattva is conceived in his final existence must have thirty-two qualities. What are these thirty-two qualities? A bodhisattva in his final existence must be conceived in the womb of a woman known by all and steadfast in conduct. She must come from a good caste and a good family. She must have an excellent figure, an excellent name, and excellent proportions.

She must not have given birth previously, and she must
have excellent discipline. She must be generous, cheerful,
and adroit. She must also be clear minded, calm, fearless,
learned, wise, honest, and without guile. She must be free
from anger, jealousy, and greed. She must not be coarse,
easily distracted, or prone to gossip. She must be patient
and good-natured, with a good conscience and sense of
modesty. She should have little attachment, anger, and
ignorance. She should be free from the faults of womankind
and be a devoted wife. In his final existence, a bodhisattva
must be conceived in the womb of a woman with all of
these excellent qualities.[87]

Queen Māyā exudes both beauty and virtue. The *Lalitavistara* expounds
upon her physical flawlessness:

Her attractive face and body
Shine like the beautiful moon in the sky
And blaze like the stainless fire of the sun.
Her body shines with an excellent light.
The complexion of this queen is resplendent,
Shining like the purest gold.
Her hair is soft, clean, and sweetly scented,
Black like the excellent bee and arranged in braids.
Her eyes are like lotus petals;
Her teeth are like stars in the sky.
Her waist is curved like a bow and her hips are ample;
Her shoulders are raised and her joints are smooth.
Her thighs and calves are like the trunk of an elephant,
And her knees have a shapely form.
The palms of her hands and the soles of her feet are
        smooth and red;
Surely she can only be a divine maiden.[88]

Her exquisite beauty and sensuality are acutely manifest in pictorial
form. In a mural on the walls of the Buddhist monastery of Ajantā
(ca. fifth century CE), Māyā appears slender but curvaceous, adorned
with exquisite jewels, leaning languorously against a column.[89]
    In an adjacent scene, she is seated next to King Śuddhodana,
bearing her breasts, swathed in necklaces, armbands, and other ornaments, all the while listening to the soothsayer interpret her dream

of the night before, in which she saw a white elephant entering her womb.[90] What is striking about this mural is the apparent congruity between Māyā's beauty and sensuality and her "sacred" role as the mother of the Buddha-to-be. We must also bear in mind that Buddhist renunciants prayed and meditated within the Ajantā caves, amidst all of this beauty and sensuality. As Dehejia observes, within the context of Indian Buddhist sacred imagery, spiritual beauty and bodily beauty are intertwined and inextricably linked.[91]

Let us turn to another possibility of female beauty and piety.

Visākhā

Visākhā is lauded for being a devout wife and generous benefactress, and for converting many to Buddhism and lavishly bestowing her wealth and services on the monastic order.[92] Visākhā is described as the Buddha's "chief benefactress" because of her donation of "ninety millions."[93] Beyond her generosity to the *sangha*, she apparently had easy access to the Buddha himself: Gotama repeatedly accepted Visākhā's invitations to come to her home, and Visākhā reportedly went to hear Gotama preach. She prompted the conversions of her father-in-law and mother-in-law to Buddhism, and "open doors were henceforth kept at their house for the religion of the Buddha."[94] Visākhā's devotion and rapport with the Buddha are epitomized in the following dialogue, in which she requests certain boons from the Blessed One:

> I desire, Lord, my life long to bestow robes for the rainy season upon the Sangha, and food for the incoming almsmen, and food for the sick and food for those that wait upon the sick, and medicine for the sick, and a constant supply of congey [rice porridge], and bathing robes for the almswomen.[95]

Gotama clearly held Visākhā in high esteem for he bestowed on her these boons, and applauded her generosity. Along with her great generosity and deeds of merit, Visākhā is celebrated for her unsurpassed beauty. According to Buddhist records, she is endowed with the five beauties: beauty of hair, of flesh, of bone, of skin, and of youth.[96]

Although she gave birth to ten sons and ten daughters, the *Dhammapada* commentary applauds her for maintaining her youth and beauty throughout: "she always seemed to be about sixteen years old" and never had a single gray hair on her head.[97] Moreover, though she was as "strong as five elephants," she was "highly civilized and feminine to her finger-tips."[98] The quintessential female patron is a woman of enthralling beauty and femininity, as the story of Visākhā testifies.[99]

Kumaradevī

Like Visākhā, Kumaradevī was a generous donor who gifted a Buddhist *vihāra* at Sarnath. A stone slab at the site is inscribed with Sanskrit verses (dating from the twelfth century) lauding the physical beauty, Buddhist devotion, and generosity of Kumaradevī, wife of King Govindachandra (king of the Gupta Empire, ca. 32 CE). The verses elaborate on her "marvelous beauty" which, according to the poet, surpass that of the goddess Pārvatī. At the same time, her devotion to the Buddha is highlighted:

> Her mind was set on religion [*dharma*] alone; her desire was bent on virtues [*guna*]; she had undertaken to lay in a store of merit [*punya*]; she found a noble satisfaction bestowing gifts [*dāna*]; . . . her appearance (was) charming to the eye.[100]

This public poem, composed as official poetry to applaud the Buddhist patroness, makes clear that "physical beauty was an expected adjunct to piety."[101] In the cases of Queen Māyā, Visākhā, and Kumaradevī, female piety and physical beauty go hand in hand, and both are publicly applauded.

Mirror, Mirror on the Wall: Reflecting on Buddhist Beauties

Comparing depictions of Buddhist laywomen to those of nuns yields striking discrepancies and biases. The "beauty myth" surrounding laywomen is laden with Buddhist female protagonists described and portrayed as being exceedingly beautiful; moreover, their beauty is a sign of their morality and spiritual prowess. In contrast, the "beauty myth" surrounding female renunciants is riddled with "ugly" and de-feminized nuns whose morality and spiritual prowess serve as catalysts for their de-beautification. One is hard pressed to find an

Indian Buddhist hagiography of a female renunciant who is lauded as beautiful, and whose body/physical appearance is commended as a sign of her virtue.

The great disparity between the treatment of laywomen (particularly generous benefactresses) and nuns/renunciant women in Buddhist texts has received scholarly attention. Nancy Falk observes that laywomen emerge more frequently, and often more positively, than do nuns in Buddhist scriptures.[102] Janice Willis expounds upon the significant role that laywomen benefactresses played in the development and sustenance of the Buddhist tradition: the support of female laity extended from "simple daily alms" to the funding of construction of *stūpas* and "more permanent and ever-larger monastic complexes."[103] Consider, here, the exaltation of Visākhā: she is arguably the most lauded woman in Indian Buddhist literature. As Uma Chakravarti observes, "It is significant that Visākhā [a laywoman] . . . is the most important woman in the Pāli texts and not Mahāpajāpatī Gotami who had renounced the world in search of liberation."[104] Likewise, Falk comments, "The grand heroine of Buddhist storytelling is not the nuns' founder Mahāpajāpatī, as one might expect, but Visākhā, a prominent merchant's daughter and wife who belonged to the early community and who never took the nuns' vows.[105] Not coincidentally, Visākhā's beauty and merit are well attested to in Buddhist narratives (particularly the *Dhammapadātthakathā*). In juxtaposition, references to Mahāpajāpatī's, or *any* nun's, beauty and merit are virtually nonexistent; a nun may be commended for her virtue, but she is surely not beautiful (again recall Rūpa Nandā, Vimalā, Ambapālī, Nanduttarā, Khemā, and Rūpyāvatī).

Diana Paul asserts that the exaltation of laywomen in Buddhist scriptures parallels the declining status of *bhikkhunīs*.[106] Thus, the lengthy and frequent passages glorifying laywomen echo their waxing status and influence in Buddhist communities, while the scarce and infrequent references to nuns (except for the *Therīgāthā*) echo their waning status and influence in Buddhist societies. Probing this disparity further, the gulf between the positive treatment of laywomen and the negative treatment of nuns/renunciant women in Buddhist texts may reflect each group's allegiance versus resistance to socially prescribed female roles. Tsultrim Allione asserts that nuns "suffered from male distrust because of their relatively emancipated position and for this reason Buddhist laywomen were often presented much more positively than nuns in Buddhist stories."[107] Allione continues: "The Buddhist laywoman was still in her correct slot according to the Hindu social system while nuns held the ambivalent position of having been accepted but with great reservation."[108] Similarly, Falk explains: "Buddhists, like Hindus, honored fecund housewives, especially if they were also pious laywomen. We can therefore suspect that many Buddhists, like Hindus, preferred to see women at the hearth rather than on the road or within a monastery's wall."[109] (Such theories are reinforced by the textual exaltation of Visākhā, the quintessential Buddhist laywoman who fulfills rather than challenges normative femininity and the prevailing stereotypes of women: she is depicted as a faithful wife, a devoted mother, a generous benefactor, and a striking beauty. Likewise, the semi-divine figures of the *yakshi*s that flank Buddhist *stūpa*s are signs of fertility, thus mirroring the same normative values of laywomen.) Eva K. Neumaier-Dargyay also draws the connection between prescribed female roles and the virtual invisibility of nuns in the public representation and enactment of culture:

> The invisibility of the Buddhist nuns in the past is an astounding fact and one that raises serious questions about gender construction within the traditional Buddhist communities. The patriarchal societies of Asia gave women a recognized and acknowledged space only when they confined themselves to the roles of mothers and subservient wives. This recognition, however, was not available to celibate nuns. Consequently, there was no public recognition whatsoever of their existence or the contribution they made to Buddhist belief and practice.[110]

All of these latter women whose beauty is depicted positively are either Buddhist laywomen or female divinities (*yakshi*s); none of them, in other words, is a nun. In contrast, the *other* women—the ugly ones who *do* de-beautify and de-feminize themselves—are all Buddhist nuns, women who have renounced the traditional role of wife and mother and instead assumed the highly anomalous role of being a female renunciant. Perhaps what is at stake here is not so much a matter of contradictory ideas about female beauty and its relationship to moral worth, but rather a matter of using female beauty as a convenient trope for expressing a deep ambivalence about the very prospect of women who renounce the world, reject the traditional roles of wife and mother, and escape from male control. Maybe the need to become ugly here has less to do with Buddhist ideas concerning the impermanence and impurity of the body, and more to do with the price exacted upon women for following a disturbingly nontraditional role.[111] In this sense, perhaps the "beauty myth" described by Naomi Wolf is even closer to this Buddhist complex of ideas than I have proposed. However, I am hesitant to leave the slippery slope of beauty once and for all in the hands of patriarchy.

Conclusion: Does Buddhist Feminism Need a Makeover?

So, where does this leave Buddhist feminists? What are the implications of all this for us today? Let us return to Wolf's *The Beauty Myth*. Wolf's bestseller was met with intensely polarized responses from the public and mainstream media; even so, it was largely embraced by feminists. Feminists lauded Wolf's book as "a clarion call to freedom" (Gloria Steinem), "essential reading for the New Woman" (novelist Fay Weldon),[112] and "a hopeful sign of a new surge of feminist consciousness" (Betty Friedan).[113] But, are beauty and feminism always and inevitably destined to be at odds? Is ugliness—the antithesis of beauty—the signifier of a liberated woman? Can a woman wear lipstick and shave her legs and still claim feminist consciousness? Is the woman who dons "hippie swag," Birkenstocks, and no makeup *more Buddhist* than the woman in eyeliner, high-heels, and a designer suit?[114] Where does beautification, or de-beautification, fit in all of this? Does Buddhist feminism need a makeover? I think, in some ways, yes.

In *Fresh Lipstick: Redressing Fashion and Feminism*, Linda Scott challenges the "antibeauty ideology" that has dominated feminist thinking for 150 years.[115] Scott, a self-identified feminist, suggests that feminism has alienated many women because of its views on beauty and fashion. Scott suggests that "feminism's anti-beauty ideology serves the interests of the few at the expense of the many."[116] She explains

> The social superiority of feminist dress reformers on dimensions of class, education, and ethnicity is recurrent: In every generation, the women with more education, more leisure, and more connections to institutions of power—from the church, to the press, to the university—have been the ones who tried to tell other women what they must wear in order to be liberated.[117]

More pointedly, she contends that such "anti-beauty" sentiments actually undermine women's agency: "Feminist writers have consistently argued that a woman's attempt to cultivate her appearance makes her a dupe of fashion, the plaything of men, and thus a collaborator in her own oppression."[118] Recognizing the complex role of beauty in human history and across cultures, Scott reminds us that people throughout history and in every culture have groomed and decorated themselves, and for a variety of reasons, not just sexual attraction. Feminists have often advocated for a more "natural" appearance, what Scott refers to as the "natural fallacy." The "natural" look, as Scott pointedly observes, is defined in negative terms:

> "Natural" is what we would look like if we did not wear corsets, hoop skirts, lipstick, push-up bras, or whatever the latest bugaboo happened to be. The alternative was presumed to be self-evident. "Natural" is what we would look like if we weren't forced to spend so many hours and use so many products making ourselves look presentable. "Natural" is the absence of artifice.[119]

The problem emerges, however, when one tries to define "natural" in positive terms. As Scott demonstrates, "natural" is just a fallacy:

> Let's imagine a woman as she would be found "in nature," without "man-made" intervention. Under this requirement, any tool or substance not occurring in the natural environment would be an artifice. There would be no scissors for haircuts, razors for shaving, soaps for cleaning. No toothbrushes or combs. All naturally occurring processes would be allowed to run their course: nails growing, hair matting, teeth rotting. A human being totally free of artifice would be unkempt, unclean, unshaven, and probably uncomfortable and unhealthy.[120]

Scott ultimately posits that around the globe and throughout time human beings have been grooming and decorating themselves.

Just as Scott exposes the "natural fallacy," so William LaFleur discerns: "We have not been natural for a very long time: spectacles, dentures, pacemakers, and condoms—even clothing—moved us over that imaginary line long ago."[121] While LaFleur's analysis of the

"natural" body centers on medical technology and biological engi-
neering and their implications for body redesign, his assessment of the
nonexistence of the "natural" body resonates with Scott's articulation
of the "natural fallacy." Indeed, LaFleur's postulation that "[d]emands
that we limit ourselves to what is 'natural' fall flat" (vis-à-vis attitudes
toward advancing forms of medical technology and biological engi-
neering) can be applied to feminism and its "anti-beauty ideology."[122]
Feminist demands that women limit themselves to what is "natural"
fall flat. If one were to extend this line of thinking to the female
renunicates of Indian Buddhist literature, even they are not "natural"
with their shaven heads and saffron robes. Clearly, the *vinaya* (monastic discipline) prohibits Buddhist renunciants from ornamentation and
adornments (save the requisite robes) and from growing their hair
longer than two inches.[123] Such body modifications serve a multiplicity of mutually reinforcing purposes, including to adhere to a life of
simplicity, to mark one's identity as a Buddhist mendicant, and to
avow one's commitment to celibacy and the holy life.[124] Returning
to LaFleur and Scott, both contend that the pejorative designation
of the "unnatural" body (in contrast to some elevated notion of the
"natural" body) is a rebuke to certain persons in society, particularly
those who modify their bodies in ways that challenge the norms of
cultural hegemony. Broadening the scope of analysis, what are the
ethical applications and implications of a purportedly "natural" and
androgynous ideal for Buddhist feminists, or any feminists, today?
While some feminists reject the trappings of beauty ideals altogether
by eschewing makeup, ornamentation, and traditionally feminine
attire in search of some "neutral" and "natural" paradigm (which
is never free from ties to one's culture), the danger emerges that the
resultant "natural androgyne" is in fact, by default, "de-feminized"
and ultimately "masculinized."

On the subject of women, femininity, and beauty, I am skepti-
cal of the transcendent androgyne as the ultimate Buddhist-feminist
goal because it seems to erase female specificity and leave us with
the seemingly unmarked default male. In *This Sex Which Is Not One*,
the French feminist philosopher Luce Irigaray exposes a "dominant
phallic economy" that privileges the male (i.e., phallus) and excludes
women as "the other"—that is, deficient, lacking, dispersed, and invisible, or "nothing to see."[125] As Irigaray intimates, the "disappearance"
of women into the "masculine-neutral" is a radical genocide (the end
of "women") that ultimately triumphs the "masculinist economy."[126]
Like Irigaray, I would like to locate an explicitly feminine and female

liberation. Women who do attain awakening often do so by deconstructing their own beauty, and, in the process, end up stripping themselves of the markers of feminine gender altogether, becoming the "transcendent androgyne" or the default male.

There is no denying that men and women can both be beautiful, and both are depicted as such in various Buddhist texts and images. There is also no denying that strict and unattainable beauty standards cause many women (and men) suffering. Yet, I am hesitant to see women as passive slaves to beauty (which was one of the critiques of Wolf's book). Likewise, I find it imperative to celebrate the female body and beauty without being muddled in the repressive demands of patriarchy.

One might conclude that the fundamental problem with beauty is not the manifestation of beauty, per se, but attachment to beauty. In other words, the desire to *be* beautiful or to *obtain* that which is deemed beautiful keeps one mired in a repetitive cycle of suffering. Disinterest in beauty itself, dispassion toward beauty, and nonattachment to beauty—coupled of course with virtue—constitute the truly beautiful person. Likewise, nonattachment implies the acceptance of impermanence: everything changes. There is an aesthetic dimension to this fundamental Buddhist teaching. The very evanescence of things is the source of their beauty and cause for joy: "A plastic flower is superficially pleasing, but only the living flower, shedding its petals and fading away at the very peak of its blossoming, is truly beautiful."[127]

An alternate conclusion might be a critique of the construction of masculine heterosexual identity—along the lines of Irigaray's criticism of the "masculinist economy." The female form does not innately create desire in males (or females). Male culture constructs the female body as a sexually desirable commodity that puts women at risk of violence and blame. The question surfaces: Is women's beauty dangerous or seductive in a world where there is not male desire? Regardless of whether the problematic issue of women's beauty is placed at the feet of men or women, from a Buddhist perspective the three poisons—ignorance, attachment, and aversion—can be seen as being at work in men's sexual desire and women's pursuit of beauty. The antidote to the three poisons—namely, wisdom, nonattachment, and compassion—offer a path for recognizing the existence of beauty and virtue united in women.

Aesthetic sensibilities and the appreciation of beauty are part of the human condition, even while such standards shift in different contexts and environments. Author and activist (and Buddhist) bell hooks reminds us that "[b]eauty can be and is present in our lives irrespective of our [class, racial, gender, or ethnic] status."[128] She challenges us: "Rather than surrendering our passion for the beautiful . . . we need to envision ways those passions can be fulfilled that do not reinforce the structures of domination we seek to change."[129] She elaborates:

> We need to theorize the meaning of beauty in our lives so that we can educate for critical consciousness, talking through the issues: how we acquire and spend money, how we feel about beauty, what the place of beauty is in our lives when we lack material privilege and basic resources for living, the meaning and significance of luxury, and the politics of envy.[130]

Like hooks, I contend that feminist (and Buddhist) thinkers "need to place aesthetics on our agenda."[131] So I end, not with a definitive conclusion *per se*, but with a vision of a fully embodied and beautiful female enlightenment, and a possibility for a Buddhist feminism in which female beauty is *not* a signifier of attachment and suffering, but instead of awakening.

Notes

1. This maxim was first stated by Sir Thomas Overbury in his poem, "A Wife" (1613): "All the carnall beauty of my wife is but skin-deep."
2. Cambridge Idioms Dictionary, 2nd ed., "Beauty is only skin deep." idioms.thefreedictionary.com/Beauty+is+only+skin+deep (accessed February 19, 2016).
3. *The American Heritage New Dictionary of Cultural Literacy*, 3rd ed. "Beauty is only skin deep." dictionary.reference.com/browse/beauty-is-only-skin-deep (accessed February 19, 2016).
4. www.merriam-webster.com/dictionary/beauty (accessed February 21, 2016).
5. Naomi Wolf, *The Beauty Myth: How Images of Beauty Are Used Against Women* (HarperCollins, 2002). (Originally published by William Morrow and Company in 1991.)
6. In *The Beauty Myth*, Wolf critiques the cosmetics, diet, pornography, and plastic-surgery industries.
7. Ibid., 10.
8. Ibid.

9. Kim Hubbard, "The Tyranny of Beauty: To Naomi Wolf, Pressure to Look Good Equals Oppression," *People*, June 24, 1991. With the publication of *The Beauty Myth*, Wolf became a leading spokeswoman of what was later described as the "third wave" of the feminist movement.

10. This method of body-focused meditation is also discussed in detail in commentarial texts such as Buddhaghosa's *Visuddhimagga* (*Path of Purification*). See Bhadantacariya Buddhaghosa (trans. Bhikkhu Ñanamoli), *The Path of Purification: Visuddhimagga* (Onalaska, WA: Pariyatti Press, 2003).

11. See Stephen Collins, "The Body in Theravāda Buddhist Monasticism," in *Religion and the Body*, ed. Sarah Coakley (Cambridge: Cambridge University Press, 1997), 185–204. Collins's explication of meditations on the body can be found on 192–94.

12. C.A.F. Rhys Davids, ed, *Visudhimagga*, 2 vols. (London: Pali Text Society, 1920–21; reprint, Routledge and Kegan Paul, 1975), 1:179–84. Cited in Liz Wilson, *Charming Cadavers: Horrific Figurations of the Feminine in Indian Buddhist Hagiographic Literature* (Chicago: The University of Chicago Press, 1996), 16.

13. On the propensity of Buddhist literature to gender the repulsive, contemplated body as specifically *female*, see Karen Lang, "Lord Death's Snare: Gender-Related Imagery in the Theragāthā and the Therīgāthā," *Journal of Feminist Studies in Religion* 2 (1986): 63–79; Liz Wilson, "The Female Body as a Source of Horror and Insight in Post-Ashokan Indian Buddhism," in *Religious Reflections on the Human Body*, ed. Jane Marie Law (Bloomington: Indiana University Press, 1995), 76–99; Wilson, *Charming Cadavers*; and Kathryn R. Blackstone, *Women in the Footsteps of the Buddha: Struggle for Liberation in the Therīgāthā* (Surrey, Great Britain: Curzon Press, 1998), 59–81.

14. Cited in Wilson, *Charming Cadavers*, 36; and Lang, "Lord Death's Snare," 69.

15. See Wilson, *Charming Cadavers*, 60, 67.

16. Lang, "Lord Death's Snare," 71.

17. *Mahāvastu*, II.147. Cited in John Powers, *A Bull of a Man: Images of Masculinity, Sex, and the Body in Indian Buddhism* (Cambridge, MA: Harvard University Press, 2009), 35.

18. *The Buddhacarita* (*Acts of the Buddha*), Part II, ed. E. H. Johnston (Calcutta: Baptist Mission Press, 1936), vv. 48–61, 70–73. See also Wilson, *Charming Cadavers*, 63–68. Accounts of the harem scene preceding the *bodhisattva*'s Great Renunciation appear in all Sanskrit biographies of the Buddha, including the *Mahāvastu*, *Lalitavistara*, and *Buddhacarita*.

19. Johnston, *Buddhacarita*, v. 64, 73.

20. As Wilson notes, "Where the other visions [i.e., the Four Sights of old age, sickness, death and a homeless renunciant] that lead Gotama to take a jaundiced view of the pleasures of *samsāra* occur some days prior to his leaving home, the harem vision occurs at a watershed point in the narrative, immediately preceding the Great Renunciation" (*Charming Cadavers*, 67).

21. Cittahattha's story can be found in a Pāli commentary to the *Dhammapada*, the *Dhammapadā hakathā*, and is cited in Wilson, *Charming Cadavers*, 80–82.

22. *Dhammapadātthakathā* cited in Wilson, *Charming Cadavers*, 80–81.

23. An *arhat* is a "worthy one," denoting a person who has attained liberation.

24. *Dhammapadātthakathā* cited in Wilson, *Charming Cadavers*, 85.

25. Ibid., 85–86.

26. Ibid., 81.

27. The story of Rūpa Nandā, told in the *Dhammapada* commentary, is cited in Wilson, *Charming Cadavers*, 157–61.

28. Ibid., 159–60.

29. Tellingly, Rūpa Nandā's name can be translated variously as: "Shapely [*rūpa*] Delight [*nanda*], "Beautiful [*rūpa*] Joy [*nanda*], or "She Who Enjoys [*nanda*] Physical From or Beauty [*rūpa*]." Ibid., 158.

30. Ibid., 152–54.

31. Ibid., 150–52.

32. Khemā's story is cited in Susan Murcott, *First Buddhist Women* (Berkeley, CA: Parallax Press, 2002), 79.

33. The story of Rūpyāvatī is found in the *Jātakamālā* (*Garland of Birth Stories*), translated by Reiko Ohnuma and reprinted in Donald S. Lopez, *Buddhist Scriptures* (New York: Penguin Books, 2004), 159–71.

34. *Jātakamālā* cited in *Buddhist Scriptures*, 165.

35. Ibid., 166–67.

36. Ibid., 168.

37. Ibid.

38. While the shaven head and formless robes speak celibacy, they also remove and mask some of the most readily discernible markers of gender. See Wilson, *Charming Cadavers*, 153.

39. Reiko Ohnuma, *Head, Eyes, Flesh, and Blood: Giving Away the Body in Indian Buddhist Literature* (New York: Columbia University Press, 2007), 225.

40. One might also add here the "woman-turned-man," as in the case of Rūpyāvatī.

41. Vidya Dehejia, *The Body Adorned: Dissolving Boundaries Between Sacred and Profane in India's Art* (New York: Columbia University Press, 2009), 1.

42. Ibid., 12.

43. Ibid., 71.

44. U. N. Roy, "Enchanting Beauties in the Early Buddhist Art: A Symbological Investigation (3rd Century B.C.–3rd Century A.D.)," in *Studies in Indian Art*, ed. Dr. Chitta Ranjan Prasad Sinha (Ramanand Vidya Bhawan: New Delhi, 1998), 62–68.

45. Female *yakshis* and *devatas* (and their male counterparts, *yakshas* and *nagarajas*) have little direct connection to Buddhist concepts. Nonetheless, their presence at sacred Buddhist sights is significant and telling.

46. See, for example, "What's Your Aesthetic? Celebrating Buddhist Culture and Beauty." www.buddhistdoor.net/features/whats-your-aesthetic-celebrating-buddhist-culture-and-beauty (accessed February 21, 2016).

47. The Bharhut *stūpa* dates to the first century BCE. Of the original pillars at the Bharhut *stūpa*, only forty-nine remain. Among the surviving image-pillars are eight male figures and seven female figures. See Dehejia, *The Body Adorned*, 81.

48. Ibid., 77.

49. Ibid., 78.

50. Ibid., 82. The "sacred narratives" to which Dehejia refers are depictions of the biography of the Buddha, his previous lives in the form of *Jātaka* tales, and later historical events like legends surrounding Emperor Aśoka.

51. It is striking to note the parallels between the Sāñchī *yakshi* bracket and imagery depicting Queen Māyā giving birth to the Buddha: both stand beneath a tree with one arm raised to grasp a branch overhead, both position their body in a similar manner, both emit a sensual quality. Indeed, both reflect the "potency of women's fertility and auspiciousness." Ibid., 93–95.

52. Ibid., 81.

53. Ibid.

54. Ibid., 84.

55. Ibid., 97–98. Dehejia concludes that the Buddhist texts, written by monastic scholars, reflect the beliefs of a narrowly defined group and not of the Buddhist lay community as a whole. She proposes that "the artistic material at the various *stūpa* sites better represents the widely held beliefs of the lay worshippers who constituted the primary group of adherents to the faith" (98). In contrast, U.N. Roy suggests that "[t]he exciting beauties of the Buddhist stūpas may reasonably be taken as symbolizing external allurements and worldly attractions, aversion to which had prompted prince Siddhāttha to renounce the pleasures of the palace" (Roy, "Enchanting Beauties," 65). I am not, however, convinced that these voluptuous, beautiful female figures flanking Buddhist *stūpa*s need to be read in such androcentric and negative terms as reminders of renunciation.

56. Dehejia, *The Body Adorned*, 22.

57. Ibid., 11, 92.

58. Powers, *A Bull of a Man*.

59. From the "Discourse to Cankī." Ibid., 3.

60. See John Powers, "You're Only as Good as You Look: Indian Buddhist Associations of Virtue and Physical Appearance," *Destroying Māra Forever: Buddhist Ethics Essays in Honor of Damien Keown*, ed. John Powers and Charles S. Prebish (Ithaca, NY: Snow Lion Publications, 2009), 67–94.

61. Ibid., 73.

62. *Lalitavistara*, cited in Powers, *A Bull of a Man*, 49. Elsewhere in the *Lalitavistara*, the Buddha states, in a direct affront to the path of extreme

asceticism, "Previously my complexion had been beautiful and smooth, but now this radiance had disappeared because of exerting myself in extreme austerities." Dharmachakra Translation Committee, trans., *Lalitavistara: The Play in Full* (2013), 192. aryanthought.files.wordpress.com/2014/05/lalitavistara-sutra.pdf (accessed August 9, 2017).

63. Powers, *A Bull of a Man*, 38.

64. Ibid.

65. Ibid.

66. Aśvaghoṣa's *Buddhacarita*. Ibid., 41.

67. Powers, "You're Only as Good as You Look," 71. As Powers notes, the association between physical beauty and morality is not confined to India. Powers, *A Bull of a Man*, 6–7.

68. Powers, *A Bull of a Man*, 5.

69. The *Lakkhana Sutta* on the thirty-two marks of a great man is found in the *Dīgha Nikāya* ("*Collection of Long Discourses*"), which is part of the Pāli Tipitaka, the canonical scriptures of the Theravāda school of Buddhism.

70. Maurice Walshe, trans., *Thus Have I Heard: The Long Discourses of the Buddha* (Dīgha Nikāya) (Boston: Wisdom Publications, 1995), 441–42. The complete list of the thirty-two marks of a Great Man includes: 1. feet with level tread; 2. soles of the feet marked with wheels with a thousand spokes; 3. projecting heels; 4. long fingers and toes; 5. soft and tender hands and feet; 6. net-like (webbed) hands and feet; 7. high-raised ankles; 8. legs like an antelope's; 9. the ability to touch one's knees with either hand without bending; 10. male organs enclosed in a sheath; 11. a bright complexion, the color of gold; 12. skin so delicate and smooth that dust cannot adhere to it; 13. separate body hairs, one to each pore; 14. bluish-black (like collyrium) body hairs that grow upwards and curl in rings to the right; 15. a divinely straight body; 16. A body with seven convex surfaces; 17. torso like a lion; 18. no hollow space between the shoulders; 19. a proportionate body like a banyan tree: the height of his body is the same as the span of his outstretched arms, and conversely; 20. an evenly rounded bust; 21. a perfect sense of taste; 22. jaw like a lion's; 23. forty teeth; 24. even teeth; 25. no spaces between his teeth; 26. very white and bright teeth; 27. a longue tongue; 28. a divine voice, like that of the *karavīka* bird; 29. deep blue eyes; 30. eyelashes like a cow's; 31. a soft and white (like cotton-down) tuft of hair between his eyes (Sanskrit, *ūrṇā*); 32. a head like a royal turban, meaning a protuberance on the top of the head (Sanskrit, *uṣṇīṣa*). Incidentally, the elongated earlobes commonly depicted in Buddha images do not figure in this list.

71. Interestingly, the Sanskrit term *lakṣaṇas* later came to be used as a synonym for "beauty" and continues to be used in reference to a person with a well-proportioned body that is also well clothed and adorned. See Dehejia, *The Body Adorned*, 65.

72. Walshe, *Thus Have I Heard*, 445, 448–50. Cited in Dehejia, *The Body Adorned*, 65.

73. Ibid., 442.

74. See Powers, *A Bull of a Man*, 31, 178.

75. John Powers, "Gender and Virtue in Indian Buddhism," *Cross Currents* 61:4(2011): 428–40.

76. Douglas Osto, "Soteriology, Asceticism and the Female Body in Two Indian Buddhist Narratives," *Buddhist Studies Review* 23:2(2006): 213.

77. Nancy Schuster Barnes, "Buddhism," *Women in World Religions*, ed. Arvind Sharma (Albany, NY: State University of New York Press, 1987), 259, n.11.

78. Dean and Juliet Flower MacCannell, "The Beauty System," *The Ideology of Conduct: Essays on Literature and the History of Sexuality*, ed. Nancy Armstrong and Leonard Tennenhouse (New York: Methuen, 1987), 209.

79. Quoted in Sabina Sawhney, "Authenticity is Such a Drag!" in *Feminism Beside Itself*, ed. Diane Elam and Robyn Wiegman (New York: Routledge, 1995), 209.

80. It is worth noting here that the thirty-two marks of a Great Man presents a vision of the ideal Indian male, not the ideal Indian female, who is conceived of as voluptuous, full-breasted, wide-hipped, and curvaceous.

81. Powers, "Gender and Virtue," 434.

82. Powers, *A Bull of a Man*, 10.

83. Ibid., 58.

84. Gwendolyn Bays, trans. *The Lalitavistara Sūtra: The Voice of the Buddha: The Beauty of Compassion* (Berkeley, CA: Dharma Publishing, 1983), 183.

85. Cited in Powers, *A Bull of a Man*, 51.

86. See Ohunma's discussion of Māyā as the idealized birth-giver in *Ties That Bind*, 66–85.

87. Lalitavistara: *The Play in Full*, 37–38.

88. Ibid., 41.

89. Dehejia, *The Body Adorned*, 42.

90. While early Buddhist texts and art celebrate Māyā's beauty, virtue, and auspicious conception, gestation, and delivery, scant attention is paid to her sudden death seven days after the Buddha's birth. For an analysis of "The Short Life-Span of the Ideal Mother," see Reiko Ohnuma, *Ties That Bind: Maternal Imagery and Discourse in Indian Buddhism* (Oxford University Press, 2012), 79–82. See also Kim Gutschow, "The Death of the Buddha's Mother," *Harvard Divinity School Bulletin* 44:1 & 2(2016). Gutschow contends that the descriptions (or lack thereof) of Maya's pregnancy, delivery, and death "may shed some light on the contradictory awe and revulsion that early Buddhist and Brahmanic authors felt toward birth and the female body."

91. Dehejia, *The Body Adorned*, 43.

92. The life of Visākhā is recounted in the *Dhammapada* commentary (*Dhammapadā hakathā*), and references to her are found in the *Udāna*, the *Aṅguttara Nikāya*, and the *jātaka*s. Incidentally, Visākhā reportedly married at age sixteen. See Horner, *Women Under Primitive Buddhism*, 28.

93. Cited in Willis, "Nuns and Benefactresses," 83–84, n.57.

94. Horner, *Women Under Primitive Buddhism*, 349.

95. Ibid., 350–351. It is noteworthy that the opportunity to practice generosity is understood to be a boon.

96. Ibid., 346.

97. Cited in Ohnuma, *Ties That Bind*, 133.

98. Cited in Horner, *Women Under Primitive Buddhism*, 346–47.

99. Interestingly, Visākhā never expressed any desire to join the order of almswomen, and the Buddha apparently never urged her to adopt the renunciant life.

100. Dehejia, *The Body Adorned*, 45.

101. Ibid.

102. Nancy Auer Falk, "The Case of the Vanishing Nuns: The Fruits of Ambivalence in Ancient Indian Buddhism," in *Unspoken Worlds: Women's Religious Lives in Non-Western Cultures*, ed. Nancy A. Falk and Rita M. Gross (San Francisco: Harper and Row, 1980), 207–24.

103. Willis, "Nuns and Benefactresses," 71.

104. Uma Chakravarti, *The Social Dimensions of Early Buddhism* (Delhi: Oxford University Press, 1987), 34.

105. Falk, "The Case of the Vanishing Nuns," 220.

106. Diana Y. Paul, *Women in Buddhism: Images of the Feminine in the Mahāyāna Tradition* (Berkeley: University of California Press, 1985), 79.

107. Tsultrim Allione, *Women of Wisdom* (New York: Arkana, 1986), 8.

108. Ibid. Here, Allione is referring to the Buddha's apparent initial hesitation to accept women into the monastic order, and the requirement that nuns accept the Eight Special Rules (*garudhammas*) as a precondition for their admission into the *saṅgha*. For an analysis of women's acceptance into the *saṅgha* and the significance of the Eight Special Rules, see Murcott, *First Buddhist Women*, 25–30, 213–17.

109. Falk, "The Case of the Vanishing Nuns," 222.

110. Eva K. Neumaier-Dargyay, "Buddhist Thought from a Feminist Perspective," *Gender, Genre and Religion: Feminist Reflections*, ed. Morny Joy and Eva K. Neumaier-Dargyay (Calgary: Wilfrid Laurier University Press, 1995), 164.

111. I am indebted to Reiko Ohnuma for her critiques and insights on an early draft of this paper that I presented at the American Academy of Religion Annual Meeting in San Diego in November 2014.

112. Quoted in Kim Hubbard, "The Tyranny of Beauty: To Naomi Wolf, Pressure to Look Good Equals Oppression," *People*, June 24, 1991.

113. Betty Friedan's comments in *Allure* magazine.

114. I am referring here to the "hippie swag" of Stephen Asma's musings. See Stephen T. Asma, *Why I Am a Buddhist: No-Nonsense Buddhism with Red Meat and Whiskey* (Charlottesville, VA: Hampton Roads Publishing, 2010), 2.

115. Linda M. Scott, *Fresh Lipstick: Redressing Fashion and Feminism* (New York: Palgrave Macmillan, 2005).

116. Ibid., 2.

117. Ibid.

118. Ibid., 1.

119. Ibid., 11.

120. Ibid.

121. William R. LaFleur, "Body," in *Critical Terms for the Study of Religion*, ed. Mark C. Taylor (University of Chicago Press, 1998), 51.

122. Ibid.

123. For an analysis of the significance of clothing in Buddhist monastic life, see Mohan Wijayaratna, *Buddhist Monastic Life: According to the Texts of the Theravāda Tradition*, trans. Claude Grangier and Steven Collins (Cambridge: Cambridge University Press, 1990), 32–55. The allowable length of hair is technically two finger-breadths, not two inches (40). For an analysis of the significance of the shaven head in Buddhist monasticism, particularly as it relates to women, see Karen Christina Lang, "Shaven Heads and Loose Hair: Buddhist Attitudes toward Hair and Sexuality," *Off with Her Head! The Denial of Women's Identity in Myth, Religion, and Culture*, ed. Howard Eilberg-Schwartz and Wendy Doniger (Berkeley: University of California Press, 1995), 32–52.

124. Wijayaratna maintains, "The clothes worn by monks and nuns are one of the most important symbols of the religious life." See Wijayaratna, *Buddhist Monastic Life*, 32.

125. Luce Irigaray (trans. Catherine Porter, *This Sex Which Is Not One* (New York: Cornell University Press, 1985), 24, 26, 69, 117.

126. See Daniel Boyarin, "Gender," in *Critical Terms for Religious Studies* (Chicago: University of Chicago Press, 1998), 117–35, for a critique of the transcendent androgyne as still male.

127. Lewis Richmond, "Buddhist Thoughts on Impermanence, Plutonium and Beauty," *Huffington Post*.

128. bell hooks, "Beauty Laid Bare: Aesthetics in the Ordinary," *To Be Real: Telling the Truth and Changing the Face of Feminism*, ed. Rebecca Walker (New York: Anchor Books, 1995), 164.

129. Ibid., 163–64.

130. Ibid., 164–65.

131. Ibid., 164.

Chapter 8

Conflicts and Compromises

The Relationship between the Nuns of Daihongan and the Monks of Daikanjin within the Zenkōji Temple Complex

MATTHEW MITCHELL

In the summer of 1945, Yamaguchi Kikujūrō, chief administrator of the popular pilgrimage temple Zenkōji, dreamt of how to mediate a conflict between the monastics of Zenkōji's two head subtemples: the Tendai monks of Daikanjin and the Pure Land nuns of Daihongan.[1] The most recent disagreement between the two subtemples began when the Religious Organizations Law came into effect in 1940. According to this law, temples must have one chief cleric, and the heads of Daihongan and Daikanjin were fighting over who should have this title, which had not been used at Zenkōji in the past. After years of arguing, the two entrusted the matter to Yamaguchi, who considered the solution for some time before he had his dream. In this dream the Amitābha icon of Zenkōji appeared before him and stated that "Daihongan's abbess [Chiei] should be the chief cleric of Zenkōji while Daikanjin's abbot should be Zenkōji's steward." The icon then delineated the roles each was to take: "The abbess is to serve the Amitābha icon, while the steward is to handle the teachings and rituals at the temple."[2] This arrangement was accepted by both sides, but it was to last only a short time because Japan surrendered in

World War II a month later, and the Religious Organizations Law was abolished and eventually replaced by the Religious Juridical Person Law. After this, the temple returned to the way it had been before, with Daikanjin and Daihongan sharing power, and neither holding the title of chief cleric of Zenkōji.

This incident demonstrates the central argument of this chapter, which is that the legal atmosphere was just as important as Buddhist doctrine (if not more so) for determining relations between monks and nuns. This becomes evident when we examine the shifting relations between the two monastic communities since the sixteenth century. In the early modern period, Daihongan started out as a part of the temple complex, but as time passed many of the nuns' administrative and ritual rights within the temple complex were slowly stripped away by Daikanjin's monks and their supporters at the powerful Tendai headquarter temple called Kan'eiji. As a result of this, and because the nuns increasingly lived away from Shinano, the nuns gradually came to be a part of and yet apart from the Zenkōji temple complex. This condition continued until the end of the early modern period when Daihongan's abbess at that time, Seien, took advantage of the changing political and legal climate to fight for ritual and administrative rights within the complex again.

In this chapter, I will discuss three periods that were formative in the relationship between Daihongan and Daikanjin: the mid-seventeenth to mid-eighteenth century when control over the temple complex was in flux, the 1860s when the warrior government was being challenged, and the 1870s to 1940s when the modern governmental and legal systems were largely in place. An examination of these three periods demonstrates the ways that changes in laws have affected the relationships between the subtemples at Zenkōji. Further, these three periods of conflict demonstrate that Daihongan's lawsuits were not fights against patriarchal systems or doctrines, but rather struggles for prestige, money, and control over Zenkōji.

By focusing on legal battles of Buddhist nuns in this chapter, I am taking part in a shift in scholarship away from doctrinal, prescriptive discussions of Buddhist womanhood. Instead of focusing on largely patriarchal/androcentric writings (or trying to find instances of female empowerment in the written record), current scholars seek to understand the ways Buddhist women actually lived, practiced, and thought about themselves within their tradition. This shift has been attributed to work on women in religions by Saba Mahmood and Dorothy Ko; in Buddhist studies, the shift is apparent in the works of scholars such as Nirmala Salgado, Lori Meeks, and Barbara Ambros, to name a few.[3]

Lawsuits are an excellent way to determine what was important to people, and they were utilized by both men and women, lay and monastic, in early modern Japan. Japanese Buddhists regularly turned to lawsuits in the early modern period because other, more violent means of conflict resolution were no longer available to them. Nuns were no different. Below we will see how the nuns of Daihongan were not afraid to pursue legal action when deemed necessary. For this reason, the example of Daihongan also challenges or expands existing understandings of Buddhist femininity and feminism. Previous scholars have portrayed Japanese Buddhist nuns as focused on cultural pursuits or rituals for the posthumous well-being of their families. However, the case of Daihongan demonstrates that Buddhist nuns were active in the legal realm. They were legally savvy—if not always successful—and willing to fight when they felt their rights were being taken away.

The case of Daihongan is particularly interesting from the standpoint of the history of Japanese Buddhist nuns. Zenkōji was the only temple in Japan where male and female Buddhist monastics shared ritual space and administrative duties. Zenkōji thus provides a prime opportunity to examine the interaction between male and female Buddhist monastics.

Daihongan within Zenkōji

The relationship between Daihongan and the other subtemples of Zenkōji varied throughout history. During the tumultuous sixteenth century, when various figures jockeyed for power, Zenkōji's buildings were destroyed, and its Amitābha icon and personnel were moved around the country by powerful warlords for almost forty years. During this period, "Hongan" nuns and its abbess were in charge of fundraising for the temple (even when it was not located in Shinano), while a separate group of male monastics were in charge of ritual activities in the temple's main hall. In 1598, Toyotomi Hideyoshi, one of the so-called unifiers of Japan, ordered that the icon be returned to its pre-1550s location in Shinano Province (what is now Nagano Prefecture).[4]

After returning to Shinano, Zenkōji's monks and nuns began to rebuild Zenkōji. They received support from both Toyotomi Hideyori (Hideyoshi's son) and later, Tokugawa Ieyasu, founder of the Tokugawa shogunate that would rule Japan until 1868. Hideyori is said to have awarded the temple a 1,000 *koku* (roughly 278,000 liters of rice) land grant in 1598, and Ieyasu reconfirmed this grant in 1601.[5]

We can understand the roles and positions of the various subtemples within Zenkōji prior to the 1640s from a document outlining the division of the yearly taxes from its temple lands, which was paid in rice.[6] Of the 1,000 *koku* of annual taxes, the monks of Daikanjin received 490 per year, Daihongan received 236, and the remaining 274 *koku* was split unevenly among the smaller Tendai, Pure Land, and Ji school subtemples.[7] Daikanjin received 100 *koku* of their 490 *koku* directly, while another 240 *koku* was for votive candles and Buddhist offerings, suggesting that Daikanjin administered the day-to-day rituals within the Zenkōji temple complex. In contrast, Daihongan received 50 *koku* directly and an additional 36 *koku* each year for hiring carpenters. Both subtemples split an additional 300 *koku* for temple maintenance, suggesting that both were to pay for such repairs equally. Donald McCallum has said that Daihongan's smaller share of the temple complex's yearly taxes is "a clear indication of lesser status" in comparison to Daikanjin.[8] However, the roles and statuses of the two main subtemples appear to have been vaguely delineated in the first half of the seventeenth century.

Daihongan and Daikanjin's roles become more clearly defined in 1642 following a suit brought before the Magistrate of Temples and Shrines (*jisha bugyō*), one of the main adjudicators of conflicts between religious institutions. The two subtemples had jointly decided to rebuild Zenkōji's main hall, which had burnt down that year, but they had begun arguing about their respective roles in the repairs. According to extant documents, Daihongan stated that though "they had been in charge of the whole process of reconstructing the temple from the distant past, now Daikanjin was causing difficulties by unjustly asserting that they be allowed to help."[9] Daikanjin countered by stating that "though both temples had worked together to rebuild the main hall in the past, this time Daihongan was causing difficulties by arguing that they alone should be in charge of the construction."[10] The Magistrate of Temples and Shrines ruled in favor of Daikanjin, and decided in the eleventh month of 1642 that both temples should split building responsibilities because they both divided 300 *koku* yearly for building maintenance.

This was a simple solution to the issue, based largely on the precedent set when the income from the temple lands was divided.

However, the Magistrate of Temples and Shrines did not stop here. They continued with two more points concerning administration of Zenkōji and the temple's lands. They stated that, first, "because Daihongan is a convent, the various duties associated with the outside [running of the temple] will be handled by [the monks of] Daikanjin after consulting with [Daihongan]."[11] Second, "because Daihongan is a convent, the rule of the townspeople and peasants living on Zenkōji's 1000 *koku* of temple lands will be handled by Daikanjin after consulting with [Daihongan]."[12] These statements, which would be cited repeatedly in later lawsuits between the two subtemples up until the 1860s, severely limited the role of Daihongan's nuns in Zenkōji by ostensibly removing the nuns from direct administrative roles in the temple complex and its lands.

The abbess at that time, Chiden (tenure as abbess 1630–1672), was unhappy with the results of this suit. Further, she became frustrated at the way that Daikanjin had come to handle things after they were given administrative control of Zenkōji's temple complex. She brought another suit before the Magistrate of Temples and Shrines in the second month of the following year (1643). In the suit she argues that since the Magistrate's decision the previous year, Daikanjin had been "ignoring the Magistrate's ruling, violating precedents, and causing difficulties by acting selfishly in all things."[13] Her statements are divided into administrative and ritual complaints. First, Daikanjin was not allowing Daihongan to be involved in the planning of the replacement main hall, nor did it allow Daihongan to pay half of the construction costs. Furthermore, in contrast with the past, Daikanjin was not passing on Daihongan's share of the yearly taxes. Additionally, they "arrogantly" used the Magistrate's ruling that control of the temple and its lands was to reside with Daikanjin to force the various subtemples, including Daihongan, into agreeing to a list of rules, and to single-handedly make decisions when in the past they were made in consultation with Daihongan. Finally, in terms of rituals, Daihongan had been left out of various rituals within the temple complex, such as the winter cleaning of the main hall or New Year's festivities; further, Daikanjin had begun performing rituals in front of Zenkōji's icon without regard for the other subtemples.[14] While Chiden does not openly argue against the Magistrate's reasoning that Daikanjin should take the lead within the temple complex "because [Daihongan] is a convent," she does argue against the strong ("arrogant" is the word she uses) central position that Daikanjin had taken since the ruling and the loss of administrative and ritual involvement that meant for

Daihongan. Unfortunately, the Magistrate's response to this suit has not survived.

The results of the Magistrate's 1642 ruling were further solidified in the seventh month of 1643, when Zenkōji was made a branch temple of Kan'eiji, the Tendai sect headquarters in eastern Japan with close and powerful connections to the ruling shogunal family.[15] Kan'eiji and Daikanjin issued rules for the inside of Zenkōji's temple complex. However, the nuns of Daihongan are not mentioned once in these rules. These regulated the day-to-day running of the temple, its ritual performances, and the interactions between the various subtemples, so Daihongan's absence in them could have effectively removed the nuns from Zenkōji's administrative and ritual life.

Sporadic conflicts between the two subtemples continued for nearly a hundred years. These ended in 1740, when Kan'eiji, backed by the Tokugawa shogunate, issued a statement that placed Daihongan under its authority.[16] The abbess of the time, Seikō (tenure 1732–1752), fought against this change, arguing in a petition to the Magistrate of Temples and Shrines that though Daihongan had been without a head temple, "many things were unclear because it was a convent," so it had recently requested in secret that it be under the control of the powerful Pure Land temple Zōjōji. Because "sectarian identity [shūmon] is particularly important," Seikō requested that if Daihongan were to be made into a branch of another temple that the shogunate allow it to be under the control of Zōjōji, a temple with which it already had some relations, instead of the Tendai temple Kan'eiji. Her request was ultimately denied, and Daihongan was placed under Kan'eiji's control, though it was to remain a Pure Land temple.[17]

Becoming a branch of Kan'eiji changed many things for Daihongan, which had until that point been "without a head temple" (muhonji), as many convents of the time were.[18] This altered Daihongan's status administratively and within the larger temple hierarchy. Afterward, the convent had to seek Kan'eiji's preapproval for many activities, including fundraising and lawsuits, before those requests could be forwarded to the Magistrate of Temples and Shrines for final approval, for instance. This had the (perhaps intended) effect of cutting down the number of suits between Daihongan and Daikanjin. Since both of them became branches of Kan'eiji, the Tendai head temple could settle conflicts before they could be forwarded to the Magistrate of Temples and Shrines. This reduced the amount of work for the Magistrate, even if only slightly. Additionally, it meant that Daihongan and Daikanjin could focus on their ritual duties to the shogunate since they were no longer busy pursuing litigation against each other.[19]

Daihongan's position within Zenkōji in the early modern period can thus be summed up as gradual stripping away of rights of its nuns. In the first half of the period, roughly from 1640 until 1740, Daihongan's nuns faced an overall gradual reduction in rights within the temple complex. They did manage to keep some rights, such as the right to be involved with the construction of the main hall and certain temple structures. Other rights they lost, regained, and lost again, such as administrative control over the fifteen Pure Land sub-temples in the complex. Other rights were gradually stripped away, such as administrative control within the temple complex or ritual rights within Zenkōji's main hall, where they were relegated to a visitor's position during major rituals and were not allowed to schedule their own independent rites. Interestingly, these reductions in administrative and ritual rights at Zenkōji were not reflected in the convent's activities in its branch temple Yanaka/Aoyama Zenkōji, where the nuns had much more freedom. This perhaps suggests that the leaders of the Tokugawa shogunate and the Magistrate of Temples and Shrines were not completely against nuns holding ritual and administrative authority at Buddhist temples. Perhaps their motivations in saying "because Daihongan is a convent . . ." may have been political (a push from Kan'eiji to solidify Tendai power within what would soon be its branch temple, for example). Whatever their motivations, however, their ruling largely removed nuns from ritual and administrative power at Zenkōji during the early modern period. In fact, in the last half of the early modern period, Daihongan's nuns spent much of their time at their branch temple in Edo instead of in their main temple at Zenkōji in Shinano.[20]

The nuns of Daihongan fought against these incursions onto their perceived rights whenever possible. We would be remiss, however, in describing these acts as resistance to the patriarchy. Daikanjin's monks were men, as were the Magistrates who handed down rulings. However, Daihongan's suits and countersuits did not directly challenge the assumption that men would administer Zenkōji and its lands. In the above example, Chiden did not fight against the Magistrate's ruling that "because Daihongan is a convent, administration of Zenkōji's lands would be handled by Daikanjin." Instead, she argued against Daikanjin's continued incursion into what Daihongan's nuns perceived as their rights. We can only speculate why she did not argue against statements such as these. Perhaps the ability to perform rituals and involvement in construction of the temple buildings were more important to the nuns than administrative issues—Chiden's specific mention of these in her countersuit would suggest that. Alternatively, Chiden may have felt that it would not help Daihongan to argue against the Magistrate's transfer of all administrative duties to Dai-kanjin. In any case, participation in these suits and countersuits was not an unusual event. Buddhist clergy regularly turned to litigation to protect (or increase) their rights or property in the early modern period.[21] Indeed, Daihongan's nuns were simply turning to the only means of resolving disputes available to the clergy in the early modern period. What is unusual is that scholars have not discussed nuns' participation in these suits more often.

Furthermore, as seen above, in some cases, Daihongan's abbesses chose between one form of patriarchal authority versus another. This is clearest when the convent faced being made the branch of the Ten-dai temple Kan'eiji. Rather than argue that the convent should remain without a head temple, Seikō instead pushed for her convent to be made a branch of the Pure Land monastery Zōjōji.

In the early modern period, Daihongan came to become a part of and yet apart from the Zenkōji temple complex. The reductions in rights during the first half of the period largely remained the status quo throughout the last half of the period, until Abbess Seien (abbess from 1837–1910) began challenging Daikanjin's position once the nascent Meiji Government introduced legal and social changes after 1868.

Meiji Era Conflicts and Compromises

In the 1850s and '60s, the Tokugawa shogunate, which had ruled Japan for more than 250 years, began to falter. They were replaced in 1868 by a group of warrior-bureaucrats supporting the rule of the emperor. Thus, in the last half of the nineteenth century, a series of governmental and legal changes affected all aspects of life in Japan, including the lives of religious institutions. As a result of these changes, Daihongan and Daikanjin once again began to struggle for power. First, in the 1860s, they sought sole control over the entire Zenkōji temple complex. After both subtemples were unsuccessful in these initial conflicts of the period, and they realized they would have to coexist in the temple complex, they negotiated their roles within the Zenkōji through four types of conflict between 1860s the 1940s. The end result of these legal changes and disputes was that Seien and her successors were able to make Daihongan a part of the Zenkōji temple complex again, with ritual and administrative duties shared with Daikanjin. In other words, this section describes how the convent went from the early modern arrangement ("a part of but apart from") to the one at the temple complex today. The events of this section are important to understanding the relationship between Daikanjin and Daihongan and to an understanding of the contemporary situation at the temple complex. Further, these events and the ways that the nuns responded to them demonstrate the peculiarities of the early modern legal system as it related to temple governance and how once this system had been removed Daihongan's nuns were able to challenge Daikanjin's authority at the Zenkōji temple complex.

Seeking to Solidify Power and Challenging the Status Quo

Prior to the Meiji Restoration, just as the Tokugawa shogunate appeared about to falter and some people began to push for the ascendency of the imperial house, Daikanjin sought to strengthen its ties to the emperor. When Emperor Kōmei passed away on the twenty-fifth day of the twelfth month of Keiō 3 (January 30, 1867, of the Gregorian calendar), Daikanjin requested that it be allowed to house the emperor's memorial tablets at Zenkōji.[22] The imperial house appears to have accepted this request, as it ordered the abbot of Daikanjin, Gijun (abbot from 1862–1873), to come to the imperial palace on the twenty-fifth day of the tenth month of the following year (November 20, 1867). Gijun made the trip with a large number of temple administrators and samurai, announcing to the regent and court liaisons that he arrived on the seventh day of the twelfth month (January 1, 1868).[23] However, two days later, on the ninth (January 3, 1868), the Meiji Emperor announced that the last Tokugawa shogun, Yoshinobu, had "returned" all powers of rule to the emperor. This seems to have laid waste to Gijun's plans as he returned to Shinano empty-handed on the fourth month of the following year (April or May 1868). If Gijun had been successful, placing Kōmei's memorial tablets within Zenkōji under Daikanjin's ritual control would have strengthened ties between the imperial household and Daikanjin, and possibly strengthened Daikanjin's position within the Zenkōji temple complex in the process.

Abbess Seien also attempted to use the change in political atmosphere to improve her subtemple's standing within the temple complex. In addition to traveling to the court in the second month of 1868 (February or March 1868), she began sending a series of requests to the nascent government, first via the imperial temple Shōgo'in, and later via the Sanada clan who were in charge of the local government of the Matsushiro Domain that retained power in the northern Shinano area until 1871. In the requests Daihongan uses the rhetoric of the Meiji government in calling for a righting of the "wrongs of the past" and "a return to the status of old" in an attempt to have the abbess granted administrative control over the Zenkōji temple complex.[24] In these requests Daihongan argues that the imperial house had given power to protect Zenkōji's icon and granted control over the complex to Daihongan's abbesses from the time of its legendary seventh-century founder, Abbess Sonkō, but that in the 1620s and '30s the Tokugawa shogunate and the monk Tenkai, an abbot from Kan'eiji, transferred that control to "[Dai]kanjin's monks, who had been administrative priests under the Daihongan's control."[25] Further, from the beginning of 1870, Daihongan petitioned to have the fifteen smaller Pure Land subtemples in Zenkōji's temple complex, which had been affiliated with Daihongan and the Pure Land school in the past but were placed under Daikanjin's control in the eighteenth century, "returned to Daihongan control." Eventually, Daihongan seems to have pressed for all of Zenkōji's subtemples to be converted to Pure Land ones, stating that Daihongan's branch temples and Kai Zenkōji where the Zenkōji Amitābha triad resided (most of the time) from 1558 until 1598 were all Pure Land temples, claiming that by extension Zenkōji itself had been Pure Land in the past until Kan'eiji and Daikanjin forced the complex to change to Tendai. Abbess Seien therefore requested that the Meiji government reverse "the wrongs of the past two hundred years" by "reinstating the Daihongan abbess as the head of all of Zenkōji as in the past and making [all temples] within Zenkōji's complex affiliate with the Pure Land school from now on or [force them to] leave the complex."[26] The abbess's plan was to release her temple and others within Zenkōji's complex from Tendai control, thereby stripping the Daikanjin monks of their power in order to claim authority over Zenkōji for herself and her temple.

In 1869, Matsushiro Domain was put in charge of investigating Daihongan's requests and offering an opinion to the Meiji govern-

ment. The administrators from Matsushiro sent requests to both Daihongan and Daikanjin asking for "detailed documents" to support
their claims for control over the temple complex.[27] While Daihongan
offered the evidence stated above, Daikanjin countered by submitting
as evidence snippets from the Kamakura shogunate's official history
(the *Azuma kagami*, which describes events from 1180 to 1266), the 1601
Deed of Land Division discussed earlier, and documents from Tenkai.
In addition, it compiled a new genealogy for itself based on existing
documents and temple histories.

In the end, Daihongan's nearly three years of petition came to
naught. In the second month of 1870, the imperial court stated (via
the Matsushiro officials) that "it is difficult to fulfill [your] request,
[and so you] should know that temple administration, rituals, and
all other items are to be as they were in the past."[28] These efforts by
Daihongan were largely unsuccessful in that control over the temple
complex did not come to reside solely with the abbess and the various subtemples did not change to Pure Land (the fifteen previously
Pure Land subtemples, however, did revert to Daihongan affiliation
in 1877). They do illustrate that struggles between Daihongan and
Daikanjin would flare up in times of transition. However, the modern
conflicts between Daihongan and Daikanjin did not come to an end
here. In fact, several later conflicts stemmed from the cryptic wording
"as they were in the past" from the court's rejection of Daihongan's
requests.

Learning to Coexist

Other disputes from the 1860s to the 1940s can be divided into four
types according to local historian Yano Tsuneo. These conflicts concerned (1) the question of who would be the chief abbot/abbess of
Zenkōji; (2) the equal division of temple administrative duties; (3) the
obstruction of rituals in Zenkōji's main hall; and (4) the ownership
of the copy of Zenkōji's Amitābha triad.[29] Though these conflicts are
incredibly interesting, and are formative in the development of the current system at Zenkōji, I only have space to briefly mention them here.

I have already touched upon the question of who would be
chief abbot or abbess of Zenkōji in the introduction to this chapter.
This problem arose twice, first in the 1870s and then again in the
1940s, because of changes in legal regulations concerning Buddhist
institutions. These laws required that there be one *jūshoku*, usually

translated as "head of temple" or "chief cleric," at each temple or convent. Zenkōji was (and is) unusual in that no one has ever held such a title over the entire temple complex, so when these laws came into effect, they caused the heads of Daihongan and Daikanjin to fight over who would hold this title. In both cases, the two subtemples first confirmed with the government that Zenkōji was indeed required to have such a post and that the post could not be shared. In the 1870s, the conflict over this between Daikanjin and Daihongan came to an end after the government changed the wording of the law to accommodate the unusual case of Zenkōji. In the 1940s, Daihongan and Daikanjin pursued litigation for almost five years before entrusting the matter to Zenkōji's chief administrator, Yamaguchi Kikujūrō who had the prophetic dream discussed in the introduction. However, as I mentioned, the requirement for Zenkōji to have a chief cleric ended when the Religious Organizations' Law came to an end in the post-war period.

Equally dividing temple administrative duties and fairly scheduling rituals in Zenkōji's main hall were two key elements to Daihongan and Daikanjin coexisting and sharing power. In the seventeenth century, the monks of Daikanjin and Kan'eiji promulgated a list of regulations for Zenkōji that largely excluded Daihongan's nuns from administrative and ritual control. In the nineteenth century, however, Seien sought to regain some ritual and administrative control within the Zenkōji temple complex in the wake of the Meiji Restoration. The heads of both subtemples lodged complaints about ritual and administrative rights with local and sectarian authorities in the mid-1870s. However, Nagano Prefecture ruled that both Daikanjin and Daihongan were to share ritual and administrative authority equally. But since this ruling did not offer specific suggestions for how to accomplish this, the conflicts continued until 1889. At that time, the heads of Daikanjin and Daihongan sought the mediation of Viscount Shinagawa Yajirō (1843–1900). With his assistance, the leaders of these two institutions signed a twenty-one-point agreement in 1893 that effectively divided ritual and administrative responsibilities for the Zenkōji temple complex and largely brought an end to the open conflicts between the two institutions.[30] Many points of this agreement are followed at Zenkōji to this day.

A final, yet vital, step to placing Daikanjin and Daihongan on equal footing in the Zenkōji temple complex was establishing who owned the temple's "Icon That Stands Before" (*maedachi honzon*). At Zenkōji, the main Amitābha triad icon is never revealed. What is shown during displays of the temple's treasures is a copy from the eleventh or twelfth century called the Icon That Stands Before. In 1906, the Icon That Stands Before was listed as a National Treasure.[31] At that time, when not on display, this icon was housed at Daikanjin, and the official paperwork listing the icon as a National Treasure stated that Daikanjin was its owner. This led to a protracted argument involving Daikanjin, Daihongan, local courts, and local residents that was only resolved in 1923 when the ownership of the Icon was transferred to the whole Zenkōji temple complex.[32]

As we can see from this, the current position of Daihongan within the Zenkōji temple complex is a result of the efforts of the convent's abbesses from the 1860s to the 1940s.[33] The reversal from the situation in the Tokugawa Period was possible in large part because of the change in legal atmosphere brought about by the Meiji Restoration. And yet they could not have happened without the efforts of the early modern and modern nuns to keep their convent afloat despite many challenges.

Conclusion

As previously noted, the case of Zenkōji is somewhat unique in Japan in that both male and female monastics controlled the temple complex. It thus provides a rare glimpse into the ways that these two groups negotiated administrative and ritual rights. Although this chapter has focused on conflicts, these two groups were not always fighting. Personnel from these two institutions regularly worked together to ensure that joint events proceeded without difficulty and that the temple complex and surrounding land were administered appropriately. However, the degree to which these two groups turned to non-Buddhist legal means—lawsuits, arbitration, and so on—to settle conflicts comes to the fore through the above examination of the seventeenth- through the early twentieth-century conflicts.

The above cases demonstrate that conflicts between Daihongan and Daikanjin developed when one group felt that its rights or duties were being abrogated by the other or when one felt it could gain an advantage over the other. However, various other factors determined if one of the subtemples would turn to lawsuits and petitions against the other. One factor was individual personalities. When the abbess was particularly strong, such as Seien, for instance, she was more likely to petition or sue. Conversely, personalities may have determined whether the heads of Daihongan and Daikanjin were more likely to come to a mutually acceptable arrangement before conflict erupted. Opportunity was also a limiting factor in lawsuits. For example, after 1740, when Daihongan was made into a branch of Kan'eiji, there are no records of the two subtemples coming into open conflict, probably because Kan'eiji forced Daihongan and Daikanjin to resolve their problems. However, when Kan'eiji's authority was removed, both Daihongan and Daikanjin began fighting again.

Though previous scholars have looked to the *vinaya*, and especially the *gurudharmas*, to understand how interactions between male and female Buddhist monastics should have occurred, the case of Daihongan suggests that the broader legal atmosphere should also be examined if one hopes to gain an understanding of the actual relationships between monks and nuns and how they negotiated or resolved conflicts. Specifically in Daihongan's case, these lawsuits enabled the nuns to maintain some of their rights in the Zenkōji temple complex in the early modern period, and to regain what they had lost once the political climate changed in the end of the nineteenth century.

Daihongan's nuns' pursuit of these lawsuits expands our understanding of Buddhist femininity in ways that have gone largely unstudied. These nuns were concerned with cultural traditions (such as tea ceremony and lute performances), and with rituals for the well-being of their ancestors, like the nuns that appear in others scholars' studies. However, in addition to these roles, Daihongan's nuns were litigants in suits, seeking to protect or regain their rights. They knew how to navigate the legal system to submit petitions and suits, and kept abreast of legal and political changes in an effort to reposition their convent within the temple complex. Thus, at Daihongan (and perhaps at other convents as well), there were politically and legally savvy nuns who navigated the complex, changing system of laws and precedents to defend their rights. As I have shown, this form of Buddhist femininity that includes legal acumen extends from the seventeenth century through the recent past, and possibly may appear in the future if the convent's rights are threatened again.

Notes

1. Japanese names are given with the family name first, followed by the personal name.

2. Chief cleric is *jūshoku*, and steward is *bettō* in Japanese. Cited in Kobayashi Keiichirō, *Zenkōjisan* (Nagano: Ginga shobō, 1973), 215.

3. Saba Mahmood, *Politics of Piety: The Islamic Revival and the Feminist Subject* (Princeton, NJ: Princeton University Press, 2005); Dorothy Ko, *Teachers of the Inner Chambers: Women and Culture in Seventeenth Century China* (Stanford, CA: Stanford University Press, 1994); Nirmala Salgado, *Buddhist Nuns and Gendered Practice: In Search of the Female Renunciant* (Oxford: Oxford University Press, 2013); Lori Meeks, *Hokkeji and the Reemergence of Female Monastic Orders in Premodern Japan* (Honolulu: University of Hawaii Press, 2010); and Barbara Ambros, *Women in Japanese Religions* (New York: New York University Press, 2015).

4. Japan did not adopt the Gregorian Calendar until 1872. In this paper, I follow convention by listing dates before 1872 with the year converted into the Gregorian year instead of the era name and year number (e.g., 1598 instead of Keichō 3), but giving months according to the historical Japanese calendar (e.g., the first day of the first month). In some cases, I express this as 1598.1.1. Dates after the switch to the Gregorian calendar are given as "January 1, 1874," for example.

5. A *koku* is a unit of rice said to be enough to feed a grown man for a year. This amounts to roughly 278 liters of rice. Zenkōji's land grant included an amount of land that had been surveyed to produce 1,000 *koku* per year.

6. This document is called the "Zenkōji ryōchiwari mokuroku." It is in Kobayashi Keiichirō, *Zenkōjishi Kenkyū* (Nagano: Shinano mainichi shinbunsha, 2000), 791–92; and Nagano Kenshi Kankōkai, ed., *Nagano Kenshi: Kinsei Shiryō Hen*, vol. 7–1 (Nagano-shi: Nagano kenshi kankōkai, 1971), 671–72.

7. The other groups of subtemples split the remaining 274 *koku* unevenly: the twenty-one Tendai temples called collectively Shūto received 168, the fifteen Pure Land temples of the Nakashū received 75, and the ten (at this point in time) Ji School temples of the Tsumado received just 31 *koku*.

8. Donald F. McCallum, *Zenkōji and Its Icon: A Study in Medieval Japanese Religious Art* (Princeton, NJ: Princeton University Press, 1994), 168.

9. This document can be found in Nagano Kenshi Kankōkai, *Nagano Kenshi*, 672; Nagano Shishi Hensan Iinkai, *Nagano shishi* (Nagano-shi: Nagano-shi, 1997), 175; and Kobayashi Keiichirō, *Zenkōjishi Kenkyū*, 802–3.

10. Ibid.

11. Ibid.

12. Ibid.

13. Nagano Kenshi Kankōkai, *Nagano Kenshi*, 673–74.

14. This reads: *Nyorai mae kuyō usuku makarinari sōrō.* Ibid., 674.

15. Kobayashi Keiichirō, *Zenkōjishi Kenkyū*, 803–4.

16. The statements and petitions mentioned in this paragraph are quoted in full in Zenkōjishi kenkyūkai, *Zenkōjishi Kenkyū*, 317–21.

17. This is apparent in documents such as the *Bugen kakiage chō* discussed above. Daihongan 1 Nagano City Public Archives fuku 2 1149.029.

234 / Matthew Mitchell

18. This statement was made within a *yuisho* written by Chizen to protest Daikanjin's attempts to reduce Daihongan's place within Zenkōji. Cited in Kobayashi Keiichirō, *Zenkōjishi Kenkyū*, 296.

19. This is similar to the ways that retired emperor Fushimi ordered a reconciliation between rival lineages within the Tendai temple complex of Shōren'in because they had "neglected their ritual practices and, through their repeated suits, contributed to the decline of the doctrinal school (Tendai), the cloister itself, and the Buddha Dharma." Brian Ruppert, "Buddhism and Law in Japan," *Buddhism and Law: An Introduction,* ed. Rebecca Redwood French and Mark A. Nathan (Cambridge: Cambridge University Press, 2014), 283.

20. This has caused some scholars to hypothesize that the nuns stayed in Aoyama Zenkōji because of the restrictions they faced at Zenkōji. However, there were fiscal reasons for not traveling as well. It cost the convent quite a lot of money to travel between Shinano and Edo, and travel was one item that was restricted in the convent's austerity measures in the early nineteenth century.

21. For example, Vesey highlights the conflicts over positioning within the head-branch temple system. Alexander Vesey, "The Buddhist Clergy and Village Society in Early Modern Japan." PhD dissertation, Princeton University, 2003, 131–36.

22. Information for this paragraph comes from Kobayashi Keiichirō, *Zenkōjishi Kenkyū*, 350.

23. Kobayashi states that Gijun returned to Shinano with at least two palanquins, twenty-one samurai, and forty-four people of retainer (*wakatō*) status and lower. Ibid.

24. The "wrongs of the past" is *kyūhei,* and "a return to the status of old" is *kikaku fukko* in Japanese. Sanadake monjo 1 Nagano City Public Archives fuku 2 1912.1144.

25. In a request dated to 1868.12 sent via Matsushiro-han. Quoted in full in Zenkōjishi kenkyūkai, *Zenkōjishi Kenkyū*, 365–68.

26. This section reads: *Kyōgo Jōdoshūmon ni aiaratame, shōnin e zuijū itashi sōrō yō, matawa taisan itashi, shōnin (no) koto korai no gotoku Zenkōji issan no jimu shujishoku ōseidasare shikarubeki gi . . .* Sanadake monjo 1 fuku 2(1912) 1144.

27. Cited in full in Zenkōjishi kenkyūkai, *Zenkōjishi Kenkyū*, 371–72.

28. This statement is *okikitodoke ainarigataku, jimu hōyō muki sonohoka subete shikitari no tōri aikokoroeru beki mune.* (cited in Sanadake monjo 1 fuku 2 1912.1144; Zenkōjishi kenkyūkai, *Zenkōjishi kenkyū*, 383.) For more on this, see Kobayashi Keiichirō, *Zenkōjishi kenkyū*, 350–51; Zenkōjishi kenkyūkai, *Zenkōjishi kenkyū*, 359–72; Nagano Shishi Hensan Iinkai, *Nagano shishi* 66:5 kindaishi.

29. Yano Tsuneo, "Meijiki ni okeru Zenkōji Daikanjin: Daihongan keisō jiken no shiteki igi," *Shinano* 36:9(1984): 10.

30. The content of the twenty-one-point agreement can be found at Yano Tsuneo, "Meijiki ni okeru Zenkōji Daikanjin," 627–29.

31. Since 1950, it has been listed as an important cultural property (*jūyō bunkazai*).

32. Yano Tsuneo, "Meijiki ni okeru Zenkōji Daikanjin," 630.

33. These abbesses were Seien, Kajūji Jōgon, and Ōmiya Chiei.

Chapter 9

Gendered Hagiography in Tibet

Comparing Clerical Representations of the Female Visionary, Khandro Tāre Lhamo

HOLLY GAYLEY

There are three rather different versions of the life of Khandro Tāre Lhamo (Mkha' 'gro Tā re lha mo, 1938–2002), a contemporary female Buddhist visionary from the Tibetan region of Golok. While all three give prominence to her miraculous deeds during the years leading up to and including the Cultural Revolution (1966–76), the models of female sanctity used by male cleric authors to characterize her religious activities diverge. The earliest account portrays Tāre Lhamo as a *ḍākinī*,[1] the emanation of the female tantric deity Vajravārāhī, and a tantric heroine who intervened to rescue fellow Tibetans during the troubled decades of the Maoist period. A later work, which includes several of the same miracle tales verbatim, characterizes her as the "wisdom consort" (*shes rab kyi grogs*) of her second husband, Namtrul Jigme Phuntsok (Nam sprul 'Jigs med phun tshogs, 1944–2011),[2] locally known as Namtrul Rinpoche, even as it describes their collaboration in the process of revealing "treasures" (*gter ma*). A third and newest version, just recently published, emphasizes local understandings of her status and religious vocation wherein Tāre Lhamo is characterized first and foremost as an emanation of the female *bodhisattva* Tārā. In that capacity, she is depicted working wonders tailored to the nomadic region of Golok, such as staving off hail storms, retrieving lost yaks, blessing amulets to protect from mastiffs, and also withstanding, through her compassionate outlook, the privations of the Maoist period. This newest version emphasizes the scope of her visionary talents from a young age, including her capacity to heal illness, to extend the life of others, to rescue the recently deceased fallen into lower states of existence, and to reveal hidden treasures that contained esoteric scriptures and sacra traced to the advent of Buddhism in Tibet during its imperial period (seventh to ninth centuries).[3]

Scholars of medieval Christianity have highlighted the relationship between the male cleric-author and female visionary-subject in European hagiographic writing. In a seminal anthology on the topic, *Gendered Voices: Medieval Saints and Their Interpreters*, Catherine Mooney and her contributors highlight the extent to which male hagiographers transform the lives of female saints according to their own "idealized notions of female sanctity."[4] The anthology illustrates the tendency among male hagiographers to emphasize women's mystical and visionary experiences, as well as bodily signs of their sanctity and miraculous healings. This is the case even as the voices of female saints themselves, when available in vernacular writings, indicate more concern with theologizing their relationship to God or recounting their socially oriented activities, including their interventions in political and ecclesiastic affairs. Moreover, male hagiographers tended to promote female paradigms of sanctity, even when those female saints themselves explicitly modeled their lives on male exemplars.

How might such reflections on the gendered dimensions of hagiographic writing help us to consider Buddhist life writings in Tibet? Given the recent focus on autobiography in Tibetan Studies, less attention has been paid to the male perspective from which the writings about eminent women usually occurred in the Tibetan genre of *namthar*, literally stories of "complete liberation" (*rnam thar*), chronicling the lives of Buddhist saints. As distinct from autobiographies, which involve complex strategies of self-representation, third-person narratives of religious figures tend to be hagiographic in tenor, casting their subject as exceptional in nature from birth and an object of veneration.[5] Drawing on issues raised in *Gendered Voices*, we can address comparable questions in available Tibetan sources for the lives of eminent Buddhist women. For example, what religious models are marshalled by male hagiographers to characterize their female subjects? What overall portrait of female sanctity is thereby constructed? Given the emphasis on past-life connections in the lives of *tertön*s or "treasure revealers" (*gter ston*) discussed by Janet Gyatso, and the importance of relationality in the autobiographies of Tibetan women as thematized by Sarah Jacoby,[6] here I am interested in when and how the noncelibate female subject of *namthar* comes to the fore in her own right amidst a web of past lives, family ties, teacher–student dynamics, and particularly, collaboration with a male tantric partner.

Tāre Lhamo and Her Hagiographers

My focus will be on the life of Khandro Tāre Lhamo, who was born into her religious vocation as the daughter of a *tertön* of high standing in Golok, Apang Terchen Orgyan Trinle Lingpa, also known as Pawo Chöying Dorje (A phang gter chen O rgyan 'phrin las gling pa, alias Dpa' bo chos dbyings rdo rje, 1895–1945). Due to her elite birth, Tāre Lhamo gained access to esoteric teachings by the prominent Nyingma masters of her day, including Rigdzin Jalu Dorje (Rig 'dzin 'ja' lus rdo rje, 1927–1961), the fourth in the prominent line of Dodrupchen (Rdo grub chen) incarnations, and Dzongter Kunzang Nyima (Rdzong gter Kun bzang nyi ma, 1904–1958), the grandson and speech emanation of a towering figure in the Golok treasure scene, Dudjom Lingpa (Bdud 'joms gling pa, 1835–1904). She married the latter's son, Mingyur Dorje (Mi 'gyur rdo rje, 1934–1959), and with him bore her only child, who died before reaching the age of ten. Her first husband and three brothers, all reincarnate lamas, were imprisoned as "class enemies" along with other elites and died in prison during the socialist transformation of Tibetan areas in the late 1950s. Spared imprisonment likely due to her gender, Tāre Lhamo was condemned to forced labor for the devastating decades to follow and subjected to periodic struggle sessions.

As one of a handful of surviving Buddhist masters in the region, Tāre Lhamo played a significant role in revitalizing Buddhist teachings, institutions, and ritual programs in Golok and northern Kham alongside her second husband, Namtrul Rinpoche, during the 1980s and '90s as economic and cultural liberalization spread across China in the post-Mao era. Due to their collaboration in revealing treasures and teaching throughout the region, Tāre Lhamo and Namtrul Rinpoche's official life stories and writings are intertwined and published together in paperback. Their joint revelations are compiled into a twelve-volume treasure corpus in traditional *pecha* (*dpe cha*) format, and their correspondence during the period of their court- ship (1978–80) is arranged into a single-volume addendum to their treasure corpus.[7] Even after her passing in 2002, images and audiovi- sual materials produced by their monastic seat, Nyenlung Monastery (Snyan lung dgon), which they rebuilt in the early 1980s in Namtrul Rinpoche's homeland, have tended to portray the couple, side by side, as objects of veneration.

In this chapter I examine and compare the three distinct versions of the life of Tāre Lhamo. Each presents a comprehensive account of her life, composed in Tibetan by male cleric-scholars who were dis- ciples of this tantric couple and based in varied locations in the region: Pema Ösal Thaye in Serta, Namtrul Rinpoche's homeland in Kandze Prefecture of Sichuan Province; Abu Karlo in Tawu, the capital of Golok Prefecture in Qinghai Province; and Rigdzin Dargye originally from Markhok, Tāre Lhamo's homeland located in Padma County of Golok. While Serta and Padma Counties neighbor one another, and Apang Terchen's activities spanned both of them, travel between them was restricted during the Maoist period. So Tāre Lhamo spent her twenties and thirties almost entirely in Padma County and then in her early forties moved to Serta to join Namtrul Rinpoche at Nyenlung. From there, in the post-Mao period, they traveled widely to discover and disseminate their treasures and those of Apang Terchen through- out Golok and beyond. This variance in each author's location, both institutional and geographic, is reflected in the three versions of her life story. All three chronicle her previous lives, prophecies at birth, early training, miraculous deeds during the Maoist period, and reli- gious activities in the post-Mao era alongside Namtrul Rinpoche. Yet each story is arranged in a distinctly original configuration and employs different models of female sanctity to frame Tāre Lhamo's activities. Moreover, the three versions diverge to varying degrees in their accounts of incidents and in the types of activities they empha- size. These variations can arguably be traced to the authors' locations and relationship to the couple, as well as the corresponding sources they were able to access in constructing their respective narratives.

The earliest version is Tāre Lhamo's official life story, inter- twined with that of Namtrul Rinpoche, commissioned by the couple, composed with their input, and published in 1997 in conjunction with a government agency in Serta. The author, Pema Ösal Thaye (Pad ma 'od gsal mtha' yas), is a cleric-scholar, local historian, and government official, working in the Bureau of Culture, History, Education, and

Health at the county seat in Serta. With input from the couple themselves and elders based in Serta, Pema Ösal Thaye presents the story
of Tāre Lhamo's youth, emphasizing her identification with female
tantric deities and antecedents, in her own *namthar*, titled *Spiraling
Vine of Faith: The Liberation of Khandro Tāre Lhamo*. Based on these
identifications, he casts Tāre Lhamo as a tantric heroine and *ḍākinī*-in-
action, who addresses the devastation of the Maoist period through a
series of miraculous deeds. Then Pema Ösal Thaye places the account
of Tāre Lhamo's religious activities later in life, traveling and teaching
with Namtrul from 1980 forward, in his *namthar*, titled *Jewel Garland:
The Liberation of Namtrul Jigme Phuntsok*. In this official version, their
life stories are intertwined and published side by side. Her life story
follows and is ultimately subsumed into his, reflecting the gendered
hierarchy at Nyenlung Monastery and their representation as a tantric
couple in his homeland of Serta.

The second version differs slightly in its structure and representation of Tāre Lhamo, yet makes a crucial modification. Largely a
derivative and abbreviated account of their official life stories, it was
published in 2001 by Abu Karlo (A bu dkar lo), a Buddhist cleric
and Tibetan doctor based at the Golok Tibetan Medical Hospital in
Tawu, the prefecture capital of Golok. Note that his location is the
farthest removed from the center of the couple's activities in Serta
and Padma Counties, but still included in their sphere of regional
influence. One difference is that Abu Karlo combined their lives into a
single *namthar*, titled *Jewel Lantern of Blessings: An Abridged Biography of
the Tertön Couple, the Lord of Siddhas Zhuchen Namtrul and Khandro Tāre
Dechen Lhamo*.[8] In this case, the account of Namtrul Rinpoche's youth
still comes first, but the chronicle of their joint activities as a couple
flows out of the section recounting Tāre Lhamo's youth. This structure
allows for the early part of Tāre Lhamo's life to be more fully integrated into the chronology, situated before the account of their joint
activities to revitalize Buddhism in the post-Mao era. Nonetheless, in
transitioning to their joint activities, Abu Karlo makes a modification
by characterizing Tāre Lhamo as the "wisdom consort" of Namtrul
Rinpoche, who occupies the position of the "great *tertön*" (*gter chen*).
In this version, Namtrul Rinpoche becomes the principle figure, with
Tāre Lhamo fashioned as his consort. Abu Karlo's version has been
the most influential among the Chinese disciples of the couple since
its brevity allowed for swift translation.[9]

Only the most recent rendition of her life, recently published
in 2017 by Khenpo Rigdzin Dargye (Mkhan po Rig 'dzin dar rgyas),

presents Tāre Lhamo's story on its own terms. In this version, she emerges as a figure in her own right without relying on an elaborate preamble of female precursors and without synthesizing her activities with those of Namtrul Rinpoche. Instead, the title of the work, *The Wonder of Divine Music: A Condensed Account of the Liberation of the Supreme Khandro Tāre Lhamo Rinpoche, the Daughter of Apang Terchen*, highlights her familial ties due to the local nature of the account and casts her as an emanation of Green Tārā, known for her compassionate salvific activities.[10] Rigdzin Dargye is a Buddhist cleric from Markhok in Padma County, sharing the same homeland and clan as Tāre Lhamo. While serving in recent years as the head disciplinarian (*dge bskos*) at Larung Buddhist Academy in Serta, his primary affiliation remains Tsimda Monastery (Rtsis mda' dgon), the monastery founded by her father Apang Terchen in Padma County in 1925. For this reason, Rigdzin Dargye had unique access to local sources, and has based his account on interviews with families in and around Markhok, especially older women in her homeland, who served as her companions in youth and through the devastating decades from 1959 to 1978 when she was in her twenties and thirties. As a result, this new rendition of her life contains a plethora of stories not found elsewhere. *The Wonder of Divine Music* sheds new light on Tāre Lhamo's early years and offers local understandings of her religious vocation. Given the differing orientations of these three authors, a comparison of their versions of Tāre Lhamo's life story promises to illuminate how Tibetan cleric hagiographers depict a visionary female subject with respect to both universalizing and localizing tendencies in crafting a representation of female sanctity.

A Tantric Heroine: The Official Story

Tāre Lhamo never stands alone in her official *namthar, Spiraling Vine of Faith*, composed by Pema Ösal Thaye and published in 1997 alongside that of Namtrul Rinpoche, *Jewel Garland*, in a 160-page paperback book.[11] Nearly half of *Spiraling Vine of Faith's* fifty-six pages consist of an extended preamble of her past lives, including excerpts from existing works by and about two of her female predecessors: Yeshe Tsogyal (Ye shes mtsho rgyal), the pre-eminent lady of treasure lore and consort to the eighth-century Indian tantric master Padmasambhava, and Sera Khandro (Se ra mkha' 'gro, 1892–1940), a female *tertön* of the preceding generation in Golok. Tāre Lhamo's own life story begins halfway through the text, chronicling her birth, early religious training, and miraculous feats during the Maoist period, and then it abruptly ends.

The second half of her life story is contained in *Jewel Garland*, where the couple serve as joint protagonists in the narration of their activities contributing to the revitalization of Buddhism during the 1980s and '90s. While Tāre Lhamo's later life, age forty onward, is subsumed into Namtrul Rinpoche's *namthar*, she nonetheless occupies an important place within its 104 pages. Namtrul Rinpoche's youth takes up the first quarter of the work (1–27). In the second quarter of the book (27–47), Tāre Lhamo makes a strong entrance into *Jewel Garland*, with excerpts from their correspondence and prophecies about their union. *Jewel Garland* includes extensive passages from her letters, featuring her voice in a way that it never appears in her own *namthar*. Moreover, for the second half (48–104) of *Jewel Garland*, Tāre Lhamo serves as joint protagonist with Namtrul Rinpoche, collaborating in the discovery and dissemination of their treasures and those of her father.

In terms of its model of female sanctity, the overarching figure in this version of Tāre Lhamo's life is the *ḍākinī*, a class of female tantric deity. In the opening lines of *Spiraling Vine of Faith*, following verses of homage, Pema Ösal Thaye identifies her as an emanation of the female tantric deity Vajravārāhī who attained buddhahood eons ago, using a longer version of her name, Khandro Rinpoche Tāre Dechen Gyalmo.

> The speech emanation of the queen mother Vajravārāhī, the supreme Khandro Rinpoche Tāre Dechen Gyalmo amassed an ocean of the two accumulations long ago in enumerable eons past. Having purified the two obscurations together with karmic residues, she reached buddhahood as the essence of blissful Samantabhadrī.[12]

Vajravārāhī is also invoked toward the end of the *namthar* in a vision that portrays Tāre Lhamo attaining realization in this life. In the vision, she tours various *ḍākinī* lands and encounters Vajravārāhī herself, who gives her sanctified feast substances. Tasting these provokes an experience of "the wisdom of nondual bliss and emptiness" (*bde stong gnyis med kyi ye shes*). Based on her identification with and close connection to Vajravārāhī, Pema Ösal Thaye refers to Tāre Lhamo as the Supreme Khandro (*mkha' 'gro mchog*) throughout the narrative,[13] where the Tibetan word *khandro* (and its extended form *khandroma*) translates the Sanskrit *ḍākinī* and is used as a title for noncelibate female figures of high religious standing.

Tāre Lhamo's exceptional nature is reinforced by recounting her illustrious past lives, and here Pema Ösal Thaye emphasizes her identifications with female figures, even though her past life genealogy includes both male and female lives. He does so by including long passages copied almost verbatim from the respective *namthars* of Yeshe Tsogyal and Sera Khandro.[14] This extensive prologue means that the reader is prepared to encounter an exceptional woman. A series of prophecies, included in the account of her birth, further serve to affirm her exceptional nature. Only then, almost halfway into her *namthar*, do we encounter the story of Tāre Lhamo herself. While the preamble to her life is filled with a panoply of female figures—divine, mythic, and human—this account of her early years focuses on her religious training and relationships with men: her father; Apang Terchen, from whom she received several major cycles of teachings, including his own corpus of revelations and the *Nyingtik Yabzhi* (*Snying thig ya bzhi*); and her main teachers, Rigdzin Jalu Dorje and Dzongter Kunzang Nyima, who provided further esoteric instructions (the latter confers his entire treasure corpus on her and appoints Tāre Lhamo as the trustee for his Yeshe Tsogyal *sādhana*). Her first husband, Mingyur Rinpoche, also receives brief mention alongside her eldest brother Wangchen Nyima (Dbang chen nyi ma), who helped to arrange their marriage.

In *Spiraling Vine of Faith*, Tāre Lhamo, as a young adult, comes of age just as Tibetan areas are being subjected to socialist transformation under Chinese Communist rule. The late 1950s witnessed the closure of monasteries in Golok and the imprisonment and death of numerous religious figures, condemned alongside other elites as class enemies. Namtrul Rinpoche was only a teenager at this time, and too young to be perceived as a threat, so he was assigned as the secretary for his work unit. For her part, Tāre Lhamo was subjected to forced labor: herding livestock, digging ditches, gathering wood, and carrying rocks for construction. While Rigdzin Dargye's rendition of her life offers the clearest picture of the hardships she endured, Pema Ösal Thaye uses the devastation of the time as a backdrop for Tāre Lhamo's miraculous activities.

In the series of miracle tales that narrate the decades from 1959 to 1978, Tāre Lhamo is cast as *ḍākinī*-in-action. Yet she is also depicted in universal terms through Buddhist paradigmatic roles that are not tied to gender, namely the *bodhisattva* (awakened being), whose altruistic mind is turned toward the benefit of others, and the tantric *siddha* (accomplished one), endowed with tantric prowess and capable of superhuman feats. Her salvific activities are thereby universalized as quintessentially Buddhist in a devastating historical period for Tibetans:

> From the ages of 22 to 41 [1959–78], because of the extreme turbulence of the times, [Khandro Tāre Lhamo] experienced a mix of myriad joys and sorrows. Nevertheless, she was able to embrace misfortune. Whatever her activities, inwardly she approached [them] with the discipline of a *bodhisattva*. Her mindstream was brimming with *bodhicitta*, and she took up with singular earnest the benefit of others, directly and indirectly.
>
> At the age of twenty-three, by the force of group karma, the whole land was devastated by widespread famine. Because the Supreme Khandro was a female *siddha* who commanded the inexhaustible treasury of the sky, each measure of rice that she cooked multiplied to be more than enough to feed eighteen people. Everyone was in a state of amazement.[15]

Pema Ösal Thaye depicts Tāre Lhamo as taking up the discipline of a *bodhisattva* by orienting her activities for the benefit of others, while her own travails and losses are glossed as "a mix of myriad joys and sorrows." He emphasizes this point by stating that her mind was "brimming with *bodhicitta*," the enlightened intent akin to altruism. Furthermore, as a sign of her tantric prowess, she is understood to command the "inexhaustible treasury of the sky," something Pema Ösal Thaye also claims for Namtrul Rinpoche in *Jewel Garland*, even though their miracles are grassroots in scale, directed at those in their immediate surroundings. Elsewhere, I argue that this serves as a distinctive way to narrate cultural trauma in a redemptive key by foregrounding the miracles of a tantric heroine while the devastation of the period looms in the background.[16]

Despite this universalizing tendency, there are other moments in which her salvific activity remains gendered in character. For example, the following account imagines Tāre Lhamo akin to the central *ḍākinī* of a *maṇḍala* (the depiction of the abode of a tantric deity), able to call on her retinue to save the day:

One time, a horseman named Norbu died. In general, during these times, because of the human and horse corpses
strewn across all the mountains and valleys, there were no
vultures [to dispose of the body in a traditional sky burial].
Before the Supreme Khandro arrived, there was nothing to
be done. [When she arrived] she commanded two corpse
cutters named Zangkyong and Tenzang, "Place the corpse
on top of a boulder." They did as she said, and five vultures
appeared—who were the emanations of five *ḍākinīs*—and
partook of [the corpse] without leaving any residual.[17]

Here we can see Pema Ösal Thaye's distinctive narrative strategy of
placing the devastation of the times in the background (the corpses
strewn across the landscape) with Tāre Lhamo's salvific activity in
the foreground (helping to resolve a dilemma by enabling the traditional sky burial in which vultures consume the corpse). Because of
her status as a *khandroma*, when the five vultures arrived to eat the
corpse, they were regarded as emanations of five *ḍākinīs* akin to the
retinue in a tantric *maṇḍala*. Another episode resonates even more
clearly with the paradigmatic role of the *ḍākinī* in Tibetan narrative
literature, appearing in the visionary experience of male figures.

Another time, when the incarnate lama, Rigdzin Sang-ngak
Lingpa (Rig 'dzin Gsang sngags gling pa), remained in
prison in Serta, Khandro Rinpoche appeared before him in
the sky by means of a magical emanation . . . and proph-
esized: "Not long from now, you will be free from jail and
we will meet." Later, in accordance with the vision of her
prophecy, the supreme precious incarnation was released
from prison like the sun freed from clouds.[18]

Here Tāre Lhamo appears in *ḍākinī* fashion, in the sky before Sang-
ngak Lingpa, alias Sera Yangtrul (Se ra yang sprul, 1925–1988), in
order to prophesize his release from prison. Note that her prophecy
is more than a prediction based on clairvoyance about the future.
Rather, it is an instance of performative speech, an illocutionary act
understood to make something the case through the utterance itself.
In this context, Tāre Lhamo announces (albeit in a vision) and thereby
is understood to effect Sang-ngak Lingpa's release.

In constructing Tāre Lhamo as a tantric heroine, saving the day
in a series of miracle tales, Pema Ösal Thaye masterfully creates a

redemptive narrative for a period of collective trauma. Endowed with *bodhicitta* and tantric prowess, Tāre Lhamo commands elemental forces and liberates others from suffering. His presentation contains a balance of universal and particular, both in terms of gender and the scale of her activities. In terms of gender, she is cast in the paradigmatically female role of a *ḍākinī* throughout the *namthar*, while the universal, nongendered models of *bodhisattva* and *siddha* are marshalled to frame her salvific activities. In terms of scale, while her activities are necessarily grassroots, given her consignment to forced labor in Padma County, the nature of the dilemmas that appear (famine, imprisonment, widespread death, and other calamities) were more universal, and, indeed, emblematic of the times for Tibetans under Chinese rule during the Maoist period. In this way, the narrative transcends her immediate context and has broader relevance, given the regional scope of her following. In fashioning a redemptive narrative, Pema Ösal Thaye attempts, in his own words, to "heal or restore faith" (*dad pa'i gso*) during the post-Mao period as Tibetans rebuilt Buddhist institutions and engaged in wide-ranging cultural preservation projects.

Consort of the Great *Tertön*: A Derivative Account

The second version of her life story, *Jewel Lantern of Blessings* by Abu Karlo, was published in 2001, only four years after *Spiraling Vine of Faith* and *Jewel Garland*. In one sense, this version serves as little more than a distillation of these texts, in a more compact and differently configured form. The motivation for its composition appears to have been the creation of a shorter work easily translated into Chinese and English, since the published translations followed shortly thereafter. Yet Abu Karlo makes several modifications in his framing of their stories. For example, Namtrul Rinpoche's youth is shortened into a preamble of seven-and-a-half pages, out of a total of twenty-eight, and an account of Tāre Lhamo's youth, including her twenties and thirties, is included thereafter, in roughly the same length, such that their activities as a couple flow out of her story. The treatment of their religious training in youth and their early miracles is comparable, while the content is almost entirely derivative of Pema Ösal Thaye's earlier work. Thereafter, their activities as a couple occupy the second half of the work, starting on page fifteen. Throughout the text, Tāre Lhamo and Namtrul Rinpoche are referred to as the "great *tertön* couple" (*gter chen yab yum*) or "venerable couple" (*rje yab yum*), combining honorific terms for male (*yab*) and female (*yum*), which seems to privilege their collaboration together rather than giving precedence to either one of them.

Although largely derivative, Abu Karlo's framing of the two-decade period from 1959 to 1978 in the section on her youth and early adulthood is less elaborate. Rather than describing Tāre Lhamo in heroic terms for this period, he matter-of-factly addresses the hardships she endured, stating: "From the age of 22, due to the strife and burden of the times, she endured countless hardships."[19] Later Abu Karlo characterizes her activities as taxing labor (*ngal rtsol*) and embellishes an episode found in *Spiraling Vine of Faith*, possibly based on an alternative account circulating orally. Here I use Tulku Thondup's translation into English, which appears in a separately published pamphlet alongside the Chinese translation:

> During the years of hardship, Khandro Rinpoche displayed many miracles. In those days, she had to carry many yak saddles on her shoulders and take them to the high lands of valleys. There she would collect firewood and load it on as many as eighteen wild yaks. Then talking to the yaks, she would bring the firewood to designated locations. However, when others tried to use the same wild yaks for transport, they remained unruly wild animals, hard to hold down, and they would throw off all the wood.[20]

This passage dramatizes Tāre Lhamo's fortitude and miraculous abilities amid arduous work. As a "yak-whisperer" of sorts, she is able to tame wild yaks and induce them into the task of carrying loads of wood. The passage emphasizes that no one else was able to do the same, as the yaks were difficult to hold in place long enough to load and unruly enough to throw off whatever loads were placed on them. This is one of the few instances of creative license Abu Karlo takes in narrating her miracles. Otherwise, his account includes half the number of episodes for this period, either verbatim or in condensed form, lifted directly from *Spiraling Vine of Faith*.

More conspicuous as a modification, in the passage closing the period, we find Tāre Lhamo subordinated to Namtrul Rinpoche as his consort and disciple. Again, here is Tulku Thondup's translation:

> As recounted earlier, Khandro Rinpoche then became the wisdom consort of Namtrul Rinpoche in accordance with

the prophecies of divinities and lamas and the prophetic signs of Dakinis. She recognized Namtrul Rinpoche as her karmic teacher for her many past successive lives. She serves his body, speech and mind with great reverence. The aspirational entrustment made by the great Padmasambhava in both Namtrul Rinpoche and Khandro Rinpoche was awakened simultaneously, when the profound interdependent causation of their three aspects, body, speech and mind were perfected.[21]

This passage captures the way that Abu Karlo indicates the couple's mutuality in the revelatory process while also portraying Tāre Lhamo as subordinate. More literally, he presents her as the "wisdom consort of the great *tertön* Orgyan Namkha Lingpa" (*gter chen o rgyan nam mkha' gling pa'i shes rab kyi grogs*), referring to Namtrul Rinpoche by his *tertön* name.[22] While this may have seemed like an innocuous decision on Abu Karlo's part, it has informed the reception of the couple among the sizeable number of Chinese disciples who converge on Nyenlung for the annual Dharma gathering (*chos tshogs*) toward the beginning of summer. It also reconfigures the seemingly neutral designation for the couple, the "great *tertön* couple" (*gter chen yab yum*), since he is fashioned as the "great *tertön*" and she as the "wisdom consort." Thus the epithet places Namtrul Rinpoche in the more prominent role around which the couple is then defined.

This difference may have as much to do with geography as gender. Tāre Lhamo's prominence in her own homeland, where she is remembered primarily as the daughter of Apang Terchen, is discernible in references to the couple. For example, at Tashi Gomang, in one of the ancillary temples, I saw a remarkable reference to the "Tāre Lhamo couple" (*Tā re lha mo yab yum*), placing her name in the prominent first position through which a tantric couple is characterized.[23] Nevertheless, the structure of *Jewel Lantern of Blessing* represents the couple with more parity, and also provides the most explicit account of their collaboration in the treasure revelation process. Abu Karlo narrates how sometimes Namtrul Rinpoche discovered the symbolic script (*brda yig*) in which treasures are encoded, and Tāre Lhamo would decode them for transcription into textual form, and at other times their roles would be reversed with Tāre Lhamo discovering the symbolic script and Namtrul Rinpoche transcribing them.[24] This description likely came directly from Namtrul Rinpoche, as it is similar to what he told me several years later. Moreover, in depicting the mutuality of their collaboration in the revelation process, Abu Karlo emphasizes the distinctiveness of their jointly revealed corpus of treasures.[25]

In thinking through the reason for this shift in hagiographic representation, it is important to note that Abu Karlo's work appeared the year before Tāre Lhamo passed away. As such, it may have provided a legitimizing mechanism for the consolidation of their lineage in Namtrul Rinpoche. In his narration of the final years of her life, during an interview in July 2006, Namtrul Rinpoche mentioned that there were already signs of her illness by 2000. Tāre Lhamo was diagnosed with what might have been esophageal cancer in 2001 and went for medical treatment in Barkam and Chengdu to no avail, passing away on March 26, 2002. Following the thread of legitimation a bit further, we can turn to another work by Abu Karlo and two collaborators compiled in 2000, titled *The History of the Medical Tradition in Golok*. This work includes the abbreviated biographies of medical doctors, who were often also religious figures, throughout the region. In a short biography of Apang Terchen published therein,[26] Abu Karlo makes public Namtrul Rinpoche's identification as one of four emanations of Tāre Lhamo's father.[27] Subsequently, in *Jewel Lantern of Blessings*, when listing Namtrul Rinpoche's previous incarnations, Abu Karlo adds the "action emanation" (*'phrin las sprul pa*) of Apang Terchen to the list,[28] an identification more obliquely referenced in the official version of their life stories by Pema Ösal Thaye.

This aspect of Namtrul Rinpoche's identity is derivative of Tāre Lhamo's own and creates a crucial connection to render him an authentic holder of Apang Terchen's treasure corpus, which they propagated throughout their teaching career together along with their own revelations. By virtue of her status as the daughter of Apang Terchen, having received the transmission directly from her father in youth, Tāre Lhamo held the position of lineage holder unequivocally, but further legitimation was required for Namtrul Rinpoche. With this in mind, there may be a way that Abu Karlo's abbreviated *namthar* represented a shift toward Namtrul Rinpoche taking full possession of their lineage inheritance. As a result of its swift translation, it became the operative understanding among Namtrul Rinpoche's Han Chinese disciples, who grew in number following Tāre Lhamo's death.

The narration from *Jewel Lantern of Blessings* has been influential due to its timely translation into Chinese and its use as the basis for the short account of their lives on a set of VCDs (video compact disc) produced by Nyenlung Monastery. On the VCD, *Melodious Songs of*

Nyenlung (*Snyan mo lung gyi sgra dbyangs*, c. 2004), it is read aloud on different soundtracks in Tibetan and Chinese, accompanied by photos of the couple and images of various figures with whom each are associated. Featuring footage taken from the late 1990s, this VCD set shows the *tertön* couple traveling to teach at different monasteries in and around Golok accompanied by devotional songs with lyrics dedicated to both of them. Whether conducting a ritual in a tent at the sacred mountain range of Nyenpo Yutse (Gnyan po g.yu rtse), giving teachings in an assembly hall at Tashi Gomang (Bkra shis sgo mang), or presiding over the consecration of the main *stūpa* in the county seat of Padma, the couple is shown leading each event in tandem at the head of the assembly. In a striking moment captured on video in this VCD set, when the couple arrives at Tashi Gomang in Padma County, Namtrul Rinpoche stands back while Tāre Lhamo receives a long line of devotees from her homeland who present ceremonial scarves to her and receive her blessings. This further illustrates the importance of location, both institutional and geographic, to the representation and reception of female sanctity.

Emanation of Tārā: The Local Rendition

The final version of her life story has recently been included in a collection of the lives and writings of Buddhist female masters from India and Tibet, published by the Ārya Tāre Publishing House at Larung Buddhist Academy. I received a draft of the work by the author, Rigdzin Dargye, in June 2014, and a scan of the published work in July 2017, titled *The Wonder of Divine Music*, totaling 120 pages.[29] The work is more substantial than previous versions of her life and focuses primarily on events in her homeland, prior to her union with Namtrul Rinpoche. In the title and early sections of the work, Tāre Lhamo is identified in local terms as the daughter of Apang Terchen. *The Wonder of Divine Music* goes so far as to refer to them as father–child lineage (*yab sras brgyud*) in the opening verses and includes a rare instance of a father–daughter treasure revelation, to be recounted below.

The opening verses also emphasize her identification with the *bodhisattva* Tārā, female embodiment of compassion, addressing her as "mother Tārā, the supreme goddess across successive lives" and "revered lady who protects from confrontation with the eight fears."[30] After two quotes, which suggest the importance of narrating the stories of Buddhist masters in order to elicit faith in the reader, the narrative

portion of the *namthar* begins by referring to her as the mind emanation of Green Tārā (*rje btsun sgrol ma ljang mo'i thugs kyi rnam sprul*).
The female *bodhisattva* Green Tārā is especially connected to protective
activity and, along these lines, Tāre Lhamo is shown protecting her
local community from the everyday hazards of nomadic life in Golok.
Her identification with Tārā comes to the fore at various points of the
narrative, including an occasion at eleven years old when her teacher
Rigdzin Jalu Dorje showered her with praise before a group of disciples as "the revered lady, noble Tārā actually appearing in human
flesh" and blessed her to perform enlightened activities as such.[31]

Her identification with Tārā in this work makes sense in local
terms for several reasons. Perhaps the most obvious reason is that
Tārā is her namesake—Tāre Lhamo means "the goddess Tārā" using
the vocative form, Tāre, as it appears in her mantra, *Oṃ Tāre Tuttāre
Ture Svāhā*. Moreover, in one of her origin myths, Tārā pledged to
always take female form in order to benefit myriad beings.[32] This
identification also makes sense, given the emphasis on Tāre Lhamo's
miracles, since Tārā is renowned for "the miraculous power to be
able to deliver devotees from all forms of physical danger."[33] Yet her
identification with Tārā is not explicit in the other versions of her life
story despite their shared emphasis on her miracle tales. In *The Wonder
of Divine Music*, this suggests the centrality of her role as a local savioress protecting the residents of the Mar Valley and areas surrounding
Tsimda Monastery, not only during the devastating decades of the
Maoist period, but also within the everyday hazards of nomadic life.
Moreover, unlike the other models of female sanctity used to frame
her life, Tārā as a female *bodhisattva* works wonders on her own without recourse to partnership with a male tantric figure.

Apart from her initial identification with Tārā, this local rendition displays less concern overall with establishing authoritative
female precedents. Perhaps for institutional and geographic reasons,
as a cleric from her father's monastery and as a member of her own
Pongyul clan (Spong/Spungs yul sde ba), among whom Tāre Lhamo
is revered, Rigdzin Dargye seems less compelled to legitimatize Tāre
Lhamo's religious authority by spending as much time on her identifications with female deities, past lives, or prophecies at birth. While
these aspects of Tāre Lhamo's identity take up almost half of *Spiraling
Vine of Faith*, they are dealt with in summary fashion in the opening pages of *The Wonder of Divine Music*. Rigdzin Dargye devotes
two pages to a preamble identifying her with female deities and past
lives, followed by brief sections on the prophecies delivered at her

birth and her own memories from previous lives.[34] The latter recounts incidents related to her status as the reincarnation of two figures from the previous generation in Golok, one female and one male, namely, Sera Khandro and Tra Gelong Tsultrim Lodrö, alt. Tsultrim Dargye (Khra dge slong Tshul khrims blo gros/alt. Tshul khrims dar rgyas, 1866–1937).[35] After that, Rigdzin Dargye turns to other topics: her religious training, treasure revelations, visionary experience, and miraculous activities. In *The Wonder of Divine Music*, the reader gains a more complete picture of Tāre Lhamo's visionary talents in her youth and early adulthood, during her twenties and thirties, and extensive salvific activities for her local community.

Due to the local nature of Rigdzin Dargye's account, several vignettes from her childhood cannot be found elsewhere. In a section on the "signs of her accomplishment" (*grub pa'i rang rtags*), one such vignette takes place in the vicinity of Dodrupchen Monastery, on an occasion when Tāre Lhamo's mother Damtsik Drolma (Dam tshig sgrol ma) and Rigdzin Jalu Dorje were sitting having a conversation.[36] Tāre Lhamo and a friend were playing near a rock outcropping, and her mother called to her to be careful lest she fall and get hurt. Tāre Lhamo thought to herself, "If I am the disciple of Dodrupchen, then even if I fall off a precipice, what harm can come of it?" So she and her friend deliberately jumped from a high point on the rock outcropping. But when she fell, no harm whatsoever came to her body. Later, when she approached Rigdzin Jalu Dorje, he said: "I had a vision of you two young disciples falling gently to the ground." Another vignette, in a section on Tāre Lhamo's "unobstructed clairvoyance" (*mngon shes thogs pa med pa*), features a hide-and-seek game with her friend Adzin (A'dzin) while they were digging for *droma* (*gro ma*), an herb, sometimes referred to as the "Tibetan sweet potato."[37] Adzin asked Tāre Lhamo to cover her head so she could hide some *droma*. When the time came to look for them, Tāre Lhamo boldly stated, "Because I am the daughter of Pawo Chöying Dorje, I know exactly where they are." And she proceeded straight to the spot to retrieve them. These are precious moments when, in childhood, Tāre Lhamo asserts her stature, either as disciple or daughter of prominent religious figures.

In *The Wonder of Divine Music*, the reader also gets a better sense for her early revelatory activity. Previous versions of Tāre Lhamo's story mention that she revealed treasures in youth but they only give a single example. This is a charming account of her stumbling on a treasure meant for Rigdzin Jalu Dorje—in the form of a stone marked by the seed syllable *Vaṃ*—when picking up rocks to protect herself from a pack of dogs near Dodrupchen Monastery.[38] Augmenting this, Rigdzin Dargye provides several more stories of her early collaborations in the revelatory process in a section dedicated to "gaining mastery over the sky repository of profound treasures" (*zab gter nam mkha' mdzod la mnga' dbang bsgyur*).[39] The most striking account is the father–daughter revelation with Apang Terchen, a phenomenon mentioned in a single line of Abu Karlo's short biography of him in *The History of the Medical Tradition in Golok*.[40] By contrast, Rigdzin Dargye provides an actual description of the process. Note that Tāre Lhamo's father died when she was only nine, so she is quite young here. What follows is a summary of the episode:

> Long ago, Apang Terchen once asked Tāre Lhamo to accompany him to the rock cliff at Serta Drongri (Gser rta 'brong ri). With his finger, he drew a circle on the rock cliff, and with his left palm, he struck it around the edges. He called to Tāre Lhamo and asked her to reach with her small hands into the cavity in the rock, entreating her to proceed gently. She retrieved a few medicinal pills to put in a metal basin brought along for the occasion, but he scolded her to be more diligent. Then Tāre Lhamo retrieved even more medicinal pills. After that, Apang Terchen restored the rock and drew out the design again, such that the rock became solid once more.[41]

Though only a paragraph, this is one of the more detailed accounts that we have of a treasure revelation by Tāre Lhamo, here guided by her father. Later, on her own, she revealed another treasure at Drongri, the sacred mountain and local protector deity of Serta, in this case a ritual implement in the form of a vajra spanning the size of a hand from the tips of thumb to middle finger. This she placed at Tsimda Monastery, and her father took it as a sign that great beings born in Markhok would have to go to another land but, for that reason, they would perform great benefit for the teachings and beings.[42] As depicted, his assessment foreshadowed Tāre Lhamo's departure for Nyenlung later in life to live with Namtrul Rinpoche.

The Wonder of Divine Music is organized thematically, rather than chronologically, allowing Rigdzin Dargye to keep Tāre Lhamo at the center of the frame throughout the work. The thematic organization consists of eleven sections, listed in an outline (*sa bcad*) following the preamble,[43] and these span the rest of the work (180–296). The transitions between sections are marked by a number and title of the section as below. While the first three acts, and the last one, on this list are necessarily chronological, the rest of the sections assemble together vignettes from different phases of her life.

1. The Manner of Her Birth as a Protector of Living Beings Extolled in Faultless Prophecies

2. The Manner of Giving Rise to Conviction among the Faithful by Remembering Past Lives

3. The Manner of Merging Minds [with the Guru] and Relying on Qualified Spiritual Guides

4. The Manner of Gaining Mastery over the Sky Repository of Profound Treasures

5. The Manner in Actuality, Visions, and Dreams of Her Encounters with Yidams and Supreme Deities and Her Journeys to Pure and Impure Realms

6. The Manner in which She Supported the Lives of the Unbiased Holders of the Teachings and Cleared Away Obstacles to Their Activities

7. The Manner of Her Engagement in Meditation Practice and Maturation of Myriad Beings through the Dharma

8. The Manner in which She Displayed Outwardly Her Signs of Accomplishment and Accepted Fortunate Ones [as Disciples]

9. The Manner in which She Guided Disciples through Her Unobstructed Clairvoyance

10. The Manner in which She Assisted the Deceased with Omniscient Wisdom

11. The Manner in which She Dissolved Her Physical Form into Dharmadhātu, Apropos of Those Clinging to Permanence

This version of her life story elucidates multiple facets of her visionary and miraculous activities. The first two sections deal with prophecies at her birth and her recollection of past lives, taking up a total of seven pages (180.14–184.11 and 184.12–186.5, respectively). The third section summarizes her training in youth in a few pages (186.6–189.6), while the fourth details her treasure revelations with a range of collaborators (189.7–198.15). The latter encompasses but is not restricted to her revelations with Namtrul Rinpoche and features testimony that Khenpo Munsel confirmed Tāre Lhamo as an authentic *tertön*.[44] The fifth section is one of the longest, taking up twenty-two pages (198.16–218.3), chronicling her visionary journeys to different realms, her interactions with tantric deities, visions in which she appeared to other Buddhist masters from the region, and visionary encounters with her own family members. The sixth section shows her extending the lives of several teachers through her ritual prowess (218.4–223.3), while the seventh features her religious activities in the post-Mao period in summary fashion across eight pages (223.4–230.9). Namtrul Rinpoche figures prominently in sections on her treasure revelations (fourth section), her extending the lives of teachers (sixth section), and her teaching and traveling during the post-Mao period (seventh section). Otherwise, the focus remains on Tāre Lhamo's own visionary and miraculous activities.

As with the other two versions of Tāre Lhamo's life, her miraculous deeds are given sustained treatment in her newest *namthar*, though Rigdzin Dargye does not restrict these to the period of 1959 to 1978 as do the others. The eighth section chronicles her outward display of "the signs of accomplishment" and takes up almost thirty pages (230.10–258.15), roughly one quarter of the work, featuring nearly fifty miracle tales. Miracles continue in the next two sections and follow the same episodic format, but with an emphasis on either her clairvoyance in the ninth section (258.16–281.15) or her visionary and ritual assistance to the recently deceased in the tenth section (281.16–294.1). The eleventh section (294.1–295.11) on her passing concludes the narrative, followed by closing verses and the colophon.

Let us consider several miracle tales to tease out a few more differences between this new *namthar* of Tāre Lhamo and the others discussed above. To begin the eighth section, Rigdzin Dargye introduces a harrowing tale, one not found in the official version of her life story, no doubt due to its politically sensitive content:

> During the period of the Cultural Revolution . . . one day while being beaten [during a struggle session], her body struck an iron stove, which was red with the fire's heat. [The Supreme Khandro] maintained compassion at the

forefront of her mind, such that great suffering did not affect her. She prayed to the bodhisattva Tārā, reciting her ten-syllable mantra, which came forth as a self-arising image on the front of her garment, tinged in green. Someone named Tsaza Oncang (Rtsa za 'on cang) from the Pongyul clan witnessed this in person. It was further attested by Lama Thöpa (Bla ma Thos pa) and many others said they encountered the cloth.[45]

This is by far the most dramatic episode in *The Wonder of Divine Music*. In this passage, in the midst of what must have been a struggle session, Tāre Lhamo invokes Tārā's beneficence by reciting her ten-syllable *mantra, Oṃ Tāre Tuttāre Ture Svāhā*, simultaneously calling on Tārā and embodying her compassion. In Rigdzin Dargye's rendering, the efficacy of her prayer results in Tāre Lhamo being spared the suffering of being burned. Heightening the miraculous tenor of the account, the *mantra* appears as a self-arising (*rang byung*) image. In an oral account, an old woman living at Tsimda Monastery, to whom Rigdzin Dargye provided me with an introduction, narrated it slightly differently. In her rendering, Tāre Lhamo's chest was placed on the iron stove, but she brought to mind the greater suffering of beings in the hell realms and so did not show any trace of being burned. While Tārā did not feature in this telling, in both cases compassion remains the central pivot of the miracle.

Another episode from the same period likewise exposes the brutality to which Tāre Lhamo was exposed during struggle sessions,[46] but again Rigdzin Dargye depicts the scene without her experiencing any suffering. It took place in the middle of winter, when Tāre Lhamo was stripped naked and placed outside overnight, her feet and hands bound.[47] Yet through her tantric practice of *tummo* (*gtum mo*), or "inner heat," she stayed warm throughout the night and remained unharmed. In these harrowing accounts, Tāre Lhamo demonstrates a heroic perseverance through her compassionate orientation and tantric prowess. *The Wonder of Divine Music* also portrays her extending compassion to others, such as imprisoned lamas. Rigdzin Dargye includes the vision in which Tāre Lhamo appears to Sangngag Lingpa to prophesize his release from prison, which also appears in *Spiraling Vine of Faith* and *Jewel Lantern of Blessings*, here referring to him by his alias Sera Yangtrul. Other stories from this period not found in earlier versions of her life story harken to her close connection with Sera Khandro's grandson, Doli Nyima (Mdo li nyi ma, b.

1946). In one such episode, credited as a miracle, she sends a cryptic message and gifts to Doli Nyima that eventuate in his release from prison.[48]

For this period of the Cultural Revolution, Rigdzin Dargye includes an account of her ongoing religious practice, presumably in secret, given that it was forbidden at the time. This is a brief account, found in the seventh section of *The Wonder of Divine Music* and not included in other versions of her life.[49] He portrays Tāre Lhamo reciting prayers while gathering yak dung, performing monthly feasts on sacred days even if she only had a little roasted barley (*rtsam pa*) to use as offerings, and even teaching the "great perfection" (*rdzogs chen*) to close disciples.[50] Strikingly, he fashions Tāre Lhamo in "the mode of being various manifestations of the twenty-one Tārās," who are the subject of well-known verses of homage in Tibetan liturgy.[51] When milking the female yak (*'bri*) by hand, she is "the goddess Tāre as milkmaid" (*bzhon ma tā re lha mo*). When gathering dung with a basket, she is "the goddess Tāre as dung collector" (*lci khur tā re lha mo*). When setting out for the mountains with a lasso, she is "the goddess Tāre as herder" (*rdzi bo tā re lha mo*). When wielding an ax and collecting wood, she is "the goddess Tāre as woodcutter" (*shing 'thu tā re lha mo*). These epithets are of course a play on her name, Tāre Lhamo, and also on the depiction of the twenty-one Tārās in different guises, each holding a different implement. In sum, her manifestation as milkmaid, dung collector, herder, and woodcutter are deemed "no different from Green Tārā as the emanation basis for all of them" (*thams cad sprul gzhi sgrol ma ljang mo gcig las med pa*). Here Rigdzin Dargye clearly invokes the beneficent presence of Green Tārā in Tāre Lhamo's own person, appearing in myriad forms in the midst of hardship.

This prepares the reader for Tāre Lhamo's exceptional status and miraculous activities in the eighth section, which are made manifest not only during the Cultural Revolution period but also, more often than not, within the everyday hazards of nomadic life on the grasslands of Golok. The episodes have a local flavor, typically introducing the families and individuals gathered together in a particular place, often camped on the grasslands together in a named valley with their herds nearby. The level of detail demonstrates the local knowledge Rigdzin Dargye was able to draw on, interviewing members of his own clan as a cleric scholar from their home monastery. Here is a prototypical story, one of several featuring a hailstorm:

On another occasion, in the Tsikyi Ridar (Rtsis kyi ri dar) valley, the Ling Nordzin (Gling nor 'dzin), Robdong Tharwa (Rob gdong thar ba), and Tsakö Pegyal (Tsha kho'i pad rgyal) households were staying together to gather medicinal herbs (specifically *rdza yung*). When Nordzin and Pegyal went to collect herbs for the Supreme Khandro, suddenly, black clouds gathered, and it was preparing to hail. In a wrathful manner, the Supreme Khandro menacingly addressed the gods, demons and humans of the whole of China, Tibet and Mongolia: "What do you need as proof? None of you can rival me." Fierce hail fell all around the surrounding area, but at the place where the households and livestock were gathered, not even one hailstone fell even though the sky remained black. Those present were amazed and gained confident faith.[52]

In this passage, Tāre Lhamo is depicted as holding sway over a considerable domain, no less than the gods, demons, and humans of China, Tibet, and Mongolia. At the same time, her activity is localized, protecting those around her in practical terms, in this case from hail that may have damaged their black yak-hair tents and wounded their livestock.

Such scenarios, related to the practical hazards of nomadic life in Golok, are reminiscent of Green Tārā's charge to rescue beings from the eight kinds of fear. The typical list of eight fears involves dangers of one sort or another: wild animals (elephants, lions, snakes), maleficent humans (bandits and captors), supernatural forces (demons or ghosts), and natural calamities (fire and drowning). Transposed onto the grasslands of Golok, we find Tāre Lhamo rescuing nomads from hailstorms, loss of livestock, and attacks by wild yak and guard dogs, usually the ferocious Tibetan mastiff. Witness the following account involving a knot shaped like a *phurba* (ritual dagger) blessed by Tāre Lhamo:

Another time, someone named Pakhung (Dpa' khyung) from Golok once wove a knotted phurba into his hair as protection from danger. A little while later a wild yak attacked him with its horns but he didn't get wounded, only a little sick. The Supreme Khandro Rinpoche made it for him and told him to wear it in his hair for protection. When a relative visited from Ngayul, he gave away the protection knot and told him to wear it without fail. Returning to Ngayul, the relative encountered a fierce black guard dog who attacked for two or three minutes and even tore at his clothing, but his body came to no harm whatsoever.[53]

In comparable fashion, Tāre Lhamo is credited with preventing wolves from attacking sheep, retrieving yak herds that got lost, rescuing the recently deceased who had fallen into hell, healing wounds, curing an old woman of cataracts, and more. As an example of her healing capacities, *The Wonder of Divine Music* includes an occasion when Tāre Lhamo visited Pegyal at his home when he was quite ill, was poured a cup of tea, took a sip, and left. By drinking the remainder of her tea, Pegyal was cured.[54] Most episodes of this nature related to life and death on the grasslands in an everyday sense; since the events are neither dated nor arranged chronologically, the reader has little sense for the timing of events.

Without a chronological flow, Rigdzin Dargye's version of her life would be difficult to follow for anyone not already familiar with Tāre Lhamo's story. This suggests a more restricted audience than the other two versions. In his preface, Pema Ösal Thaye offers *Spiraling Vine of Faith* and *Jewel Garland* to two types of readers, ordinary people with faith in Buddhism and researchers with an interest in Tibetan culture and history,[55] suggesting a public audience of some magnitude and breadth. Meanwhile, the colophon to *Jewel Lantern of Blessings* mentions Tibetan, Chinese, and foreign disciples specifically as its target audience, perhaps in anticipation of its translation into Chinese and English.[56] Given its publication in the Ārya Tāre collection, following Pema Ösal Thaye's version of her life, Rigdzin Dargye's piece provides an important complement detailing new facets of Tāre Lhamo's life. Unlike his eminently readable works of advice to the laity using simple Tibetan,[57] *The Wonder of Divine Music* is a dense work, episodic in fashion, without a clear narrative frame to hold the various vignettes together, even within a single theme. In this regard, it is less well crafted as a piece of literature than Pema Ösal Thaye's work.

Although the work was published in 2017, one wonders whether a twelfth section will be added in a future iteration, given the prototypical Tibetan arrangement of the life of the Buddha into twelve acts. In 2014, Rigdzin Dargye had mentioned planning to add something about Tāre Lhamo's rebirth before completing the *namthar*, so at some point another section might be added to round out his rendition of her life.

With its emphasis on specific family and place names, *The Wonder of Divine Music* is localizing in two senses, prioritizing geography as much as gender in the depiction of Tāre Lhamo's salvific activities. In the first sense of the local, Rigdzin Dargye focuses his account geographically on the Mar Valley and on the myriad ways that Tāre Lhamo assisted members of the Pongyul clan and others in the area with whom she had a close connection. In a second sense, its gendered specificity is accomplished through the choice of Tārā as the central model through which to frame her life and in the mundane household-level setting of her miracles. In pan-Tibetan myths, the male *bodhisattva* of compassion, Avalokiteśvara, is said to give birth to the Tibetan people in the form of a monkey who copulates with an ogress, and he is also identified retrospectively with the seventh-century Tibetan emperor Songtsan Gampo (Srong btsan sgam po) and with the line of Dalai Lamas who ruled over Central Tibet for three centuries. While Tārā can be regarded as his partner in these activities (emanating as Songtsan Gampo's wives, for example), she is more typically depicted in murals and scroll paintings intervening within the travails of everyday life, particular in her aspect of saving beings from the eight fears. In this way, she is more like Guanyin, the female embodiment of Avalokiteśvara in China, whose legends include mundane appearances—as a fisherwoman, for example. This model of female sanctity seems well suited to frame Tāre Lhamo's local activities, addressing both the everyday perils of nomadic life and the devastating decades of the Maoist period.

Overall in his rendition, along similar lines to Catherine Mooney's observation regarding the construction of the "female mystic" in medieval Europe, Tāre Lhamo is fashioned as the visionary "other" to the male cleric. Rigdzin Dargye himself is enmeshed in managing monastic affairs at the largest Buddhist institution on the Tibetan plateau as the head disciplinarian at Larung Buddhist Academy. While invested in recuperating stories about Tāre Lhamo, he includes far more episodes in sections dedicated to her miracles and visionary experience than to her religious training and teaching activities. In addition, although contributing a large body of new material from Tāre Lhamo's youth and early adulthood in her homeland, in the process he downplays the scope of her regional influence by focusing on the local. Perhaps this is the cost of highlighting Tāre Lhamo as a figure in her own right, given that her more widespread influence came later in life after her second marriage to Namtrul Rinpoche in 1980, which coincided with economic and cultural liberalization in

China. But, then again, Rigdzin Dargye may not have felt the need to repeat an account of her later life with Namtrul Rinpoche, beyond what is summarized in the seventh section, since it is so thoroughly chronicled by Pema Ösal Thaye in *Jewel Garland*.

Conclusion: Framing Gender?

What can we take away from these rather different hagiographic portraits of Tāre Lhamo by her male cleric disciples? All three versions emphasize her miracles during the years leading up to and including the Cultural Revolution, while *Spiraling Vine of Faith* and *The Wonder of Divine Music* both dedicate sections to her visionary experience. Each adds information not found in the others and draws attention to different aspects of her identity and activities. While the content of episodes included in each version is an important contributor to this, I have called attention to the framing devices used by her hagiographers to characterize the primary role for which Tāre Lhamo should be remembered, whether as a tantric heroine during troubled times, the "wisdom consort" of Namtrul Rinpoche, or an emanation of Tārā manifesting in the Mar Valley. As argued, these differences involve the male authors' situatedness in terms of their geographic and institutional locations, as it pertains to the relative prominence of Tāre Lhamo and Namtrul Rinpoche in their respective homelands. While Pema Ösal Thaye and Abu Karlo universalize Tāre Lhamo's story by framing it within recognizable tropes of the Tibetan Buddhist imaginaire (whether *ḍākinī*, *bodhisattva*, *siddha*, or consort), Rigdzin Dargye localizes her story in the particulars of her homeland, rendering her as Tārā of the Mar Valley.

Given that the most active and public phase of Tāre Lhamo's teaching career occurred in partnership with Namtrul Rinpoche, it is important to have these diverse hagiographic portraits. Otherwise, it would be easy for Tāre Lhamo's own career to disappear into the homogenizing category of the "consort" that prompts the easy assumption that she served mainly in a supporting role to Namtrul Rinpoche. As a cautionary, we might remember Rita Gross's notion of "androcentric recordkeeping," which tends to erase women's contributions from the historical record over time.[58] In *The Wonder of Divine Music*, Rigdzin Dargye is more *comprehensive* and catalogue-like in chronicling her activities in youth and early adulthood, due to his unique access to oral tradition in and around Markhok as a cleric-scholar from Tsimda Monastery. Many of the details of Tāre Lhamo's early life would be lost without his considerable efforts to gather and compile local remembrances. By contrast, Pema Ösal Thaye's version is more *selective*, in part out of necessity in order to avoid politically sensitive topics, given his post in a government office and the publication of *Spiraling Vine of Faith* and *Jewel Garland* in conjunction with a government agency. Yet his selectivity is also likely, in part, a reflection of his own sense of craft as a writer in creating a compelling narrative. His version is masterfully written, highlighting the universal appeal for Tibetans of Tāre Lhamo's salvific activities during the Maoist period and choosing those situations most emblematic of the years leading up to and including the Cultural Revolution. Indeed, Pema Ösal Thaye is original in the way he fashions a redemptive narrative out of the wreckage of that period, telling a new kind of *namthar* in order to heal cultural trauma.

In *Jewel Lantern of Blessings*, Abu Karlo offers the most *distilled* version of Tāre Lhamo's life story. In terms of impact, it has been influential as the basis of the earliest translation of the lives of Tāre Lhamo and Namtrul Rinpoche into Chinese, circulating widely among their Han Chinese disciples and informing their representation in audiovisual materials produced by Nyenlung Monastery. Otherwise, so far in the Tibetan, *Spiraling Vine of Faith* has the widest reach, since it has been reproduced twice, detached from *Jewel Garland* in both cases. It was reprinted in a 2003 journal issue devoted to the lives of prominent Tibetan women in the Nyingma tradition, published by the Ngakmang Research Institute.[59] More recently, it appeared with a new title in a 2013 compilation of the lives of Buddhist women in India and Tibet, published by Larung Buddhist Academy.[60] It is hard to predict the impact of Rigdzin Dargye's rendition of her *namthar* now that it is published. Certainly, it will make clear for the historical record that Tāre Lhamo was already an accomplished practitioner, visionary, teacher, and *tertön* prior to joining with Namtrul Rinpoche in her early forties.

In light of the material provided in *The Wonder of Divine Music*, their twenty-some years revealing treasures and teaching together can be seen as an extension of Tāre Lhamo's already well-established role and standing in Padma County. In fact, an episode in *Jewel Garland* illustrates the way that her own regional prominence helped launch their teaching career as a *tertön* couple, since Tāre Lhamo and Namtrul Rinpoche gave their first large-scale public teaching in 1985 at Tsimda Monastery, where they disseminated anew the treasures of her father, Apang Terchen, alongside their own revelations. In the end, how Tāre Lhamo is remembered may turn out to be a factor of geography as much as gender with discrete representational practices based at Nyenlung and Tsimda Monasteries and extending beyond.

Notes

1. This term will be defined later in the chapter. The most comprehensive study on the *ḍākinī* to date is Judith Simmer-Brown, *Dakini's Warm Breath: The Feminine Principle in Tibetan Buddhism* (Boston: Shambhala Publications, 2001).

2. Namtrul Rinpoche is to be distinguished from Khenpo Jigme Phuntsok (Mkhan po 'Jigs med phun tshogs, 1933–2004), the monastic founder of Larung Buddhist Academy in Serta.

3. For an overview of the treasure tradition, see Tulku Thondup, *Hidden Teachings of Tibet* (Boston: Wisdom Publications, 1997); and Janet Gyatso, "Drawn from the Tibetan Treasury: The gTer ma Literature," in *Tibetan Literature: Studies in Genre*, ed. José Cabezón and Roger Jackson (Ithaca, NY: Snow Lion Publications. 1996).

4. Catherine Mooney, *Gendered Voices: Medieval Saints and their Interpreters* (Philadelphia: University of Pennsylvania Press, 1999), 3.

5. For strategies of self-representation in Tibetan autobiographical writing, see Janet Gyatso, *Apparitions of the Self: The Secret Autobiographies of a Tibetan Visionary* (Princeton, NJ: Princeton University Press, 1998). Gyatso distinguishes between the first-person and third-person voice in Tibetan *namthar* as follows: "The self-written account, due to powerful constraints in Tibetan linguistic convention on how one should talk about oneself, typically exhibits a studied diffidence, whereas the life written by someone else typically exhibits an equally studied reverence" (105). Her assessment of the latter mirrors observations made by Patrick Geary regarding the hagiographic construction of saints as objects of veneration in his chapter, "Saints, Scholars, and Society: The Elusive Goal," *Saints: Studies in Hagiography*, ed. Sandro Sticca (Binghamton, NY: Medieval & Renaissance Texts & Studies, 1996).

6. See Janet Gyatso, *Apparitions of the Self*; and Sarah Jacoby, *Love and Liberation: Autobiographical Writings of the Tibetan Buddhist Visionary Sera Khandro* (New York: Columbia University Press, 2014).

7. Their treasure corpus was first published as *O rgyan 'jigs med nam mkha' gling pa dang ḍāk ki tā re bde chen rgyal mo rnam gnyis kyi zab gter chos* in a facsimile edition in twelve volumes (Gser rta: Snyan lung dgon, n.d.). This collection has more recently been combined into a fourteen-volume paperback edition that includes their correspondence and biographies, *Khyab bdag gter chen bla ma 'ja' lus pa dpal mnyam med nam mkha' gling pa rin po che dang*

mkha' 'gro rin po che tā re lha mo zung gi zab gter nam mkha' mdzod (Chengdu: Si khron mi rigs dpe skrun khang, 2013).

8. A bu dkar lo, *Gter ston grub pa'i dbang phyug gzhi chen nam sprul dang mkha' 'gro tā re bde chen lha mo zung gi mdzad rnam nyer bsdus byin rlabs nor bu'i sgron me* (Xining: Mtsho sngon nang bstan rtsom sgrig khang, 2001). Hereafter, in the notes, I abbreviate this text to JLB.

9. The English translation of his work by Tulku Thondup under the title, *Blessing Light of Jewels* (no publication information), never gained a readership, but its companion Chinese translation, *Nianlong shangshi fumu renboqie lüezhuan*, has been reproduced in multiple formats, including a glossy pamphlet with photographs. Other published sources about the couple in Chinese, featuring selections from their teachings and biographical accounts, include *Nianlong shangshi fumu guang zhuan: Wugou moni baoman* and *Yanjiao Huibian: Erli renyun moni baoman* (Gser rta: Snyan lung dgon, c. 2009).

10. Rig 'dzin dar rgyas, *A paṃ [alt: phang] gter chen gyi sras mo mkha' 'gro tā re lha mo mchog gi rnam par thar ba mdo tsam brjod pa ngo mtshar lha yi rol mo*, in *Mkha' 'gro'i chos mdzod chen mo* published by Bla rung ā rya tā re'i dpe tshogs rtsom sgrig khang (Lhasa: Bod ljongs bod yig dpe rnying dpe skrun khang, 2017), vol. 16, 177–296. The colophon references the author as Golok Rigdar (Mgo log Rig dar), since there are two clerics known as Khenpo Rigdzin Dargye at Larung Buddhist Academy. The date of completion is given as the first day of the third month of the fire bird year (late April, 2017). Hereafter, I will use WDM to abbreviate this work in the notes.

11. This version of her life story, alongside the letters she exchanged with Namtrul Rinpoche during the period of their courtship in the late 1970s, are discussed in more details in my book, *Love Letters from Golok: A Tantric Couple in Modern Tibet* (New York: Columbia University Press, 2016). Their biographies, *Spiraling Vine of Faith: The Liberation of Khandro Tāre Lhamo* (*Mkha' 'gro tā re lha mo'i rnam thar dad pa'i 'khri shing*, hereafter SVF in the notes) and *Jewel Garland: The Liberation of Namtrul Jigme Phuntsok* (*Nam sprul 'jigs med phun tshogs kyi rnam thar nor bu'i do shal*, hereafter JG in the notes) were first published in Pad ma 'od gsal mtha' yas, *Skyabs rje nam sprul rin po che 'jigs med phun tshogs dang mkha' 'gro tā re lha mo mchog gi rnam thar rig 'dzin mkha' 'gro dgyes pa'i mchod sprin* (Chengdu: Si khron mi rigs dpe skrun khang, 1997).

12. SVF 106.8–12. The translations in this article are my own except where indicated.

13. This same epithet is also employed by Abu Karlo and Rigdzin Dargye. In youth, Pema Ösal Thaye refers to her as "the supreme maiden" (*sras mo mchog*).

14. Note that Tāre Lhamo is recorded in *Spiraling Vine of Faith* as an emanation of two figures from the preceding generation, one male and one female, namely Tra Gelong Tsultrim Lodrö/Tsultrim Dargye (Khra dge slong Tshul khrims blo gros/Tshul khrims dar rgyas) and Sera Khandro, otherwise

known as Uza Khandro Dewe Dorje (Dbus bza' mkha' 'gro Bde ba'i rdo rje). Yet Pema Ösal Thaye chooses to highlight her female antecedents by excerpting long passages from the *namthar*s of Yeshe Tsogyal and Sera Khandro. Specifically, he excerpts chapter 6 from the well-known version of Yeshe Tsogyal's life by Taksham Nuden Dorje (Stag sham Nus ldan rdo rje), *Bod kyi jo mo ye shes mtsho rgyal gyi mdzad tshul rnam par thar pa gab pa mngon byung rgyud mangs dri za'i glu phreng* (Kalimpong: Bdud 'joms rin po che, 1972): 134.1–137.3 and the short autobiography of Sera Khandro, titled *Ku su lu'i nyams byung gi gnas tshul mdor bsdus rdo rje'i spun gyis dris lan mos pa'i lam bzang* in *The Collected Revelations (gter chos) of Se ra mkha' 'gro Bde chen rdo rje*, vol. 4 (Kalimpong, India: Dupjung Lama, 1978), 103–29. There are published translations of the former by Keith Dowman, *Sky Dancer: The Secret Life & Songs of the Lady Yeshe Tsogyal* (Ithaca, NY: Snow Lion Publications, 1996) and the Padmakara Translation Committee, *Lady of the Lotus-Born: The Life and Enlightenment of Yeshe Tsogyal* (Boston: Shambhala Publications, 2002) and of the latter by Christine Monson, *The Excellent Path of Devotion: An Abridged Story of a Mendicant's Experiences in Response to Questions by Vajra Kin* (Boulder, CO: Kama Terma Publications, 2013) and Sarah Jacoby, "The Excellent Path of Devotion: An Annotated Translation of Sera Khandro's Short Autobiography," *Himalayan Passages: Tibetan and Newar Studies in Honor of Hubert Decleer* (Boston: Wisdom Publications, 2014), especially chapter 2.

15. SVF 139.16–140.8.

16. See Gayley, *Love Letters from Golok*.

17. SVF 140.8–15.

18. SVF 143.11–17.

19. JLB 12.12–14. The Tibetan reads: *gdung grangs nyer gnyis par dus kyi ru 'dzing dang 'khel bas tshad med pa'i o brgyal bzhes*.

20. JLB 13.5–12. Translated by Tulku Thondup in *Blessing Light of Jewels*, 9.

21. JLB 15.1–8. Translated by Tulku Thondup in *Blessing Light of Jewels*, 10.

22. Note that Pema Ösal Thaye uses the designation "great *tertön*" (*gter chen*) for Namtrul Rinpoche on two occasions, but does not pair that with a characterization of Tāre Lhamo as the consort to the great *tertön*. See Pad ma 'od gsal mtha' yas, *Rig 'dzin mkha' 'gro dgyes pa'i mchod sprin*, i.1 and JG 3.13.

23. There is no hard and fast rule being put forward here, given that *Wonder of Divine Music* features an episode in which Tāre Lhamo's cousin, Jigme Wangdrak [Dorje], one of the main teachers at Adzo Monastery (A bzod dgon) in Jigdril County of Golok, refers to the couple as the "Namtrul couple" (Nam sprul yab yum, WDM 194.10). Note that this figure remained close to Namtrul Rinpoche after Tāre Lhamo's passing.

24. JLB 23.17–24.4.

25. JLB 24.1–4. The Tibetan reads: *gter ston gzhan dang gzhan las khyad par du 'phags pa thabs shes zung ldan gyi zab chos glegs bam pod bcu gsum tsam 'gro ba'i spyi nor du byon pa*.

26. A bu dkar lo, Dung gces, and Gsang bdag tshe ring, *Mgo log sman rtsis rig pa'i lo rgyus ngo mtshar nor bu'i rlabs phreng* (Xining: Qinghai Minorities Publishing House, 2000): 203–14.

27. Apang Terchen's more widely recognized emanations were the previous Sakya Tridzin (Sa skya khri 'dzin), the 41st throne-holder of the Sakya lineage who now lives in Dehradun, India, and Jigme Wangdrak Dorje ('Jigs med dbang drag rdo rje), the only one to be enthroned as such and the nephew of Apang Terchen. There is also a local *siddha* named Tulku Wulo (Sprul sku Bu lo) on the list of incarnations.

28. JLB 2.11–12.

29. To the 2014 draft, the 2017 complete version added a title, opening verses, a paragraph-long preamble, one or more episodes and closing verses for each section, closing verses to the text as a whole, and a colophon. Editorial corrections were also made along the way.

30. WDM 177.9–10. The Tibetan reads: *tshe rabs lhag pa'i lha mchog sgrol ma yum* and *'jigs brgyad g.yul las skyob mdzad rje btsun ma.*

31. WDM 186.15–16. The Tibetan reads: *rje btsun ā rya tā re dngos mi'i sha tshugs su byon pa.*

32. This pledge is contained in one of the origin myths for the *bodhisattva* Tārā given in Stephan Beyer, *The Cult of Tārā: Magic and Ritual in Tibet* (Berkeley: University of California Press, 1973): 64–65.

33. Robert Buswell and Donald Lopez, *The Princeton Dictionary of Buddhism* (Princeton, NJ: Princeton University Press, 2014): 895.

34. Following the opening verses of praise, the narrative begins by identifying her as the mind emanation of Green Tārā (*rje btsun sgrol ma ljang mo'i thugs kyi rnam sprul*), followed by her more standard *trikāya* identification as Samantabhadrī, Vajravārāhī, and Yeshe Tsogyal as found in *Spiraling Vine of Faith* (WDM 178.14–179.3). The section on prophecies at birth can be found at 180.14–184.11 and the section on her recollection of past lives at 184.12–186.5.

35. Given the disparity in their dates—Sera Khandro passed away in 1940, and Tāre Lhamo was born in 1938—Rigdzin Dargye is explicit in stating that Tāre Lhamo was a "pre-mortem reincarnation" (*ma 'das sprul sku*) of her predecessor (WDM 181.15), referring to the rare phenomenon of a reincarnation being recognized prior to the death of his or her predecessor. This is the first use of the term in reference to Tāre Lhamo's past lives that I have seen. In addition to her identification with Sera Khandro and Tra Gelong, as found in the other two accounts of her life, here Rigdzin Dargye adds a third identification as an emanation of Apang Tulku Shedrup Tenpai Nyima (A pang [alt: phang] sprul sku bshad sgrub bstan pa'i nyi ma).

36. WDM 237.17–238.8.

37. WDM 278.13–18.

38. SVF 136.14–137.8 and JLB 11.13–17. In *The Wonder of Divine Music*, it is her other main teacher, Dzongter Kunzang Nyima, who reveals a *sādhana* based on this treasure (WDM 190.3–14).

39. For example, one episode shows her revealing a treasure with Dzongter Kunzang Nyima's daughter, Lhacam Chökyi Drolma (Lha lcam Chos kyi sgrol ma), also considered to be an emanation of Sera Khandro (WDM 191.6–192.6). This is then used when she conducts rituals to extend the lives of other Buddhist masters, a capacity with which Pema Ösal Thaye also credits her.

40. Abu Karlo references a treasure revealed by this father and daughter pair in Gyalrong in *Mgo log sman rtsis rig pa'i lo rgyus*, 211.

41. WDM 189.7–190.3.

42. WDM 190.15–191.5.

43. WDM 180.3–13.

44. WDM 194.4–196.4. This is an episode not found in the 2014 draft version. It was added to the completed 2017 *namthar* and includes testimony to how unusual Tāre Lhamo's treasures are. Khenpo Munsel's comments are embedded in a conversation between Tāre Lhamo's cousin, Jigme Wangdrak [Dorje], who is the only enthroned reincarnation of her father, and Khenpo Shiten (Mkhan po Zhi bstan) of Tarthang Monastery (Dar thang dgon) in Jigdril County.

45. WDM 230.11–231.1.

46. The term Rigdzin Dargye uses for struggle session is *'thab rtsod* instead of the more common *'thab 'dzing*.

47. WDM 251.13–17. The "heat of *tummo*" (*gtum mo'i me drod*) is explicit in the 2014 draft that Rigdzin Dargye shared with me.

48. WDM 254.7–255.3.

49. The theme of practicing in secret during this period can be found in the *namthar* of other Buddhist masters from the region who survived and spearheaded the revitalization of Buddhism in the post-Mao period, including Khenpo Jigme Phuntsok (Mkhan po 'Jigs med phun tshogs, 1933–2004) and Pema Tumbo, better known as Kusum Lingpa (Pad ma gtum bo, alias Sku gsum gling pa, 1934–2009). See Tshul khrims blo gros, *Snyigs dus bstan pa'i gsal byed cig bu chos rje dam pa yid bzhin nor bu 'jigs med phun tshogs 'byung gnas dpal bzang po'i rnam thar bsdus pa dad pa'i gsos sman* in *Chos rje dam pa yid bzhin nor bu 'jigs med phun tshogs 'byung gnas dpal bzang po'i gsung 'bum* (Hong Kong: Xianggang xinzhi chubanshe, 2002), vol. 3: 364–418 and A bu dkar lo, *Gter ston grub pa'i dbang phyug o rgyan sku gsum gling pa'i rnam thar mdo tsam brjod pa ma tshogs rig 'dzin bzhad pa'i rang gdangs* (Zhang kang then mā dpe skrun khang, 2003).

50. WDM 223.5–14 and 224.5–8.

51. WDM 224.8–17. The Tibetan reads: *sgrol ma nyer cig po'ang sprul gzhi gcig gi sprul ba sna tshogs yin tshul*. Omitted in my abbreviated translation is the phrase "sharing a single emanation basis" (referenced later in the paragraph). On liturgical praises to the twenty-one Tārās, see Martin Wilson, *In Praise of Tārā: Songs to the Savioress* (Boston: Wisdom Publication, 1986). That Tārā would manifest as a herder or wood collector is reminiscent of Guanyin emanating as a fisherwoman and other mundane female forms in China.

52. WDM 233.9–234.1.

53. WDM 238.9–239.2.

54. WDM 232.17–233.9.

55. Pad ma 'od gsal mtha' yas, *Rig 'dzin mkha' 'gro dgyes pa'i mchod sprin*, iii.5–6.

56. JLB 27.18–19.

57. See, for example, Rig 'dzin dar rgyas, *Chos rje dam pa 'Jigs med phun tshogs 'byung gnas dpal bzang po mchog gi mjug mtha'i zhal gdams rang tshugs ma shor/ gzhan sems ma dkrugs zhes pa'i 'grel ba lugs gnyis blang dor gsal ba'i sgron me* (c. 2004) and Go 'jo ba Sgron skyabs, *Mthun 'brel gyi slob gso* (c. 2013), centered on a speech of that title by Khenpo Rigdzin Dargye as transcribed by Konpopa Thubten Lungtok (Kong po pa Thub bstan lung rtogs).

58. Rita Gross, *Buddhism After Patriarchy: A Feminist History, Analysis, and Reconstruction of Buddhism* (Albany: State University of New York Press, 1992).

59. See *Sngags pa'i shes rigs dus deb* 5:1 (2003): 117–132.

60. See *'Phags bod kyi skyes chen ma dag gi rnam par thar ba pad ma dkar po'i phreng ba*, vol. 12, 121–54. At the time of publication, this compilation had expanded to fifty-two volumes. While *Spiraling Vine of Faith* is excerpted and reproduced almost in its entirety, the title has been changed to *The Ladder Traversing to Akaniṣṭha: The Liberation of Khandro Tāre Lhamo* (*Mkha' 'gro tā re lha mo'i rnam thar 'og min bgrod pa'i them skas*). This reflects how it appears in the fourteen-volume paperback version of the couple's treasure corpus, mentioned in note 7 above. See *'Phags bod kyi skyes chen ma dag gi rnam par thar ba pad ma dkar po'i phreng ba*, vol. 12, 121–54 (2013 version) and vol. 16, 133–176 (2017 version) within the larger 52-volume collection, *Mkha' 'gro'i chos mdzod chen mo*.

Chapter 10

Feminine Identities in Buddhist *Chöd*

Michelle J. Sorensen

In this chapter, I explore the problem of female embodiment in Buddhism. Drawing on interviews and field research I have conducted in Nepal and India, I discuss how Tibetan Buddhist women practitioners of *chöd* (*gcod*) negotiate the idea of inferior female embodiment. In particular, I discuss how Tibetan women construct their gender identity through the tensions between religious forces and cultural forces. By examining how lay and celibate women in Nepal and India understand their gender identities through the practice of *chöd*, I explore how women reflect on and adapt to their own experiences of being embodied as female. Finally, I suggest that researchers might productively combine Western feminist perspectives with empathetic responses to Buddhist experience in order to understand fully what it means to be a woman Buddhist practitioner in Tibetan cultures.

Buddhist Problems of Female Embodiment

The fundamental challenge faced by women practitioners of Buddhism is a structural inferiority within the tradition. From the earliest Buddhist teachings, women have faced more impediments to enlightenment than men. Female celibates must obey more precepts than males: the "Eight Conditions," or "heavy laws" (*garudhamma*), prescribe the behavior of renunciant women and effectively render them inferior in status to all male members of the *sangha*. Many Buddhist texts suggest that one must be reborn as a man before becoming a fully enlightened being, a complete and perfect Buddha. Naomi Appleton explains that while a woman can become an awakened *arhat* in the Theravāda Buddhist tradition, she cannot become a *bodhisattva*, as the *Bahudhātuka Sutta* (*Majjhima Nikāya* 115) infamously records the Buddha asserting. Nor can a woman practitioner become a fully awakened *buddha*.[1]

In Mahāyāna Buddhism, the story of the Nāga Princess in the *Lotus Sūtra* (*Saddharmapundarīka Sūtra*) and the story of the Goddess in the *Vimalakīrtinirdeśa Sūtra* are often interpreted as examples of equal opportunities provided for both males and females to become enlightened. However, these *sūtras* emphasize that one needs to transcend all dichotomizations, including gender, in order to become enlightened and thus might not illustrate that a woman can attain enlightenment in a female form. Another infamous passage, from the *Bodhisattvabhūmi* written by Asanga in the fourth century, is often cited in discussions on the status of women in Buddhism. In this text, Asanga explains that "completely perfected Buddhas are not women," not only because they have transcended the status of womanhood, but also, "All women are by nature full of defilement and of weak intelligence. And not by one who is full of defilement and of weak intelligence is completely perfected Buddhahood attained."[2] Rita Gross calls this "[a] particularly virulent example" of misogyny,[3] one that stands out, according to Miranda Shaw, for articulating a belief that has "negative implications for women insofar as it communicated the insufficiency of the female body as a locus of enlightenment."[4]

In addition, as scholars such as Liz Wilson have pointed out, women's bodies have often been used in Buddhist literature to symbolize all that is repugnant, corrupting, and horrific about existence in samsara. Wilson's study of Buddhist hagiographic texts from multiple traditions demonstrates "how disgust-inspiring representations of women figure in the religious achievements of members of the men's monastic order."[5] Such texts demonstrate how meditations focusing on women in states of unconsciousness, disfiguration, and death are useful for men who aspire to spiritual accomplishment. Although gender discriminations are understood to be mundane conventions—as opposed to actual characteristics—within Buddhist philosophical exegesis, the teaching that female embodiment is a barrier to enlightenment clearly has profoundly negative effects on women practitioners. Unlike their male counterparts, many women practitioners focus on attaining rebirth as a human male as the next necessary stage in attaining enlightenment.

Gender and *Chöd*

While the women I met in Nepal and India struggle with traditional representations of women's bodies as inferior, one means they have of countering these representations is the practice of Tibetan Buddhist *chöd*. Buddhist *chöd* appeals to both lay and renunciant women for a number of reasons. First, *chöd* traces its lineage to the foremost woman philosopher-adept in Tibetan Buddhism, Machik Labdrön (*ma gcig lab sgron*, c. 1055–1153). Second, as I will discuss in a subsequent section, practice texts within the *chöd* tradition often invoke the feminine in forms of wisdom *ḍākinīs* or *yoginīs*—enlightened supramundane beings who assist others on the path to enlightenment. Perhaps most importantly, *chöd* offers women practitioners a vehicle through which they can attain enlightenment in a female embodiment.

Machik Labdrön is one of the most renowned historical women in Tibetan Buddhism. From a young age, Machik distinguished herself by her keen interest in and comprehension of Buddhism. She became a student of Drapa Ngonshé (*grwa pa mngon shes*, 1012–1090), reciting the *Prajñāpāramitāsūtra* texts for lay persons on behalf of her teacher. Following further study with Kyotön Sonam Lama (*skyo ston bsod nams bla ma*, b. eleventh century), she became involved with an Indian *yogi* known as Töpa Baré (*thod pa 'ba' re*) and had three sons and two daughters with him. Later in her adult life, Machik returned to dressing as a spiritual practitioner as she had in her youth and traveled widely to receive teachings. She eventually settled in a cave at Zangri Khangmar (*zangs ri khang dmar*), where a community of disciples formed around her. The *chöd* praxis of Machik, grounded in the Mahāyāna Buddhist *Prajñāpāramitā* teachings, is directed toward cutting through ego-clinging and erroneous patterns of thinking.

Chöd emphasizes the practice of visualizing the dissection of one's own body into aggregates and offering them as food to a variety of sentient beings. Using *chöd* methods, women practitioners can imagine their own female bodies as transformed into offerings that will satisfy any and all beings. A prototypical practice of body offering is described in *The Distinctive Eightfold Supplementary Section*, an early text attributed to Machik Labdrön.[6] According to *The Distinctive*

Eightfold Supplementary Section, the practice has three parts: a preliminary meditation on cultivating compassion and loving kindness; the
main practice of giving one's body, which is possessed of the six perfections; and the conclusion of dedicating the merit one has generated
through the practice to the unsurpassed spirit of enlightenment.[7] The
preliminary meditation requires the practitioner to generate compassion for all sentient beings, paying special attention to beings that
have caused harm to (*gnod byed*) or obstructed (*bgegs*) the practitioner. During this meditation, the practitioner cultivates the intention to
offer her body and visualizes those to whom she will offer her body.

In the main part of the practice, the practitioner visualizes her
body as very large; with an envisioned sword of wisdom, she cuts
through her neck and makes her body an offering to the harmdoers
(*gnod byed*), satisfying them all according to their particular desires for
meat, blood, or bones. By visualizing her body as totally consumed,
the practitioner's mind is no longer attached to concerns about the
past, present, or future. Instead, she can dwell in a natural state of
open awareness: "the mind (*sems*) does not hanker after the past, does
not anticipate the future, and does not notice the present. You rest
softly and very loosely. Then, meditatively cultivating compassion
you give your body as food; the mind rests in the state of reality
(*gnas lugs*). In that way, visualize the tip of day and the fading away
of night cycling (*khor ro ro*) in turn (*re mos*)."[8] For the conclusion
of the practice, the practitioner recites a variation on the traditional
Buddhist statement of going for refuge and dedicating the merit of
her actions, repeating three times: "I myself go for refuge to the Buddha, Dharma, and the Sangha[9] until enlightenment. By the merit of
the actions including the giving of myself for the benefit of beings,
may I attain buddhahood." At this point in the teaching, there is the
imperative to the practitioner: "Your activity should be comfortable!"[10]
The *chöd* practitioner must be advanced enough in her practice that
visualizing the distribution of one's body as food should be helpful
on the Buddhist path and not a further obstruction or distraction.

Through such practices, *chöd* allows women to counter representations of inferior, disgusting, or horrific female bodies by visualizing
their own bodies as offerings that will benefit all sentient beings. These
practices of sacrificing oneself for the sake of others also emulate idealized *bodhisattva* practices recorded throughout Buddhist literature,
including in the stories of the previous lives of Śākyamuni Buddha.
By means of the process of body offering, women can perform the
perfection of generosity and cultivate the wisdom of nonattachment

and emptiness; practicing *chöd* allows them to embody themselves as *bodhisattva*s. Although *chöd* offers the possibility of enlightenment to women, women practitioners must also confront the inferior status of women in Buddhism through the socially constructed gender norms they face in their everyday lives. As I have observed first-hand, female Buddhist *chöd* practitioners must negotiate their own spiritual experiences with teachings that position them as inferior, reinterpret teachings to accommodate women's experiences, and resist gender norms that would limit their spiritual practice.

My examples of how Tibetan Buddhist women develop their embodied subjectivity through moments of negotiation, reinterpretation, and resistance are drawn from fieldwork in Pharping, Nepal, in 2014, and in Dharamsala, India, in 2006 and 2007. The village of Pharping, known by Tibetans as Yangley shod (*yang le shod*), is notable for its congeniality to Buddhist women practitioners: it has temples dedicated to the tantric goddess Vajrayoginī and the celestial female *bodhisattva* Tārā. The highly respected Nyingma lama Kyabjé Chatral Sangyé Dorjé Rinpoche (*khyab rje bya bral sangs rgyas rdo rje*), recently deceased,[11] has given teachings to and guided the practice of a resident community of Buddhists, including Tibetan and Nepalese laywomen who have shared their experiences with me. Many women in this community practice Machik Thröma Nagmo (*ma gcig khros ma nag mo*), a *chöd* teaching revealed by Dudjom Lingpa (*bdud 'joms gling pa*, 1835–1904) that centers on a form of Vajrayoginī, in the wrathful feminine form of Thröma Nagmo. As I mentioned earlier, such practices focusing on supramundane entities in female form give women practitioners the opportunity to reinterpret teachings on the inferiority of women. Women in this community are empowered by this practice and inspired by the form of Thröma Nagmo as a feminine embodiment of wisdom and compassion. However, they are also subject to Buddhist gender norms that they think limit their attainments.

Complementing the research in this community of lay practitioners in Nepal, I conducted research at two renunciant communities of the Shuksep (*shug gseb*) lineage: one in Himachal Pradesh, India, and another in the Kathmandu Valley, Nepal. These communities are named and modeled after the original Shuksep nunnery, located outside of Lhasa, which was founded by a reincarnation of Machik Labdrön, Lochen Jétsün Chönyi Zangmo (*lo chen rje btsun chos nyid bzang mo*, c. 1852–1953). These communities in India and Nepal were initially established by and for female refugees from the original Shuksep community; many of the women who currently live there have left the Tibetan Autonomous Region (TAR) in China in order to study in these Shuksep communities in exile. All of the female renunciants in the community in Nepal and many in the community in India practice some form of Buddhist *chöd*, individually and/or collectively. Women in both communities take seriously their role in keeping *chöd* praxis alive through their regular practice of rituals and through their personalized interpretations of ritual performances and meditative practices.

Tsok Effigies and Women's Bodies

In Pharping, I lived and participated in *chöd* practices with a village matriarch who has become a role model for Buddhist practitioners in the village community. This woman, known locally as Amala (or "Mother"), is well regarded not only for her devotion to and practice of Buddhism, but also for her generosity in materially supporting Buddhist renunciants by providing them with lodging and stipends. Belief in the transformative potential of *chöd* for women has led Amala to become a lay spiritual leader in the community, teaching her female friends the rituals and practices associated with Thröma Nagmo *chöd*. Amala learned Thröma Nagmo *chöd* from Semo Dechen Yudron (*sras mo bde chen g.yu sgron*, d. 2007). Semo Dechen Yudron was the eldest daughter of the incarnation of Dudjom Rinpoche, the Tibetan virtuoso mentioned above who revealed the *terma* teaching of Thröma Nagmo *chöd*. Semo Dechen Yudron herself was considered to be an emanation of Thröma Nagmo, the dark wrathful ḍākinī associated with this form of *chöd*. As with many practices of *chöd*, the visualized offering of one's own body is central to Thröma Nagmo *chöd*. Practitioners of Thröma Nagmo *chöd* can follow various versions of the liturgy, but even the short ritual performance takes approximately three hours. As in the longer practices, the practitioner of the short practice of Thröma Nagmo *chöd* must not only provide edible items for offering and sharing during the ritual feast, but must also construct ritual sculptures, called *torma*, made out of butter, roasted barley flour, and dyes. These torma are relatively small sculptures that symbolize various esoteric tantric concepts and ideals. In addition to torma, a ritual sculpture particular to the practice of body offering in Thröma Nagmo *chöd* takes the form of a human being. Although it is made out of the same substances as the torma, this sculpture is referred to as a "*tsok*" (*tshogs*), which is the same term used for the feast ritual itself.

The *tsok* thus symbolizes both the body that is to be offered and the ritual of offering. This ritual sculpture is an effigy of one's own body that is fed to both literal and imagined others who are the guests of the ritual feast. Among contemporary female practitioners of Thröma Nagmo *chöd*, this figurine can take on a distinctly feminine form.

In order to illustrate the significance of this *tsok* effigy sculpture, I will describe my experiences at an intimate Thröma Nagmo *chöd* feast performance that included only three participants, all lay women: Amala, who acted as the head ritual specialist, an attendant, and myself. Amala constructs a new effigy sculpture for each *chöd* performance. This figurine is sculpted by hand to represent herself—a feminine form with breasts, an indented waist, rounded hips, and so forth—and covered with a red dye.[12] Amala explicitly identified the *tsok* figurine with herself, noting that the effigy sculpture to be offered should simulate the main person leading the offering.[13] Significantly, Amala chose to mold the *tsok* to represent her own female embodiment, though she might have used a male form. While Amala does see women as spiritually inferior to men, as I will discuss further, using a female form for this practice clearly allows Amala to use her own embodiment as a means to enlightenment. Following the liturgical instructions, this form was dissected and distributed to the real and imagined guests of the ritual feast for consumption. This performance of body offering takes place in several stages. The first stage is the symbolic dissection by a ritual assistant of the ritual specialist's form: the effigy sculpture is cut through with an X from each shoulder to opposite hip. In the second stage, the head is severed and the body is cut through, yielding six pieces that are distributed onto offering plates. These plates are also filled to abundance with other offerings common in non-*chöd* Tibetan Buddhist offering feasts, such as fruit, cookies, candy, juices, and snack foods. The plates are then distributed to each participant, who donates part of her allotment to feeding the less fortunate, including the hungry ghosts and hell-beings that populate the Buddhist cosmos. These plates of edibles are left outside the building to feed birds, animals, insects, and other beings as further acts of generosity and compassion. Each participant then eats a small part of the dough effigy that symbolizes the donor. Through the creation and dissection of this effigy of Amala's own body—and by figurative extension their own bodies—participants "cut through" their own obstacles to enlightenment. The ritual thus revalues women's bodies as instruments for the attainment of enlightenment, rather than as barriers to enlightenment. As these women consciously craft dough effigies in the form of their own embodiments, they are reinterpreting teachings that would limit their spiritual attainments and reimagining their women's bodies as beneficial to their spiritual practices.

I witnessed a similar negotiation of gender identity through the practice of *chöd* at the former location of Shuksep near McLeod Ganj in Himachal Pradesh, India (it has since moved to another location in Himachal Pradesh). While living in the area and visiting this site frequently in 2006–2007, I observed the women of this nunnery performing a communal *chöd tsok* from the Longchen Nyingthig (*klong chen snying thig*) tradition. For this *tsok*, a ritual sculpture was prepared in a distinctly female form. In contrast to the *tsok* sculpture made by Amala that was explicitly made in her own image, this effigy was fashioned to represent more generally the young women participating in the *tsok*. This figurine was made out of the traditional materials of roasted barley flour and water, and was thus a somewhat neutral oatmeal hue. But what was particularly striking to me is that the figurine's facial features were carefully delineated. The eyes, eyelashes, and eyebrows had been drawn in black; in addition, the lips had been drawn in red. Overall, the effect of these colors against the muted dough suggested a female figure that had been made up with cosmetics. This figurine was meant synecdochally to represent females who practice the offering of the body within the context of the Longchen Nyingthig *chöd*, and this was the only time that I have seen the *tsok* effigy adorned in this way. Although none of the women at this practice were obviously using cosmetics during any of the practices, one does sometimes see Tibetan Buddhist celibate women in India and Nepal wearing their robes tailored in a body-flattering fashion, shaping their eyebrows through threading, and wearing eye makeup and lipstick. Given that many young nuns now are living in close proximity to centers where Western dharma practitioners congregate and where young local women are increasingly leaving behind traditional South Asian ideas of modesty, the "made-up" effigy figurine was an intriguing representation of the nuns' embodiment. Clearly the effects of globalization are changing the ways in which many Tibetan renunciant women understand their embodied subjectivity. While contemporary standards of attractiveness and the associated distractions of vanity are projected onto the *tsok* effigy in this instance, when I asked the female renunciants about the makeup, they laughed quietly without verbal elaboration. By "making up" the effigy, the women seem to be simultaneously negotiating their own identities as unadorned renunciants while also imagining other subjectivities for themselves that would underscore their conventional femininity.

As with Amala's *tsok* figurine, the figurine created by the nuns allows them to negotiate their gender identities. For both groups, the construction and subsequent destruction of the *chöd* effigy not only manifests the subjective form of consciousness but also helps women practitioners assert their agency in resistance to the patriarchal aspects of Buddhist ideology and South Asian society. Unlike in other Tibetan Buddhist ritual offering practices, in *chöd tsok* the effigy is shaped like a human body. Moreover, this practice can be led by a female ritual specialist, and the *tsok* effigy can take her own distinctly female form. Within a predominantly patriarchal social environment, a woman practitioner who fashions a female form as a key material element of the *chöd* ritual can be seen as literally performing an act of self-representation and figuratively performing an act of resistance to the status quo. By using representations of their own bodies to fulfill spiritual goals, these women perform resistance to the cultural belief in the inferiority of women.

Supramundane Femininities and Women Practitioners

As I mentioned previously, *chöd* also allows women practitioners to visualize themselves as supramundane feminine beings. In addition to using *tsok* figurines to represent their embodiments, *chöd* practitioners frequently invoke feminine embodiments of enlightenment in their rituals. The most popular forms for such visualizations in *chöd* are Dorjé Neljorma (Vajrayoginī) and her related manifestations as the wrathful Thröma Nagmo (Khrodakālī) or the sow-headed Dorjé Phagmo (Vajravārāhī). In Amala's practice, the centrality of the feminine figure of Thröma Nagmo is potentially empowering for women. As mentioned previously, Thröma Nagmo is a wisdom *ḍākinī*, a supramundane female figure who represents the ideal of enlightenment and assists others in attaining this goal. In this practice, the practitioner visualizes herself "becoming" Thröma Nagmo, and the practitioner as Thröma Nagmo then performs the sacrifice of the symbolized self of the effigy. Thröma Nagmo not only functions as a symbol of enlightenment in this practice, but she herself is considered an enlightened being: a *buddha* or *bodhisattva*. By invoking Thröma Nagmo for this practice, women practitioners are implicitly challenging the view that a woman cannot become a *buddha*. Practitioners' perspectives on such deities, however, tend to be more ambivalent. Many of the women I spoke with in Nepal viewed figures such as Thröma Nagmo as *bodhisattva*s who adopt a female form through their practice of *upāya*, or skillful techniques for the liberation of others. In other words, these beings chose to take a female form, but they are not really women. Even historical women such as Machik Labdrön are viewed in the same light. Such potentially inspiring persons are not seen as mundane historical women but as supramundane enlightened beings who have embodied themselves as women.

The founder of the original Shuksep nunnery in Tibet, Lochen Chönyi Zangmo, is considered by many Tibetans to be a reincarnation of Machik Labdrön. On a recent visit to the Shuksep location in Nepal, I was surprised to learn that many of the women who reside there do not consider Lochen Chönyi Zangmo as a historical woman who could serve as an inspiration to their practice. Rather, they viewed Lochen Chönyi Zangmo as they do Machik Labdrön: a supramundane manifestation of enlightenment, not an actual woman whom they might emulate. This was especially interesting considering that the image of Lochen Chönyi Zangmo was not as prominently displayed on the altar at this Shuksep; rather, a photo of the male Nyingma lama Chatrul Rinpoche I mentioned above was in the place of honor. The women at this Shuksep also told me that they do not do perform the practices associated with remembering Lochen Chönyi Zangmo as often as the women at the original Shuksep in Tibet. From one perspective, we might think that enlightened beings such as Machik Labdrön would take female embodiments to inspire women. However, many women I spoke with did not view such historical women as figures they could aspire to emulate. Such practitioners distinguish the feminine in enlightened and "divinized" form from their own mundane and human embodiment. While such figures might be inspiring to women, then, they do not obviously encourage women to resist prevailing gender norms. As Janet Gyatso and Hanna Havnevik argue, the "deified figure of the *dākinī*" does not necessarily function as a "model of female personality formation" for Tibetan Buddhist women. In their view, "the use of the term *dākinī* . . . in certain outstanding women's titles" "hardly demonstrates that women have been 'empowered' to think of themselves as *dākinī*s on a regular basis."[14] Although divinized forms of women might be inspiring in some way, women practitioners are not encouraged to think they can *become dākinī*s.

This same ambivalence toward women's bodies and enlightenment was revealed in a discussion I had with Amala. As noted,

Amala was able to use the ritual space to transvalue her own body as a vehicle to cultivate enlightenment. By representing herself as the symbolic effigy sculpture, she was able to generate the wisdom of emptiness through the severing of ego attachment and the accumulation of merit through the generosity of feeding others her own body. But Amala, like other women who practice *chöd*, leaves the ritual space to return to her quotidian existence, where women are inferior to men. Amala believes that women are inferior to men in many practical respects: women are mentally and physically weaker than men, they bear children and raise families, their lives hold many distractions, and they have fewer opportunities and resources than men. Amala also stresses that women are inferior to men in terms of *karma* in that they are not "fit vessels" for Dharma teachings and practices. Despite her position as a laywoman who is also a religious specialist and spiritual advisor to women in her community, Amala includes the wish to be reborn in a male body in her aspiration prayers, and she attests that other women in her community do likewise. This is not a unique wish, as Karma Lekshe Tsomo acknowledges: "It is common for Buddhist women to denigrate their own potential."[15] Not only lay *yoginī*s such as Amala, but profound female spiritual adepts such as Orgyan Chokyi (1675–1729) include such a prayer in their daily practices.[16] Tsomo elaborates that women who pray for a rebirth as a man in the next life "abdicate" the responsibility for their spiritual life to men. In my view, Amala's negotiations of gender norms and spiritual practices are more complex. Not only lay *yoginī*s such as Amala, but profound female spiritual adepts such as Orgyan Chokyi, include such a prayer in their daily practices.[17] We can see these prayers not simply as a renunciation of responsibility, but as a rhetorical technique for placing oneself firmly within a tradition of female practitioners.

Amala's prayers to be reborn in a male body can be seen as profoundly ambivalent, both acknowledging her social subordination to men and proudly situating herself within a tradition of female Buddhist adepts. We might be tempted to read her predicament, and the predicaments of other women Buddhists, through the lens of Western feminism. From this perspective, we might read Amala's ambivalence as an alienating experience produced by a patriarchal society. But Tsomo warns, "Western feminist responses to patterns of gender discrimination are sometimes limited by a lack of understanding of the lives of women in non-Western cultures. In the process of gaining an understanding, moreover, there is a danger of overlaying one's own cultural presumptions and expectations on a starkly different realm of experience."[18] By privileging a Western feminist perspective, in other words, we risk losing sight of the particularly Buddhist elements of these women's experiences. In her work on Buddhist nuns in Ladakh, Kim Gutschow suggests a way forward from this interpretive problem. Drawing on a concept from Donna Haraway,[19] Gutschow advocates for a "passionate detachment" as a means for understanding Buddhist women's experience: a "perspective which combines a passionate feminism with Buddhist detachment.[20] Gutschow consciously seeks a "middle way . . . between feminist and Buddhist perspectives" on interdependence, indeterminacy, and subjectivity."[21] A feminist orientation might help us to understand how Amala resists normative gendered experiences, while a Buddhist orientation might help us to understand the particular forms such resistance might take. In other terms, we can strive to recognize what Saba Mahmood would call Amala's "modalities of agency" without imposing abstract Western feminist ideals on her experiences.[22] Using the perspective of "passionate detachment," we might read Amala's ambivalence in a few other ways. Amala's perspective may be a way of emphasizing her own humility, which is a Buddhist virtue for both men and women in canonical and mundane contexts. Or it might be read as a critique of the inadequate efforts of Buddhist men, who have optimal conditions for attaining enlightenment, yet do not progress on the path despite their perceived advantages. Or Amala's ambivalence might simply reflect an inability to reconcile religious ideals with social realities. Nevertheless, despite their ambivalence about their gender identities in patriarchal cultures, Amala and other practitioners are still able to use their female bodies to work toward their own enlightenment. By symbolizing themselves donating their own bodies, they are emulating the actions of great *bodhisattvas*, sacrificing themselves for the benefit of all sentient beings.

Notes

1. Appleton points out that even though this limitation on women's abilities is echoed in the *Atthānavagga* in the Anguttara Nikāya and in various Chinese sources, scholars such as Kajiyama Yuichi have argued that these passages are interpolations. Naomi Appleton, "In the Footsteps of the Buddha? Women and the *Bodhisatta* Path in Theravāda Buddhism," *Journal of Feminist Studies in Religion* 27:1(2011): 33.

2. Quoted in Janice D. Willis, "Nuns and Benefactresses: the Role of Women in the Development of Buddhism," *Women, Religion, and Social Change*, ed. Yvonne Haddad and Ellison Banks Findley (Albany: State University of New York Press, 69; Rita M. Gross, *Buddhism After Patriarchy: A Feminist History, Analysis, and Reconstruction of Buddhism* (Albany: State University of New York Press, 1993), 61; Miranda Shaw, *Passionate Enlightenment: Women in Tantric Buddhism* (Princeton, NJ: Princeton University Press, 1994), 27; and Serinity Young, *Courtesans and Tantric Consorts: Sexualities in Buddhist Narrative, Iconography and Ritual* (New York: Routledge, 2004), 198.

3. Gross, *Buddhism After Patriarchy*, 61.

4. Shaw, *Passionate Enlightenment*, 27.

5. Liz Wilson, *Charming Cadavers: Horrific Figurations of the Feminine in Indian Buddhist Hagiographic Literature* (Chicago: University of Chicago Press, 1996), 8.

6. The following is adapted from my dissertation. Ma gcig Lab sgron, "*Khyad par gyi le lag brgyad pa*," *Gdams ngag mdzod*, vol. 14, ed. 'Jam mgon kong sprul (Paro, Bhutan: Lama Ngodrup and Sherab Drimey, 1979), 155–64; and vol. 9 (Delhi: N. Lungtok and N. Gyaltsen, 1971), 601–10. Translated and discussed in Michelle J. Sorensen, "The Distinctive Eightfold Supplementary Section," *Making the Old New Again and Again: Legitimation and Innovation in the Tibetan Buddhist Chöd Tradition*. Dissertation, Columbia University, 2013.

7. Ibid., 465–86.

8. Ibid., 480.

9. Described here as the supreme assembly (*tshogs kyi mchog rnams*; *gaṇānāmagraṃ*). Ibid., 454.

10. *Agang bde'i spyod lam bya'o*. Ibid.

11. 1913–2016.

12. Other sculptures used in Buddhist rituals represent various types of sentient beings and have the region of their Brahman apertures (Brahmarandhra, the area of the cranium fontanelle, or "third eye"), their hearts, and their genitalia marked by disks made out of the dough material; however, they are not explicitly formed to represent a particular gender or sexuality.

13. However, female practitioners have been known to choose to mold the *tsok* figure in the form of a male body.

14. Janet Gyatso and Hanna Havnevik, "Introduction," *Women in Tibet* (New York: Columbia University Press, 2005), 8.

15. Karma Lekshe Tsomo, "Mahāprajāpatī's Legacy: The Buddhist Women's Movement: An Introduction," *Buddhist Women Across Cultures*, ed. Karma Lekshe Tsomo (Albany: State University of New York Press, 1999), 31.

16. Kurtis R. Schaeffer, "The Autobiography of a Medieval Hermitess: Orgyan Chokyi (1675–1729)," *Women in Tibet*, ed. Janet Gyatso and Hanna Havnevik (New York: Columbia University Press, 2005), 83–109; and Kurtis R. Schaeffer, *Himalayan Hermitess: The Life of a Tibetan Buddhist Nun* (New York: Oxford University Press, 2004).

17. Kurtis R. Schaeffer, "The Autobiography of a Medieval Hermitess: Orgyan Chokyi (1675–1729)," *Women in Tibet*, ed. Janet Gyatso and Hanna Havnevik (New York: Columbia University Press, 2005), 83–109; and Kurtis R. Schaeffer, *Himalayan Hermitess: The Life of a Tibetan Buddhist Nun* (New York: Oxford University Press, 2004).

18. Karma Lekshe Tsomo, "Change in Consciousness: Women's Religious Identity in Himalayan Buddhist Cultures," *Buddhist Women Across Cultures*, ed. Karma Lekshe Tsomo (Albany: State University of New York, 1999), 173.

19. Donna Haraway, "Situated Knowledges: The Science Question in Feminism and the Privilege of Partial Perspective." In *Simians, Cyborgs, and Women*. London: Free Association Books, 1991.

20. Kim Gutschow, *Being a Buddhist Nun: The Struggle for Enlightenment in the Himalayas* (Cambridge, MA: Harvard University Press, 2004), 12.

21. Ibid., 13.

22. Saba Mahmood, *Politics of Piety: The Islamic Revival and the Feminist Project* (Chicago: University of Chicago Press, 2004).

Chapter 11

Mindfully Feminine?

The Role of Meditation in the Production and Marketing of Gendered Lifestyles

Jeff Wilson

From the cover of *Time* magazine to your child's elementary school, mindfulness practice has hit the big time in North America. Originating in Buddhist monastic contexts, the practice of *sati* ("mindfulness") has been adapted to new circumstances in the West, where it is applied as a decontextualized spiritual practice that can be pursued for the purposes of life enhancement.[1] My focus in this essay is on the role played by mindfulness in producing contemporary visions of femininity at various life stages, and how these gendered lifestyles are marketed to different demographics of North American women. Buddhist meditation practice is transformed in these applications into a technique for building an empowered and sexy identity, managing the multitasking stresses of lay life with aplomb, and projecting a confident, enviable self-image to others.

Both the producers and consumers of such quasi-Buddhist femininities are women, who use mindfulness and its associated values as sites at which to display and negotiate contemporary understandings of proper womanhood. To demonstrate the range of gendered mindful lifestyles being marketed to contemporary American women, I focus especially on three case studies, paying close attention to the visions

of femininity being deployed, how Buddhism is selectively appropriated to enhance these visions, the ways that these models reveal the
opportunities and constraints acting on American women's ideas of
femininity, and the economic motives embedded in such depictions.

Getting a Grip on Mindfulness

The mindfulness movement challenges many presuppositions of religious scholars about how religion operates, or even what religion *is*.
Therefore, it is necessary to discuss theoretical framing before plung-
ing into the chaotic churn of the ever-growing, ever-changing mindfulness movement in North America. I take as my guiding perspective
Thomas Tweed's translocative approach to the study of Buddhism.
Tweed states:

> There is no pure substratum, no static and independent
> core called 'Buddhism'—either in the founder's day or
> in any later generation. What we have come to call 'Bud-
> dhism' was always becoming, being made and remade
> over and over again in contact and exchange, as it was
> carried along in the flow of things. Buddhist leaders have
> the right—even the role-specific obligation—to determine
> what constitutes 'authentic' Buddhism; but scholars—and
> Buddhist practitioners when they contribute to academic
> conversations—have another duty, I suggest: to follow the
> flows wherever they lead. To study the historical or con-
> temporary expressions of Buddhism is to trace the flow
> of people, rituals, artifacts, beliefs, and institutions across
> spatial and temporal boundaries.[2]

Building on this perspective, one of my primary research interests is the intersection of Buddhism with non-Buddhist culture, and
the mutual influence and transformation that takes place. The mindfulness movement in North America is a perfect arena in which to
examine these concerns; it is through mindfulness that Buddhism has
had the largest impact on contemporary American and Canadian society. Mindfulness meditation, drawn directly from Asian Buddhism
and then recontextualized, medicalized, psychologized, and reap-
plied to this-worldly concerns, is a multibillion dollar industry that

has produced dozens of best-selling books, transformed entire fields of medicine and psychological counseling, altered military training, and developed its own successful periodicals. Mindfulness meditation has reached nearly every segment of the population, from the ghetto to the highest halls of power. And one of the most interesting facts about this movement is that only a relatively small percentage of this output is created by authorized Buddhist teachers. Rather, this Buddhist practice has been released into the wild, so to speak, and is now often taught by non-Buddhists to non-Buddhists for applications entirely unrelated to concepts such as *nirvāna*, impermanence, no-self, rebirth, or *karma*.

The sources used here, therefore, are not *sūtra*s. Often, they are not even overtly Buddhist, though in many cases they are penned by Buddhists who hide or downplay their religious identities in order to appeal to the broadest possible audience. To study the mindfulness movement, one must look at what happens when Buddhist practice is discussed in self-help manuals, medical journals, online pop psychology forums, afternoon talk shows, and similar sources rarely investigated by traditional Buddhologists. Examination of such sources reveals that the key to understanding which Buddhist practices are successfully taken up by the wider culture is often related to their potential for being economically profitable. Mindfulness is not just a religious practice—it is a commodity offered for consumption in a capitalist marketplace where promoters simultaneously seek to benefit their clients and make money off the exchange. Savvy marketers tap into gendered roles, representations, and concerns to sell their mindful products and, in doing so, introduce new elements of Buddhism into North American discussions of femininity, while still usually remaining within the confines of dominant discourses over what should and should not be considered appropriate behavior and self-presentation for women.

Mindfulness as Postfeminist Lifestyle Enhancement

Often, what is being sold is mindfulness as a lifestyle embodied in the iconic form of an expert self-help author, as we see in my first example of mindful femininity. The book is Kimberly Wilson's 2010 text *Tranquilista: Mastering the Art of Enlightened Work and Mindful Play.* Here's how she starts:

You may be wondering, "What in the world is a tranquilista?" So glad you asked! A tranquilista is a woman
who embraces her many sides: she is spiritual (she's a
tranquility-seeker), creative (loves style), and entrepreneurial
(calls her own shots). She hearts fashion and philanthropy.
Parties and prayer. Entertaining and enlightenment. The
golden rule and layers of vintage gold bangles. She is you
and she is moi. She is full of aspirations and always seeking inspiration. Oh, and she sparkles. Literally.[3]

So explains Wilson, who is a yoga teacher, a successful author, an
admirer of Buddhist monk Thich Nhat Hanh and Mindfulness-Based
Stress Reduction founder Jon Kabat-Zinn. Wilson is a tranquilista, and
as she points out to the reader, you ought to be one too. A tranquilista
is "mindfully extravagant," a person who embraces "flair-filled must-
haves such as shiny chandeliers, kitten heels, and little black dresses
while also practicing yoga, meditating, caring for the environment,
and be-ing a do-gooder."[4] Such modern divas go about "designing our
lives as self-defined entrepreneurs who care about blending balance,
bliss, and beauty. . . . A tranquilista mixes spiritualty, creativity, and
entrepreneurship in varied amounts to bake the perfect concoction
that will help her attain her individual dreams and desires while
making a positive impact."[5]

What we have here is mindfulness filtered through a classic post-
feminist mindset. As sociologist Jayne Raisborough explains:

What's apparent in the postfeminist sensibility is a cel-
ebration and encouragement of women's uniqueness and
their agency. There is a positive endorsement here to live
life to the full, pursue desires, and shrug off any inhibi-
tion, imagined as keeping past generations of women tied
to a life of self-sacrifice and duty. The neoliberal terrain
is imagined then as opening up unparalleled opportunities for women and girls, suggesting that now they are
"untethered by gender constraints" and entitled to "have
it all."[6] Women are invited to follow the rhythms of their
choices and desires to create life in the image of their inner
self. . . . The postfeminist sensibility constructs a young (or
youth-aspiring) heterosexual woman who exudes confidence,
sexual desire and power.[7]

Tranquilista is an example of lifestyle commodification and expertise based on being a cool chick in the city. As Raisborough notes: "It is within lifestyle media that prevailing idealisations about what we should be, who we should *become* and how we should manage our lives appears to circulate most energetically, seemingly harmlessly and with widespread popularity."[8] *Tranquilista*, like a large number of other mindfulness books, can be located within the self-help and lifestyle media genres, and it actively seeks to mold perceptions of how one should be as a woman, as well as how one may attain that envisioned feminine lifestyle. Wilson suggests that the reader identify with the author, be like her, and become popular, stylish, pretty, fit, happy, successful, in control, modern, urban, helpful, vivacious, and feminine. A whole vision of contemporary femininity is conveyed in this book and it uses mindfulness to achieve these goals. The book promotes mindfulness as a part of gender identity itself. It promises a satisfying balance between traditional North American female concerns such as style and beauty with the quasi-feminist appeal to women as workers in the modern economy. Her subsequent book, *The Tranquility du Jour Daybook*, follows a similar pattern, simultaneously soothing readers with mindfulness and admonishing them to smile, project a good attitude, and dress fashionably.[9]

Wilson is pitching to a very particular demographic here, one that does not include most North Americans. As Wilson's author bio points out, "She lives in a petite raspberry-colored flat in Washington, DC, with two fancy felines named after French impressionists, a supportive beau, and a black pug."[10] For many young urban women, this is the new American dream, and Wilson seeks to both inspire and milk that dream through her books, blogs, fashion line, media appearances, website, online courses, and podcast. But we should note that this lifestyle, which is supposedly generated and maintained by the practices of mindfulness and yoga, is also deeply dependent on very particular choices and compromises, and is accessible only to women in certain geographical, class, and perhaps racial situations. There is no home mortgage, only an apartment to look after; no children, only fashion-accessory pets; no husband, only a nice live-in guy; no medical issues (and especially, no age-related health concerns) to attend to, only a sexy young body to adorn; and the author lives in a place where public transportation is readily available to take her to the endless parade of swanky restaurants, bookstores, concerts, and other diversions that fill her life as a tranquilista.

Without a family to care for, conventional North American female patterns of nurturance are available in Wilson's promoted lifestyle to be redirected inward toward self-care and outward toward fulfilling social and environmental activism. Should the excluded aspects of life (husbands, children, houses, health issues, and so on) that figure strongly in the experiences of many North American women reappear, the mindful and fun life of the tranquilista might quickly evaporate. As Raisborough notes: "The doing of a self, then, in particular the doing of an *individual* self, might not be an achievement that is freely open to all but the very grounds and consequences of embattled power relations. It is here that we find class, gender, and 'race' and so on far from being irrelevant, emerging as revitalized battle lines. At least, it may then be appropriate to argue for a *structured individualism* whereby individualism is mediated through existing social and cultural divisions."[11] In other words, while *Tranquilista* rhapsodizes about the freedom of choice and individuality available to smart, forward-thinking women today, this rhetoric may mask the limited and socially conditioned range of actual choices and forms of individuality accessible to readers. The freedom available is more one of assertion of being free and enacting freedom through choice of hairstyle, attire, and perhaps profession than one of being actually free from the conditions of North American living circumstances and the ongoing gender expectations placed on women.

This sort of lifestyle marketing has a long history in American encounters with Asian religion, as Jane Naomi Iwamura points out in her book *Virtual Orientalism*:

> Like Zen in the late 1950s, Americans approached Transcendental Meditation as stylized religion that signified a way of life, that is, an identity, more than something that transformed one's consciousness. One could sample this alternative perspective and subscribe to its outlook simply by wearing Indian attire and listening to the inspired sitar of Ravi Shankar. Inversely, by adopting this particular style of clothing and/or music, one demonstrated openness to such spiritual alternatives.[12]

Iwamura points out how Americans need not actually join Buddhist or Hindu groups in order to participate in the aura assigned to such "alternative" religions. Likewise, mindfulness can be promoted outside of Buddhism, and its Buddhist connections can even be explicitly denied, while it continues to do the cultural work of associating the consumer with the values of freedom, health, peacefulness, awareness, and so on that American culture has often attributed to Buddhism.

The emphasis that Iwamura puts on fashion in the quote above is important, and we see these strategies reflected in the way that mindfulness is marketed and how mindfulness is appropriated to market other commodities. Consider, for example, the jewelry and fashion company BuDhaGirl, whose tagline is "Mindful Glamour." Advertising in popular magazines such as *Tricycle: The Buddhist Review* and *Mindful*, BuDhaGirl claims that by paying mindful attention to what you are doing as you put on their jewelry in the morning, you are conducting a sacred ritual that will benefit you throughout the day. As their promotional materials state,

> BuDhaGirl is the first fashion company that uses daily rituals to bring mindfulness into people's everyday lives. We do this through a series of visual intentions and Reminders™ [pendants]. We work with our scientific board comprised of neuroscientists, psychologists, and mindfulness coaches to bring optimum product interaction. Through daily mindful glamour, BuDhaGirl allows people to create their own ritual, by adding intention to the acts they already perform. Choosing a Reminder™ in the morning or pausing to put on the All Weather™ Bangles, allows people to stop and think about what they really want to celebrate and accomplish that day. We provide the physical tools people need to remind them of the importance of being present and mindful throughout their day.[13]

So what distinguishes these bracelets and other products in the crowded fashion marketplace is that they are somehow more mindful than other jewelry, and thus when a woman wears them she is cultivating her spirituality, not her vanity. This helps to justify the $150 expense. Here we see where a tranquilista potentially gets her literal sparkles, and we can note again that these rituals of mindful glamour are available only to women with a degree of wealth. There is little hint in the mainstream mindfulness literature that such marketing might be an abuse of mindfulness's purposes, likely because they align with an unchallenged cultural assumption that such uses are natural and positive. As Mike Featherstone observes: "Rather than unreflexively adopting a lifestyle, through tradition or habit, the new heroes of consumer culture make lifestyle a life project and display their individuality and sense of style in the particularity of the assemblage of goods, clothes, practices, experiences, appearance and bodily dispositions they design together into a lifestyle."[14] Tranquilistas and similar women are, therefore, following a script approved by neoliberal norms in North America, and employed by entrepreneurs to attract consumer dollars via associating their products with mindfulness.

The mindfulness movement is entirely cognizant of the power of marketing lifestyles. Witness the full-page advertisement for the magazine *Mindful* that appears on page seventeen of the magazine's first issue. "It's who you are," the ad proclaims in huge letters at the top of the page.[15] "You want the best for your family and friends. You enjoy work that is meaningful and satisfying. You're dedicated to a more caring and sustainable society. You know the simple practice of being in the moment brings out the best in who you are. You are mindful. And this is your magazine."[16] Placed directly above the smiling picture of a happy young white woman from the magazine's cover, the advertisement speaks directly in the second person to the readers, telling them that they are already part of the mindfulness movement, and that their participation in this lifestyle is meaningful, caring, and self-nurturing. By being mindful you are living a positive lifestyle, and buying *Mindful* helps you support that lifestyle. In case anyone does not get the point, the ad continues: "Mindful is the groundbreaking new magazine dedicated to helping you live mindfully."[17] The advertisement is less thoroughly gendered than *Tranquilista*, though with its fashionably dressed female model and text about nurturing behaviors, at a minimum it is designed to appeal to female readers, if not exclusively. *Mindful*'s readership is, in fact, overwhelmingly female, as are the consumers of self-help media in general. Mindfulness entrepreneurs are well aware of this, and it is no mistake that the literal face of mindfulness—as represented by innumerable book and magazine covers and product advertising—is most often female.

Mindful Mothering: Mindfulness at Middle-Age

Compared to *Tranquilista*, completely different gender identities are promulgated in books such as *Momfulness* by Denise Roy.[18] Books such as this one target an older, settled, married, more suburban audience with children (for example, Roy's other book is *My Monastery is a Min-*

ivan), thus speaking to this demographic's desired mindful lifestyles.[19] Here the advice is dispensed amidst houses with porch swings and backyards, while carpooling, doing laundry, and failing to live up to a seven-nights-in-a-row mindful sex commitment with one's husband. It is a less enticing vision than being a tranquilista, especially because it does not offer a plan for how to become something exciting, being instead a pragmatic (and hopefully comforting) battle strategy for using mindfulness to enhance one's mothering skills, in order to carry out triage on an already overwhelming situation.

Here the lifestyle is a world away from "Sex and the City": motherhood is painted as difficult, tiring, body-destroying, time-consuming, stressful, and messy. One of Roy's mindfulness exercises involves locking yourself in the bathroom in order to "create a little zone of quiet," an act of desperate retreat familiar to many modern mothers.[20] Motherhood is challenging stuff, as Roy asserts: "As the mother of four children (and the foster mom of a fifth), I can attest to the fact that motherhood leaves stretch marks on us—in so many ways! I have been stretched physically, mentally, emotionally, spiritually. My limited notion of what constitutes a family has widened, and I have been pulled (sometimes kicking and screaming) into the present moment."[21]

Mindful motherhood, then, is a world away from the fabulous bodies and seemingly effortless existence of the tranquilista. It is hard, exhausting, body-damaging work. And yet, Roy also suggests that it is profoundly rewarding—or can be, if approached mindfully. As she continues:

> Through great challenges and even greater love, my heart has grown to hold more than I ever thought possible. Motherhood continues to stretch me to this day, and I see no end in sight. It teaches lessons that many spiritual disciplines teach: the transforming effect of true presence, the importance of close attention, the need for deep compassion, the celebration of embodiment, the recognition of the sacred in all things, and the power of community. Momfulness is the word I use for this spiritual practice of conscious mothering. When we mother with mindfulness and compassion and a willingness to let this vocation awaken our hearts and transform our lives, we walk a spiritual path. We discover that care for our children and family is not a distraction from sacred practice but is the very essence of it.[22]

Women in Roy's book do not identify with kitten heels and bangles, but with laps, hugs, and "Mama Bear Instincts."[23] They find fulfillment through mothering, through transferring their responsibility solely from themselves, and society in the abstract, into nurturance for very specific small people who have nightmares, stubborn opinions, developing breasts, and bowls of spaghetti upside-down on their heads. Roy is selling mindfulness wrapped in a gender identity possible only because of children, lifelong partners, and settled housing, and which conversely needs mindfulness in order to juggle all those things and appreciate them to the greatest possible depth. This is a gendered mindful lifestyle consumption as unobtainable for the tranquilistas as the tranquilista's lifestyle is for Roy, and thus they are marketed in different ways to capture the attention of different audiences.

Just as Wilson's mindful lifestyle does not challenge contemporary postfeminist ideas about femininity, Roy's mindful lifestyle is meant to enhance, not deconstruct, a traditional pattern of female identity based on being a wife, mother, and settled suburban dweller. The liberations sought in both cases are neither Buddhist liberations from the round of *saṃsāra*, nor political liberations from the oppressions of patriarchy or capitalism. They are small-scale assaults on mundane suffering within the system, meant to help readers adjust themselves better to their situations and thus experience less friction, rather than to overturn the situation itself. Such understanding of the purpose of mindfulness in a woman's life is on clear display in another book, *Mindful Motherhood: Practical Tools for Staying Sane During Pregnancy and Your Child's First Year*, by Cassandra Vieten. Drawing on the example of being up all night with a screaming baby, Vieten suggests that mindfulness can help new mothers accept the situation and even appreciate it:

> When approached mindfully, even distressing experiences can be met with some degree of acceptance. And when you take an accepting stance toward the experience, your whole state of being often changes. Even when your state *remains* agitated and upset, this too can be met with mindful awareness and with fewer of the judging thoughts and anxiety-provoking stories that so often ratchet up the discomfort. By approaching the situation and your feelings about it with a willingness to have them be what they are, rather than resisting them or struggling to change them, you can reduce a lot of unnecessary suffering.[24]

Often in mindful mothering books, the nursery or playground is implicitly inscribed over a model of the Buddhist monastery, with the child playing the role of the Zen master and the parent, somewhat ironically, placed in the role of student. Either by some natural innocence that connects children more spiritually to the world, or by the facts of the situation that demand a mother to stretch her limits of patience, awareness, and compassion, rearing children is depicted as a supreme opportunity to engage in Buddhist/spiritual practice, as well as mindfulness being necessary to survive the situation. In these moments, the woman's spiritual potential is sewn into her emerging identity as a mother first and foremost. As Vieten remarks: "Young infants have a way of demanding that you attend to the present moment. Even if you get distracted, a baby's needs will bring you back to the 'now' again and again. And for most women, being fully engaged in the moment with a newborn baby can be extremely rewarding. . . . Nearly everyone experiences a depth of love, a stretching open of the heart, a true, deep, and unshakable desire to *be with* this other little being in ways that they never had before."[25] These then are the rewards for stepping out of the carefree lifestyle of the tranquilista and embracing a feminine lifestyle of sublimation to the needs of children (and the other domestic arrangements that tend to be necessary to make middle-class motherhood viable). If the keyword for young women's mindful lifestyles is "beauty," then for mindful mothers it is "heart."

Mindful Crones

A third gendered lifestyle is captured in *The Mindful Woman*.[26] Sue Patton Thoele states upfront that she is not an expert on mindfulness. She is, however, a woman with considerable life experience, which she marshals as sufficient qualification to write a book on mindfulness for women. Thoele is a grandmother who has passed through the intensive motherhood phase and emerged to the other side in a life stage that mirrors that of the tranquilista in certain ways, yet is utterly different. She is still in the suburbs, divorced and remarried, still busy, but now has relative freedom to devote to hobbies, exploring spirituality, and female friends. Her anecdotes involve dealing with health issues, young people who tailgate her while she drives too slowly, and "croning" ceremonies wherein friends celebrate a woman's entrance into her later years. Her intended audience is older women who have spent decades putting others' needs ahead of their own, and who now find themselves with the time but not the know-how to try to cultivate a healthier lifestyle.

Thoele's solution is mindfulness, which she feels is particularly appropriate for women. As she constructs them, women have many innate qualities, all of them positive, which make them who they are and provide them with rich social and inner lives. Mindfulness enhances these inherent feminine aspects:

> Even though the practice of mindfulness is deeply rooted in ancient, monastic traditions, I believe women are uniquely suited to its practice because we are naturally blessed with qualities such as sensitivity and diffuse awareness. Diffuse awareness is the ability to comfortably perceive and understand many things at once. Sensitivity is having feelings about what is seen, understood, and experienced. Women are multifocused, multifaceted, multitasking wonders. We are aware of and can pay attention to multiple things at once while also noting how we are feeling within the process. These are natural talents conducive to mindful living.[27]

Thoele here repeats the conventional wisdom of contemporary American society that women are somehow naturally able to perform several tasks simultaneously in a manner impossible for men (who are usually depicted as having the capacity to handle only one task at a time). Without irony, she marries mindfulness—which involves the practice of close attention to a particular focus—with the twenty-first-century association of women with multitasking, the practice of simultaneously performing multiple activities. The result is a gendered lifestyle that conjoins seemingly opposed values. Rather than using mindfulness to slow down modern life's hectic pace, she believes being mindful simply allows a woman to enjoy her frenetic life more:

> Because women possess an innate ability to perceive an expanded range of feelings, thoughts, and experiences, we are adept at *consciously* handling several things at once. That doesn't mean you don't get frazzled and frustrated. It does mean you can feel even better and more productive by attentively, purposefully, nonjudgmentally staying in the present moment. . . . With awareness and attention, you can be mindful *within* your busyness.[28]

Because, according to Thoele, mindfulness is an especially female aspect, it is important to cultivate it in a manner that best suits the reader's intrinsic feminine qualities: "Becoming mindful is an excellent avenue for self-care and self-realization. In order to get the most out of mindfulness, you need to practice it in ways that are harmonious with your basic nature—a woman's way. The practices contained in The Mindful Woman concentrate on feminine strengths, qualities, and energies."[29] Thoele then provides a list of relevant, naturally possessed feminine qualities, including emotionally grounded, intuitive, relational, compassionate, empowered, gentle, forgiving, receptive, and healing.[30] She claims that women love to connect with others and implies that they have a psychic connection with their female friends.[31]

A strong theme of The Mindful Woman is that women are powerful and should recognize their power. In Thoele's conception, power appears to derive from their biological status as child bearers and social roles as matriarchs, rather than conscious choices they make as liberated individuals. "As bearers and givers of life and the core around which our families revolve, women are incredibly strong and amazingly powerful."[32] In particular, Thoele as an older woman spends time stressing the ways in which women are wise, a trope absent from mindful lifestyles pitched at women in books such as Wilson's, and of limited application (mainly, to the practice of child-drearing) in mindful mothering works. If the basic positive affirmation of tranquilista-type books is "Go get it!" and that of mindfulness for moms is "You can handle it," the pop mantra of works such as Thoele's is "You are wise and in control." As Thoele states: "We women are wonderfully powerful and wise, plus more influential that we dare imagine. Which, of course, means that you are powerfully wise and influential. As with all worthwhile endeavors, being aware of and accepting your own radical wisdom begins internally. Paying attention to the wisdom, grace, and courage you express in the moment provides a treasure trove of insight into your own incredible qualities and gives you the audacity to rebel in conscious, peaceful ways."[33] The assertion that one may need to "rebel" is a small hint that women in Thoele's age group have spent a lifetime subordinating their desires to the needs or whims of others, and now must struggle to find their own direction as they emerge from the all-encompassing cocoon of family life. The sense of being peaceful even while exercising one's alleged amazing power, which mindfulness allows, is a high concern for Thoele. She fears sacrificing the sensitive and nurturing vision of femininity that she values (and claims as indelible) through overly assertive expression of power, and turns to mindfulness for support in being powerful in a specifically feminine manner. "By mindfully and lovingly clearing away emotional debris and honoring our authentic selves, we can bless those we care about—and the world in general—by naturally generating and expressing the soft power that is our fundamental nature."[34]

Conclusion

In *Selling Yoga: From Counterculture to Pop Culture*, Andrea Jain draws on Jean Baudrillard and Robert Bocock to discuss how yoga (which has traveled similar trajectories to mindfulness through contemporary North American culture) is related to lifestyle consumption. As Jain notes:

> According to Jean Baudrillard, consumers construct the self-identity they desire by consuming what they think signifies that self-identity (Baudrillard 2002). This occurs through the use of signs and symbols (Bocock 1993: 3). Market researchers and advertising campaign managers link products and services to consumer desires by establishing brand images for everything from dish soaps to sporting goods (Bocock 1993: 22). In other words, branding discourses operate to link consumer desires to a certain brand's products and services.[35]

Wilson, Roy, and Thoele all use gender in very overt ways to market their books on mindfulness, but they target their brands to reach different target audiences of women experiencing different stages of life. Each offers a particular vision of how mindfulness might enhance life and help build or manage an identity as a modern woman, so that mindfulness practice becomes an expression of one's femininity and provides practical benefits appropriate to one's particular situation. And while each author is also an accomplished career woman, they market their expertise at teaching mindfulness primarily through the vehicle of their own personal status as a woman in the same circumstances as their imagined readers. The femininity they assert has little in the way of revolutionary feminism about it— there is no sense that society at large or male patriarchy in particular limit the options of North American women. Instead, each life stage is presented as natural and appropriate. This is just how women are, the books teach—they *are* multitaskers, they *are* maternal, they *are* really into sparkly things, right? Furthermore, these feminine mindfulness lifestyles are always presented in terms of care and nurturance. Tranquilistas care for themselves through mindful extravagance, yoga, and meditation, while nurturing the world through charity work or sustainable entrepreneurship. Mothers use mindfulness to regain their sanity and momfulness to nurture their families. And older women are told to use their natural feminine qualities to gain access to mindfulness, which will allow them to wisely care for themselves and thereby have a positive impact on those around them.

Tranquilista, Momfulness, and *The Mindful Woman* are just three examples, but they, and the mindful femininities they promulgate, are representative of trends that I find replicated in innumerable books that discuss mindfulness, which is a female-dominated publishing industry, despite the presence of many important male authors, researchers, and promoters. Whole subgenres of the industry are overwhelmingly directed toward female readerships, such as mindful eating (which uses mindfulness to gain control over one's diet and figure) and mindful parenting (which uses mindfulness to help soccer moms connect better with their overstimulated children). Thus it seems that mindfulness, when it is connected to gender—as it often is—is primarily attached to views of proper social roles for women. These books acknowledge that these roles come with a high cost of stress and other health hazards, but rather than challenge the perpetuation of such roles, they seek to manage the attendant stress through mindfulness while leaving the basic notions of femininity intact. They reinforce the sense of gender identity, participate in the commodification of Buddhist practice, and help move authority over Buddhist meditation from the provenance of monks to professionals and laypeople, especially women.

In a sense, then, one could argue that mindfulness is being liberated through the actions of women, rather than women being liberated through the practice of mindfulness. It is lifted out of earlier, male-dominated, renunciatory environments and approaches, and applied to the everyday concerns of women in their ordinary lives. In the process, it appears to lose any revolutionary potential it may have had as a critique of gender images and consumerist lifestyles, but it also seems that many women are simply uninterested in such critiques. For these authors and readers, the utility of Buddhist meditation lies not in its ability to overturn conventional lifestyles and thought processes, but in helping to live them more comfortably.

Notes

1. For further information about the history, size, and success of the mindfulness movement, see Jeff Wilson, *Mindful America: The Mutual Transformation of Buddhist Meditation and American Culture* (Oxford and New York: Oxford University Press, 2014). This paper partially overlaps with material on pages 142–47 of *Mindful America* but is designed to explore the topic in a different forum. The incorporated material from *Mindful America* is used with the acknowledgment of Oxford University Press.

2. Thomas A. Tweed, "Theory and Method in the Study of Buddhism: Toward 'Translocative' Analysis," *Journal of Global Buddhism* 12(2011): 23.

3. Kimberly Wilson, *Tranquilista: Mastering the Art of Enlightened Work and Mindful Play* (Novato, CA: New World Library, 2010), xi.

4. Ibid.

5. Ibid., xii.

6. Joanne Baker, "Claiming Volition and Evading Victimhood: Post-Feminist Obligations for Young Women," *Feminism and Psychology* 20:2(2010): 187.

7. Jayne Raisborough, *Lifestyle Media and the Formation of the Self* (Hampshire, UK: Palgrave Macmillan, 2011), 149.

8. Ibid., 5.

9. Kimberly Wilson, *The Tranquility du Jour Daybook* (Washington, DC: Hip Tranquil Ventures, 2012).

10. Wilson, *Tranquilista*, 185.

11. Roberts et al., 1994. Cited in Raisborough, *Lifestyle Media*, 40–41.

12. Jane Naomi Iwamura, *Virtual Orientalism: Asian Religion and American Popular Culture* (Oxford and New York: Oxford University Press, 2011), 93.

13. budhagirl.com/videos (accessed November 24, 2014).

14. Mike Featherstone, *Consumer Culture and Postmodernism* (London: Sage, 1991), 86.

15. *Mindfulness* 1:1(2013): 17.

16. Ibid.

17. Ibid.

18. Denise Roy, *Momfulness: Mothering with Mindfulness, Compassion, and Grace* (San Francisco: Jossey-Bass, 2007).

19. Denise Roy, *My Monastery is a Minivan: Where the Daily is Divine and Routine Becomes Prayer* (Chicago: Loyola Press, 2001).

20. Roy, *Momfulness*, 48.

21. Ibid., x.

22. Ibid.

23. Ibid., 118.

24. Cassandra Vieten, *Mindful Motherhood: Practical Tools for Staying Sane During Pregnancy and Your Child's First Year* (Oakland, CA: New Harbinger, 2009), 3.

25. Ibid., 8.

26. Sue Patton Thoele, *The Mindful Woman: Gentle Practices for Restoring Calm, Finding Balance, and Opening Your Heart* (Oakland, CA: New Harbinger, 2008).

27. Ibid., 21.

28. Ibid., 27.

29. Ibid., 23.

30. Ibid., 24–25.

31. Ibid., 100–101.

32. Ibid., 145.

33. Ibid., 80.

34. Ibid., 146.

35. Andrea R. Jain. *Selling Yoga: From Counterculture to Pop Culture* (New York: Oxford University Press, 2015), 77.

Insights and Imaginations

An Epilogue

KARMA LEKSHE TSOMO

Since the 1960s, interest in Buddhism has grown exponentially throughout the world. This has been facilitated by great Buddhist teachers, new research and publications on Buddhism in modern languages, the Internet, the growth of outstanding Buddhist educational centers, and an abundance of vibrant Buddhist social service activities. Especially in Western countries, the Buddha's teachings on peace, compassion, ethics, and human psychology have had a significant impact. This new wave of interest in Buddhism has brought greater educational and professional opportunities for women and has increased awareness of women's capabilities and potential. Attention to the topic of women in Buddhism has expanded dramatically. Although the Buddha taught a path to liberation for the benefit of all beings, full recognition and equal opportunity do not extend to women in many Buddhist traditions. Many women still do not have access to Buddhist education, and women are still not equally represented in Buddhist institutions.

As the world advances scientifically and technologically, it is obvious that many areas of human development have not kept pace. We can now communicate to any precise point on the planet in a fraction of a second and disseminate information to hundreds of thousands of people with the touch of a screen, yet human beings remain enslaved by the same negative emotions that have plagued humanity for millennia. Wars and corruption rage. Greed and hatred spin out brutish strategies to control others and their resources. Sadly, as time goes by, we become more skilled at killing and cheating greater numbers of people with far less effort. Today, more human beings live in slavery than ever before in human history. Children, including many Buddhist children, as young as six years old are sold into the sex trade. Shortages of basic necessities like food and water affect billions of people, while a tiny fraction amass obscene wealth. Virtues like loving kindness and compassion seem to be in short supply.

As the Buddha taught, recognizing and eliminating the sources of human suffering—greed, hatred, and ignorance—is our best hope for transforming the world. This practical solution can also change the course of human history. However, greed, hatred, and ignorance will not go away without effort. More living examples of people with a heart of compassion, insightful wisdom, and skillful methods are needed to motivate others on the path. This is where Buddhist women come in. For if humanity is to survive, we need all the help we can get.

Since women constitute half the population of Planet Earth, their help is needed to address the serious problems that affect humanity today. We can no longer afford to squander half our precious human resources by ignoring or devaluing the spiritual potential of women. Given the opportunity, women can assume greater responsibility for global transformation. All beings, male and female, have the potential to liberate living beings from suffering. One of my Tibetan teachers said, "The only difference between us and Buddha Śhakyamuni is that we are lazy."

Since human life is precious and fleeting, we have no time to lose in realizing our spiritual potential. Every compassionate action can be a *bodhisattva* practice. We need not wait until we are perfectly awakened to start relieving the sufferings of the world. Our *bodhisattva* activity need not wait for a male rebirth or ideal circumstances. As the essays in this volume have shown, re-evaluating and revaluing women's capabilities within and beyond cultural constraints is liberating. If particular constructions of gender are helpful, then well and good. If they are restrictive and self-defeating, they need to go. Women's profound potential for compassion and wisdom can bring benefit to beings wherever they are, influencing the family, community, workplace, and polling place. A radical rethinking of what it means to be human can liberate that potential.

Contemporary debates about the exploitation and sexual abuse of women require that we draw on all cultural resources to examine attitudes toward women and investigate the roots of patriarchy. All human beings are implicated in the perpetuation of the myths about gender, sexuality, and identity. The essays here have raised questions about constructions of femininity and what gender looks like cross-culturally. To question women's complicity in the subordination and subjugation of women politically, economically, and socially is itself a revolutionary act. The silk ceilings of Buddhist societies, which have seemed so solid for centuries, are now rent.

The contemporary transnational character of Buddhist teachings and traditions provides unprecedented opportunities for questioning outdated attitudes toward women at every level. Healthy exchanges about gender equity and more egalitarian organizational structures are becoming increasingly common. Just in the nick of time, age-old Buddhist myths about women's potential and personalities are being exposed and shattered. At this pivotal juncture, classic constructions of race, class, sexuality, ethnicity, gender, and authority are all equally open to challenge and critique. In such a revolutionary environment, the theoretical ideal of liberation can no longer be used to deny social inequities. The pervasive rhetoric of liberating all beings from suffering can no longer be used to mask the structural injustices at the root of human suffering. If women are not free from poverty and illiteracy, they will have a tough time becoming Buddhas.

The recent spotlight on sexual violence raises questions about gender injustice internationally, including in Buddhist societies. Some women may be included in meetings, a few may even get on stage, but patterns of male privilege remain strong in Buddhist societies. Standard policies acknowledged by universities, and nongovernmental organizations internationally, are largely unknown in Buddhist communities.

A growing transnational movement is freeing Buddhist women to question social expectations and limitations. Exchanges across national and cultural boundaries are creating solidarity and powerful connections. Although women in Buddhist settings challenging patriarchy may feel as if they are spitting in the wind, through deft turns and insights they are carefully ensuring that women can no longer be ignored. Using new technologies to at once illuminate and transcend cultural differences, they are creatively expanding the Buddhist feminist imagination beyond their dreams.

A healthy exchange of mutual influences continues to travel back and forth between Asia and the West. The translation of cultures is not a simple binary equation, but a dynamic multidimensional process. The notion that achieving gender equality is the white woman's burden is both simplistic, patronizing, and makes no logical sense in a globalized Buddhist community. Even if Buddhist enlighten-ment remains more ideal than reality, much like gender equality in North America, the very notion of liberation can be transformative for women as well as men. If all sentient beings, even mosquitos, can become liberated, surely women can too.

Globally, gender equality is the new normal and sexist behavior has become taboo in polite company, but this memo has not reached most of the Buddhist world. Hundreds, even thousands of monks may be seated on stage with nary a nun in sight. A monk who dares to ordain a nun still risks censure or expulsion. How can a tradi-tion dedicated to relieving suffering ignore the sufferings of women? When will Buddhists move beyond social welfare activities to eradi-cate the root causes of social injustice that make charity necessary?

Women, with first-hand experience and insight into the suffer-ings and indignities of poverty, war, and economic injustice, are key to eradicating social injustice, exploitation, and brutality. Development organizations have repeatedly demonstrated that addressing these human calamities depends on empowering women and girls. The question is how women can exert a decisive influence and begin to dismantle the culture of greed and violence that dominates our world. The challenge is to extend the benefits of gender empowerment to the millions of women in Buddhist societies who are politically, edu-cationally, and economically repressed or neglected.

Sadly, many Buddhists still hesitate to admit that their cherished religious tradition has a gender problem, even when it is glaringly obvious. The patriarchal cast of ancient religions is not surprising. Buddhism was founded in a staunchly male-dominated environ-ment, but that was 2,500 years ago. What is surprising is that so many Buddhists today continue to overlook the gender discrimina-tion hidden in plain sight all around them. This is true not only of Asian Buddhism; North American temples and Dharma centers are also frequently out of kilter, with men enjoying positions of authority and women working behind the scenes. Transforming sexist attitudes in Buddhist communities will require a revolution of consciousness. Social transformation requires more than charity and meditation.

In the last decades of the twentieth century, Buddhist women around the world gained new visibility as they became more socially active. Some of the most visible were Buddhist nuns in Taiwan, includ-ing Bhiksuni Zhengyen and Bhiksuni Chao-hwei, fearless advocates of human rights, women's rights, animal rights, and environmental justice. An international, socially engaged Buddhist women's movement initiated by Sakyadhita International Association of Buddhist Women quickly gained momentum.

In 2009, Ajahn Brahm, a British monk, garnered international acclaim when he participated in the full ordination ceremony of four nuns in Australia and was subsequently expelled from the Ajahn Chah Forest Sangha. In 2014, he was invited to present a paper at the 11th United Nations Day of Vesak in Vietnam, but his pre-approved paper on gender equality in Theravāda Buddhism was summarily cancelled. The irony of banning a paper on the empowerment of women at a conference dedicated to the U.N. Millennium Development Goals (number 3 being the empowerment of women!) was not lost on the more than five thousand people from ninety-three countries who signed a petition to protest the ban. As a consequence of the ban, the monk's paper reached a far wider audience than originally intended.

A gender-balanced Buddhist society can no longer assume that monks are more worthy of support than nuns or that boys are more deserving of education than girls. Donating alms to monks may be very meaningful and fulfilling for Buddhist women, but consigning women to the role of donor rather than beneficiary of the merit system has created deep social maladies. A gendered system of merit, polluted by sexist preconceptions, skews the virtue of generosity in favor of males, further exacerbating gender inequalities. This gender-biased economy of merit, shared by hundreds of millions of Buddhists worldwide and perpetuated by women as well as men, has had serious social and economic consequences, including corruption, domestic violence, and sex trafficking.

Mobilizing hundreds of millions of women equipped with wisdom and awareness will provide a formidable force for global transformation. As idealistic as gender equality may sound, the transformative power of enacting wisdom and compassion is enormous. There is nothing in the Buddhist scriptures to prevent such a revolution, and much to support it. Buddhists could then go down on the right side of history. At the end of 2016, nineteen Himalayan nuns became the first women in the history of the world to earn the prestigious *geshema* degree in Buddhist philosophy. At the beginning of 2017, Orgyen Trinley Dorje, the Seventeenth Gyalwang Karmapa, took steps to restore full ordination for women in the Tibetan tradition. These are auspicious signs of good things to come.

Bibliography

Allione, Tsultrim. *Women of Wisdom*. New York: Arkana, 1986.

Anālayo, Bhikkhu. "The *Bahudhātuka-sutta* and its Parallels on Women's Inabilities." *Journal of Buddhist Ethics* 16(2009): 137–90.

Anālayo, Bhikkhu. "The Buddha's Past Life as a Princess in the *Ekottarika-āgama*." *Journal of Buddhist Ethics* 22(2015): 95–137.

Anālayo, Bhikkhu. "Chos sbyin gyi mdo: Bhiksunī Dharmadinnā Proves Her Wisdom." *Chung-Hwa Buddhist Journal* 24(2011): 3–34.

Anālayo, Bhikkhu. "The Going Forth of Mahāpajāpatī Gotamī in T 60." *Journal of Buddhist Ethics* 23(2016): 1–31.

Anālayo, Bhikkhu, "Karma and Female Birth," *Journal of Buddhist Ethics* 21(2014): 109–53.

Anālayo, Bhikkhu. "Mahāpajāpatī's Going Forth in the Madhyama-āgama." *Journal of Buddhist Ethics* 18(2011): 268–317.

Anālayo. Bhikkhu. "Outstanding Bhikkhunīs in the Ekottarika-āgama." In *Women in Early Indian Buddhism: Comparative Textual Studies*, edited by Alice Collett. New York: Oxford University Press, 2014.

Anālayo. "The Revival of the *Bhikkhunī* Order and the Decline of the *Sāsana*. *Journal of Buddhist Ethics* 20(2013) 111–193.

Anderson, Carol S. "The Agency of Buddhist Nuns," *Buddhist Studies Review* 27:1(2010) 41–60.

Anderson, Carol S. "Changing Sex or Changing Gender in Pāli Buddhist Literature." *The Scholar & Feminist Online: Queer/Religion* 14:2(2017) 1–6.

Anderson, Carol S. "Changing Sex in Pali Buddhist Monastic Literature." In *Queering Paradigms VI: Interventions, Ethics and Glocalities*, edited by Bee Scherer. Oxford: Peter Lang, 2016.

Anderson, Carol S. "Defning Women's Bodies in Indian Buddhist Literature." In *Re-figuring the Body: Embodiment in South Asian Religions*, edited by Barbara A. Holdrege and Karen Pechilis. Albany: State University of New York Press, 2016.

Anderson, Carol S. "Gender in Pali Buddhist Traditions." In *Gender in Indian Philosophy*, edited by Veena Howard. London: Bloomsbury, 2017.

Appleton, Naomi. "In the Footsteps of the Buddha? Women and the *Bodhisatta* Path in Theravāda Buddhism." *Journal of Feminist Studies in Religion* 27:1(2011): 33–51.

Appleton, Naomi. *Jātaka Stories in Theravāda Buddhism: Narrating the Bodhisatta Path.* Surrey: Ashgate, 2010.

Arai, Paula. *Bringing Zen Home: The Healing Heart of Japanese Women's Rituals.* Honolulu: University of Hawai'i Press, 2011.

Arai, Paula Kane Robinson. *Women Living Zen: Japanese Sōtō Buddhist Nuns.* New York: Oxford University Press, 1999.

Asma, Stephen T. *Why I Am a Buddhist: No-Nonsense Buddhism with Red Meat and Whiskey.* Charlottesville, VA: Hampton Roads Publishing, 2010.

Baker, Joanne. "Claiming Volition and Evading Victimhood: Post-Feminist Obligations for Young Women." *Feminism and Psychology* 20:2(2010).

Balkwill, Stephanie. "The Sūtra on Transforming the Female Form: Unpacking an Early Medieval Chinese Buddhist Text," *Journal of Chinese Religions* 44:2(2016): 127–48.

Bardsley, Jan. *The Bluestocking of Japan: New Women Fiction and Essays from Seito, 1911–1916.* Ann Arbor, MI: Center for Japanese Studies, 2007.

Barnes, Nancy Schuster. "Buddhism." In *Women in World Religions,* edited by Arvind Sharma. Albany: State University of New York Press, 1987.

Barnes, Nancy. "The Nuns at the Stūpa: Inscriptional Evidence for the Lives and Activities of Early Buddhist Nuns in India." In *Women's Buddhism, Buddhist Women,* edited by Ellison Banks Findly. Somerville: Wisdom Press, 2000.

Barrett, Michele. *Women's Oppression Today: The Marxist/Feminist Encounter.* London: Verso, 1980.

Batchelor, Martine. *Women in Korean Zen: Lives and Practices.* Syracuse, NY: Syracuse University Press, 2006.

Bays, Gwendolyn, trans. *The Lalitavistara Sūtra: The Voice of the Buddha: The Beauty of Compassion.* Berkeley, CA: Dharma Publishing, 1983.

Benard, Elisabeth A., and Beverly A. Moon, eds. *Goddesses Who Rule.* New York: Oxford University Press, 2000.

Bhikkhu, Thanissaro [Geoffrey DeGraff]. *The Buddhist Monastic Code II,* 3rd ed. Valley Center, CA: Metta Forest Monastery, 2013.

Blackburn, Anne. *Locations of Buddhism.* Chicago: Chicago University Press, 2010.

Blackstone, Kate R. *Women in the Footsteps of the Buddha: Struggle for Liberation in the Therīgāthā.* Surrey, UK Curzon Press, 1998.

Blackstone, Kate R. "Damning the Dhamma: Problems with *Bhikkhunīs* in the Pāli *Vinaya.*" *Journal of Buddhist Ethics* 6(1999): 292–312.

Bode, Mabel. "Women Leaders of the Buddhist Reformation." *Journal of the Royal Asiatic Society of Great Britain and Ireland* (1893): 517–66, 763–98.

Bodhi, Bhikkhu. *Discourses of the Ancient Nuns.* Kandy: Buddhist Publication Society, 1997.

Bodhi, Bhikkhu. *The Connected Discourses of the Buddha: A New Translation of the Samyutta Nikāya*. Boston: Wisdom Publications, 2000.

Bodhi, Bhikkhu. *The Numerical Discourses of the Buddha: A Translation of the Anguttara Nikāya*. Boston: Wisdom Publications, 2012.

Boucher, Sandy. *Turning the Wheel: American Women Creating the New Buddhism*. Boston: Beacon Press, 1993.

Boyarin, Daniel. "Gender." In *Critical Terms for Religious Studies*, edited by Mark C. Taylor. Chicago: University of Chicago Press, 1998.

Buckley, Sandra. "Altered States: The Body Politics of 'Being-woman.'" In *Postwar Japan as History*, edited by Andrew Gordon. Berkeley: University of California Press, 1993.

Buddhaghosa, Bhadantacariya (trans. Bhikkhu Ñanamoli), *The Path of Purification: Visuddhimagga*. Onalaska, WA: Pariyatti Press, 2003.

Buswell, Jr., Robert E., ed. *Encyclopedia of Buddhism*. New York: Macmillan Reference, 2004.

Buswell, Robert, and Donald Lopez. *The Princeton Dictionary of Buddhism*. Princeton, NJ: Princeton University Press, 2014.

Byrne, Jean. "Why I Am Not a Buddhist Feminist: A Critical Examination of 'Buddhist Feminism.'" *Feminist Theology: The Journal of the Britain & Ireland School of Feminist Theology* 21:2(2013): 180–94.

Cabezón, José Ignacio. *Buddhism, Sexuality, and Gender*. Albany: State University of New York Press, 1992.

Cabezón, José Ignacio. *Sexuality in Classical South Asian Buddhism*. Somerville, MA: Wisdom Publications, 2017.

Caplow, Florence, and Susan Moon, eds. *The Hidden Lamp: Stories from Twenty-Five Centuries of Awakened Women*. Boston: Wisdom Publications 2013.

Carbonnel, Laure. "On the Ambivalence of Female Monasticism in Theravāda Buddhism: A Contribution to the Study of the Monastic System in Myanmar." *Asian Ethnology* 68:2(2009): 265–82.

Carrithers, Michael. "Jainism and Buddhism as Enduring Historical Streams." *Journal of the Anthropological Society of Oxford* 21:2(1990): 141–63.

Chakravarti, Uma. *The Social Dimensions of Early Buddhism*. Delhi: Oxford University Press, 1987.

Chamsanit, Varaporn. "Reconnecting the Lost Lineage: Challenges to Institutional Denial of Buddhist Women's Monasticism in Thailand." PhD dissertation, Australia National University, 2006.

Cho, Eun-su, ed. *Korean Buddhist Nuns and Laywomen: Hidden Histories, Enduring Vitality* (Albany: State University of New York Press, 2011).

Chung, In Young. "A Buddhist View of Women: A Comparative Study of the Rules for *Bhiksunīs* and *Bhiksus* Based on the Chinese *Prātimoksa*." *Journal of Buddhist Ethics* 6:2(1999): 9–105.

Cogan, Gina. "Time Capsules for Tradition: Repositioning Imperial Convents for the Meiji Period. *U.S.-Japan Women's Journal English Supplement* 30/31(2006): 80–104.

Cogan, Gina. *The Princess Nun: Bunchi, Buddhist Reform, and Gender in Early Edo Japan.* Cambridge, MA: Harvard University Asia Center, 2014.

Collcutt, Martin. *Buddhism: The Threat of Eradication.* In *Japan in Transition: From Tokugawa to Meiji,* edited by Marius B. Jansen and Gilbert Rozman. Princeton, NJ: Princeton University Press, 1986.

Collett, Alice. "Buddhism and Gender, Reframing and Refocusing the Debate." *Journal of Feminist Studies in Religion* 22:2(2006): 55–84.

Collett, Alice. "The Female Past in Early Indian Buddhism: The Shared Narrative of the Seven Sisters in the *Therī-Apadāna.*" In *Religions of South Asia* 5:1/2(2011): 209–226.

Collett, Alice. "Historio-Critical Hermeneutics in the Study of Women in Early Indian Buddhism." *Numen* 56(2009): 91–117.

Collett, Alice. *Lives of Early Buddhist Nuns: Biographies as History.* New Delhi: Oxford University Press, 2016.

Collett, Alice, and Bhikkhu Anālayo. "Bhikkhave and Bhikkhu as Gender-inclusive Terminology in Early Buddhist Texts." *Journal of Buddhist Ethics* 22(2014): 760–97.

Collins, Steven. "The Body in Theravāda Buddhist Monasticism." In *Religion and the Body,* edited by Sarah Coakley. Cambridge: Cambridge University Press, 1997.

Collins, Steven. "Remarks on the Third Precept: Adultery and Prostitution in Pali Texts." *Journal of the Pali Text Society* 29(2007): 263–84.

Collins, Steven, and Justin McDaniel. "Buddhist 'Nuns' (*mae chi*) and the Teaching of Pali in Contemporary Thailand." *Modern Asian Studies* 44(2010): 1373–1408.

Como, Michael. *Weaving and Binding: Immigrant Gods and Female Immortals in Ancient Japan.* Honolulu: University of Hawai'i Press, 2009.

Conze, Edward, trans. *The Perfection of Wisdom in Eight Thousand Lines and Its Verse Summary.* Bolinas, CA: Four Seasons Foundation, 1973.

Cook, Joanna. "Hagiographic Narrative and Monastic Practice: Buddhist Morality and Mastery Amongst Thai Buddhist Nuns." *Journal of the Royal Anthropological Institute* 15(2009): 349–64.

Cook, Joanna *Meditation in Modern Buddhism: Renunciation and Change in Thai Monastic Life.* New York: Cambridge University Press, 2010.

Cowell, E. B., and R. Neil, eds. *The Divyāvadāna: A Collection of Early Buddhist Legends.* Amsterdam: Oriental Press, 1970.

Crane, Hillary. "Becoming a Nun, Becoming a Man: Taiwanese Buddhist Nuns' Gender Transformation." *Religion* 37(2007): 117–32.

Dehejia, Vidya. *The Body Adorned: Dissolving Boundaries Between Sacred and Profane in India's Art.* New York: Columbia University Press, 2009.

Derris, Karen. "My Sister's Future Buddhahood: A Jātaka of the Buddha's Lifetime as a Woman." In *Eminent Buddhist Women,* edited by Karma Lekshe Tsomo. Albany: State University of New York Press, 2014.

Derris, Karen. "When the Buddha Was a Woman: Reimagining Tradition in the Theravāda." *Journal of Feminist Studies in Religion* 24:2(2008): 29–44.

Dhammadinā, Bhikkhunī. "The Parinirvāna of Mahāprajāpatī Gautamī and Her Followers in the Mūlasarvāstivāda Vinaya." *The Indian International Journal of Buddhist Studies* 16(2015): 29–61.

Dhammananda, Bhikkhuni. "Bhiksuni Ta Tao: Paving the Way for Future Generations." In *Eminent Buddhist Women*, edited by Karma Lekshe Tsomo. Albany: State University of New York Press, 2014.

Dhammadinnā, Bhikkunī. "Predictions of Women to Buddhahood in Middle-Period Literature." *Journal of Buddhist Ethics* 22(2015): 481–531.

Diemberger, Hildegard. *When a Woman Becomes a Religious Dynasty: The Samding Dorje Phagmo of Tibet*. New York: Columbia University Press, 2007.

Dimitrov, Dragomir. "Two Female Bodhisattvas in Flesh and Blood." In *Aspects of the Female in Indian Culture: Proceedings of the Symposium in Marburg, Germany, July 7–8, 2000*, edited by Ulriche Roesler and Jayandra Soni. Marburg: Indica et Tibetica Verlag, 2000.

Dowman, Keith. *Sky Dancer: The Secret Life & Songs of the Lady Yeshe Tsogyal*. Ithaca, NY: Snow Lion Publications, 1996.

Dragseth, Jennifer Hockenbery. *Thinking Woman: A Philosophical Approach to the Quandary of Gender*. Eugene, OR: Cascade Books, 2015.

Eichman, Jennifer. "Prominent Nuns: Influential Taiwanese Voices." *CrossCurrents* 61:3(2011): 345–73.

Elam, Diane and Robyn Wiegman, eds. *Feminism Beside Itself*. New York and London: Routledge, 1995.

Engelmajer, Pascale. *Women in Pāli Buddhism: Walking the Spiritual Paths in Mutual Dependence*. London: Routledge, 2015.

Essen, Juliana. *Right Development: The Santi Asoke Buddhist Reform Movement of Thailand*. Oxford: Lexington Books, 2005.

Falk, Monica Lindberg. *Making Fields of Merit: Buddhist Female Ascetics and Gendered Orders in Thailand*. Seattle: University of Washington Press, 2008.

Falk, Nancy Auer. "The Case of the Vanishing Nuns: The Fruits of Ambivalence in Ancient Indian Buddhism." In *Unspoken Worlds: Women's Religious Lives in Non-Western Cultures*, edited by Nancy A. Falk and Rita M. Gross. San Francisco: Harper and Row, 1980.

Faure, Bernard. 2003. *The Power of Denial: Buddhism, Purity, and Gender*. Princeton, NJ: Princeton University Press.

Faure, Bernard. *The Red Thread: Buddhist Approaches to Sexuality*. Princeton, NJ: Princeton University Press, 1998.

Featherstone, Mike. *Consumer Culture and Postmodernism*. London: Sage, 1991.

Findly, Ellison Banks. "Ānanda's Case for Women." *The International Journal of Indian Studies* 3:2(1993): 1–31.

Findly, Ellison Banks. "Women Teachers of Women: Early Nuns: 'Worthy of My Confidence.'" In *Women's Buddhism, Buddhism's Women: Tradition, Revision, Renewal*. Boston: Wisdom Publications, 2000.

Findly, Ellison Banks. *Women's Buddhism, Buddhism's Women: Tradition, Revision, Renewal*. Boston: Wisdom Publications, 2000.

Finnegan, Damchö Diana. "'For the Sake of Women, Too': Ethics and Gender in the Narratives of the Mūlasarvāstivāda Vinaya." PhD dissertation, University of Wisconsin-Madison, 2009.

Fister, Patricia. "Creating Devotional Art with Body Fragments: The Buddhist Nun Bunchi and Her Father, Emperor Gomizuno-o." *Japanese Journal of Religious Studies* 27:3/4(2000): 213–38.

Foster, Barbara, and Michael Foster. *The Secret Lives of Alexandra David-Neel*. New York: Overlook Press, 2002.

Franklin, Jeffrey. *The Lotus and the Lion*. Ithaca, NY: Cornell University Press, 2008.

Fuengfusakul, Apinya. "Buddhist Reform Movements in Contemporary Thai Urban Context: Thammakai and Santi Asoke." PhD thesis, University of Bielefeld, Germany, 1993.

Gandhi, Leela. *Affective Communities*. Durham, NC: Duke University Press, 2006.

Gayley, Holly. *Love Letters from Golok: A Tantric Couple in Modern Tibet*. New York: Columbia University Press, 2017.

Geary, Patrick. "Saints, Scholars, and Society: The Elusive Goal." In *Saints: Studies in Hagiography*, edited by Sandro Sticca. Binghamton, NY: Medieval & Renaissance Texts & Studies, 1996.

Gethin, Rupert. *The Foundations of Buddhism*. New York: Oxford University Press, 1998.

Goldman, Robert P. "Transsexualism, Gender, and Anxiety in Traditional India." *Journal of the American Oriental Society* 113:3(1993): 374–401.

Grant, Beata. "Da Zhangfu: The Rhetoric of Female Heroism in Seventeenth-Century Buddhist Writings." *Nan Nü: Men, Women and Gender in China* 10:2(2008): 177–211.

Grant, Beata. *Eminent Nuns: Women Chan Masters of Seventeenth-century China*. Honolulu: University of Hawai'i Press, 2009.

Grant, Beate. "Female Holder of the Lineage: Linji Chan Master Zhiyuan Xinggang (1597–1654)," *Late Imperial China* 17:2(1996): 51–76.

Gross, Rita M. *Buddhism beyond Gender: Liberation from Attachment to Identity*. Boulder, CO: Shambhala Publications, 2018.

Gross, Rita M. *Buddhism after Patriarchy: A Feminist History, Analysis, and Reconstruction of Buddhism*. Albany: State University of New York Press, 1993.

Gutschow, Kim. *Being a Buddhist Nun: The Struggle for Enlightenment in the Himalayas*. Cambridge, MA: Harvard University Press, 2004.

Gutschow, Kim. "The Death of the Buddha's Mother." *Harvard Divinity School Bulletin* 44:1/2(2016).

Gyatso, Janet. *Apparitions of the Self: The Secret Autobiographies of a Tibetan Visionary*. Princeton, NJ: Princeton University Press, 1998.

Gyatso, Janet. "Drawn from the Tibetan Treasury: The gTer ma Literature." In *Tibetan Literature: Studies in Genre*, edited by José Cabezón and Roger Jackson. Ithaca, NY: Snow Lion Publications, 1996.

Gyatso, Janet. "One Plus One Makes Three: Buddhist Gender, Monasticism, and the Law of the Non-Excluded Middle." *History of Religions* 43:2(2003): 89–115.

Gyatso, Janet, and Hanna Havnevik. *Women in Tibet.* New York: Columbia University Press, 2005.

Haas, Michaela. *Dakini Power: Twelve Extraordinary Women Shaping the Transmission of Tibetan Buddhism in the West.* Boston: Snow Lion Publications, 2013.

Hahn, Michael, "In Defence of Haribhatt in *Pramānakīrtih: Papers Dedicated to Ernst Steinkellner on the Occasion of His 70th Birthday,* Part 1, edited by B. Kellner, H. Krasser, Horst Lasic, M.T. Much, and H. Tauscher. Vienna: Wiener Studien zur Tibetologie und Buddhismuskunde, 2007.

Hahn, Michael. *Haribhatta and Gopadatta, Two Authors in the Succession of Âryaśūra. On the Rediscovery of Parts of Their* Jātakamālās, 2nd ed. Tokyo: Studia Philologica, 1992.

Halafoff, Anna, and Praveena Rajkobal. "Sakyadhita International: Gender Equity in Ultramodern Buddhism." *Feminist Theology: The Journal of the Britain & Ireland School of Feminist Theology* 23:2(2015): 111–27.

Hallisey, Charles. *Therīgāthā: Poems of the First Buddhist Women.* Cambridge, MA: Harvard University Press, 2015.

Hannah, Michelle. "Transmigratory Buddhists and Traveling Feminism: Globalization and Cross-Cultural Differences." *The Australian Journal of Anthropology* 21:3(2010): 332–49.

Hansen, Anne. *How to Behave.* Honolulu: University of Hawai'i, 2007.

Haraway, Donna. "Situated Knowledges: The Science Question in Feminism and the Privilege of Partial Perspective." *Simians, Cyborgs, and Women.* London: Free Association Books, 1991.

Harding, Sarah. *Machik's Complete Explanation: Clarifying the Meaning of Chöd.* Ithaca, NY: Snow Lion Publications, 2003.

Harris, Clare. *The Museum on the Roof of the World.* Chicago: Chicago University Press, 2012.

Harris, Elizabeth. "Reclaiming the Sacred: Buddhist Women in Sri Lanka." *Feminist Theology: The Journal of the Britain & Ireland School of Feminist Theology* 15(1997): 100.

Harrison, Paul. "Who Gets to Ride in the Great Vehicle? Self-Image and Identity among the Followers of the Early Mahāyāna." *Journal of the International Association of Buddhist Studies* 10:1(1987): 67–89.

Heikkilä-Horn, Marja-Leena. *Buddhism with Open Eyes: Belief and Practice of Santi Asoke.* Bangkok: Fah Apai, Ltd., 1997.

Heikkilä-Horn, Marja-Leena. "Santi Asoke Buddhism and the Occupation of Bangkok International Airport." *Austrian Journal of South-East Asian Studies* (2009): 31–47.

Heim, Maria. "She Who Heard Much: Notes on Receiving, Interpreting, and Transmitting Buddhavacana." *International Journal of Hindu Studies* 19:1/2(2015): 139–56.

Heirman, Ann. "Chinese Nuns and Their Ordination in Fifth Century China." *Journal of the International Association of Buddhist Studies* 24:2(2001): 275–304.

Heirman, Ann. "Fifth-century Chinese Nuns: An Exemplary Case." *Buddhist Studies Review* 27:1(2010): 61–76.

Heirman, Ann, trans. *The Discipline in Four Parts: Rules for Nuns According to the* Dharmaguptakavinaya. Delhi: Motilal Banarsidass, 2002.

Heirman, Ann. "Washing and Dyeing Buddhist Monastic Robes." *Acta Orientalia Academiae Scientiarum Hungaricae* 67:4(2014): 467–88.

Hirakawa, Akira (ed. and trans.). *Monastic Discipline for the Buddhist Nuns: English Translation of the Chinese Text of the Mahasanghika-Bhikṣuṇī-Vinaya.* Patna: Kashi Prasad Jayaswal Research Institute, 1982.

Hirakawa, Akira (trans. Karma Lekshe Tsomo). "The History of Buddhist Nuns in Japan." *Buddhist-Christian Studies* 12(1992): 143–58.

Hiratsuka, Raicho (Teruko Craig, trans.). *In the Beginning, Woman Was the Sun: The Autobiography of a Japanese Feminist.* New York: Columbia University Press, 2006.

hooks, bell. *Ain't I a Woman?* Boston: South End Press, 1981.

hooks, bell. "Beauty Laid Bare: Aesthetics in the Ordinary." In *To Be Real: Telling the Truth and Changing the Face of Feminism*, edited by Rebecca Walker. New York: Anchor Books, 1995.

hooks, bell. *Talking Back: Thinking Feminist, Thinking Black.* Cambridge, MA: South End Press: 1999.

Horner, I. B., trans. *The Book of the Discipline* (Vinaya-pitaka), 6 vols. London: Pali Text Society, 1896–1981.

Horner, I. B. *Women Under Primitive Buddhism: Laywomen and Almswomen.* London: George Routledge & Sons, 1930.

Hsieh, Ding-hua E. "Images of Women in Ch'an Buddhist Literature of the Sung Period." In *Buddhism in the Sung*, edited by Peter N. Gregory and Daniel A. Getz, Jr. Honolulu: University of Hawai'i Press, 2002.

Ikeya, Chie. "The 'Traditional' High Status of Women in Burma: A Historical Reconsideration." *Journal of Burma Studies* 10(2005–2006): 51–81.

Iryop, Kim (trans. Jin Park). *Reflections of a Zen Buddhist Nun.* Honolulu: University of Hawai'i Press, 2014.

Ito, Tomomi. "Ordained Women in Yellow Robes: An Unfamiliar 'Tradition' in Contemporary Thailand." *Out of the Shadows: Socially Engaged Buddhist Women*, edited by Karma Lekshe Tsomo. Delhi: Sri Satguru, 2006.

Ito, Tomomi. "Questions of Ordination Legitimacy for Newly Ordained Theravāda Bhikkhunī in Thailand." *Journal of Southeast Asian Studies* 43(2012): 55–76.

Itoh, Ayako. "The Emergence of the Bhikkhunī-Sangha in Thailand: Contexts, Strategies and Challenges." PhD dissertation, École Pratique des Hautes Études, 2013.

Iwamoto, Akemi. "'New Women' and Zen in Early 20th-Century Japan: Raichō Hiratsuka and D. T. Suzuki." *Buddhism at the Grassroots*, edited by Karma Lekshe Tsomo. Delhi: Sakyadhita, 2012.

Iwamura, Jane Naomi. *Virtual Orientalism: Asian Religion and American Popular Culture*. Oxford and New York: Oxford University Press, 2011.

Jackson, Peter. *Buddhism, Legitimation, and Conflict: The Political Functions of Urban Thai Buddhism*. Singapore: Institute of Southeast Asian Studies, 1989.

Jacoby, Sarah. "The Excellent Path of Devotion: An Annotated Translation of Sera Khandro's Short Autobiography." In *Himalayan Passages: Tibetan and Newar Studies in Honor of Hubert Decleer*. Boston: Wisdom Publications, 2014.

Jacoby, Sarah H. *Love and Liberation: Autobiographical Writings of the Tibetan Buddhist Visionary Sera Khandro*. New York: Columbia University Press, 2014.

Jaffe, Richard M., and Michel Mohr. "Editor's Introduction: Meiji Zen." *Japanese Journal of Religious Studies* 25:1/2(1998): 1–10.

Jaffe, Richard. "Seeking Shakyamuni: Travel and the Reconstruction of Japanese Buddhism." *Journal of Japanese Studies* 30:1(2004): 65–96.

Jain, Andrea R. *Selling Yoga: From Counterculture to Pop Culture*. New York: Oxford University Press, 2015.

Jamison, Stephanie W. *Sacrificed Wife/Sacrificer's Wife*. New York: Oxford University Press, 1996.

Jay, Jennifer W. "Imagining Matriarchy: 'Kingdoms of Women' in Tang China." *Journal of the American Oriental Society* 116.2(1996): 220–29.

Jnaanavira, Dharmacari. "A Mirror for Women? Reflections of the Feminine in Japanese Buddhism." *Western Buddhist Review: Journal of the Western Buddhist Order* 4(2003).

Johnston, E. H., ed. *The Buddhacarita (Acts of the Buddha)*, Part II. Calcutta: Baptist Mission Press, 1936.

Jones, Constance A., and James D. Ryan, eds. *Encyclopedia of Hinduism*. New York: Facts on File, 2007.

Jones, Lindsay, ed. *Encyclopedia of Religion*, 2nd ed., vol. 1. Detroit: Thomson Gale, 2005.

Jordt, Ingrid. "Bhikkhuni, Thilashin, Mae-chii: Women Who Renounce the World in Burma, Thailand, and the Classical Pali Buddhist Texts." *Crossroads* 4:1(1988): 31–39.

Kabilsingh, Chatsumarn. *Thai Women in Buddhism*. Berkeley, CA: Parallax Press, 1991.

Kieschnick, John. "The Symbolism of the Monk's Robe in China." *Asia Major* 12:1(2000): 9–32.

318 / Bibliography

Klein, Anne C. *Meeting the Great Bliss Queen: Buddhists, Feminists, and the Art of the Self*. Boston: Beacon Press, 1996.

Kloppenborg, Ria. "Female Stereotypes in Early Buddhism: The Women of the Therīgāthā," *Female Stereotypes in Religious Traditions*, edited by Ria Kloppenborg and Wouter J. Hanegraaff. Leiden, New York, Köln: E. J. Brill, 1995.

Krey, Gisela. "On Women as Teachers in Early Buddhism: Dhammadinnā and Khemā." *Buddhist Studies Review* 27:1(2010): 18.

Krey, Gisela. "Some Remarks on the Status of Nuns and Laywomen in Early Buddhism." In *Dignity and Discipline: Reviving Full Ordination for Buddhist Nuns*, edited by Thea Mohr and Jampa Tsedron. Boston: Wisdom Publications, 2010.

Kuo, Karen. "Japanese Women Are Like Volcanoes." *Frontiers: A Journal of Women Studies* 36:1(2015): 77.

Insook Kwon. "The New Women's Movement in 1920s Korea: Rethinking the Relationship between Imperialism and Women." *Gender and History* 10:3(1998): 381–405.

Lab sgron, Ma gcig. *Khyad par gyi le lag brgyad pa*. In *Gdams ngag mdzod*, edited by 'Jam mgon kong sprul, vol. 14. Paro, Bhutan: Lama Ngodrup and Sherab Drimey, 1979.

LaFleur, William R. "Body." In *Critical Terms for the Study of Religion*, edited by Mark C. Taylor. University of Chicago Press, 1998.

LaFleur, William R. *Liquid Life: Abortion and Buddhism in Japan*. Princeton, NJ: Princeton University Press, 1992.

LaMacchia, Linda. *Songs and Lives of the Jomo (Nuns) of Kinnaur, Northwest India: Women's Religious Expression in Tibetan Buddhism*. Delhi: Sri Satguru Publications, 2008.

Lang, Karen Christina. "Lord Death's Snare: Gender-Related Imagery in the *Theragāthā* and the *Therīgāthā*." *Journal of Feminist Studies in Religion* 2:2(1986): 63–79.

Lang, Karen Christina. "Shaven Heads and Loose Hair: Buddhist Attitudes toward Hair and Sexuality." In *Off with Her Head! The Denial of Women's Identity in Myth, Religion, and Culture*, edited by Howard Eilberg-Schwartz and Wendy Doniger. Berkeley: University of California Press, 1995.

Langenberg, Amy Paris. "*Mahāsanghika-Lokottaravāda Bhiksunī Vinaya*: Intersection of Womanly Virtue and Buddhist Asceticism." In *Women in Early Indian Buddhism: Comparative Textual Studies*, edited by Alice Collett. Oxford: Oxford University Press, 2014.

Langenberg, Amy Paris. "Female Monastic Healing and Midwifery: A View from the *Vinaya* Tradition." *Journal of Buddhist Ethics* 21(2014): 155–90.

Levering, Miriam. "The Dragon Girl and the Abbess of Mo-Shan: Gender and Status in the Ch'an Buddhist Tradition," *Journal of the International Association of Buddhist Studies*, 5:1(1982): 19–35.

Levering, Miriam. "Lin-chi (Rinzai) Ch'an and Gender: The Rhetoric of Equality and the Rhetoric of Heroism." In *Buddhism, Sexuality, and Gender*, edited by José Ignacio Cabezón. Albany: State University of New York Press, 1992.

Levering, Miriam. "Miao-tao and Her Teacher Ta-hui." In *Buddhism in the Sung*, edited by Peter N. Gregory and Daniel A. Getz, Jr. Honolulu: University of Hawai'i Press, 2002.

Lhamo, Rinchen. *We Tibetans*. New York: Potala Publications, 1985 [1926].

Loos, Tamara. *Subject Siam*. Ithaca, NY: Cornell University Press, 2006.

Lopez, Jr., Donald S. *Prisoners of Shangri-La: Tibetan Buddhism and the West*. Chicago: Chicago University Press, 1998.

Lopez, Donald S. *Buddhist Scriptures*. New York: Penguin Books, 2004.

Lowy, Dina. "Love and Marriage: Ellen Key and Hiratsuka Raichō Explore Alternatives." *Women's Studies* 33:4(2004): 361–80.

Mahmood, Saba. *Politics of Piety: The Islamic Revival and the Feminist Project*. Chicago: University of Chicago Press, 2004.

Malalasekera, G. P. *Dictionary of Pâli Proper Names*. Oxford: The Pāli Text Society, 1997.

McGill, Justine. "The Silencing of Women." In *Women in Philosophy: What Needs to Change?* Edited by Katrina Hutchison and Fiona Jenkins. New York: Oxford University Press, 2013.

MacCannell, Dean, and Juliet Flower. "The Beauty System." In *The Ideology of Conduct: Essays on Literature and the History of Sexuality*, edited by Nancy Armstrong and Leonard Tennenhouse. New York: Methuen, 1987.

Mackenzie, Rory. *New Buddhist Movements in Thailand: Towards an Understanding of Wat Phra Dhammakaya and Santi Asoke*. New York: Routledge, 2007.

Mackenzie, Vicki. *Cave in the Snow: Tenzin Palmo's Quest for Enlightenment*. New York: Bloomsbury, 1998.

McCallum, Donald F. *Zenkōji and Its Icon: A Study in Medieval Japanese Religious Art*. Princeton, NJ: Princeton University Press, 1994.

McCargo, Duncan. *Chamlong Srimuang and the New Thai Politics*. New York: St. Martin's Press, 1997.

McClintock, Anne. *Imperial Leather*. New York: Routledge, 1995.

McMahan, David. *Buddhist Modernism*. Oxford University Press, 2008.

McRae, John. *Vimalakīrti Sūtra*. Berkeley, CA: Numata Center for Buddhist Translations and Research, 2004.

Meeks, Lori Rachelle. "Buddhist Renunciation and the Female Lifecycle: Understanding Nunhood in Heian and Kamakura Japan." *Harvard Journal of Asiatic Studies* 70:1(2010): 1–59.

Meeks, Lori Rachelle. *Hokkeji and the Reemergence of Female Monastic Orders in Premodern Japan*. Honolulu: University of Hawai'i Press, 2010.

Minamoto, Junko. "Buddhism and the Historical Construction of Sexuality in Japan." *U.S.-Japan Women's Journal*, English Supplement, 5(1993).

Mitchell, Scott A. *Buddhism in America: Global Religion, Local Contexts*. London and New York: Bloomsbury Academic, 2016.

Mitchell, Scott A., and Natalie E. F. Quli. *Buddhism beyond Borders: New Perspectives on Buddhism in the United States*. Albany: State University of New York Press, 2016.

Mohanty, Chandra Talpade. *Feminism without Borders: Decolonizing Theory*. Durham, NC: Duke University Press, 2003.

Mohanty, Chandra Talpade. "Under Western Eyes: Feminist Scholarship and Colonial Discourses." *Boundary 2* 12:3/13:1(1984): 333–58.

Mohr, Michel. "Japanese Zen Schools and the Transition to Meiji: A Plurality of Responses in the Nineteenth Century." *Japanese Journal of Religious Studies* 25:1/2(1998): 167–213.

Mohr, Thea, and Jampa Tsedroen, eds. *Dignity & Discipline: Reviving Full Ordination for Buddhist Nuns*. Somerville, MA: Wisdom Publications, 2010.

Mollier, Christine. *Buddhism and Taoism Face to Face: Scripture, Ritual, and Iconographic Exchange in Medieval China*. Honolulu: University of Hawai'i Press, 2008.

Monson, Christine. *The Excellent Path of Devotion: An Abridged Story of a Mendicant's Experiences in Response to Questions by Vajra Kin*. Boulder: Kama Terma Publications, 2013.

Morrell, Robert. "Mirror for Women: Muju Ichien's Tsuma Kagami." *Monumenta Nipponica* 35:1(1980).

Morris, Rosalind C., ed. *Can the Subaltern Speak? Reflections on the History of an Idea*. New York: Columbia University Press, 2010.

Mooney, Catherine. *Gendered Voices: Medieval Saints and their Interpreters*. Philadelphia: University of Pennsylvania Press, 1999.

Mrozik, Suzanne. *Virtuous Bodies: The Physical Dimensions of Morality in Buddhist Ethics*. Oxford: Oxford University Press, 2007.

Mueggler, Erik. *The Paper Road*. Berkeley: University of California Press, 2011.

Murcott, Susan. *The First Buddhist Women: Translations and Commentary on the Therīgāthā*. Berkeley, CA: Parallax Press, 1991.

Nanayon, Upasika Kee (trans. Thanissaro Bhjikkhu). *An Unentangled Knowing: The Teachings of a Thai Buddhist Lay Woman*. Barre, MA: Dhamma Dana Publications, 1995.

Nattier, Jan. *Once Upon a Future Time: Studies in a Buddhist Prophecy of Decline*. Nagoya: Nanzen Institute for Religion and Culture, 1991.

Nattier, Jan. "Gender and Hierarchy in the *Lotus Sutra*." In *Readings of the Lotus Sutra*, edited by Jacqueline Stone and Stephen Teiser. New York: Columbia University Press, 2009.

Neary, Ian. "In the Beginning, Woman was the Sun: The Autobiography of a Japanese Feminist." *English Historical Review* 123:500(2008): 247–48.

Neumaier-Dargyay, Eva K. "Buddhist Thought from a Feminist Perspective." In *Gender, Genre and Religion: Feminist Reflections*, edited by Morny Joy and Eva K. Neumaier-Dargyay. Calgary: Wilfrid Laurier University Press, 1995.

Norman, K. R. *The Elders' Verses II: Therīgāthā*, 2nd ed. London: Pāli Text Society, 2007.

Obeyesekere, Ranjini. *Portraits of Buddhist Women: Stories from the Saddharma-ratnavaliya*. Albany: State University of New York Press, 2001.

Oh, Bonnie B. C. "Kim Iryop: Pioneer Writer/Reformer in Colonial Korea." *Transactions of the Royal Asiatic Society, Korea Branch* 71(1996): 18.

Ohnuma, Reiko. "Bad Nun: Thullananda in Pali Canonical and Commentarial Sources," *Journal of Buddhist Ethics* 20(2013): 17–66.

Ohnuma, Reiko. "Debt to the Mother: A Neglected Aspect of the Founding of the Buddhist Nun's Order." *Journal of the American Academy of Religion* 74:4(2006): 861–901.

Ohnuma, Reiko. *Head, Eyes, Flesh, and Blood: Giving Away the Body in Indian Literature*. New York: Columbia University Press, 2006.

Ohnuma, Reiko. "Mother-Love and Mother Grief: Pan Asian Buddhist Variations on a Theme" *Journal of Feminist Studies in Religion* 23:1(2007) 95–106.

Ohnuma, Reiko. "The Story of Rūpavatī: A Female Past Birth of the Buddha." *Journal of the International Association of Buddhist Studies* 23:1(2000): 103–45.

Ohumna, Reiko. *Ties That Bind: Maternal Imagery and Discourse in Indian Buddhism*. Oxford: Oxford University Press, 2012.

Ohumna, Reiko. "Woman, Bodhisattva, and Buddha." *Journal of Feminist Studies in Religion* 17:1(2001): 63–83.

Oldenberg, Hermann, and Richard Pischel, eds. *Thera- and Therī-Gāthā*, 2nd ed. London: Luzac & Company, 1966.

Osto, Douglas. "The Supreme Array Scripture: A New Interpretation of the Title 'Gandhavyūha-sūtra.' " *Journal of Indian Philosophy* 37(2009): 273–90.

Osto, Douglas. *Power, Wealth, and Women in Indian Mahāyāna Buddhism: The Gandavyūha-sūtra*. London: Routledge, 2008.

Osto, Douglas. "Soteriology, Asceticism and the Female Body in Two Indian Buddhist Narratives." *Buddhist Studies Review* 23:2(2006): 203–20.

Osto, Douglas. "Proto-Tantric" Elements in the *Gandavyūha-sūtra*." *Journal of Religious History* 33:2(2009): 165–77.

Oung, Kim Thida. *A Twentieth Century Burmese Matriarch*. Yangon: Author, 2009.

Owen, Lisa Battaglia. "On Gendered Discourse and the Maintenance of Boundaries: A Feminist Analysis of the Bhikkhunī Order in Indian Buddhism." *Asian Journal of Women's Studies* 4:3(1998): 8–60.

Owen, Lisa Battaglia. "Toward a Buddhism Feminism: Mahayana Sutras, Feminist Theory, and the Transformation of Sex." *Asian Journal of Women's Studies* 3:4(1997): 1–11.

Padmakara Translation Committee. *Lady of the Lotus-Born: The Life and Enlightenment of Yeshe Tsogyal*. Boston: Shambhala Publications, 2002.

Park, Jin Y. *Women and Buddhist Philosophy: Engaging Zen Master Kim Iryŏp*. Honolulu: University of Hawai'i Press, 2017.

Paul, Diana Y. *Women in Buddhism: Images of the Feminine in the Mahāyāna Tradition*. Berkeley: University of California Press, 1985.

Paul, Diana, trans. *The Sūtra of Queen Śrīmālā of the Lion's Roar*. Berkeley, CA: Numata Center for Buddhist Translations and Research, 2004.

Peach, Lucinda J. "Social Responsibility, Sex Change, and Salvation: Gender Justice in the Lotus Sutra." *Philosophy East and West* 52:1(2002): 50–74.

Poompanna, A. *Insight into Santi Asoke, Part 2*. Bangkok: Kittiya Veerapan, 1991.

Powers, John. *A Bull of a Man: Images of Masculinity, Sex, and the Body in Indian Buddhism*. Boston: Harvard University Press, 2009.

Powers, John. "Gender and Virtue in Indian Buddhism." *CrossCurrents* 61:4(2011): 428–40.

Powers, John. "You're Only as Good as You Look: Indian Buddhist Associations of Virtue and Physical Appearance," In *Destroying Māra Forever: Buddhist Ethics Essays in Honor of Damien Keown*, edited by John Powers and Charles S. Prebish. Ithaca, NY: Snow Lion Publications, 2009.

Pruitt, William, trans. *The Commentary on the Verses of the Therīs*. Oxford: Pali Text Society, 1999.

Pruitt, William, ed. *Therīgāthā-atthakathā*. Oxford: Pali Text Society, 1998.

Pruitt, William. "The Career of Women Disciple Bodhisattas." *Journal of the Pali Text Society* 29(2007): 389–405.

Raisborough, Jayne. *Lifestyle Media and the Formation of the Self*. Hampshire, UK: Palgrave Macmillan, 2011.

Rhys Davids, C.A.F., ed. *Visudhimagga*, 2 vols. London: Pali Text Society, 1920–21 (reprint, Routledge and Kegan Paul, 1975).

Rhys-Davids, C.A.F., and K. R. Norman, trans. *Poems of Early Buddhist Nuns*. Oxford: Pali Text Society, 2009.

Roy, Denise. *Momfulness: Mothering with Mindfulness, Compassion, and Grace*. San Francisco: Jossey-Bass, 2007.

Roy, Denise. *My Monastery is a Minivan: Where the Daily is Divine and Routine Becomes Prayer*. Chicago: Loyola Press, 2001.

Roy, U. N. "Enchanting Beauties in the Early Buddhist Art: A Symbological Investigation (3rd Century B.C.–3rd Century A.D.)." In *Studies in Indian Art*, edited by Chitta Ranjan Prasad Sinha. New Delhi: Ramanand Vidya Bhawan, 1998.

Ruch, Barbara. *Engendering Faith: Women and Buddhism in Premodern Japan*. Ann Arbor, MI: Center for Japanese Studies, University of Michigan, 2003.

Ruppert, Brian. "Buddhism and Law in Japan." In *Buddhism and Law: An Introduction*, edited by Rebecca Redwood French and Mark A. Nathan. Cambridge: Cambridge University Press, 2014.

Said, Edward. *Orientalism*. New York: Pantheon, 1978.

Salgado, Nirmala. *Buddhist Nuns and Gendered Practice: in Search of the Female Renunciant*. New York: Oxford University Press, 2013.

Sang, Tze-lan D. *The Emerging Lesbian: Female Same-Sex Desire in Modern China.* Chicago: University of Chicago Press, 2003.

Sawhney, Sabina. "Authenticity is Such a Drag!" In *Feminism Beside Itself,* edited by Diane Elam and Robyn Wiegman. New York: Routledge, 1995.

Schaeffer, Kurtis R. *Himalayan Hermitess: The Life of a Tibetan Buddhist Nun.* New York: Oxford University Press, 2004.

Schaeffer, Kurtis R. "The Autobiography of a Medieval Hermitess: Orgyan Chokyi (1675–1729)." In *Women in Tibet,* edited by Janet Gyatso and Hanna Havnevik. New York: Columbia University Press, 2005.

Scherer, Burkhard. "Gender Transformed and Meta-gendered Enlightenment: Reading Buddhist Narratives as Paradigms of Inclusiveness." *Revista de Estudos da Religião* 3(2006): 65–76.

Scherer, Burkhard. "Macho Buddhism: Gender and Sexuality in the Diamond Way." *Religion and Gender* 1:1(2011): 85–103.

Schneider, Jane, and Annette Weiner, "Cloth and the Organization of Human Experience." *Current Anthropology* 27:2(1986): 178.

Schopen, Gregory. *Bones, Stones, and Buddhist Monks: Collected Papers on the Archaeology, Epigraphy, and Texts of Monastic Buddhism in India.* Honolulu: University of Hawai'i, 1997.

Schopen, Gregory. *Buddhist Nuns, Monks, and Other Worldly Matters: Recent Papers on Monastic Buddhism in India.* Honolulu: University of Hawai'i Press, 2014.

Schopen, Gregory. "On Emptying Chamber Pots Without Looking and the Urban Location of Buddhist Nunneries in Early India Again." *Journal Asiastique* 296:2(2008) 229–256.

Schopen, Gregory. "On Incompetent Monks and Able Urbane Nuns in a Buddhist Monastic Code." *Journal of Indian Philosophy* 38(2010): 107–31.

Schopen, Gregory. "Separate but Equal: Property Rights and the Legal Independence of Buddhist Nuns and Monks in Early North India." *Journal of the American Oriental Society* 128:4(2008): 625–40.

Schopen, Gregory. "The Urban Buddhist Nun and a Protective Rite for Children in Early North India." *Pāsādikadāna?" Festschrift für Bhikkhu Pasadika,* edited by M. Straube, et al. Marburg: Indica et Tibetica Verlag, 2009.

Scott, Linda M. *Fresh Lipstick: Redressing Fashion and Feminism.* New York: Palgrave Macmillan, 2005.

Scott, Rachelle M. "Buddhism, Miraculous Powers, and Gender: Rethinking the Stories of Theravada Nuns." *Journal of the International Association of Buddhist Studies* 33:1/2(2011): 489–511.

Sedgwick, Eve Kosofsky. *Touching Feeling: Affect, Pedagogy, Performativity.* London & Durham, NC: Duke University Press, 2003.

Seeger, Martin. "The Bhikkhuni-Ordination Controversy in Thailand." *Journal of the International Association of Buddhist Studies* 29(2006): 155–83.

Seeger, Martin. "Reversal of Female Power, Transcendentality, and Gender in Thai Buddhism: The Thai Buddhist Female Saint Khun Mao Bunruean Tongbuntoem (1895–1964)." *Modern Asian Studies* 47:5(2013): 1488–1519.

Shaw, Miranda. *Passionate Enlightenment: Women in Tantric Buddhism*. Princeton, NJ: Princeton University Press, 1994.

Shih, Heng-ching. "Chinese Bhiksunis in the Ch'an Tradition." *National Taiwan University Philosophical Review* 15(1992): 181–207.

Shih, Pao-ch'ang (trans. Kathryn Ann Tsai), *Lives of the Nuns: Biographies of Chinese Buddhist Nuns from the Fourth to Sixth Centuries*. Honolulu: University of Hawai'i Press, 1994.

Shikibu, Murasaki (trans. Royall Tyler). *The Tale of Genji*. New York: Penguin Classics, 2002.

Simmer-Brown, Judith. *Dakini's Warm Breath: The Feminine Principle in Tibetan Buddhism*. Boston: Shambhala Publications, 2001.

Skilling, Peter. *Esā āgra*: Images of Nuns in (Mūla-)Sarvāstivādin Literature," *Journal of the International Association of Buddhist Studies* 24:2(2001): 135–57.

Skilling, Peter. "Nuns, Laywomen, Donors, Goddesses: Female Roles in Early Indian Buddhism," *Journal of the International Association of Buddhist Studies* 24:2(2001): 241–74.

Sorensen, Michelle J. "Making the Old New Again and Again: Legitimation and Innovation in the Tibetan Buddhist Chöd Tradition." PhD dissertation, Columbia University, 2013.

Spender, Dale. *Man Made Language*. London: Pandora, 1980.

Sponberg, Alan. "Attitudes toward Women and the Feminine in Early Buddhism." In *Buddhism, Sexuality, and Gender*, edited by José Ignacio Cabezón. Albany: State University of New York Press, 1992.

Suh, Sharon A. *Silver Screen Buddha: Buddhism in Asian and Western*. London and New York: Bloomsbury Academic, 2015.

Suksamran, Somboon. *Buddhism and Politics in Thailand: A Study of Socio-political Change and Political Activism of the Thai Sangha*. Singapore: Institute of Southeast Asian Studies, 1982.

Swearer, Donald. *The Buddhist World of Southeast Asia*. Albany: State University of New York Press, 2010.

Takemi, Momoko. "'Menstruation Sutra' Belief in Japan," *Japanese Journal of Religious Studies* 10:2–3(1983): 229–46.

Thera, Nyanaponika and Hellmuth Hecker, *Great Disciples of the Buddha: Their Lives, Their Works, Their Legacy*. Somerville, MA: Wisdom Publications, 2003.

Thoele, Sue Patton. *The Mindful Woman: Gentle Practices for Restoring Calm, Finding Balance, and Opening Your Heart*. Oakland, CA: New Harbinger, 2008.

Thondup, Tulku. *Hidden Teachings of Tibet*. Boston: Wisdom Publications, 1997.

Todeschini, Alberto, "The Maiden Who Fell in Love with a Thief: Considerations on the Story of the Nun Bhaddā Kundalakesī." *Dharma Drum Journal of Buddhist Studies* 13(2013): 153–86.

Tomalin, Emma. "The Thai Bhikkhuni Movement and Women's Empowerment." *Gender and Development* 14:3(2006): 385–97.

Trainor, Kevin. "In the Eye of the Béholder: Nonattachment and the Body in Subhā's Versé (*Thetīgāthā* 71)." *Journal of the American Academy of Religion* 61(1993): 57–79.

Tsomo, Karma Lekshe. "Buddhist Feminist Reflections." In *Buddhist Philosophy: Selected Primary Texts*, edited by Jay Garfield and William Edelglass. New York: Oxford University Press, 2009.

Tsomo, Karma Lekshe. "Buddhism and Human Rights," *A Companion to Buddhist Philosophy*, edited by Steven Emmanuel. Chichester, West Sussex, U.K.: Wiley-Blackwell, 2013.

Tsomo, Karma Lekshe, ed. *Buddhist Women across Cultures: Realizations*. Albany: State University of New York Press, 1999.

Tsomo, Karma Lekshe, ed. *Buddhist Women in a Global Multicultural Community*. Kuala Lumpur: Sukhi Hotu Press, 2008.

Tsomo, Karma Lekshe, ed. *Buddhist Women and Social Justice: Ideals, Challenges, and Achievements*. Albany: State University of New York Press, 2004.

Tsomo, Karma Lekshe. "Change in Consciousness: Women's Religious Identity in Himalayan Buddhist Cultures." In *Buddhist Women Across Cultures*, edited by Karma Lekshe Tsomo. Albany: State University of New York, 1999.

Tsomo, Karma Lekshe, ed. *Eminent Buddhist Women*. Albany: State University of New York Press, 2014.

Tsomo, Karma Lekshe, ed. *Innovative Buddhist Women: Swimming against the Stream*. Surrey, England: Curzon Press, 2000.

Tsomo, Karma Lekshe. *Into the Jaws of Yama, Lord of Death: Buddhism, Bioethics, and Death*. Albany: State University of New York Press, 2006.

Tsomo, Karma Lekshe. "Lao Buddhist Women: Quietly Negotiating Religious Authority." *Buddhist Studies Review* 27:1(2010): 85–106.

Tsomo, Karma Lekshe. *Sisters in Solitude: Two Traditions of Buddhist Monastic Ethics for Women, A Comparative Analysis of the Dharmagupta and Mūlasarvāstivāda Bhikṣuṇī Prātimokṣa Sūtras*. Albany: State University of New York Press, 1996.

Turner, Alicia, Laurence Cox, and Brian Bocking. "Beachcombing, Going Native and Freethinking: Rewriting the History of Early Western Buddhist Monastics." *Contemporary Buddhism* 11:2(2010): 125–47.

Tweed, Thomas A. "Theory and Method in the Study of Buddhism: Toward 'Translocative' Analysis," *Journal of Global Buddhism* 12(2011): 23.

Uno, Kathleen S. "Death of 'Good Wife, Wise Mother'? In *Postwar Japan as History*, edited by Andrew Gordon. Berkeley: University of California Press, 1993.

Vesey, Alexander. "The Buddhist Clergy and Village Society in Early Modern Japan." PhD dissertation, Princeton University, 2003.

Vieten, Cassandra. *Mindful Motherhood: Practical Tools for Staying Sane During Pregnancy and Your Child's First Year*. Oakland, CA: New Harbinger, 2009.

Walshe, Maurice, trans. *Thus Have I Heard: The Long Discourses of the Buddha* (Dīgha Nikāya). Boston: Wisdom Publications, 1995.

Walters, Jonathan. *"Apadāna: Therī-apadāna:* Wives of the Saints: Marriage and Kamma in the Path to Arahantship." *Women in Early Indian Buddhism: Comparative Textual Studies,* edited by Alice Collett. Oxford: Oxford University Press, 2014.

Walters, Jonathan. "Gotamī's Story: Introduction and Translation." In *Buddhism in Practice,* edited by Donald S. Lopez, Jr. Princeton, NJ: Princeton University Press, 1995.

Walters, Jonathan. "A Voice from the Silence: The Buddha's Mother's Story." *History of Religions* 33:4(1994): 358–79.

Wayman, Alex, and Hideko Wayman, trans. *The Lion's Roar of Queen Śrīmālā.* New York: Columbia University Press, 1974.

Wijayaratna, Mohan (trans. Claude Grangier and Steven Collins). *Buddhist Monastic Life: According to the Texts of the Theravada Tradition.* Cambridge: Cambridge University Press, 1990.

Williams, Liz. "A Whisper in the Silence: Nuns Before Mahāpājapatī." *Buddhist Studies Review* (2000): 167–73.

Willis, Janice D. "Nuns and Benefactresses: The Role of Women in the Development of Buddhism." In *Women, Religion, and Social Change,* edited by Yvonne Haddad and Ellison Banks Findley. Albany: State University of New York Press, 1985.

Wilson, Jeff. *Mindful America: The Mutual Transformation of Buddhist Meditation and American Culture.* Oxford and New York: Oxford University Press, 2014.

Wilson, Kimberly. *Tranquilista: Mastering the Art of Enlightened Work and Mindful Play.* Novato, CA: New World Library, 2010.

Wilson, Kimberly. *The Tranquility du Jour Daybook.* Washington, DC: Hip Tranquil Ventures, 2012.

Wilson, Liz. "Buddhism and Gender." In *Buddhism in the Modern World,* edited by David L. McMahan. New York: Routledge, 2012.

Wilson, Liz. *Charming Cadavers: Horrific Figurations of the Feminine in Indian Buddhist Hagiographic Literature.* Chicago: University of Chicago Press, 1996.

Wolf, Naomi. *The Beauty Myth: How Images of Beauty Are Used against Women.* HarperCollins, 2002.

Wu, Judy Tzu-Chun. *Radicals on the Road: Internationalism, Orientalism, and Feminism during the Vietnam Era.* Ithaca, NY: Cornell University Press, 2013.

Yosano, Akiko. "The Day the Mountains Move." In *Feminist Theory Reader: Local and Global Perspectives,* 2nd ed., edited by Carole R. McCann and Seung-kyung Kim. New York: Routledge 2010.

Young, Serinity. *Courtesans and Tantric Consorts: Sexualities in Buddhist Narrative, Iconography, and Ritual.* New York: Routledge, 2004.

Young, Serinity. "Female Mutability and Male Anxiety in an Early Buddhist Legend." *Journal of the History of Sexuality* 16:1(2007): 14–39.

Yü, Chün-Fang. *Kuan-yin: The Chinese Transformation of Avalokitesvara*. New York: Columbia University Press, 2000.

Yü, Chün-Fang. *Passing of the Light: The Incense Light Community and Buddhist Nuns in Contemporary Taiwan*. Honolulu: University of Hawai'i Press, 2013.

Yuan, Yuan. "Chinese Buddhist Nuns in the Twentieth Century: A Case Study of Wuhan." *Journal of Global Buddhism* 10(2009): 375–412.

Contributors

Lisa Battaglia is an associate professor of Religion in the Howard College of Arts and Sciences at Samford University. She received her BA in Religion from Duke University, an MA in Women's Studies from the University of Alabama, and an MA and PhD in History and Critical Theories of Religion from Vanderbilt University. She is a comparative religionist with scholarly interest in Asian religious traditions and critical methods in the study of religion. Her research focuses on women's ordination in Theravāda Buddhism, women's alternative renunciant communities in Buddhist Thailand, and representations of beauty and the female body in Buddhism.

Eunsu Cho is a professor in the Department of Philosophy at Seoul National University. She received her PhD in 1997 from the University of California, Berkeley. She has published articles ranging from Indian Abhidharma Buddhism to Korean Buddhist thought and history. She edited an anthology on Korean Buddhist nuns, *Korean Buddhist Nuns and Laywomen: Hidden Histories, Enduring Vitality,* and co-translated (with John Jorgensen) the *Jikji: The Essential Passages Directly Pointing at the Essence of the Mind.*

Holly Gayley is an associate professor of Buddhism at the University of Colorado Boulder. Her research focuses on contemporary Buddhist literature in Tibet and its lived context with a special interest in issues of gender, agency, ethics, and identity. Her first book, *Love Letters from Golok: A Tantric Couple in Modern Tibet,* explores the lives and letters of an eminent contemporary couple, Khandro Tare Lhamo and Namtrul Rinpoche, who played a significant role in reinvigorating Buddhist practices, teachings, and institutions during the post-Mao period in the nomadic region of Golok. Her second project traces the emergence of an ethical reform movement, spearheaded by cleric-scholars at Larung Buddhist Academy in eastern Tibet, with published articles on the topic in the *Journal of Buddhist Ethics*, *Himalaya Journal*, *Contemporary Buddhism*, and the *Journal of Religious Ethics*.

Amy Holmes-Tagchungdarpa is an associate professor in the Department of Religious Studies at Occidental College. She is the author of *The Social Life of Tibetan Biography Textuality, Community, and Authority in the Lineage of Tokden Shakya Shri*. She completed her PhD in Asian Religions and History at Australian National University.

Christine A. James is a professor of Philosophy and Religious Studies at Valdosta State University in Valdosta, Georgia. Her dissertation on "Objectivity in Philosophy of Science and the History of Sonar Technology and Underwater Imaging" was completed at the University of South Carolina. Although her specialization is Philosophy of Science, she has published a variety of articles and book chapters in scholarly journals, including *The Journal for Philosophical Practice*, *The International Journal of Sociology and Social Policy*, *Essays in Philosophy*, *The Southwest Philosophy Review*, *The Journal of Consciousness Studies*, *Biosemiotics*, and the *Journal for Human Rights*.

Karen Lang is a professor emerita in the Religious Studies Department of the University of Virginia, where she taught courses on Buddhist history and philosophy. Her publications include *Āryadeva's Four Hundred Verses: On the Bodhisattva's Cultivation of Merit and Knowledge*, and *Four Illusions: Candrakirti's Advice on the Bodhisattva's Practice of Yoga* and numerous articles on Indian Buddhist philosophy and literature.

Matthew Mitchell is a graduate from the Asian Religions Track of Duke University's Graduate Program in Religion. His dissertation, which was awarded the Stanley Weinstein Dissertation Prize for best dissertation on East Asian Buddhism 2014–2016, focused on a group of Buddhist nuns of the Daihongan subtemple of Zenkoji in Japan's early modern period. His research in Japan and writing have been funded by the Japan Foundation's Dissertation Fellowship, the Anne T. and Robert M. Bass Fellowship for Undergraduate Instruction, and the Robert H. N. Ho Family Foundation Dissertation Fellowship. He received his MA from the Religion Department of the University of Hawaii at Mānoa.

Robekkah Ritchie is currently a doctoral candidate at the Dahlem Research School, Department of History and Cultural Studies, Freie Universität, Berlin. Her research interests include contemporary transformations in the representation of women monastics in Thailand and the intersections of meditation, contemplation, culture, and dress. She co-teaches a survey course on Buddhism in the Religious Studies Department at Freie Universität.

Michelle J. Sorensen completed her doctoral degree at Columbia University under the supervision of Dr. Robert A. F. Thurman. Her dissertation, "Making the Old New Again and Again: Legitimation and Innovation in the Tibetan Buddhist Chöd Tradition," offers a revisionary history of the early development of *chöd*. It includes English translations of six *chöd* texts attributed to Machik Labdrön and two commentaries by the Third Karmapa, Rangjung Dorje. She has given numerous presentations at national and international conferences and has published several articles and book chapters on historical and contemporary *chöd* philosophy and practice. She is an assistant professor in the Department of Philosophy and Religion at Western Carolina University and is currently working on a book about Machik Labdrön and the development of the *chöd* tradition in Tibet.

Karma Lekshe Tsomo is a professor of Buddhist Studies at the University of San Diego, where she teaches Buddhist Thought and Culture and other courses. She received a doctorate in Comparative Philosophy from the University of Hawaii at Mānoa. She is past-president of Sakyadhita International Association of Buddhist Women and the founder and director of Jamyang Foundation, an educational initiative for women in developing countries. Her publications include *Into the Jaws of Yama: Buddhism, Bioethics, and Death*; *Sisters in Solitude: Two Traditions of Monastic Ethics for Women*; and a number of edited volumes on women in Buddhism.

Ching-ning Wang (Chang-shen Shih) received her PhD in the Sociology and Women's Studies Program at the Graduate Center of the City University of New York in 2004. She is a Buddhist nun from Dharma Drum Mountain, Taiwan, and was a lecturer at the Dharma Institute of Liberal Arts from 2010 to 2015. In 2016–17, she was a research associate and visiting faculty at the Women's Studies in Religion Program, Harvard Divinity School. She is currently a visiting scholar at the

Center for the Study of World Religions, Harvard Divinity School, and is working on a monograph titled "The Making of a Modern Female Chan Teacher: Gender, Buddhism, and Modernity."

Jeff Wilson is a professor of Religious Studies and East Asian Studies at Renison University College, University of Waterloo. He earned a PhD in Religious Studies at the University of North Carolina at Chapel Hill. He is the author of *Mourning the Unborn Dead*, *Dixie Dharma*, and *Mindful America*. With Tomoe Moriya, he is the co-editor of *Selected Works of D.T. Suzuki, Volume III: Comparative Religion*.

Index